GODS, SAGES AND KINGS

Vedic Secrets of Ancient Civilization

Other Passage Press Books by David Frawley

AYURVEDIC HEALING
A Comprehensive Guide

THE ASTROLOGY OF THE SEERS
A Guide to Hindu (Vedic) Astrology

BEYOND THE MIND
(Forthcoming)

FROM THE RIVER OF HEAVEN
Hindu and Vedic Knowledge for the Modern Age

THE UPANISHADIC VISION
(Forthcoming)

WISDOM OF THE ANCIENT SEERS
Secrets of the *Rig Veda*
(Forthcoming)

GODS, SAGES AND KINGS

Vedic Secrets of Ancient Civilization

by David Frawley

Passage Press
Salt Lake City, Utah

Passage Press is a division of Morson Publishing
Morson Publishing
P.O. Box 21713
Salt Lake City, Utah 84121-0713

Published 1991

Printed in the United States of America

All translations from the Sanskrit by David Frawley unless otherwise indicated
Cover design by Ted Nagata Graphic Design
Maps by Gail Frawley
Backcover Photograph by John Domont

Printed on acid-free paper

ISBN 1-878423-08-8

ॐ

This book is dedicated to our ancient spiritual fathers, the great Vedic Rishis.

To the great seer families of the Angirasas, Bhrigus, Atharvans, Atris, Kanwas, Bharadwajas, Gotamas, Vasishtas, and Vishwamitras.

To the seers Manu, Yama, Brihaspati, Ayasya, Ushanas, Dirghatamas, Kakshivan, Kutsa, Agastya, Dadhyak, Kashyapa, Vamadeva, Shyavashwa, Sobhari, Jamadagni, Madhucchandas, Parashara, Ghora, Krishna, and Virupa, whose names merge into the eternal and infinite.

Namah Paramarishibhyah!
Reverence to the Supreme Seers!

And to the great sages of the late Vedic age and the kings who took such great effort to compile and preserve the Vedas:

Tura Kavasheya, Yajñavalkya, Uddalaka Aruni, Shandilya, Aitareya, Kaushitaki, Pippalada, Vyasa, and the avatar Krishna and the great kings of the Kurus and the Pañcalas, of Ayodhya, and Videha.

And to the great Saraswati river, which flowed from the foot of Mount Kailas, the Himalayan home of the Vedas, to the sea, before her banks changed marking the end of the Vedic age. May her waters flow again!

CONTENTS

PART II: The Throne of Indra
Stories of Vedic Kings

PART III: Vedic Astronomy
The Testimony of the Stars

PART IV: Vedic Religion

PART V: Peoples of the Ancient World The Fall from Grace

APPENDICES

FOREWORD

By Vyaas Houston

David Frawley's book *Gods, Sages and Kings* is, as the author himself acknowledges in its preface, not a conservative book. It calls into question our entire view of human history, and therefore our primary understanding of who we are as human beings inhabiting the planet earth. Although the book on one level is a fascinating and colorful revelation of a highly developed ancient culture, it is much more significantly a truly spiritual vision of where we come from and who we are. *Gods, Sages and Kings* is a very important book. It fills a major void in our understanding of human history, and grants us the possibility of actually redefining ourselves in the light of our origins.

Twenty years ago, I had the good fortune of discovering the world's oldest living language: Sanskrit, the language of ancient India and Vedic civilization. It was an unmistakable homecoming, a return to a spiritual source. It was perfectly clear to me that I had come upon a perfect language, a language that invokes the spirit, an inexhaustible wellspring of spiritual inspiration. The ancients called it *devavani*, the language of the gods.

Where did it come from? — a language infinitely more sophisticated than any of our modern tongues. How could language have been so much more refined in ancient times, especially among a people, the Vedic Aryans, whom scholars tell us were nomadic barbarians from the north? The discrepancy between the language and what has been traditionally offered as its origin is so great that either we have been thoroughly at a loss, or have tended at times to resort to supernatural explanations. The obvious truth is that there must have been an equally refined and advanced civilization, which evolved along with the language over a very long period of time. *Gods, Sages and Kings* is the first book I have seen that skillfully uncovers precisely how time and cultural bias have obscured this fact. This was possible because we do have a perfectly preserved account of that ancient culture, the Vedas, and because David Frawley, more than any other researcher to date, has been able to fathom its spiritual symbolism, as well as its historical and cultural orientation and chronology.

This book also solves a long standing dilemma, encountered by those who have cherished a spiritual vision of life. Whereas, on the one hand, we have inherited a lofty spiritual vision through the Sanskrit language and an inspired body of literature, we have at the same time seemingly had no historical source, no established order by which we could ground this vision, and bring it to earth. The predominant elements of our historical identity have been war, technology and trade. Our human identity has been captured in a belief in domination by force as a necessary condition of survival. Under such circumstances, spiritual life, be it yoga and meditation, or prayer and devotion has tended to be largely a means of escaping domination — hence life denying and therefore unfruitful. What should be obvious to us after millennia of spiritual striving with limited success is that we have had no foundation on which to build. Yet it is not that we have really lacked a spiritual foundation — but that we have not recognized the one which existed.

The Sanskrit language alone is a certain testimony that it did exist, and at that, for a very long time. We simply have never turned on the light to see that it has always been there, in the Vedas themselves, the world's oldest, most perfectly preserved and comprehensive scriptural history.

David Frawley has turned on the light in a big way. For the first time we see a rich and radiant vision of the origins of human civilization in a spiritual culture, based upon yogic knowledge. Rather than taking pride in our technological and intellectual progress, it would serve us far more and be much closer to the truth to acknowledge that we are the children of great seers, rishis, and we have somewhat lost our way. It is indeed a great reassurance, even more, a healing balm to our souls and minds to know that for at least 5,000 years, in the relatively recent past (c. 6000-1000 BC), a culture based upon the yogic knowledge of the absolute oneness of all life flourished.

David Frawley is not the first to expostulate a spiritual interpretation of the Vedas. But he is the first to give us the full panoramic view of their magnificence, revealing layer by layer the culture, the politics, the ritual, the astrology, the geography, and the deep spiritual understanding which connected it all so perfectly. No one to my knowledge has ever presented us with such a convincing and thorough proof of the spiritual origins of civilization.

I am deeply grateful to David Frawley for writing this book. Even more than a remarkable piece of brilliant scholarship, it is a work which reflects Dr. Frawley's deep commitment to the awakening of self knowledge for all human beings, and the reemergence of our true spiritual heritage. For me personally, it has put some very large and nagging doubts to rest, once and for all. At the same time, it has brought into the light of the sun, what were before only faint memory traces and dim intuitions of an ancient spiritual home.

Vyaas Houston
Warwick, New York
February 1991

PREFACE

There is much ground for believing that ancient India was more central to the origins of civilization than is presently considered, that it may be the source of civilization as we know it. This has been the main belief of the Hindu and Buddhist traditions, and many Western mystical and occult groups like the Theosophists have held similar ideas. A few Western historians have also inclined to this view. Though most Western scholars and the current view of history still see a Middle Eastern origin for civilization, much new information is coming out that may challenge this view.

Gods, Sages and Kings proposes the idea of an ancient Indian and Himalayan home for world civilization. It proceeds primarily through a reexamination of the Vedic literature of ancient India and proposes a new decipherment of Vedic symbolism on three levels:

1. The *Rig Veda,* the oldest of the Vedic texts, portrays the geography of north India as it was thousands of years ago, probably before 3000 BC.

   The *Veda* shows a very early era prior to the coming into being of the Rajasthan desert of western India when a mighty river — the Vedic Saraswati — flowed through what was then the central Vedic land. The existence and extent of this river has now been proved by modern research, which has traced its ancient course from the Himalayan foothills to the Rann of Kutch on the Arabian Sea.

   The Vedic rivers can be identified with the main rivers of modern India and Pakistan. The *Veda* also shows a maritime culture that knew of and travelled on more than one sea.

2. The Vedic people had a calendar based upon astronomical sightings relative to the equinoctial positions going back from 2000 BC to at least 6000 BC, from the age of Taurus to that of Cancer.

   This Vedic calendar was modified periodically according to precessional changes which can be documented up to the positions found in Hindu calendars today. It indicates that astronomy and astrology may have originated in India.

3. The Vedic hymns reflect the practice of Yoga and meditation, including a knowledge of the seven chakras of the subtle body — the foundation of all later yogic practices both Hindu and Buddhist.

This indicates a profound spiritual culture existing at the dawn of human history and a spiritual rather than materialistic origin for human culture as a whole.

Gods, Sages and Kings also examines the different kings and dynasties of ancient India and the regions they ruled. On this basis, it attempts to reveal how the peoples of the ancient world relate to and may be descendants of the Vedic people. This includes peoples of similar languages to the Vedic, like the Iranians and Europeans, and people of similar religions, like the ancient Egyptians and Babylonians. It can be extended perhaps to include all the peoples of the ancient world. Ancient civilization as a whole was probably much more advanced, particularly along spiritual lines, and older than prevalent scholarly models today propose.

***

I approach the *Vedas* here not primarily from an academic standpoint, as an historian, archaeologist or linguist. Though aspects of these studies are brought into play, the approach is primarily of one who perceives the spiritual nature of ancient culture and takes their teachings seriously, not as primitive utterances but as the secret wisdom of the sages.

In the course of nearly twenty years of study, whenever I found something in the *Vedas* that appeared superstitious, primitive or irrational I have never just accepted it as such. I always looked deeper as to whether such apparent primitiveness may merely reflect my own lack of understanding of the background or orientation of the ancient mind. So doing, I found that what may appear to be a deficiency in the ancients is usually a lack of empathy and insight in the modern mind which distorts the ancient language according to the superficial framework of modern thought. It is our own failure to understand the ancient language of mantra, myth and symbol that causes us to see ancient teachings as primitive. The wisdom of the ancient seers, like that of the deeper psyche, proceeds by a poetic and imagistic expression, not by the rational terms of the surface mind.

My larger study has involved the spiritual and yogic implications of the *Vedas*. This book has grown out of that work and is meant as a supplement to it, dealing with the outer aspects of the Vedic culture. My other books on the subject, like *Wisdom of the Ancient Seers, Secrets of the Rig Veda,* are concerned specifically with the inner truth.

In the course of my studies I found that the *Rig Veda* has a deeper spiritual meaning than is usually ascribed to it, even by traditional Hindus. I also noticed that the modern interpretation of the nature of the society and the geographical context of the Vedic hymns was often far afield from what is actually presented in them — that the *Vedas* came from a much earlier time and greater area than is acknowledged. Gradually putting together various pieces of information on these issues, a totally different picture of Vedic civilization emerged and evolved into this book.

We will focus here on what is actually said in the *Vedas*. The main references are from the *Rig Veda* itself, and we will explore what can be substantiated within it relative to the Vedic tradition as a whole. I use primarily my own translations here, as the older English translations are often quite Victorian and cumbersome, not to mention often insensitive to any deeper meaning of the hymns. The modern intellectual mind, predominantly materialistic, humanistic and scientific in nature, can have a limited ability to understand ancient spiritual texts. The view of one open to the tradition, as I try to be, may be closer to the truth and certainly is at least worthy of consideration as an alternative.

By the standards of our times, aspects of this book may be viewed as mystical fiction, though some academicians, it is hoped, will find its information worthy of examination and accurate on some important points. I could have written a more conservative book, as even its lesser contentions require a radical shift of our view of ancient history, but I felt compelled to reveal as much of the more complete story as I could. Even a point as simple as the maritime nature of Vedic culture calls into question the entire modern interpretation of the *Vedas* and through it all our ideas about the ancient world. For those less academically minded, they may want to focus on the material presented in the sections 'Peoples of the Ancient World'. This is of greater relevance for those who already accept a spiritual meaning to history.

Please note that in this book footnotes are listed by letter. Numbers refer to a special Sanskrit Appendix which gives the transliteration of the main Vedic verses translated, for those who are interested in the original Sanskrit. All references unless specified are to the *Rig Veda*. Text abbreviations used are explained in the Bibliography.

One point of controversy I have not tried to solve is the date of Krishna. One view places him at 3102 BC. A Puranic tradition and the archaeological work at Dwaraka suggest around 1500 BC. My point is that even if we use the later date for Krishna the antiquity of the *Vedas* and the Vedic nature of early ancient Indian culture is still affirmed. This I believe is the essential point to establish to allow for a proper reexamination of ancient Indian and world history. I am, however, completing a concordance between Puranic and Vedic historical accounts. This will be a separate work but will fill in many of the gaps left out here.

I would like to express my appreciation to the many people, groups and publications who have supported my Vedic work through the years, particularly in India. These include M. P. Pandit, who first helped publish my Vedic work in India over ten years ago, Motilal Banarsidass publishers and their journal *Glory of India,* the *Mountain Path* of the Sri Ramanashramam, and the many helpful reviews this work has received throughout India. Dr. B. L. Vashta requires a special acknowledgment for his support and the connections with the Hindu community he has developed for me. Subhash Kak, a modern Vedic scholar and linguist, now working on the decipherment of the Indus Valley script, has been helpful in providing information, including recent articles, many of which are his own, to substantiate the propositions of this book. Ken Gilbert's proofing of the book has been helpful, as has Ken Johnson's.

I think we are beginning a new era in the study of the ancient world, based on an appreciation of the spiritual and yogic knowledge these cultures possessed. In particular, a new era of Vedic studies is dawning which allies these spiritual studies with new archaeological work in India, like the excavations at Dwaraka or the tracing of the ancient flow of the Saraswati river. This may change most of the views of ancient history we have held for the past century and show that most of our interpretations of the history of India, like the Aryan invasion, are incorrect. We may soon discover that the yogic culture of the *Vedas* may be central to world history and the development of civilization, even that of the so-called Western world.

May the insight and the grace of that spiritual humanity again come to us that we may once more establish a spiritual culture on Earth!

David Frawley
Santa Fe, New Mexico
August 1990

INTRODUCTION

ANCIENT HISTORY FROM THE VISION OF THE SEERS

From our Mother, the Dawn, may we be born as the seven seers, the original men of wisdom. May we become the sons of Heaven, the Angirasa seers. May we break open the mountain and illuminate the reality.

Just as our ancient and supreme Fathers, oh sacred Fire, seeking the truth, following the clear insight, sustaining the chant, broke through Heaven and Earth and revealed the radiant Spirit. — *Rig Veda IV.2.15–6*

THROUGH THE GLASS DARKLY

Confronting the Veil of Time

All cultures look back to their predecessors and like to see in them the origins of civilization. In the modern technological world we look to the ancient Greeks, as they first developed the scientific cultural model we follow. We also look back to the ancient Middle East, to the region where Christianity was born, as it represents the religious side of our culture. As both Greece and the Middle East are not far removed from each other, we regard civilization to have developed first in the Middle East and then traveled and developed further in Greece and Europe. We ignore or limit the role of the great Asiatic civilizations of India and China, making them mere footnotes to what we see as the main progress of civilization through the Western world. Yet we should note that India and China have also had their interpretations of world history, which prevailed in their regions of the world for thousands of years. In their views of history our culture has not appeared very prominent either. Until the advent of technology, Europe was just a footnote in culture to the larger and more enduring civilizations of Asia.

Each culture likes to rewrite history in its own image. Each age, as an ancient Hindu philosopher noted, has the arrogance to call itself modern and regard previous generations as out of date. Our era is no different in this respect. While we think we have gone beyond the bias of older interpretations of history, we may have only created a bias of another sort.

Technology and science may not be the ultimate or enlightened things they seem for us today. They may still reflect a narrowness of vision. Certainly they have had a more destructive effect upon our environment than anything human culture has done so far. After all, science and technology are still based upon manipulating the outer world on the crude level of machines. They are not based on a mastery of the inner world of the mind. They do not necessarily reflect a love of nature or of God. Perhaps the greatest achievements of humanity — those of philosophy, art and religion — are, not surprisingly, accomplishments of non-technological ages. In fact, most of our world religions, our most profound connections with the transcendent, are the products of ancient times long before the advent of science. For the teachings that address the ultimate issues of life and death, we still go back to our oldest books.

This is not to say that technology has no benefit, or that it cannot be made into something wholly beneficial. The point is that the mind-set technology creates may be no more appropriate for understanding the ancient world and human origins than it is for understanding religion. Religion, after all, was the main project of ancient man and remains so for much of the world today.

Our interpretation of history may be no more real or objective than those of other ages and cultures. We are simply still trapped in our own modern mind-set and unable to see the limitations it puts upon us. As the modern idea of history is the most removed of all interpretations from any spiritual view, it may be the most untrue of all of them. While we have a better idea of the outer world — the quantitative factors of life — we have a more deficient perception of the inner world, the domain of our soul. In this respect ancient scriptures and myths may be closer to the truth, as they give emphasis to inner rather than outer realities (which is why the latter were not so well portrayed by them).

Changing our view of history is not just an academic issue. Our view of history determines the field in which we think and act; how we view ourselves both individually and collectively. To change ourselves and bring a greater consciousness into the world we must first change our idea of what the world is and how it has developed. Even a number of liberal or New Age thinkers, when it comes to their view of history, accept the standard chronology invented by modern materialistic historians and archaeologists, whose views on life they would otherwise question or reject. This has caused some good thinkers today to make major mistakes in their interpretations of humanity. Even many thinkers of Asia have accepted this modern, materialistic, generally Western interpretation of their history which has caused them to denigrate their own usually more spiritual heritage. Such people, in trying to be rational, scientific, or modern, have reduced their own cultural background to fit into the narrow mold of the materialistic mind.

To gain a more spiritual idea as to the origins of civilization we must examine the ancient teachings and historical records of India. India has maintained the greatest continuity of civilization since ancient times. In some respects it is a living relic of our ancient past. Indeed, much of the form of Hindu culture today, with its temple worship and caste system, appears the same as it was three thousand years ago. It is very similar to what we find in ancient Egypt and Babylonia of that era.

Ancient India has provided us with an extensive literary record, the largest of the ancient world. In its Vedic texts, which number many thousands of pages, we have preserved, in what appears to be the original language and accent, the teachings of at least three thousand years ago. We have old commentaries on many of these books as well, some dating from before the time of the Buddha. While we have found some of the written records of the ancient Middle East, they are largely fragmentary and mutilated and their interpretation is often a matter of conjecture. Their cultures passed away and the continuity of their traditions was broken.

The oldest literary sources we have from the ancient Greek world are the works of Homer (c.700 BC). From the Middle East, the oldest extant books are those of the Hebrew *Bible*. While parts of the Old Testament are much older, as a whole much of it was redone after 500 BC. It endured the vicissitudes of Egyptian and Assyrian conquests and the Babylonian captivity. The *Gathas* of Zoroaster are also old, dating from before the founding of the ancient Persian empire (525 BC), but they are later than the Vedic. They are also fragmentary since their greater portions were destroyed by the Greek and Muslim conquests of Persia. From China the oldest book is the *I Ching*, though only its core portions date to 1000 BC or earlier. While *The Egyptian Book of the Dead* is much older than these (to 3000 BC), no living tradition or record of its interpretation has survived for us.

Vedic literature thus provides us with more original ancient teachings than what we have from all the rest of the world put together. This is not to say that the rest of the world did not have such books. Even many Vedic teachings are known to have been lost. However, the *Vedas* preserve more unaltered teachings from an early ancient era than we can find elsewhere.

Even by the most conservative estimates the four *Vedas* date from 1500-1000 BC and have remained virtually unchanged since. The extensive *Brahmanas* and early *Upanishads* precede the time of the Buddha. Such preservation is particularly remarkable in a tropical country like India where written records decay quickly. India also endured many conquests — some, like the long Muslim attacks, extremely violent and destructive — but it was able to maintain its ancient records. Even today Brahmins recite the *Vedas* much as they did some three thousand years ago or more. This shows a singular dedication to the teaching and tradition, which should at least be worthy of notice. The ancient world did not entirely die. It has remained in India and is still accessible through it.

Vedic literature has been examined and translated in modern times, largely in the late nineteenth and early twentieth centuries, by such Western Vedic scholars as Muller, Keith, Griffith, Wilson and Bergaine. While they did much to bring attention to the *Vedas* and their views are often interesting, we do not find that they really understood these ancient texts. They had little sensitivity for their deeper meaning and were often content with a casual and superficial rendering of them as primitive. Difficulties in understanding the *Vedas* were not seen as a basis for questioning their inadequate methods of interpretation but rather as proof of the confused nature of the Vedic mind. If these scholars could not make sense of something in the *Vedas* they usually blamed the Vedic seers for being unintelligible, not themselves for missing something of the right way of approach to such mystic teachings. They dissected the *Vedas* according to a materialistic and intellectual mind, not by a mind sensitive to the spiritual life or to symbolic language. Hence we can still say that the real meaning of the *Vedas* is yet unknown to us. Such translators and interpreters mainly served to categorize Vedic grammar but they did not have the background to understand the spiritual secrets of the *Vedas*.

The *Vedas* are filled with mantras, symbols and cryptic statements and codes. They do not reveal themselves readily to those who do not look deeply. It is not enough to have the records of the ancients if we do not know how to read them. Nor is it enough to translate them into our language if we do not understand the background and orientation of the language in which they were composed. Interpretations unaware of these points only create confusion, just as an unfocused lens only serves to give us a blurred image of an object.

So far we have interpreted the culture and history of India according to our own social, intellectual, and religious preconceptions and have thereby created a distortion of it. By distorting it we have distorted our own history and that of the world as a whole, which is all interrelated. In fact, our treatment of the ancient spiritual teachings of India is just the most evident way in which we have misinterpreted the ancient world and its spiritual background. We interpret ancient scriptures and mystical texts by modern social and psychological ideas and quite naturally find them to be chaotic or primitive. By the spiritual standards of the ancients our modern intellectual and materialistic culture may be found lacking as well.

Such cultural ethnocentricity will not take us very far in understanding humanity but will only serve to glorify ourselves.

While we cannot uncover all aspects of Vedic culture in a single book, we can at least open up a different way of looking at it and at ancient humanity. I think this direction of approach which takes seriously the spiritual orientation of the ancients is much closer to the truth than those which ignore or denigrate it. If we look at these teachings with an openness to the spiritual life, we find the ancient teachings to be radically different than how they are portrayed by the modern mind and the so-called authoritative views of them. We find that there was much more to these ancient cultures than is even yet suspected in academic circles today.

For those of us who value the spiritual life, we cannot simply accept the modern materialistic idea of man as defined by Western history. We cannot believe that human culture originated in a mechanical way through the development of tools and equipment. Yet we also cannot simply accept the common Western religious view that the world was created by the will of some personal God either. We are inclined to see the role of conscious seers, sages and meditators as our true guides and leaders. We see their role in ancient culture, which developed on a strong religious and spiritual foundation all over the world.

The main source of our inquiry is the *Rig Veda,* the most ancient of the books of India or of any Indo-European language. The *Rig Veda* may be, if this interpretation is correct, the most ancient book in the world. By most accounts, even those of modern scholars, it is the longest and best preserved of any book that we have from before 1000 BC. I believe it may provide us with the key to both ancient Indian and world culture.

The *Rig Veda* as a spiritual book may not be understood from a non-spiritual perspective, any more than a book on science can be understood by one who is not a scientist. What would we think of a book on science by one who is not a scientist, who has never done any experiments and does not know mathematics? Interpretations of spiritual texts by those who are not of a spiritual bent of mind, who do not practice meditation and do not understand the meaning of mantra and symbols, may be equally questionable. Hence it is not surprising that interpretations within such an inappropriate background could not even understand the outer aspects of the Vedic teaching. The ancient language is symbolic and imagistic. This does not preclude philosophical ideas or even a great knowledge of the world, but it clothes such knowledge in symbols that a more literal mind may take only on the most evident level.

Yet in this book we will often hold to a more literal meaning of Vedic terms than do many modern interpretations. For example, the view in this book that the Vedic is a maritime culture is based upon the many references and symbolisms of the ocean and ships in the hymns. I cannot ignore or scale down these references because it is hard to place the civilization of the *Rig Veda* in proximity to the ocean and still preserve our modern ideas about ancient history. We should not interpret an ancient text according to our preconceptions of where and by whom it should have been written. We must first of all try to hear its own voice.

References to seas and oceans and a vision of the universe as a series of oceans cannot be explained away by supposing that some big river was imagined to be the ocean by the primitive mind. This is not a rational interpretation of what is said but an irrational reduction of it according to the imposition of outside ideas and preconceptions. Yet this has been part of the general and accepted method of Vedic scholarship. Most of what has been done on the *Vedas* so far remains largely the unquestioned work of nineteenth century Western scholars who were often trapped in the cultural and sometimes imperialistic bias of their times.

In addition, this approach brings to bear the knowledge of other religious and spiritual traditions and the views of the ancient peoples themselves. When all ancient civilizations refer to themselves as having been preceded by many others, we cannot pretend they were the first. While the Egyptians and Sumerians refer to themselves even in their earliest period as old cultures and look to many civilizations before and around them, it is ludicrous for us to say that they invented civilization. Certainly whatever culture invented civilization would have known it. It would not have regarded itself as simply one in a long line of such cultures. Yet such views are now taken for granted by our historians and archaeologists.

We observe a certain homogeneity in ancient culture throughout the world. The solar religions which once dominated the ancient world from Mexico and Peru to Egypt, Europe, India and China, must have been related. Their priestly and warrior cultures and temple worship reflect a certain commonality of culture. We cannot isolate humanity into local cultures in ancient times any more than in modern times. Contact between cultures may have been more difficult but as human beings we always find a way to learn about our neighbors. Evidences of diffusion in art and literature abound. Hence it is not surprising to find that some of the people mentioned in the *Rig Veda* may include the Assyrians, Egyptians, Phoenicians, Persians, and perhaps even American Indians.

We have narrowed down our picture of the ancient world to fit into our ideas of human history. Ancient cultures relate their origins to various sages, usually seven seers, who are often identified with the stars of the Big Dipper or the Pleiades. We ignore such ideas and explain human civilization as developing through various practical inventions like pottery, writing, or the wheel. This is not based on an understanding of the ancient world, nor is it the view of the ancients themselves. It is what is convenient to our own particular mind-set and our technological and materialistic values. It is important that we examine what the ancients themselves say and how the statements of different ancient cultures fit together, not how it would appear to us today as if our values pertained to all of human history.

In interpreting history we have made our type of culture the pinnacle of human civilization, as if it represented its most important trend. Yet the kind of culture we have does not appear to be typical of human culture even through the historical period we know of. Human culture has always been of a primarily religious orientation, except for modern times, and even today the place of religion is strong over much of the world. Our culture actually appears to be more of a temporary sidetrack from the general religious trend of human civilization as a whole and should not be made to serve as the measurement for all of it. What it means to be a human being, or what human civilization means, must be examined in its total context, all of history, not just that of modern man. This is not to say that these religious cultures did not have many corruptions, some of which modern culture has corrected. Yet there was also much that was very good in them which we have lost, particularly if we go back to their original teachings before their decline through time.

Our historians have systematically rejected the testimony of the ancients as unreliable and have branded most of their statements about the origins of human civilization as mythological or superstitious and without much historical basis. We have even dismissed their ideas about themselves and have imposed upon them our own interpretation of who they were. While we have learned to accept such places as Troy as real and not just legendary, we have dismissed most of the literature of the other ancient cultures as not referring to anything actual or substantial. The great Indian epic, the *Mahabharata,* for example, refers to a civil war involving all of north India that occurred some time before that of the Buddha. Kings from throughout the whole country of the time are mentioned as having been involved in the battle. This we have turned into a local skirmish among petty princes in the northwest corner of India, which was later exaggerated by poets. We assume exaggeration, if not deception, on the part of the ancients rather than giving them credit for what they actually say when it goes against what we believe possible for them.

We have dug up ancient ruins and have used scientific methods to date them but we have interpreted them according to the preconceptions of our own culture. Ruins may be interpreted in many ways, including some quite different than what our textbooks say today. The interpretation we have given these ruins may tell more about us than about them. We cannot assume that the ruins we have found are complete. Much of the potential ground of civilization has not been excavated. Much of it cannot be excavated, nor can all of it ever be found. Nor do cultures always leave ruins. They must build in stone, end suddenly, or be left in a suitable climate to do so. Nor do ruins speak. We give them a voice. We often have trouble understanding modern India or modern China. How can we expect to understand haphazard ruins of ancient India or China? The fact that we have found the main remains of civilization in the Middle East may not reflect the truth of history. It may just reflect the region's proximity to our own cultural matrix and the desert climate of the region suitable to preserve ruins. It may be an accident, not a real uncovering of the origins of human culture.

The question of the history of India is particularly difficult because it is a culture with which we have not had a direct link, unlike those of the ancient Middle East. In our history of the world, we reduce India and China, where the largest number of human beings have always lived and where civilizations have retained the greatest continuity, to be of only minor interest. A typical study of world history today focuses on modern European history and casts but a side glance on all ancient and Eastern cultures, as if they were not of real significance.

We have ignored ancient historical dates and records, including calendars going back to 3000 BC or earlier, as baseless mythology or as a mere invention of later times.[a] If the ancients were as primitive and circumscribed in their understanding of the world as we claim, why is their sense of history longer than ours? It is not only the Babylonians and Greeks who developed astronomy and astrology; so did the Hindus, Chinese, and Mayans. Yet we ignore the information yielded by Hindu astronomy because it reflects an earlier period of history than we can conveniently ascribe to it.

The question of the *Rig Veda* is even more difficult because many ideas about it have become accepted as fact, even though they are highly speculative and not proven by the actual text. The modern idea is that the Vedic people were a racial type (Aryans). They are said to have invaded India in the second millennium BC as primitive nomads from Central Asia. The *Rig Veda* is said to have been composed in the Punjab region of northwest India as the first step of this invasion. These are ideas used to interpret the text. They are not found within it. In fact, they require altering the meaning of words and changing the orientation of the text to make them credible. However, no one seems to really read the *Rig Veda* these days in the original Sanskrit. We read it through the interpretations and naturally it proves the interpretations. If we find astronomical references to early eras (before 2000 BC) in the *Vedas,* we cannot say that these are too early for them to be real. This is not scholarship, it is prejudice, which literally means prejudgment.

The *Rig Veda,* as its language and culture has great affinities with those of ancient Europe, is more threatening to our modern ideas of man. The more credibility we give it, the more credibility we give to a possible Indian origin to our own European culture, which many of us may not particularly like to be true. The *Rig Veda* may cause us to reassess our own ancient heritage and we may find that there is a spiritual side to our own pre-Christian culture that may be of great value to us even today.

Hopefully, recent excavations in India, particularly of Dwaraka, a newly discovered ancient Indian city that is perhaps the city of Krishna long ago submerged into the sea, will serve to dispel many of these notions. They suggest that the Vedic people (called Aryans, though not to be confused with the modern European usage of this term) were already in India by 1500 BC and built magnificent stone port cities at the furthest point of Gujarat. This would show that the massive ancient Indus Valley civilization that preceded such sites — and has already been well excavated in India and Pakistan — was also Vedic and that the entry of the Vedic people into India would have to come before the beginning of this civilization, before 3000 BC. My view here is that it was even earlier than this.

However, it is not the purpose here to explore accounts of recent excavations. This is the work of archaeologists. This book is meant to give a different and more accurate literary interpretation of the *Rig Veda* that should substantiate such finds and take them back further. While we can use both literary and archaeological accounts to supplement each other, we should not make one hostage to the other. We cannot say that since archaeological evidence does not substantiate that the Vedic people were near the ocean, their common words for the ocean must therefore refer to something else. We may not be able to fit a literary record into an archaeological mold but that should not be the basis for interpreting it. Otherwise it will only substantiate whatever may be our latest archaeological idea.

Nor can we say that we have no archaeological evidence of Vedic culture. The extensive Indus Valley culture of ancient India (dated 3000–1500 BC) is located right in the Saraswati river area described in the *Vedas.* The river went dry before the end of the Indus Valley culture. How could the Vedic people know of a river that declined and went dry before they supposedly entered the region? The *Vedas* also use an astronomical calendar of this same time period (2000 BC and earlier). Archaeological evidence is not enough if our interpretation of it is incorrect. Nor can we find archaeological evidence to support a literary text that we have wrongly interpreted. In approaching the *Vedas*, a literary misinterpretation has given rise to an archaeological misinterpretation. While more excavations may uncover this error, it is also evident if we examine the literary record with more sensitivity.

It is surprising that we have not been able to find a place in ancient history for the largest preserved ancient literary tradition. We have placed it in some apparent dark age between the end of the Indus Valley culture and the time of the Buddha. Yet this dark age is rapidly disappearing with new discoveries. It is also strange to place the most extensive and enduring literary record of ancient civilization in an archaeological dark age. Is that explaining it or ignoring it?

On the basis of the *Vedas,* we will be able to explore the origin of humanity and world civilization. Our concern is not just with the origins of Indian culture but that of the whole of humanity. We will see the story of man centered in an area of the world that is as likely to be the source of early civilization as is the Middle East. India and its surrounding region is the home of the majority of the religions of humanity. The religions of India, of course, originate here: those of the Hindus, Buddhists, Jains and Sikhs. These have dominated the Eastern world including China, Japan, Indochina and Indonesia, and have had some effect on the Western world as well.

The ancient Persian religion, the Zoroastrian, had a similar form to the Vedic and greatly influenced the religions of the Middle East, including both Judaism and Christianity. The idea of the 'savior' appears to have originated with it. It influenced Rome and such medieval mystical movements found in Europe as the Manicheans and the Freemasons. The older pre-Christian religions of the Greeks, Romans, Kelts, Germans and Slavs — the Indo-European peoples from which most of us in the West have descended — resembled the Vedic just as their languages are related to Sanskrit. Much of our European mythology has a Vedic counterpart. Even such modern religions as Islam, which invaded India, were very much influenced by the teachings of India and adopted some of them, particularly on a mystical level. The history of humanity is as much the history of religion as anything else, as religion has always been closest to the heart of man and the most enduring aspect of civilization. In this regard we should look to India, the land of Yoga and religion.

What emerges in light of this view is the Vedic as the possible original or prototypal culture for the human race in this World Age; the Vedic as the root of all human civilization of the last ten thousand years or so. This does not imply a mere glorification of India or Hinduism either. Vedic or

Aryan culture extended beyond India, as is visible in its ancient European and Persian varieties. Most of its forms predate those of later Hinduism, though they are related to them. Vedic culture appears to have its spiritual center in an area now in Tibet (Mount Kailas) and it probably included members of the Oriental as well as the Caucasian races. I think that the origin of all religions can be found in the *Rig Veda.*

Hence let us start a new journey into the ancient world, not viewing the ancients from the outside but from the inside, with respect for the ancients themselves and the legacy they struggled with such great labor to pass on to us. Teachings passed on over millennia must have represented truths so crucial for humanity that we cannot simply dismiss them carelessly. We are beginning to recognize the power of myth. In this regard the religions of India have the most complex mythology in all the world. Their basis in the *Rig Veda* must thereby be central to our understanding of world mythology.

***

> *Four are the levels of speech. Three concealed in mystery cannot be manipulated. The wise who have knowledge know all of these, common men speak only with the fourth.*
> — *Rig Veda I.164.39*

THE SYMBOLISM OF LIGHT

Ways of Interpreting the Veda

The Gods and myths of the *Rig Veda* have been interpreted primarily in a naturalistic way. Both the older native scholars, like Sayana (c. 1400 AD) and Yaska (c. 600 BC), and modern Western scholars have followed this approach, though the older commentators also admitted deeper meanings and spiritual interpretations. European scholars read the *Veda* as primitive poetry of nomadic Aryans, as they invaded India around 1500 BC overthrowing a previous high civilization that they little understood. Older Hindu scholars saw a development from a ritualistic religion in the *Vedas* to the meditative philosophy of the *Upanishads.* They did not see a barbaric invasion but an organic growth within the same culture. Only a few rare thinkers have ascribed a deeper meaning to the ancient Vedic hymns themselves.

The great Vedic myth is of the winning of the Light and the Waters by the Gods. This is achieved by the help of man through the sacrifice which gives power to the Gods. It involves a battle against the forces of darkness, negativity and drought. The lights that are sought are the dawn, day and the Sun. Winning the Waters is gaining the release of the rivers to flow into the sea. Central to this is the myth of Indra, the main Vedic God, like the Greek God Zeus, who slays the dragon who withholds the Waters and thereby brings about their release. This has been regarded mainly as a myth of the bringing of rain, so sought after by primitive people, simple farmers and herdsmen. The winning of the dawn and the Sun has been interpreted as a worshipping of the powers of light through the day.

While we can take this naturalistic approach as a starting off point in viewing the *Rig Veda,* it is only scratching the surface. It can be taken in different ways and can prove much more than has been allowed for it. In itself it does not prove that the *Rig Veda* was composed in Central Asia or northwest India by primitive nomads who knew nothing of the wider world or the greater arts of civilization. A culture would not likely have developed the myth of the winning of the rivers to flow into the sea if it had never seen the ocean. Moreover, the winning of the Waters and the winning of the Light are presented in the *Rig Veda* as a single victory; the Waters are those of the Sun world. Why should a culture equate a daily light myth with a yearly water-rain myth? In north India there is a unique climatic condition wherein the rains occur at the summer solstice, the time when the days are longest. Inhabitants of such a land would quite naturally associate the light with the rains. Equating the rains with the year and the Sun would thus suggest north India as the land wherein this myth originated.

I have followed out this winning of the Waters myth and used it to prove a much different point than the ordinary one. I believe it shows that the *Rig Veda* portrays the sacred geography of north India in its river, ocean, and mountain symbolism. It shows a land between two mountain ranges, between two oceans, between Heaven and Earth, the land of the Gods or the atmosphere, a land of seven great rivers flowing to the sea, of which the great Indus is only one. This is the specific geographical domain of north India. Hence the *Rig Veda* must have been composed primarily in north India, not just a corner of it, but with knowledge of the entire domain.

We can accept that the Waters and the Light are an important aspect of the Vedic myth and can be used to make sense of the hymns. It can even show a culture with a broad geographic extent. But I do not think that such a naturalistic view explains everything, nor that it reveals the secret of the Veda, however we interpret it. Light and water are themselves symbols which can mean any number of things. They are not just rain and sunlight. Ancient man had enough spiritual preoccupations, as is obvious from the ritualistic nature of his culture, that he could see something more to life than the gaining of rain and sunlight. Such things are not so unpredictable in nature that they require constant ritual worship to assure. Light may also stand for the spiritual light, the winning of enlightenment or Self-realization.

Just because we have an interpretation that can make some sense of a thing does not mean that we can rest content with it as explaining all of it. Even today most human behavior can be interpreted as a seeking of food, which is one of the main interpretations of the solicitations of ancient peoples. Yet that does not take us very far in understanding different human cultures. While we might be satisfied with such a superficial view of the ancients, whom we don't have to deal with and may not want to bother with, it is explaining things away, not understanding them, and is not acceptable to a deeper inquiry.

While this simple naturalistic interpretation has been the main view, it can be extended yet further. Some scholars, like Tilak,[b] have interpreted the Vedic winning of the Light as a yearly rather than daily myth, reflecting the seasons and solstices. That the victory of the Sun is the winning of the year is well known in later Vedic literature, like the *Brahmanas,* wherein the sacrifice follows the movement of the Sun and is marked by the solstices. Such an interpretation reveals some very ancient stellar positions, suggesting the *Rig Veda* dates back much earlier than we have thought. I certainly accept that approach here also and take it back yet further. Just as the winning of the seven rivers to flow into the sea shows us the larger geographical domain of north India, the yearly winning of the Sun at the solstice shows us a much more ancient time period for the hymns than is usually acknowledged. Through these two interpretations we can take the *Veda* back not only to a much larger area but to a much earlier time.

Yet even this, though it reveals the antiquity of the *Vedas,* does not show everything. If we were to stop here we would regard the Vedic as a very ancient and extensive civilization, perhaps the root of all human culture. While this would be a great step in the right direction, we might still interpret it as a spiritually primitive culture or even an early scientific-poetic culture.

The Sun and the Waters have an inner reality in the *Vedas.* The inner Sun that is won is the enlightened mind or the consciousness of the Self. The Vedic myth reflects the practice of Yoga. The main Vedic God Indra, the wielder of the thunderbolt, destroys the dragon who lies coiled at the foot of the mountain and thereby releases the seven rivers to flow into the sea. Indra represents the awakened mind or the state of 'seeing'. The dragon or serpent is the Kundalini which lies at the base of the mountain of the spine. The mountain-spine equation is very common in yogic and mythological literature. The seven rivers are the seven chakras or yogic centers in the subtle body. Their waters are the streams of bliss that flow from them. The Vedic myth thus has in essence a spiritual meaning. It is a myth of enlightenment from an ancient culture that valued enlightenment perhaps more so than any culture in history. It reflects the spiritual glory of the Vedic people.

I suggest three major points in interpreting the Vedic myth:

1. The geographic domain it presents: its homeland, portrayed through its sacred geography, is that of north India from sea to sea.

2. According to its calendar, its astrology and astronomy, it shows a time period as early as 6000 BC.

3. According to its spiritual meaning, it shows a symbolism of the practice of Yoga and meditation. The Vedic seers not only had spiritual knowledge but they named and interpreted their spacio-temporal environment according to its symbolism.

Some may object to such a multidimensional interpretation. How can we say that the *Rig Veda* can be interpreted in terms of a geographical area, an astrological calendar and the practice of Yoga? Are these not mutually exclusive? We should note that the idea of several levels of meanings is common in the interpretation of scriptures all over the world. The four or seven levels of interpretation of the *Koran* or *Bible* are well known. Why should the scripture of India and of Sanskrit, the most multileveled of all languages, be different? The Sanskrit language has a tremendous range for plays on words and double meanings. The whole literature is full of it. How can we exclude this from the enigmatic, cryptic *Vedas,* which speak frequently of secret meanings and different levels of speech? Vedic Sanskrit can be interpreted in more different ways even than later Sanskrit. This is why there are so many varied and contrary interpretations of it.

While it is sacred geography and sacred time which are mentioned in the *Rig Veda,* these were also used to structure the outer time and space. The people named their places and rivers after their Gods and their stories. They oriented their calendar in a similar way. Hence from Vedic sacred time and space we can also understand when and where the *Vedas* were composed or gathered.

Those of more spiritual bent may object to describing the holy *Vedas* in geographic or temporal terms. They have their point. The spiritual meaning is the essential thing. It goes beyond all outer concerns. From its perspective, when and where the *Vedas* were compiled is irrelevant. It is their inner truth which ultimately matters. Yet these outer facets are important for communicating with the mind of our times and putting the *Vedas* in their proper place in human culture. As long as we do not make these outer meanings primary or final, they have their value. However, if they are all we see, our vision is indeed narrow.

What has been most curious in the modern interpretations of the *Veda*, both by western and native scholars, is their non-religious and unspiritual nature. The *Rig Veda* is said to be the 'Shruti', the scripture or book of revelation, the Hindu Bible. Yet it has been interpreted in naturalistic and sociological terms, as a kind of cultural document. The same thing has often been done with the *Bible* and other ancient scriptures. We cannot understand the *Rig Veda* unless we view it primarily as a religious or spiritual document and only secondarily as a cultural statement. Hence if the *Rig Veda* is filled with a sevenfold symbolism this must primarily reflect the nature of the universe as having seven planes of consciousness, as we know from all occult and religious teachings. It was not because their domain encompassed exactly seven rivers. At the same time they would not have used the symbolism of a land of great rivers if they lived in a riverless desert like the Central Asian area from which they were supposed to be nomadic invaders.

PREVIEW OF CONCLUSIONS

Before we examine the conclusions proposed in this book, it is helpful to review the prevalent views on the ancient history of India through the *Vedas*.

Traditional Hindu View of the Vedas

The *Vedas* are the scriptures of the Hindu religion. They are regarded as the mantras of the great ancient seers and sages, said to have been enlightened sages comparable to Krishna, Buddha, or Christ in their realizations. The *Vedas* are seen as originating from earlier ages of light, the mythical Golden Age of truth. Seers of the *Rig Veda* like Vasishta, Vishwamitra, and Agastya are referred to throughout Hindu literature as its great teachers. The Aryan peoples of India, including the Hindu Dravidians of the south, place themselves in the lineages of the Vedic seers and their families as their descendants. The Vedic religion was founded by Manu, the mythical 'first man', who was said to have come down from the Himalayas after a great flood in early ancient times and established the Vedic culture on the banks of the Saraswati river. India was thus the original home of Vedic culture from which it spread throughout the world.

Prevalent Historical View of the Vedas

The prevalent Western textbook view of Vedic culture is quite different than the Hindu view, which it regards as a typical product of the so-called primitive mythic imagination. The Vedic people are regarded as nomadic tribes, who came from the steppes of southern Russia, entering India through Afghanistan around 1500 BC. They are assumed to have been fair-skinned, blue-eyed, and light-haired, which distinguished them from the dark-complexioned natives whom they discriminated against. The Vedic invaders are described as nomadic cattle breeders who, with horse-drawn chariots and iron weapons, defeated the native population of India by the crude force of arms. By this view, the Vedic people gradually took over a superior urban Indus Valley culture of Dravidian origin which had flourished in India already for a thousand years (though perhaps was already in a state of decline). While the Vedic people were racially assimilated into the native culture whose superior civilization they adopted, and which probably included the spiritual system of Yoga, they still managed to impress the land with their language and with reverence for their literature and sages as the greatest of humanity. All memory of the invasion appears to have been eradicated in what may have been one of the greatest cover-ups in the history of the world.

Revised View of the Vedas Presented in this Book

The interpretation presented here moves in the direction of the older Hindu view of the *Vedas*. If we examine the *Vedas* with a sensitivity to their spiritual meaning, and with an understanding of their symbolism, the following points become probable:

1. Woven into the entire fabric of the *Vedas*, from beginning to end, is an oceanic symbolism. The *Rig Veda* is a product of a maritime culture, that undertook travel, trade, and colonization by sea. The ocean was known in the earliest period. If the Vedic people did migrate into India, it is likely that at least some of them came by sea or from a land that bordered the ocean. This we explore in our first chapter 'The Image of the Ocean'.

2. The main site of habitation for the Vedic people was along the rivers of northern India, most centrally the Saraswati river region, which existed between the modern Ravi and Yamuna rivers all the way down to the sea in an area which is now the desert of Rajasthan. Some of the rivers of India were different

at this early era. Some of their courses have changed and others have gone dry, as modern geographical studies confirm.

Additional areas of Vedic culture included the Ganges river basin down to the Bay of Bengal and the Indus basin and its rivers down to the Arabian Sea. There are also references to rivers in Afghanistan, in what was called Gandhara. Central spiritually to Vedic culture were the Himalayan lands of the Soma to Mount Kailas in Tibet. The seven Vedic rivers are the great rivers of north India from sea to sea. These we explore in our second and third chapters 'The Saraswati River' and 'The Land of the Seven Rivers'.

3. One of the most important and last legends of the *Rig Veda,* that of Sudas or the 'Battle of the Ten Kings', is a battle between Aryan kings in north India for the control of the entire region. This shows that the Aryans had been in India some time before the *Rig Veda* was finished. The *Rig Veda* culminates with an Aryan civil war in India. The chapter 'Stories of Vedic Kings from the *Rig Veda*' centers on this issue.

4. A Vedic or Aryan renovation of India (such as the legend of Divodasa) did occur but at a much earlier period of the hymns, apparently after a great Flood. Even here, the Aryans overthrew a related but spiritually fallen culture, which had oppressed them and which at least some of them had fled from. They did not fight with unfamiliar peoples but with the members of their own culture who failed to maintain the spiritual law of the land. Hence, an 'Aryan revolt' is a more appropriate term than an 'Aryan invasion'.

The Vedic people appear to have come down from the Himalayan river valleys, where some of them may have fled as refugees. Other Vedic hymns speak of the Vedic ancestors as coming from across the sea or having been saved from a Flood. Hence some of them may have come to India by sea. The main Vedic era began after a great deluge that destroyed an earlier, fallen culture, the remnants of which the Vedic Aryans fought and overcame as their evil ancestors (like the myth of the destruction of Atlantis or the Biblical Flood). Vedic Kings created large empires encompassing most of modern India and perhaps beyond. These issues we will also explore mainly in our section on 'Stories of the Vedic Kings', particularly the second part 'From the *Brahmanas* and *Puranas*'.

5. The date of the *Rig Veda* is much earlier than usually accepted. Such river and oceanic references by themselves put the Vedic people from sea to sea in north India at an early period of the text.

The most reliable source for dating is the Vedic calendar. This can be dated in two ways: relative to the equinox and to the solstice. The Taurus (Krittika) vernal equinox and the summer solstice in Leo (Magha), which indicate a date of around 2000 BC, were introduced near the end of the Vedic age. The Gemini (Mrigashira) vernal equinox and the summer solstice in Virgo (Phalguni), which indicate a date of around 4000 BC, occur toward the later period of the *Rig Veda* and in the early period of the other *Vedas*. The Cancer (Purnarvasu) vernal equinox and the summer solstice in Libra (Chitra), a period of around 6000 BC, appear in an earlier period of the *Rig Veda*, with suggestions of yet earlier calendars existing in the text. These we will explore in detail in the two chapters on 'Vedic Astronomy'.

6. The priests or Brahmins had special occult knowledge that allowed them to control some of the forces of nature. They had yogic knowledge that afforded them many powers beyond those of ordinary humanity. While they knew a great deal about the secret forces of nature, their knowledge worked through the mind rather than through technology. Meditation or mantra was the main force they used. It allowed them to travel great distances, to bring on the rain and to part the rivers for people to cross. They kept their knowledge secret, veiled in a mystery religion, and allowed the majority of people to follow a simple outer life in harmony with nature.

The great spiritual knowledge of the Brahmins included a highly developed system of Yoga. This is also reflected in the symbolism of the hymns, whose prime goal is enlightenment or liberation, which we examine specifically in the chapter 'Vedic Religion'.

7. Based on this interpretation of the *Vedas* we can correlate most of the peoples and cultures of the ancient world with the

Vedic. We can begin to discern a world-civilization in early ancient times of a technologically simple but spiritually sophisticated nature, possessing also much occult knowledge and power. We are the fallen descendants of that era, the children of the seers who have wandered far. This is the culminating part of the book in the three chapters of the section 'Peoples of the Ancient World'.

To support this material there is additional information in the Appendix. The Vedic people had a broad view of the physical world with a knowledge of oceans, mountains, deserts, and forests. They also had a broad knowledge of the subtle worlds, the realms of the Gods, and understood all the different levels of cosmic existence from dense physical matter to pure consciousness itself. This we explore in the appendix on 'Vedic Cosmology'.

The Vedic culture had cities, villages, and nomadic people under its rule. Cities were made of stone, plastered brick, and metal reinforcement. Both agriculture and cattle raising were practiced. They had herds of cattle, horses, and camels in the tens of thousands. They had horse-drawn chariots and ships with oars and sails for travel. They worked in gold, metal, clay, stone, wood, leather, and wool and had a high development of arts and crafts, as well as astrology, medicine, music, dance, and poetry. The Vedic people not only conquered cities but had many of their own. They were a culture of smaller kingdoms under a central king or emperor. These issues are explored primarily in the Appendix on 'Vedic Civilization'.

The *Vedas* thus appear to be our best record of the ancient spiritual teachings of humanity. They contain a timeless wisdom, a mantric code in which the wisdom of the race was passed down from World Age to World Age, for how many millennia we can only speculate. The Vedic people were probably in India by 6000 BC and before and may be the native people of that region.

Many spiritual and occult teachings, including those of India, look back to earlier eras than these. The *Rig Veda* itself looks back upon earlier ages and reflects the knowledge of long cosmic time cycles. However, the hymns of the *Rig Veda* treat these earlier eras as current. We do not have any other ancient teachings, at least not among known books and scriptures, that were set down at such an early time.

This interpretation of the *Vedas* fractures our modern view of the ancients. It shows that cultures existed in early ancient times that were much more highly advanced spiritually than ours is today; they were not mere primitive barbarians. While they did not develop technology as we know it, they had occult and spiritual knowledge and powers in many respects quite superior to it, though these were often hidden.

This new view of the *Rig Veda* requires a complete reevaluation of our view of history and our idea as to who we are as human beings. We are children of the ancient seers, not just the offspring of primitive hunters, farmers, or traders. Our legacy is in cosmic consciousness, not just in tools and machines. These great seers even fathered our ancient European ancestors. We Westerners also come from the same spiritual roots as the people of the East, of India. All the world may literally be as the *Vedas* say, of one family.

INTERPRETATIONS OF HISTORY

A Spiritual Model

Our interpretations of history follow our social values and beliefs. Our modern interpretation is essentially a commercial and technological one. We see civilization as developing through the invention of the wheel, writing and so on. It reflects the view of a culture that holds wealth and equipment to be the highest reality and is attached to the outer world of the senses as the truth. Such commercial and technological ideas of humanity do not show much sensitivity to the spiritual view of life. They are economic ideas and reflect the bias of the business class. They are a merchant's view of history and reality. They are the products of an outgoing mind, seeking not so much to understand the world as to dominate it.

We also have a strong political orientation in our interpretation of history. Our history is largely one of governments and political power struggles. This reflects the bias of the political mind and its worldly power seeking motives. While there is little human activity for which we cannot ascribe some economic or political motivation, this creates much distortion when we apply it to the spiritual life.

The ancients, particularly those in spiritual cultures like India and Egypt, looked up to their sages. They did not look up to the commercial man as their cultural ideal (though they also struggled with these same social value issues). The idea that civilization was invented by farmers, merchants, or craftsmen was foreign to them. They looked to the Gods and the priests as their culture bearers.

They preserved their traditions largely through oral transmissions. We call them illiterate because they may not have known how to write. Yet many such ancient bards memorized thousands of verses and could extemporize poetry of a complex metrical order that few of us today, particularly the passive generation of the mass media, could ever do. They looked upon the written word as something profane, best used for business, but not for the sacred literature that was their greatest treasure. The *Rig Veda,* which was not written down for long periods of time, is probably the best preserved of these oral texts.

Who founded civilization? This depends upon what we define civilization to be. A commercial view will take us back to the first businessmen. A scientific view will give us the first scientist. A religious view will take us back to the first teachers of a particular religion. If the essence of civilization is technology then the modern view may be right, but if it is the culture of the spirit, it is quite wrong. By my interpretation civilization was founded by the yogis, seers, and sages. A 'spiritual model' of history like the one proposed in this book was also the testimony of the ancients. It describes civilization as a fall from grace or the eternal. It reflects the Divine or the Self as the highest reality and remains detached from the outer world of appearances.

There is a class of human beings, perhaps very small in number, who have always looked over humanity. These are the great gurus, avatars and spiritual teachers. In ancient times they had a much greater role developing and shaping human culture. As humanity declined from the ancient ages of light they gradually withdrew into seclusion. Today they still exist, though they may be hard to find by the outer mind. We read of such great masters who look over the world in all the religious teachings of the world. The prime area they relate to is the Himalayas. There are the Islamic Sufis in the western Himalayas or Hindu Kush, the Tibetan Buddhists in the north, the Chinese Taoists and Buddhists in the east and the great Hindu Yogis in the south and central area. It is to this region I think we should look for the origins of human culture. While many occult teachings glorify such masters and may put a cloak of illusion or mystery about them, there is still a core of truth about them which we cannot ignore. It is not so much as miracle men that we should look at them but as enlightened beings, those who have mastered the ego and have found the entire universe to exist within themselves.

Our political and economic interpretations of history cannot be true if enlightenment or spiritual realization is the real goal of humanity. Such views remain subjective, childish and bound by the biases of the mind and ego. As we mature spiritually we must give them up and recognize our higher source and purpose. This is to acknowledge our spiritual ancestors and guides.

We also have an occult, science fiction view of history as involving beings from other worlds or ancient technology. Ancient Gods may be turned into astronauts, temples into space ships etc. While the ancients were much more evolved than our current estimation of them admits, this view is quite often a product of the modern science fiction imagination. The origin of humanity is not in the outer world, not even by beings in spaceships. It is in the Divine consciousness within us.

The ancients were more aware of subtle and astral realities than we are. They communicated with beings of these worlds, some of whom were very spiritual and benefic, others who were quite malicious. They mention them as Gods, titans, and demons. While some of them were beings from other physical worlds, most were contacted in the mind, though some did materialize themselves or gain a connection to the physical world by the power of the worship afforded to them. Humanity did become involved with wars between the Gods and the demons. Yet this is only a symbolism for the eternal battle between truth and falsehood within us that we always have to face. In fact, earlier humanity fell from its spiritual heights by allying itself with the inferior Gods or powers of darkness, the beings of the lower astral plane.

The great high Gods of the ancients were spiritual truth-forces. They were transmitted by the power of the sages to limit or eliminate negative influences on Earth. The *Rig Veda* celebrates a great victory of the Gods over the demons, the powers of enlightenment over those of ignorance and unconsciousness. Many people, particularly in the New Age and occult fields, are opening up to the astral plane again. It is important that we do so with great caution and insight. Otherwise we may just draw back some of these same forces of darkness and illusion and bring more confusion into the world. The *Vedas* give us much insight in this regard.

The *Rig Veda* shows us a spiritual origin for human civilization. A similar conclusion may be arrived at if we examine seriously the teachings of any of the ancient cultures. Yet the *Rig Veda* possesses perhaps the largest scope of any of them and is worthy of examination by those of us who are concerned with this greater truth of humanity.

PART I

THE VEDIC WORLD

1

THE IMAGE OF THE OCEAN

THE MARITIME NATURE OF VEDIC CULTURE

All the universe rests within your nature, in the ocean, in the heart, in all life. — *Rig Veda IV.58.11*

The modern, generally Western idea, is that the *Rig Veda* is the product of a nomadic people invading India from the northwest, who, therefore, could not have known anything of the sea. They were crude warriors of the steppes and so we would not expect them to have any sense of, much less poetic and religious feeling for, the sea they had never seen.

However, this idea does not come from the *Veda* itself. It is a preconception used to interpret it. We can only discountenance the many references to the ocean in the *Rig Veda* by redefining the regular Sanskrit terms for ocean presented in it to have meant nothing more than any large body of water, river or lake. If we take them as they appear, as is done here, they fairly clearly show a maritime culture. Even a modern scholar like Griffith, though he does not allow that the early Vedic people had any contact with the ocean, is compelled to translate various Vedic terms as 'ocean' or 'sea' nearly a hundred times in his translation of the text. While the Vedic 'ocean' may also refer to that of Heaven or the atmosphere, such images do not reflect a lack of contact with the earthly ocean but the usage of it as a metaphor for the whole universe. They show great intimacy with the sea, not just as practical fact but as a poetic image impressed on them by life in proximity to it.

The image of the ocean permeates the entire text of the *Rig Veda.* This is not to say that the Vedic people were unfamiliar with mountains or rivers. Large forests and deserts are mentioned, but familiarity with these does not prove non-familiarity with the ocean. The scope of Vedic geography is quite large, with great mountains, plains, rivers and seas. This allowed scholars to focus on one side of it and become caught up in that one aspect. Yet the oceanic symbolism appears to be the most common. In this chapter we will explore the numerous Vedic references to oceans and ships and see how such statements cannot be explained except by assuming that the Vedic culture grew up by the sea — that the *Vedas* are the product of a maritime culture.

CREATION FROM THE COSMIC SEA

The Vedic idea of creation is from an original cosmic ocean, which overflows and thereby produces the manifest world. We see this in the Vedic creation hymns:

> Law and truth from the power of meditation were enkindled. Thence the night was born and thence the flooding ocean. From the flooding ocean the year was born. The Lord of all that moves ordained the days and nights. The Creator formed the Sun and Moon according to previous worlds; Heaven and Earth, the atmosphere and the realm of light (X.190).
>
> The creative Sun upheld the Earth with lines of force. He strengthened Heaven where there was no support. As a powerful horse he drew out the atmosphere. He bound fast the ocean in the boundless realm. Where the ocean overflows its boundaries, the creative Sun, as the Son of the Waters knows that. Thence came the world and the upper region, thence Heaven and Earth were extended (X.149.1-2).

What is perhaps the most famous Vedic creation hymn uses an entirely oceanic symbolism for the world's origin:

> In the beginning there was darkness hidden in darkness, all this universe was an unillumined sea (X.129.3).

Another hymn of the world's beginning speaks of the creation of the Sun, the light of the world, from an original cosmic sea:

> When the Gods stood together in the sea. Then as dancers they generated a swirling dust. When, like ascetics, the Gods overflowed the worlds, then from hidden in the ocean, they brought forth the Sun (X.72.6-7).

This idea of an original cosmic ocean is not limited to hymns of the tenth and last book of the *Rig Veda.* A hymn of the fourth book describes creation as from the cosmic sea and the gaining of immortality, the great goal of the Vedic sages, as mergence back into it. The hymn begins:

> From the ocean the blissful wave has arisen, together with its wave it attained immortality.

It ends:

> All the universe rests within your nature, in the ocean, in the heart, in all life. That which is borne in the confluence of the waters, may we attain that blissful wave of yours, oh Gods (IV.58.1, 11).[1]

A hymn of the fifth book identifies the Sun with the ocean as the Divine Son or source of the worlds, which in turn is one with the Divine Father or transcendent Spirit:

> Endless wide paths encompass Heaven and Earth from all sides. The bull, the ocean, the radiant bird, has entered into the home of the original Father (V.47.2–3).[2]

A culture which has never seen the ocean, or was just recently or vaguely acquainted with it, does not mythologize the origin of creation according to it.

Vedic Terms for the Sea

There are a number of terms in the *Rig Veda* that mean ocean or sea. 'Samudra', the main term in classical Sanskrit for the ocean, is very common in the *Rig Veda* and this meaning for it makes sense in all passages. It is the main such term we will explore in subsequent references. Samudra is the ocean, particularly as the great body of water into which all the rivers flow.

Some Western scholars have said that since samudra means etymologically 'a collection of waters' it could mean any large river or lake, particularly the Indus river, which in the Punjab is quite large. If samudra means ocean in classical Sanskrit we cannot explain it away by assuming that it meant something else originally. Nor does a culture mythologize so extensively about the ocean if they have only imagined it from a big river. We could just as well say that because our English word 'sea' may refer to a large inland lake, like the Caspian or Aral Sea, that it indicates that our knowledge of the ocean is faulty. Some overlapping of meaning of terms for ocean, sea, flood, or water may occur as language naturally develops.

Other Vedic terms that appear to mean ocean include 'salila', which refers more to the ocean depths or the unbounded sea. 'Arnas', which means flood or billowing overflowing waves of water, also at times appears to have a more general sense as the ocean. 'Apas', which means water generally, often refers to the expanse of the unbounded heavenly waters or celestial ocean. 'Purisha' is a name for the heavenly ocean as the source of the rains and is contrasted with the samudra as the earthly ocean, though there also occurs a higher and lower samudra as the heavenly and earthly seas. We also read of the waves, 'urmi', that come from the sea. In addition there are terms for lakes like 'saras', 'kula' and 'hlada'.

'Sindhu', which means river generally, not just the Indus river, sometimes appears in the more general sense of sea or large body of water. The Saraswati river also means sea or ocean in several passages. Let us examine a number of typical Vedic references to the ocean.

INDRA AND THE OCEAN

Vedic hymns are frequently compared to rivers that flow into the ocean which is the deity. This is particularly true of Indra, the most frequently invoked Vedic God. Indra is the great lord of the chants which flow to him like rivers to the sea.

> All songs give increase to Indra who is as expansive as the sea (I.11.1).[3]

The Vedic deity is thus the ocean to whom our hymns flow like rivers. Many such verses to Indra as the ocean can be found in the *Rig Veda.*

> Indra has an extent like the sea (I.30.3).[4]
> Indra, an ocean of wealth (I.51.1).
> Indra, extensive as the sea (I.52.4).[5]
> Hymns to Indra like the ocean in their convergence (I.56.2).[6]
> As rivers to the ocean strong hymns and songs have entered Indra whose extent is vast (VI.36.3).[7]
> The Soma drops, like rivers into the sea enter into Indra (III.46.4).[8]
> In the slope of the mountains, in the concourse of the rivers, by the power of the hymn the sage (Indra) was born. Hence, arisen conscious he looks down upon the sea, from which awakening he stirs (VIII.6.28-9).[9]

This last hymn to Indra lauds him along the whole course of rivers from the mountains to the sea.

The main Vedic myth also has an oceanic symbolism. It is of Indra who slays the dragon who withholds the waters and thereby releases the seven rivers to flow into the sea:

> You destroyed the dragon who withheld the waters. Earth in her awareness furthered your thunderbolt. You gave energy to the ocean-going floods. You became the Lord through strength, thou daring hero (IV.16.7).[10]
>
> He slew the dragon lying at the mountain. The creator fashioned for him his flashing thunderbolt. As milch cows bellowing as they flowed, directly the waters entered the ocean (I.32.2).[11]
>
> You slew the serpent who encompassed the floods. You released the waters to the ocean (VI.30.4).[12]
>
> By which you released the great floods to the ocean, Indra that power of yours is vigorous (VIII.3.10).[13]
>
> As rivers according to their impulse go forth, the floods as if chariot borne entered into the sea. As rivers uniting to the sea, to Indra they carry the well-pressed Soma (III.36.6–7).[14]
>
> Indra and Soma, the serpent, the withholder of the waters, you slew. You destroyed the dragon and Heaven approved. You sent forth the flood of the rivers and filled manifold seas (VI.72.2).[15]

Not only Indra but the other Gods like Soma aid in this work of killing the serpent and freeing the rivers to travel to the sea or seas.

This release of the seven rivers is sometimes compared to the pouring of the heavenly ocean which has seven foundations, an unlikely metaphor for a large river or lake.

> To Indra and Agni, like the seer Nabhaka, direct your prayers, who poured out the sea with seven foundations, whose opening is above (VIII.40.5).[16]

Indra and Agni, the two main Vedic Gods, win the Waters of the realm of light. This is the higher ocean above Heaven, the cosmic waters. The great Vedic war between the Gods and demons, between good and evil men, is for the heavenly Waters. The Waters are one of the great prizes of the Aryan people, along with the light, and are also symbolized by the cow. It is only contact with an earthly ocean that would give rise to the metaphor of a heavenly one.

Not only is Indra compared to the sea, his thunderbolt, vajra, with which he slays the dragon is found in the ocean. Indra's chariot also encompasses the seas.

> The thunderbolt lies within the ocean enclosed by the waters (VIII.100.9).[17]
>
> Indra, not by the seas or mountains is your chariot contained (II.16.3).[18]

This also symbolizes Indra's chariot as a vehicle or ship that travels on the seas.

The Vedic ocean, as we see, is not infrequently mentioned in the plural, showing a knowledge of more than one sea. The ocean is one of the dwelling places of Indra as it is of all the Gods.

> Whether you are in the luminous realm of Heaven or in the domain of the sea, whether in the station of the Earth or in the atmosphere, come to us, Indra (VIII.97.5).[19]
>
> Whether in the east, the south, the north or the west you are called by men, come quickly with your powers; whether you exult yourself on the slope of Heaven, in the Sun-world or in the ocean of Soma (VIII.65.2-3).[20]
>
> Come to us quickly, Indra, from Heaven or Earth, from the ocean or the heavenly sea (IV.21.3).[21]

We see both Heaven and Earth compared to two oceans. The hymns are also compared to the currents of the ocean that rise up from the bottom of the sea. The term for ocean used in this next reference, sagara, was later specific for the eastern sea or Bay of Bengal.

> To Indra I direct my songs in an unceasing flow, like waters from the bottom of the sea (X.89.4).[22]

AGNI AND THE OCEAN

Agni, the sacred fire, is the second major Vedic God after Indra in terms of the number of hymns to him. The Vedic is a religion of fire worship and fire rituals. Agni, like Indra, is frequently related to the ocean and the waters.

> All delights converge in Agni, as seven mighty streams into the ocean (I.71.7).[23]

> Oh Agni, for your firm law our words like cattle are spoken, as rivers to the sea (VIII.44.25).[24]
>
> Agni, whose vesture is the ocean. (VIII.102.4-6).[25]

The idea of the fire dwelling in the ocean, the submarine fire, is a common Vedic concept. In Vedic cosmology the worlds are sometimes three: Heaven and Earth and the Divine Waters beyond.

> From Heaven, Agni first was born; second on Earth from us as the knower of all births; third, in the Waters as the God-mind, enkindled perpetually, those of wisdom laud him. In the ocean, in the Waters, as the God-mind, you are enkindled as the Divine vision, oh Agni, in the udder of Heaven. Standing in the third region, in the lap of the Waters, the bull has grown (X.45.1, 3).

Agni thus has an ocean dwelling form, which is his highest form and original home. Agni is also said to dwell in all the rivers. He is identified with the ocean.

> Agni who possesses a sevenfold humanity is placed in all the rivers (VIII.39.8).
>
> Agni, the one ocean, the upholder of treasures (X.5.1).[26]

This strong familiarity with the rivers itself suggests knowledge of the ocean, as a maritime culture would extend down the rivers to the sea. The mingling of river and ocean symbolism thus tends to reinforce, not deny, the latter. All great ancient civilizations grew up in river plains by the sea. The Vedic was no different.

The *Vedas* describe creation as a series of oceans of light, which are cosmic forms of the great fire God, Agni.

> Agni, your splendor that is in Heaven and on the Earth, which has entered the plants and the waters, by which the wide atmosphere is extended, it is a brilliant ocean of light. Agni, you move to the ocean of Heaven ... to the waters which are beyond the luminous heaven of the Sun and to those which stand below it (III.22.2-3).[27]

There are waters or oceans both above and below the Sun, which itself is often identified with the sea.

Agni as Vaishwanara, the Universal Man, is the king who receives tribute from men, including those conquered by him, by the earthly sea, and from the Gods by the heavenly sea. This suggests trade or colonization by sea by the Vedic people.

> Having controlled the Nahusha people, Agni made them tribute bearers by his strength. In whose peace all people stand seeking grace according to their nature, the Universal Man sits at the supreme place of Heaven and Earth, in the lap of the parents. The Divine Fire, as the universal ruler, received the foundation treasures in the rising of the Sun. From the inferior and superior oceans, he received them, from Heaven and Earth (VII.6.5–7).[28]

DELIVERANCE ACROSS THE SEA

The symbolism of ships is as pervasive in the *Vedas* as that of the sea, which it tends to reinforce. The saving action of Agni, the sacred fire, is frequently compared to a ship that carries us across the river or sea.

> As a ship across the river (or sea), Agni, take us across to safety (I.97.8).[29]
>
> Agni will deliver us across all difficulties, as a ship across the river (or sea; I.99.1).[30]
>
> Agni, destroyer of difficulties, deliver us across all danger as a ship across the river (or sea; V.5.9).[31]

This image of wisdom, symbolized by fire, taking us across the river or ocean of worldly difficulties, remains in all Indian philosophy and is found in both Hindu and Buddhist works.

Other Vedic Gods save their worshippers from across the sea through a ship. The Ashwins are the main saviours and miracle workers of the Gods and this is one of their most famous actions.

> When he was lost in the supportless, foundationless, ungraspable ocean, you put forth your strength, oh Ashwins. You bore Bhujyu home, mounted on a ship with a hundred oars (I.116.5).[32]

Earlier in this hymn we read:

> For three nights and three days, oh Ashwins, you carried Bhujyu with your swift birds. To the other shore of the wet ocean, with three vehicles with a hundred feet and six horses (I.116.4).[33]

This is not a confused image of ocean travel. Bhujyu stands for the Sun. The three vehicles with a hundred feet and six horses are the 360 days of the year or degrees of the zodiac. The three days and three nights are a period at the end of the year wherein the Sun renews its light. Ocean travel is thus interwoven with the solar myth. The yearly return of the Sun follows the myth of crossing the ocean — an apt symbol for a maritime people. The sunset on the sea would give rise to such an image.

These ships that travel in the atmosphere and are often compared to birds or horses must be sailing vessels. The poetic vision of sailing ships would see them as birds flying in the blue of the sea, like the blue of the sky. We read of Bhujyu's rescue:

> With ships of the nature of the wind that travel through the atmosphere and keep the water away (I.116.3).[34]

This story of Bhujyu and his rescue from the ocean by the Ashwins and their mystic ship is a common Vedic myth.

> Ashwins, you bore Bhujyu from the flooding ocean with straight moving bird-horses (I.117.14).[35]
>
> Ashwins, you delivered Taugrya (Bhujyu) across the ocean (I.118.6).[36]
>
> You carried Bhujyu, the son of Tugra, from the watery ocean by birds, through the air (VI.62.6).[37]
>
> Ashwins, Bhujyu cast in the ocean, you bore across the floods with your unfailing horses (VII.69.7).[38]
>
> When the son of Tugra served you, abandoned in the sea, then with wings your vehicle flew (VIII.5.22).

Bhujyu is also one of the main mythic ancestors of the Vedic people, who call themselves 'Tugra' or 'Taugra' after his ancestry. The implication is that the Vedic people in part were refugees from some hostile land across the sea.

Turvasha and Yadu are the founders of two of the five main Aryan peoples. They are brought from afar across the flood. Like the story of Bhujyu, their story gives the image of Vedic ancestors as saved across the sea or flood by the grace of the Gods. In this regard, the Vedic Manu is himself a flood figure and he may be related to such early Vedic ancestors.

> Indra, you delivered across the sea, Turvasha and Yadu to safety (I.174.9).[39]
>
> For Turvasha and Yadu, you calmed the gushing waters on the farther shore (V.31.8).

The Vishwedevas, the Universal Gods, also deliver their worshippers across all difficulties like a ship across the waters, as do the great Vedic God of the sea, Varuna, and Soma, the Vedic God of immortality.

> Deliver us across all difficulties, oh Universal Gods, as ships across the waters (VIII.83.3).[40]
>
> Oh Divine Varuna, guide this hymn of your worshipper with wisdom and skill, by it may we cross over all difficulties; may we mount it as a saving ship (VIII.42.3).[41]
>
> Soma, deliver us as a ship across the river (or sea; IX.70.10).[42]

The Gods save their worshippers by the ship of prayer or wisdom. Why would a supposed group of cattle rearing nomads from Central Asia use such an image? The Vedic rite, the sacrifice, is also called a ship.

> The ships of truth have delivered the righteous. Varuna takes us across the great ocean (IX.73.1,3).[43]
>
> Those who do not have the power to ascend the sacrificial ship trembling fall into calamity (X.44.6).[44]

The Vedic hymn is frequently compared to a ship with oars, as it is the means of deliverance across the ocean of the world.

> At dawn, the new vehicle is employed. With four yokes, three whips, seven rays and ten oars, human and winning the light, it should be hastened with wishes and thoughts (II.18.1).

The Vedic word for ship, nau, is also a synonym for Vak, the Word Goddess. The *Veda* gives not metaphors of mountain nomads but of insightful poets using the image of the cosmic boat.

> Come with the ship of our thoughts to take us to the other shore, Ashwins, employ your vehicle. Your oar that is as wide as Heaven, your vehicle in the ford of the rivers, by thought the drops of Soma are employed (I.46.7–8).[45]

Ocean-going ships are the messengers of the Gods. Bearing delights, they appear as trading vessels. As sailing ships in the sunlight on the sea, they are compared to birds flying through the atmosphere.

> Pushan, your ships that are within the sea, golden in the atmosphere which travel, by them you go on the embassy of the Sun, made by love, desiring glory (VI.58.3).[46]
>
> When, oh Ashwins, you cross the ocean, men bring you fruits and delights (V.73.8).[47]

These travels of the Ashwins by sea are not to foreign peoples but to the Nahushas (V.73.3), descendants of Nahusha, who derive from Manu, thus suggesting Vedic colonies across the sea.

THE IMAGE OF THE FLOOD AND STOPPING THE WATERS

The flood is a common ancient myth. In any large river plain like north India floods and changes of river courses occur periodically. Naturally a culture that grew up in such a region would have many flood myths. Not only are the Vedic Gods compared to ships, they stop the waters and deliver the righteous miraculously over the floods.

> The great flowing stream of all rivers, Indra, you brought to rest by prayer the flood and made the rivers easy to cross for Turviti and Vaya (IV.19.6).
>
> The river Vibalyam, extending over the Earth, Indra, you stopped by your magic wisdom power (IV.30.12).

The Gods, in fact, release the flood to destroy evil men and to give the Earth to the Vedic or Aryan people to freely extend over. Indra speaks:

> I was the Father of the human race and the Sun. I am the seer Kakshivan. I humbled the sage Kutsa. I am the seer Ushanas, behold me. I gave the Earth to the Aryans, the rain to my mortal worshipper. I led the roaring floods. The Gods moved according to my direction (IV.26.1–2).

The Vedic people had the grace of the Waters. They preferred to live along large rivers and the sea. The great Vedic sages also have, among their miraculous powers, the power to stop the rivers and make them easy to cross. They communed with the great water spirits.

> The great seer, born of the Divine, directed by the Divine, wise in vision, stopped the flooding river, when Vishwamitra favored king Sudas (III.54.9).

The Gods provide the Vedic people the leadership to cross the waters. If the Aryans were a river and ocean going culture, they would have traveled to other lands and established similar cultures or colonies in other river basins.

> Maruts, let there be for us a powerful hero, who is the almighty ruler of men, through whom we may cross the waters to good habitations and dwell in our own home with you (VII.56.24).[48]

The Vedic battle is also for the Waters, perhaps a battle along the rivers and on the sea.

> The peoples direct their will in this work, fierce, powerful, contending with each other in the battle for the floods (IV.24.4).[49]

The Vedic people fight their enemies, the Dasyus, along the rivers. The rivers aid the Aryans (as Saraswati aids King Divodasa), and the Dasyus are defeated by the floods or in the convergence of the waters (VI.47.21). The Vedic war is not just for the light, it is for the waters, the rivers, perhaps even for the ocean. Indra speaks:

> As a bull I uphold seven rivers, wealth-flowing currents over the Earth. Of strong will I cross the floods, by war I made for man a way to goodness (X.49.9).[50]

Indra's enemy, the defeated serpent or dragon, lies slain in the middle of the sea.

> Not ceasing, not coming to rest, his body is hidden in the middle of their depths. The waters move around the

secret body of the serpent. Indra's enemy lies in extended darkness (I.32.10).

THE DIVINE SHIP, VARUNA AND OCEAN TRAVEL

With their enemies defeated by the flood and the release of the Waters, this leaves the Aryans free to travel over the Earth, which is compared to a Divine Ship.

> Heaven and Earth, the incomparable good protector, the Goddess Aditi who gives protection and guidance, may we ascend the Divine ship, free of sin, that has good oars which does not sink, to happiness.[51]
>
> Auspicious be our paths along the shores, auspicious in the convergence of the waters that bear the light of Heaven (X.63.10, 15).[52]

The Earth itself and the great Vedic Mother Goddess called Aditi are compared to a ship. This is only possible as an image for a people who traveled by ship and used ships for spreading over the Earth.

We read not only of using a ship for a house — living on boats — but using large ships to carry masses of people across significant expanses of water. This is hardly a mere ferry across a river that is mentioned here.

> Agni, give us a ship for our vehicle and house, with constant oars and quarters, which can take across our heroes and benefactors and our people to safety (I.140.12).[53]

Some Vedic Gods, like the Ashwins, the Vedic miracle workers who deliver Bhujyu across the sea, are said to live in a house on the sea. Their house must be a ship, or perhaps an island, like that in the Rann of Kutch, or a city like Dwaraka said to be built on the sea.

> Ashwins, whether you are in a distant habitation, or beyond in the luminous realm of Heaven or in a house built upon the sea, come thence to us (VIII.10.1).[54]

There are also images of the Sun as the Divine ocean or as a Divine ship.

> The Sun mounted the luminous ocean, having yoked his straight-backed horses. The wise have led him like a ship through the water. The Waters, listening, have come here. We hold in the waters your vessel (or thought) that wins the light, by which the seers of the nine rays crossed over the ten months. By this vessel may we gain the protection of the Gods, by this vessel may we cross over all narrowness (V.45.10–11).

The myth of the Navagwas or the 'seers of the nine rays', is one of the oldest in the *Rig Veda.* They help win the Sun out of darkness and gain the release of the heavenly waters. The Sun is often pictured as carried across the Heavens in the boat. We find this image both in ancient Egypt and in ancient India. The Vedic word for 'boat', 'nau', means also 'word'. The word for 'thought' or 'prayer', 'dhi', means also 'vessel'. Here the seers of the nine rays take the Sun in its vessel of prayer through the waters for a period of ten months or a year, the time of the sacrifice or human gestation, to reach the other shore beyond darkness. Ten months on the waters is an image of ocean travel, not crossing a river. Hence we see not only the image of the sea but of ocean travel at the core of the Vedic myth. The movement of the Sun through the year follows the image of crossing the sea. This would not be possible for a river.

The Maruts, the Vedic storm Gods, work on the sea. The Vedic storm includes the image of a storm on the sea:

> The Gods who dwell in the luminous realm of Heaven above the firmament, who make the mountains shake across the flooding ocean; who extend with their rays with strength across the ocean, Indra come with the Maruts (I.19.7–8).[55]

What are these mountains that are across the sea? They are surely not hills across a river. They must be a mountainous shoreline region or island, which again indicates the ocean-going nature of Vedic culture.

The Maruts as Gods of the storm draw the waters up from the ocean and make them rain.

> Oh Maruts, you draw up the rain from the ocean and, full of the heavenly waters, make it pour (V.55.5).[56]

A people must have had some knowledge and proximity to the ocean to know how the rains come from the evaporation of its waters.

Varuna, the ocean God, is a prominent Vedic God. By the opinions of a number of scholars, he is perhaps the oldest God of the Aryans.

> Varuna knows the station of the birds who fly through the atmosphere. He knows the ocean-going ships (I.25.7).[57]

Varuna, the God of the ocean in later times, is a much more prominent God in the *Rig Veda* and has an oceanic symbolism there also. He appears to be an ocean god from the beginning.

> Varuna is a secret ocean (VIII.41.8).[58]
>
> That is the great magic power of this divine greatest seer, Varuna, that no one can challenge, when the diverse flowing streams cannot fill the one ocean with their water (V.85.6).[59]

This shows a knowledge of several great rivers flowing into the sea. We find a variation on this same idea in another verse:

> Varuna dug a path for the Sun and led forth the ocean-going floods of the rivers (VII.87.1).[60]

Varuna as the God of the sea is communed with during ocean travel:

> When Varuna and I ascend into the ship, when we go forth to the middle of the sea, then we move with the waves of the waters and swing back and forth as if on a swing for joy. Varuna placed Vasishta in a ship. Skillful, he made him into a seer by his greatness. A sage, he made him a singer in the brightness of the days, as far as the heavens extended, as far as the dawns VII.88.3-4).[61]

Here we have the image of traveling on the ocean, riding on the waves for a period of days. Moreover, the enlightenment of the sage is compared to ocean travel in a ship. We have the image of the unbounded skies, of a long ocean journey. The seer of this hymn, Vasishta, is the most famous of the Vedic sages and has the most hymns in the *Rig Veda* of any seer. He is not just a minor seer but the foremost of them all. Hence if he knew of the sea why not the rest? His name is Maitrivaruni. He is the son of Mitra and of Varuna, the God of the sea. The great seer Agastya, who is brother to Vasishta, is also descended from Varuna and the sea. Hence it is not surprising that he is attributed with taking the Vedic teaching to south India and beyond by sea to Indonesia. Bhrigu, the father of the Bhrigu line of seers, the second most important seer-family in the *Vedas,* is also a son of Varuna or the God of the sea, and has among his descendants Turvasha and Yadu, two of the five Vedic people who are saved by the Gods from across the sea.

Vedic cosmology thus includes a great ocean God and the knowledge of several seas:

> The Maruts move through Heaven, Agni through the Earth, the Wind moves through the atmosphere. Through the Waters and the oceans, Varuna moves (I.161.14).[62]

THE OCEAN GOD AND WATER GODDESSES

The ocean itself is also invoked in the hymns to the Universal Gods, Vishwedevas:

> May the Creator with the Gods and their wives in accord, Heaven with the Gods and the Earth with the oceans, and the Dragon of the Depths hear us, along with the One-horned Goat, the Earth and the Ocean (VI.50.13-14).[63]

As in other passages more than one ocean is indicated; also we find the idea here of the Earth being encompassed by oceans. The Earth itself is compared to and called the sea, suggesting a knowledge that the ocean is much larger than the land mass on Earth.

The Dragon of the Depths, Ahir Budhnya, mentioned in this verse and in many of the hymns to the Universal Gods, appears to be a sea dragon. The One-horned or One-footed Goat, Aja Ekapat, is also associated with the ocean and must be some mythical sea monster. In another hymn to the Universal Gods, peace is asked from the various deities including the ocean:

> May the Divine One-footed Goat give us peace, peaceful be the Dragon of the Depths, peaceful the Ocean. May the Son of the Waters who is a ship be peaceful to us (VII.35.13).[64]

The Waters, Apas, have several hymns to them in the *Rig Veda.* They are worshipped as Divine, and ritual bathing was an integral part of the

Vedic religion. They often symbolize the heavenly waters and may mean the ocean in many passages. A hymn to the Waters starts out with the image of the ocean.

> Whose eldest is the ocean, from the middle of the sea, the Waters continue flowing unceasingly. The Waters which are heavenly or those which flow, which are dug out or those which come forth of themselves, whose goal is the sea (VII.49.1-2).[65]

Another Vedic God is called the "Son of the Waters," Apam Napat; the Waters being the cosmic waters. He is the Vedic version of Neptune, the Roman God of the sea, whose name comes from the same root (nap). Several hymns and many verses in the *Rig Veda* are addressed to him. He is obviously the ocean deified.

> Some unite to him, others flow to him, the rivers fill a common wideness. Shining pure, the Son of the Waters, the pure waters converge into him. All the worlds are like branches of him (II.35.3, 8).
>
> Priests, go to the ocean, worship with offerings the Son of the Waters (X.30.3).

The rivers in the *Rig Veda* are described even by name as flowing to the sea.

> Saraswati, pure in her course from the mountains to the sea (VII.95.2).[66]
>
> From the lap of the mountains, happy, smiling, like two running mares, like two bright mother cows licking their calf, Vipas and Shutudri run with fluid. Directed by Indra, seeking power, as chariots they travel to the sea (III.33.1-2).[67]
>
> Oh Maruts, what medicine of yours is in the Indus and in the Asikni rivers, what is in the oceans or what is in the mountains (VIII.20.25).[68]

Saraswati is the most famous Vedic river. Vipas and Shutudri are said to be the modern Beas and Sutlej. Asikni is the modern Chenab. We have the image of the mountains, rivers and oceans, or evidence of Vedic culture existing from the Himalayas to the sea.

Saraswati, the main Vedic river Goddess, can symbolize the boundless waters. As symbolizing water she indicates the one resort of all rivers.

> Saraswati, who is like a great ocean (or flood; I.3.12).
> Saraswati, whose endless, unencompassed, brilliant, mobile flood with power continues to roar (VI.61.8).[69]

SOMA AND THE SEA

While Varuna is the most specific Vedic ocean God, the most general is Soma, who is the God of the flowing waters. After Indra and Agni, hymns to him are of the most frequency in the *Rig Veda.* The Soma hymns are the pinnacle of the hymns of the *Rig Veda* and form a special book. Soma is also the Moon, whose mythological association with the sea is well known. Through Soma's common identification with the ocean, both earthly and celestial, we see how the oceanic symbolism of the *Rig Veda* is part of its greatest expression of joy and rapture.

As the "Lord of the rivers" (IX.15.5),[70] Soma is obviously the sea.

> The king of the river plunges into the sea, lodged in the rivers, he holds to the wave of the waters (IX.86.8).[71]
> Soma flows as the first of the rivers (IX.86.12).
> Thus like rivers down to the sea, the Soma drops have poured into the chalices (IX.88.6).[72]
> The king of the rivers has put on the vesture. He has mounted the most righteous ship of truth (IX.89.2).[73]

The roar of the ocean is well known to anyone who sees it, and it is not surprising to find it mythologized by a maritime culture.

> The ocean roars in the original laws, generating creation as the king of the world (IX.97.40).[74]

We read also of the Moon's influence on the ocean with the winds and tides.

> Soma (the Moon) stirs the ocean with the winds (IX.84.4).[75]

One of the most beautiful utterances in the *Rig Veda* is a praise of Soma as the Divine ocean. Soma is the cosmic ocean from which all creation comes, in which it abides, and into which it must return — the ocean of the bliss of consciousness.

> You are the all knowing ocean, oh seer, yours are the five directions in the law, you transcend Heaven and Earth, yours are the constellations, flowing Soma, who are the Sun (IX.86.29).[76]

The Vedic hymns themselves are not only compared to rivers entering into the sea. They themselves become the sea.

> Flow on Soma as peace for us, draw out for our milk an ambrosial juice, increase the ocean of the hymn (IX.61.15).[77]

All life, through the mystic chants, is an overflowing of the Divine ocean. By purifying our minds we are able to enter into the ocean of truth.

> Forming the ray from Heaven, you flow through all forms. Soma, as the ocean you overflow. Cleansing themselves, the living ones, as to the sea, the Soma drops have come to the source of truth. Soma, beloved, enter the ocean (IX.64.8, 17, 27).[78]
>
> To the ocean the Soma drops, like cows to their home, have come to the source of truth (IX.66.12).[79]

The Apsarasas are celestial nymphs or angels who dwell in the cosmic sea. They are common throughout Hindu mythology since the time of the *Rig Veda.*

> The ocean-going angels have flowed to the wise Soma (IX.78.3).[80]

Soma is lauded as the king who delivers us from across the sea. Soma crossing the sea suggests that the Aryans themselves crossed the sea.

> Flowing Soma, the Divine King, the vast truth, crosses the ocean by the wave (IX.107.15).[81]

Other verses identify Soma with the primal or great ocean:

> Soma, as the ecstatic, you were the first to extend the ocean for the Gods (IX.107.23).[82]
>
> Flow on Soma as the great ocean, the Father of the Gods through all the laws (IX.109.2).[83]

The ocean is the Father of all the Gods, the support of all cosmic laws. Calling Soma the great ocean indicates that the Aryans knew there were larger and smaller seas. How could the great ocean be the Indus River?

Not only is Soma associated with the ocean in many ways, several oceans are recognized. The four directions of space are compared to four oceans:

> Flow on Soma as wealth from four oceans to us, a thousandfold and from every side (IX.33.6).[84]
>
> The Soma libations have extended like the oceans (IX.80.1).[85]

In the same way other Vedic Gods are related to more than one ocean:

> Indra is a fourfold ocean, the support of treasures (X.47.2).[86]

What are these several oceans if not the Arabian Sea, Bay of Bengal, or the Persian Gulf, all of which are not too distant if the Aryans knew of the sea?

Such are typical references. More exist in the hymns but these are enough to prove our point. We have references to rivers flowing to the sea, to the Earth being bounded by several seas, to travel on and across the sea, and to the images in Vedic mythology of an oceanic cosmos. The main Vedic myth is of Indra who releases the seven rivers to flow into the sea. Hence Indra is frequently referred to as the sea. Varuna, a main Vedic God, is specifically the God of the sea. Soma is commonly referred to as the ocean, as he is a watery God. Agni, the God of fire, has an oceanic form. Even the Sun as the source of the cosmic Waters is compared to the ocean. Other specific ocean and water deities exist. The Gods are compared to ships and their saving action said to be like a ship. There is perhaps not a single Vedic God or group of Gods that is not somewhere related to the ocean or ships. In addition, the Vedic sages and ancestor figures are often saved from across the sea or descend from ocean Gods like Varuna.

As the Vedic culture is maritime, the Vedic people lived by the sea for some time before the hymns of the *Rig Veda* were composed. A period of some centuries would be required to allow the ocean to become an integral part of their thinking. They were hardly limited to northwest India and we must place them along the coast, most likely both to the east and west of India, as part of their original homeland. As we define the rest of Vedic culture, its extent of contact with the ocean will become clear, particularly after our examination of the rivers, which comes next.

If we grant that the *Rig Veda* shows a maritime culture, this in itself would cause our whole view of history to change. It would require a much greater antiquity for the *Vedas* and give a much more sophisticated idea of Vedic culture.

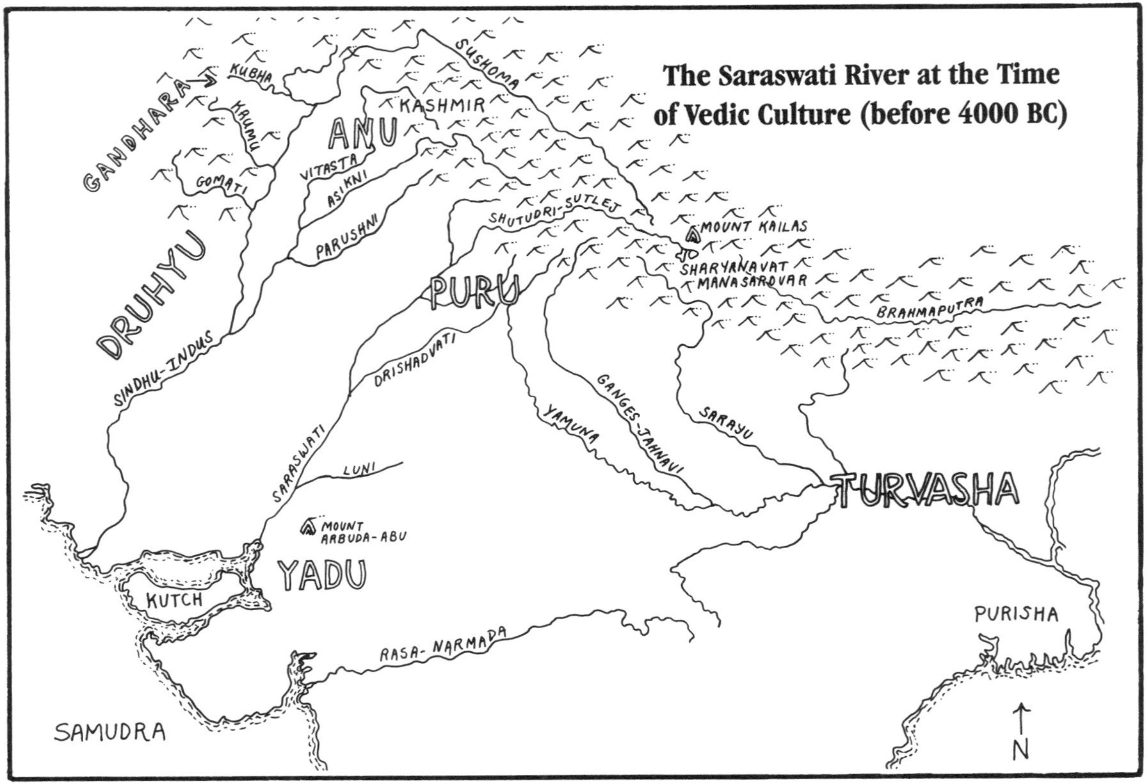
The Saraswati River at the Time of Vedic Culture (before 4000 BC)
GANDHARA
KUBHA
KRUMU
GOMATI
DRUHYU
ANU
KASHMIR
SUSHOMA
VITASTA
ASIKNI
PARUSHNI
SHUTUDRI-SUTLEJ
MOUNT KAILAS
SHARYANAVAT
MANASAROVAR
BRAHMAPUTRA
PURU
DRISHADVATI
SINDHU-INDUS
SARASWATI
LUNI
MOUNT ARBUDA-ABU
YADU
KUTCH
YAMUNA
GANGES-JAHNAVI
SARAYU
TURVASHA
PURISHA
RASA-NARMADA
SAMUDRA
N

2
THE SARASWATI RIVER
THE HOMELAND OF VEDIC CIVILIZATION

We set you down, oh sacred fire, at the most holy place on Earth, in the land of Ila, in the clear brightness of the days. On the Drishadvati, the Apaya and the Saraswati rivers, shine out brilliantly for men.

— *Rig Veda III.23.4*

Splendor is the king, all others are princes, who dwell along the Saraswati river. Like the Rain God extending with rain he grants a thousand times ten thousand cattle.

— *Rig Veda VIII.21.18*

THE IMAGE OF THE RIVERS

The *Rig Veda* contains not only a vast oceanic symbolism, it is pervaded with the image of the rivers — seven great streams flowing into the sea. India itself is the land of rivers, containing the most extensive group of large rivers in the world flowing from the Himalayas, the world's highest mountains. It is not surprising that a people from this region would portray the rivers in their mythology. Yet it would be surprising if people from Central Asia, a land of desert and few real rivers, would create images of this order. Nor do we find this river-ocean symbolism imposed upon some earlier desert symbolism. We find the worship of the rivers and the sea at the very heart of the Vedic mind. The *Rig Veda* itself is filled with the waters. It is fertile, flooding and flowing in its language, just like the land of India.

The exact location and extent of the Vedic culture has been a matter of disagreement and speculation. Modern scholars have primarily limited the Vedic civilization (and by "Vedic" we mean the culture of the *Rig Veda*) to the Punjab, the five-river region of northwest India. They claim the *Rig Veda* reflects a nomadic invasion from Central Asia through this region, which did not reach to the ocean until the latest period of the book. Certainly the Punjab has been an important region for Vedic and Hindu culture of all periods. The rivers of the Punjab are mentioned in the *Rig Veda;* their later names are often traceable to original Vedic ones. Yet many other rivers are found in the text; some of which are names of rivers to the east and a number also whose location is not definitely known.

References to the ocean in the *Rig Veda* are more frequent than references to specific rivers. Terms like samudra meaning ocean, are more common than the names of particular rivers. Names of specific rivers are also uncommon next to generic names for rivers. The ancient Hindu index of the *Rig Veda* lists twenty-seven synonyms for river,[a] many of which appear commonly in the text. This is a similar number to that of specific river names, many of which only occur once or twice in the text. It is not only in the *Rig Veda* that we seldom find names of specific rivers mentioned, it is true of all other branches of Vedic literature, even more so.

As the name for the Indus river, Sindhu, is a generic for 'river', many scholars have reduced all the important rivers in the *Rig Veda* to tributaries of the Indus, often minor affluents in the Punjab. This kind of semantic reductionism, however, completely fails to explain the oceanic symbolism. Moreover as the Indus is commonly mentioned as one of the rivers, one of seven, it would appear that the others had an equal stature and were not just tributaries of it. We should note that in the *Rig Veda* there are only a few passages where Sindhu means a specific river and not river in general. There are also several rivers called Sindhu in central and eastern India, as well as traces of this name for rivers in Afghanistan.

The fact that some of the rivers of Afghanistan originally had Vedic names does place the Vedic people in that region, but it does not serve to make it their primary habitation, as some scholars would have it. We cannot use an infrequent mentioning of small mountain rivers to override a greater mass of oceanic and maritime symbolism and a more common mentioning of large Indian rivers like Indus, Saraswati, and Yamuna.

Proving that the Vedic people were in one region, or had some influence upon it, does not serve to disprove their existence elsewhere. That Americans are found in California cannot be used to prove they don't live in New York. The influence of the Vedic language on place names can be found into Europe to the West and Indonesia to the East. This shows the power of the culture and should not be used to reduce it to one corner of this area. Many rivers of east India have Vedic equivalents as well. Yet these are dismissed as coming from a later time period because they do not fit in with the Punjab theory, not because they do not exist. For an interpretation to be plausible, it must make sense of Vedic symbolism as a whole. This is only possible through an integral symbolism of a land of large rivers, more than one ocean and extensive mountain ranges.

When people of a new language invade an area, river and other geographical names from the older culture are usually retained. Many rivers of America, like the Mississippi, have older American Indian names. The non-Sumerian names of Mesopotamian rivers have similarly caused scholars to postulate an earlier non-Sumerian culture in the region. However, all the ancient river names known in India are traceable to Sanskrit. No pre-Aryan names for Indian rivers like the Indus or Ganges have ever been pointed out by anyone. This also does not fit in with the idea of an Aryan invasion into India in late ancient times. When rivers are named in the *Rig Veda* their names are entirely Sanskrit in origin and they have equivalents in later river names in India.

As some river names were standard for the Aryans, we may find them given to more than one stream even in India. We may also find, as in later Hindu literature, that some rivers had more than one name. This was owing to the greater familiarity with them. Sometimes the names given to rivers changed with time, as most of the Vedic names for rivers were replaced in time.

Rivers were used to delineate kingdoms in ancient times and often indicated their boundaries. Usually great cities were built on rivers or in their confluences. Hence even lands that did not have great rivers were still named after their rivers or identified according to them. We may, therefore, expect certain rivers to serve as boundaries for different regions of the Vedic people.

THE SARASWATI RIVER: THE PLACE OF ORIGINS

The Indus, the main river of the Punjab, is an important river in the *Rig Veda*. We find mention of the Vedic people all along it, from its mountain regions to the sea. The Vedic name of the Indus, Sindhu, means 'river' in general or even 'sea'. Yet the river called Saraswati is the most important of the rivers in the *Rig Veda*, the most frequently and intimately mentioned. The image of this "great Goddess stream" dominates the text. She is not only the most sacred river but the Goddess of wisdom, of the Divine Word. She is said to be the Mother of the *Veda* and the hymns are said to have been envisioned through her grace and in her presence. Vedic texts like the *Brahmanas* speak of the great sattras or sessions of the ritual done along her banks.[b]

A hymn of the *Rig Veda* states:

> May the rivers overflowing grant us their grace (VI.52.4).

This might cause us to think that of the Vedic rivers the Indus is most important, since its name Sindhu is generic. A further verse in the same hymn tells us:

> May Indra be most close to us with his grace and Saraswati overflowing with the rivers (VI.42.6).

Saraswati is thus more important than the Indus. As Indra is the foremost of the Gods, the Saraswati is foremost of the rivers. Vedic rivers are generally feminine in nature. The Vedic culture grew up along the rivers and worshipped the rivers as their mothers. Of these mother streams the Saraswati is the greatest. Saraswati is deified as the Mother Goddess of the Aryan people.

> The best mother, the best river, the best Goddess, Saraswati (II.41.16).[1]

Saraswati is also lauded in a male form as Saraswan several times in the *Rig Veda* (i.e. VII.96.4-6).

It is said of the Saraswati:

> She flows with a nourishing stream, Saraswati a support like a bronze city. She moves as if on a chariot *by greatness surpassing all other rivers and waters.* Saraswati has appeared unique among the rivers, *pure in her course from the mountains to the sea.* Revealing wealth and the abundance of the world she yields milk and ghee to the descendants of Nahusha (VII.95.1-2).[2]

Nahusha is one of the great ancestors of the Vedic people, following shortly after Manu, the Vedic original man. We see here that the Saraswati was a definite river — the largest of all the rivers of the Vedic region — and that it flowed all the way to the ocean, along whose banks the Vedic people resided going back to their original progenitors. Like the Biblical Jordan the Saraswati yields milk and honey, and also ghee.

The Saraswati, rich in plants, is inhabited on both sides by the Vedic Aryans. Leaving the land of the sacred river was looked upon with disfavor, so great was the attachment to it.

> When on both your banks full of plants the peoples dwell, luminous Saraswati, may you awaken as our protectress (VII.96.2).
>
> Saraswati, may we not leave you for other lands (VI.61.14).

Saraswati thus appears as the prototype of all rivers, or as the sea or ocean.

> Who fills the earthly regions and the wide atmosphere, may Saraswati protect us from blame; who has three stations and seven levels, increasing the five peoples of men, in all battles she is to be invoked (VI.61.11-12).[3]

To do this the Saraswati must have been a massive river like the Indus. Yet the Saraswati also retains a more intimate character. She is not just called a river but is deified as the Divine Mother and Goddess. She is intimately connected with Agni, the Vedic sacred fire, and appears as one of his attendant Goddesses or consorts (as in the Apri hymns). The Vedic culture was a culture of the sacred fire along the sacred river of the Saraswati.

The Saraswati is the only river in the *Rig Veda* lauded in hymns of its own. She is the only river that enters the Vedic pantheon as a great Goddess.

> Saraswati like a great ocean appears with her ray, she rules all inspirations (I.3.12).[4]

As such, she continued as the Goddess of wisdom lauded in India today.

According to the ancient Hindu law book, the *Manu Samhita,* the Vedic culture began and was centered in the Saraswati region, west of the Yamuna river.

> The land, created by the Gods, which lies between the two Divine rivers, Saraswati and Drishadvati, the sages call 'the land of the Brahmins'. The custom, handed down in regular succession since time immemorial among the four classes and mixed peoples of that country, is called 'the conduct of the Aryans' (MS II.17-8).[c]

In this regard the *Rig Veda* says:

> We set you down, oh sacred fire, at the most holy place on Earth, in the land of Ila, in the clear brightness of the days. On the Drishadvati, the Apaya and the Saraswati rivers, shine out brilliantly for men (III.23.4).[5]

This shows that the region of the Saraswati, also called "the land of Ila," was the most sacred place on Earth, and the central homeland of the Vedic Aryans.

> You, oh sacred fire, are the first living one for living men. The Gods made you as the lord of the peoples of Nahusha. They made Ila the teacher of men (I.31.11).[6]

Nahusha is an important early descendant of Manu. The land of Ila or Saraswati is indicated as the place where the great early Aryan kings and sages lived and ruled like Manu and Nahusha. Divodasa, the great Aryan king and one of the earliest kings in Vedic mythology, is specifically said to be a gift of the Saraswati river (VI.61.1-2).

THE SARASWATI REDISCOVERED

It is thus clear from the *Rig Veda* and the Vedic tradition that the homeland of its people is the Saraswati river. The Saraswati is regarded as the most central and greatest of the rivers, and a lush and fertile region. The Indus was an important site of habitation but not as central as the Saraswati. However, the river in India said traditionally to be the Saraswati is a minor stream in the Punjab that dries out in the desert of Rajasthan — hardly the great stream of the *Veda*. This turned the great Vedic lauding of this river into something questionable or fanciful. It caused nineteenth century scholars to regard the original Saraswati to be a small stream in western Afghanistan — the Haraquiti of the Persians — where the Vedic culture was supposed to have started before the so-called Aryan invasion of India, whose name was later transposed to this small river in India. Some of them considered that the Saraswati, lauded as a great river, must have been another name for the Indus, though Vedic texts are quite clear about her location and difference from it.

Was there ever a time in which this Saraswati river was a great river, perhaps the largest in India, as the *Vedas* say? Further archaeological and geographical examination of India over the past few years has made a great and very important discovery about the Saraswati, one that should change our view of human history. The minor Saraswati (now called Ghaggar), traditionally identified as the great Saraswati of the *Rig Veda*, was a much larger river in ancient times and its dried river bed, when irrigated, is very fertile. Parts of its course are quite visible from aerial and satellite photography. Many sites of the Indus Valley culture, which flourished in the third and second millennia BC, have been found along its dried course showing that it was indeed an important site of ancient Indian civilization. Hence the Saraswati has been found to have been a great river, perhaps the greatest in India, as the *Vedas* say, but this takes us back to early ancient times, to the Indus Valley culture or before — much earlier than the time period given to the *Vedas* by modern scholars.

Another related stream also now going dry in the desert, the Naiwala, corresponds to the Drishadvati, the second main river by which Manu marked the source land of Vedic culture. In addition, the Sutlej (Shutudri of the *Vedas*) has also been found to have emptied into the Saraswati in ancient times. It also has a large dried river bed culminating in the Saraswati. Now it empties along with the Beas into the Indus as one of the five rivers of the Punjab. In fact, the Sutlej appears to have been the largest of the rivers in the Saraswati system. These combined flows made for an imposing river, the dried river bank appearing about five miles across (as satellite photography reveals from Hanumangarh in Rajasthan to Marot in Pakistan).[d, e]

Much work in India is being done tracing the extent of this river using aerial data, land surveys and the testing of well water. It has yielded information of extreme importance about the Saraswati and her earlier greatness. *It now has been found that the Saraswati changed its course at least four times and originally flowed to the sea straight through what is now the desert of Rajasthan.* Its earlier flow joined the Luni river and entered the ocean at the center of the Rann of Kutch. We know from ancient Greek records that Kutch was still an island when the Greeks visited India after the time of Alexander the Great. Kutch appears as the ancient delta of the Saraswati. The most ancient course of the Saraswati apparently also drained the great Yamuna river, which first flowed west and only later flowed east into the Ganges as it does today. Yet earlier in the prehistoric era the Ganges also appears to have flowed west into the Saraswati, like the Yamuna. Perhaps the Vedic myth of the descent of the Ganges, which appears in the literature that shifts the emphasis of Vedic culture away from the Saraswati, reflects this change of course for that river. In any case, there is ample evidence that the further back in time we go, the larger the Saraswati river becomes until it becomes the largest river in India just as the *Vedas* say, but this takes us back many thousands of years into prehistory.

In later ancient times, apparently that of the Indus Valley era, the Saraswati shifted its flow to the west. It then turned south again around Anupagarh in Rajasthan and entered the Arabian Sea on the west side of the Rann of Kutch, where a stream called the Nara flows today. At a yet later time, definitely during the Indus era, it moved yet more to the west, ending up in Marot in Pakistan, and perhaps flowed into the Indus river from there. The last stage of the Saraswati occurred when the Sutlej shifted its banks and flowed west into the Indus through the Ravi instead of south into the Saraswati. After this time the Saraswati ceased as a major river and dried up in the desert (which is how it is described in later texts like the *Manu Samhita* and *Mahabharata*).[f, g]

Indus Valley sites, like Kalibangan, are found mainly along the later courses of the Saraswati, when it was flowing to the west and already in its decline. In fact, we should rename the Indus Valley culture the Indus-Saraswati culture as many Hindu scholars are now proposing, since the great majority of Indus sites are east of the Indus and toward the Saraswati.[h]

We see that in Vedic times the Punjab, which means 'the region of the five rivers', did not even exist. Another major stream flowed between the Indus and Ganges comparable in size to them. There was no separation between the Punjab and the Ganges plain to clearly divide them but rather a continuous series of rivers from the Indus in the west to the Ganges in the east. The Rajasthan desert had not yet come into being to divide these two river systems. Not surprisingly the Vedic texts speak of a land of seven rivers, not one of five. The central and foremost of these seven rivers is the Saraswati. This indicates that there were as many rivers to the east of the Saraswati as to the west.[i]

The Vedic land, the land of the seven rivers, was not the Punjab, though it included that region, and its central river was the Saraswati, not the Indus. The Vedic land included the course of these rivers down to the sea and was not limited to their upper regions. As it included rivers in the Punjab to the west of the central Saraswati, it also included rivers to the east, and indeed a number of them are mentioned in the *Rig Veda* as Yamuna, Ganges, and Sarayu.

The Saraswati region is lauded in the Vedas as yielding milk and ghee (VII.95.2). Saraswati is compared to a cow in her richness. The Saraswati region appears to have been a good pasture land, and the central region for the Vedic cult of the cow. This shows a much different climate than the present desert of Rajasthan.

If we identify the Saraswati as the central region of the Vedic Aryans, the Indus Valley culture must be post-Vedic. The Saraswati stopped flowing about the time of the end of the Indus Valley culture. Thus the end of the Vedic and that of the Indus Valley culture coincide. If the Vedic people are later than the Indus Valley culture they could not have known of the Saraswati or described it as they do. In this regard, we should note that at Indus valley sites, including at Kalibangan, located on the Saraswati near its joining the Drishadvati, we find evidences of fire altars, with animal sacrifices, offerings of potsherds, beads and gold, much as in the Vedic Brahmanical rituals.[j, k, l]

Such finds further indicate that the Indus Valley culture must have been Vedic. The Vedic Aryans would not have attributed their culture to the banks of a river that went dry before they got there. Thus the Vedic glorification of the Saraswati, and its tradition of relating it to this minor stream, proves the antiquity of Vedic culture, the authenticity of the region it demarcates, and its identity with or precedence over the Indus Valley culture. The earlier, probably pre-Indus valley culture, and southern course of the Saraswati appears to more appropriately mark the Vedic age, as the vastness and uniqueness afforded this river in the *Rig Veda* makes most sense for this phase of it. Yet this takes us back much earlier than the Indus culture. Modern scientific studies indicate that the Saraswati river dried up around 1800 BC, while its previous ocean-going flow ended perhaps as early as 8000 BC.[m]

Archaeologists first assumed the Indus Valley culture was destroyed by outside invasion (supposedly by the Vedic people). Now that has been shown not to have been the case. There is no evidence of a violent end to this culture. Climate changes and a shifting of rivers may have done it. There is also evidence of earthquakes in ancient India as in the ancient Middle East, like those that destroyed the Minoan culture. We find a progressive drying up of the region from the Sahara to the Indus in ancient times. The Indus Valley shows evidence of having been wetter in ancient times (for example, we know Palestine was also wetter). The Indian monsoon may have reached further west and gradually retreated to the east, perhaps as part of the deforestation that ancient civilization caused. The drying up of this region would have caused the flow in the Saraswati to be reduced.

When the Sutlej shifted its bank and began to flow into the Indus, the Indus region would have had severe flooding and its banks may have changed, devastating the whole region. The Saraswati would have dried up further. Such a change of rivers could have brought down or marked the end of an era for a culture dependent upon them.

While such geological changes may at first glance appear to be far fetched ways of rationalizing traditions, they are indicated geologically and archaeologically. We now know that the sea coast of India sunk in late ancient times (as the excavations at Dwaraka and along the coast of India show). In fact, this shift may have occurred about the time that the Saraswati ceased to flow, though I am not certain what the connection may be. In a flat river plain like north India many floods and shifting of rivers have been recorded through history, often causing great damage.

The Saraswati river in the *Vedas* is thus not just a mythical stream but an actual river on which the Aryans lived.

> Splendor is the king, all others are princes, who dwell along the Saraswati river. Like the Rain God extending with rain he grants a thousand times ten thousand cattle (VIII.21.18).[7]

The Saraswati was the central land of the great Aryan kings of north India. If we expect to find remains of the Vedic culture we should excavate the Saraswati region under the sands of the Rajasthan desert. The drying up of the Saraswati came at the end of the Vedic age, for a people that had found it to be a great river since their earliest recollections. To place the *Vedas* after the Indus Valley culture is a great mistake in the interpretation of history, which hopefully we can begin to move beyond.[n]

There is thus little doubt that the main homeland of the Vedic people was this Saraswati region and that they had resided there for a long time before the hymns of the *Rig Veda* were finished, so intimate is her place within them. As this was the central Vedic homeland, we would be inclined to see the greater Vedic land as north India, spreading as far east as west from the Saraswati and from sea to sea in line with the oceanic symbolism. Hence we have the firm facts of ancient geography to support the antiquity of the *Vedas.* While our interpretation of ancient texts may be wrong, we cannot deny the courses of ancient rivers. The Vedic people could not have known that this river flowed of its own accord into the sea as the greatest river in India if they entered India in 1500 BC when the river had already dried up in the desert. It took many thousands of years for the Saraswati to change its course four times and then dry up by the time of the *Mahabharata.* That the *Vedas* knew of this river and its greatness certainly calls into question our entire view of human history.[o]

3

THE LAND OF THE SEVEN RIVERS: THE GREATER VEDIC LAND

The powerful bull with seven rays, who releases the seven rivers to flow; he, oh men, is Indra.

— *Rig Veda II.15.12*

THE VEDIC HYMN TO THE RIVERS: The Main Rivers of India

There is one specific hymn in the *Rig Veda* to the rivers (X.75). It describes the rivers in the domain of Vivaswan, the creator, whose son is Manu, the founder of Vedic culture. These therefore are the rivers in the domain of Manu, the land of the Aryans. The hymn uses the generic term for river as Sindhu, which in the *Vedas* is not always the name of the Indus river, as we see here. The hymn lauds the rivers as different aspects of the same great river, mentioning many rivers, of which the Indus is very important, but not even the first mentioned.

> 1. Oh Waters let the singer, in the seat of the creative Sun (Vivaswan), declare that supreme greatness of yours. Threefold, seven by seven, they flow. Of the streams, the river is the fastest with power.
>
> 2. For you, Varuna made a path to flow, oh River, when you ran to victory. You descend through the summits of the Earth, when as the first of the moving ones, you rule.
>
> 3. His roar extends above the Earth to Heaven; he raises an endless vigor with the light. Like a cloud the rains give forth their thunder, when the River flows roaring like a bull.
>
> 4. Oh River, like mothers to their child, the milch cows flow to you with milk. As a king to battle you lead their sides, when you go forth as the first of the torrents.
>
> 5. Oh Ganga, Yamuna, Saraswati, follow my hymn, Shutudri with the Parushni. Listen to me, with Asikni, Marudvridha with Vitasta, Arjikiya with Sushoma.

6. With Trishtama you are first to flow, together with Susartu, Rasa and Shweta, Oh Sindhu with such as the Kubha and Mehatnu, you seek the Gomati and Krumu.

7. Straight, shining, white, she encompasses the regions in greatness. The inviolable River, the most artful of the artful, like a dappled mare, has a beautiful form.

8. Like a good horse, like a good chariot, like a good garment, the River is golden, well made and full of power, young, dressed in wool, rich in plants, auspicious you wear a growth of honey.

9. The River yokes her chariot moved by horses, by which she will win the prize in the race. Great, her glory is lauded, of her inviolable, self-effulgent and rapturous.

The Vedic rivers are numerous, usually three groups of seven (X.64.8). This reflects a land of many closely placed rivers, not a few scattered and variable mountain or desert run-off streams. It shows that there was not just one large river drainage system but several. The three groups of seven are probably the rivers of the Indus system, the Saraswati system, and the Ganges system. Sometimes Saraswati is lauded as the foremost of the seven or twenty-one rivers (VI.61.12).

Varuna is the God of the sea, both earthly and heavenly. The Vedic rivers flow from the mountains (Himalayas) to the sea. They are often spoken of as flowing in floods or torrents and as being very difficult to cross, often requiring boats to do so.

This hymn begins with the main rivers of India from the Ganges in the east (V.5): "Oh Ganga, Yamuna, Saraswati, Shutudri, Parushni." Each is westward of the previous, so it appears like a geographical index.

Modern scholars, not wanting to place the Vedic people too far into the east of India, have assumed that the hymn begins listing the rivers with those most distant and unimportant. This is highly unlikely. Any hymn to the rivers of a land would start out with those most prominent. An American hymn to the rivers would start out with such rivers as the Mississippi and Missouri, not the Sacramento or Columbia. The early inclusion of the Saraswati, the main Vedic river, proves this point. It is probable that these were the main rivers of Vedic culture with the Saraswati in the center. Parushni is the modern Ravi, and Shutudri the Sutlej.

The first three, Ganga (Ganges), Yamuna, and Saraswati became the prototype of the three great rivers in later Indian literature. The region around the Ganges, Yamuna, and Saraswati has been traditionally identified with Manu, and was said to be passed on to his descendants. These three rivers are very close to each other in their upper regions. Hence a culture that knew of one would probably know of the others.

There follow some less certain but mainly identifiable rivers in the second half of the verse: the Asikni, Marudvridha, Vitasta, Arjikiya, and Sushoma. Asikni is well-known to be the next river west of Parushni (Ravi), now called the Chenab. Asikni is mentioned several times in the *Rig Veda:*

> Holy Maruts, what medicine is on the Indus, in the Asikni, in the oceans or in the mountains, with that bless us (VIII.20.25-26).

The Vedic people thus knew of an Asikni river with the Indus and the connection of both with the ocean.

The Vitasta is similarly well-known as the earlier name for the Jhelum west of the Asikni. It flows through Kashmir. Marudvridha, "what increases the Maruts," must be a river near these two. With the Vedic association of the Maruts with the mountains it may be further up in the Himalayas. Wherever it is it shows intimacy with the Punjab region.

THE MOUNTAIN LANDS OF THE SOMA

Sushoma is said by the ancient scholar Yaska to be the Indus. This would make perfect sense in the geographical order of this hymn as it is the main river of the Punjab to the west after Vitasta, but most modern scholars with their Indus fixation would not allow this. They would turn everything into a minor tributary of the Indus but not have the Indus mentioned according to another name, even though most Vedic and Hindu rivers, particularly those large or famous, have several names.

Sushoma, su-soma, meaning "good soma," also makes sense as the name of the Indus, particularly in its upper reaches, as there it was famous for its Soma. The great ancient Ayurvedic doctor Sushrut in his classic text *Sushrut Samhita,* indicates the Indus river as a major place of the Soma.

> The one and the same Divine Soma plant may be classified into twenty-four species according to the difference of their habitats, structures, epithets, and potencies. They are as follows: Amshumat, Munjavat, Chandramah, Rajataprabha, Durvasoma, Kaniyan, Svetaksha, Kanakaprabha, Pratanavan, Talavrinta, Karavira, Amshavan, Svayamprabha, Mahasoma, Garudahrita, Gayatrya, Traishtubha, Pankta, Jagata, Shankara,

> Agnishtoma, Raivata, Yathokta, and Udupati. All these kinds of Somas secure for the user a mastery of the Vedic chant and are known by the above auspicious names mentioned in the *Vedas.*[a]
>
> In the Himalayas, Arbudas, Sahyas, Mahendras, Malayas, Sriparvatas, Devagiris, Giris, Devasahas, Pariyatras, Vindhyas, Devasundas and Hladas are the inhabitants of the Soma plants.[b]

Soma is said to grow in all the different mountain ranges of India, north and south. Soma is thus the plant of all the mountain ranges of India but specifically the higher ones, the Himalayas. Then Sushrut mentions the places of the best Somas.

> Somas of the best kind, the Chandramah species, are often found to be floating here and there on the mighty stream of the river Sindhu (Indus), which flows down at the foot of five large mountains beyond the north bank of the Vitasta. The Munjavat and the Amshumat species may also be found in the same region, while those known as the Gayatri, Traishtubha, Pankta, Jagata, Shankara, and others looking as beautiful as the Moon are found to float on the surface of the divine lake known as the little Manasa in Kashmir.[c]

The Chandramah Soma, called the best Soma, comes from the upper Indus region. The greatest diversity of Somas, however, comes from Kashmir. In the upper Indus region, an area called Baltistan, are some of the highest mountains in the world, including the highest after Everest, Mount K-2. There are several great mountain ranges in the region: the Himalayas end here, as do trans-Himalayan ranges. The Karakoram range, including K-2, is nearby, as are the Pamirs and the Hindu Kush. All these ranges have mountains over 20,000 feet. This region is thus the meeting place of the great mountain ranges of the world, the veritable roof of the world. Here we see a great land of the Soma. Sushoma thus appears as a name for the Indus, particularly above Kashmir in the Himalayas. One of the main accesses to this upper Indus region from lower India is through the passes north of Kashmir.

A hymn of the *Atharva Veda* (AV V.22.5, 7) relates Mujavat with Balkh, the region of Bactria in northern Afghanistan. Balkh is often mentioned as the furthest western land of India, and was later a stronghold of the ancient Persian Zoroastrian religion. The same Atharva hymn (V.14) relates Mujavat with Gandhara, or eastern Afghanistan. Mujavat is named in the *Rig Veda* as a place of the Soma (Maujavata; X.34.1). Even today we find a Munjan region just north of the Hindu Kush in Afghanistan, across the mountains from the Indus. It is along the Kokcha river, a tributary of the Amu Darya, in a region called Badakshan, located between Bactria and northwest India. It is also the prime lapis lazuli bearing region of the ancient world. Perhaps it is Vedic Mujavat or some part of its region.[d]

This gives us two main regions of the Soma in the northwest India vicinity: the upper Indus and Kashmir. Yet though Vedic culture included parts of Afghanistan, this appears to be only its western fringe. The same hymn of the *Atharva Veda* (AV V.22.17) that recognizes Mujavat lists not only Balkh, Gandhara and Mujavat as distant lands to the west, it also mentions Anga and Magadha, or Bengal and Bihar, which would be the distant lands of the Aryans to the east. This may outline the same region as the land of the *Rig Veda,* from the Amu Darya to the Bay of Bengal, with the far eastern and western regions criticized for being unorthodox in their practices.

Going back to the River hymn, this leaves Arjikiya unaccounted for. It should be nearby the Indus (Sushoma) and the Vitasta. Yaska identifies it as the Vipas (Beas). This would be out of place here, as the Beas is east of the Parushni, but we must respect it as a possibility, as his opinion on Sushoma was correct. Based on Sushrut, I think that Arjika, mentioned as a land and an important region of the Soma, is Kashmir or greater Kashmir, the second great land of Soma. Arjikiya may be the name of some important river in Arjika or the greater Kashmir area (which may have extended east into the Beas or north into Ladakh and Leh). Yet wherever Arjikiya may be, it is somewhere in the western Himalayan region above the Punjab.

In other verses in the *Rig Veda,* there is an association of Sushoma, Arjika, and Sharyanavat (VIII.7.29, VIII.64.11) as lands of the Soma. The lands of the Soma are described:

> Which Somas are in the superior region, which are in the inferior region, or which are in Sharyanavat, which are in the well-made Arjikas, which are in the middle of the Pastyas (home regions), or which are among the five peoples (IX.65.22-3).

These may be names of Soma mountain regions of the Himalayas. The superior region may be the Himalayas, while the inferior region may be the Vindhyas or southern mountains of India, the traditional boundaries of the Vedic land. Sharyanavat, Arjika, and the Pastyas must be other areas or mountain ranges in the Himalayas. The land of the five peoples is the plains of India below.

Sharyanavat is said by the medieval commentator Sayana to be a lake in the Saraswati region near Kurukshetra region, but it elsewhere appears associated with a large region with a mountain range and the source of the rivers. Sharyanavat is perhaps the most important Vedic region of the Soma.

> I choose the grace of Heaven and Earth, of the mother rivers, and the mountains of Sharyanavat (X.35.2).[1]
>
> Indra, dragon-slayer, drink the Soma at Sharyanavat. Flow, oh compassionate Soma, lord of the directions, from Arjika ... Flow, oh Soma, to Indra (IX.113.1-2).

As a lake Sharyanavat could be the greater Manasa lake (Manasarovar) at the foot of the sacred mountain, Kailas or Meru in Tibet, from which flows the Sutlej, the main branch of the ancient Saraswati system. Soma is also closely linked with Saraswati. The Soma verses themselves are called Saraswati (IX.67.32). We will examine this issue shortly.

Therefore, the second half of this verse (5) of the River hymn (X.75) portrays the rivers of the Punjab and Himalayan areas to their north, from Asikni (Chenab) to Sushoma (Indus). Hence we see in one verse of this hymn a delineation east to west of the rivers from the Ganges to the Indus — the main rivers of all north India. They indicate perhaps the main dwelling places of the Aryans in the plains of India and in the Himalayas. In the plains it is the Ganges-Yamuna-Saraswati that is their central land. In the mountains it is Kashmir and the upper reaches of the Indus in the Himalayas, the lands of Soma.

GANDHARA

Into Afghanistan

The next verse of the River Hymn (6) continues with a series of rivers whose locations are not known. Those in the first half, Trishtama etc., are the most questionable in identity, so we will return to them after tentatively identifying those of the second half. They are named the Sindhu, Kubha, Gomati, Krumu, and Mehatnu. In this group we can recognize the Indus and the Kabul (Kubha), which flows from Afghanistan. The Gomati, Krumu and Mehantu appear to be western affluents of the Indus south of the Kabul. The Krumu has been identified with the modern Kuram and the Gomati with the modern Gomal, both west of the Indus. These rivers mark western India and nearby Afghanistan, or essentially the western drainage of the Indus.

Why should this hymn to the rivers mention these small mountain rivers? Some scholars have used their designation to connect the Vedic people with some home in Afghanistan and Central Asia. Actually there is a more simple and obvious reason for their inclusion. They are the rivers of a region known as Gandhara, the western uplands of India. The name of this region can be found in the *Rig Veda* itself as associated with sheep (I.126.7). It is an important source for wool, as sheep do well in mountain areas. Yet the main importance for Gandhara is that it dominates the paths of entry into India and the trade routes overland from it. No doubt it had a similar importance in Vedic times. Even though the rivers of this region are small they served to delineate this important kingdom, which is still within the drainage system of the main rivers of northern India.

Gandhara connects not only to regions to the west and north but to land routes to the east. Any trade from ancient India overland to either China or the Middle East would have gone through this region. Along this path Buddhism traveled from India to China. Ancient Vedic culture also appears to have traveled from here in the same way. Certainly the connection between ancient India and Persia would have been primarily through this region. Perhaps the Aryan peoples of Central Asia and Europe migrated from India via Gandhara.

As a place of trade and the interchange of ideas, Gandhara was a region of great learning. Much of Indian art and sculpture developed there as it was a center for trade and the exchange of ideas. Panini, who was the foremost of the Sanskrit grammarians, came from this region. Hence Gandhara was probably in Vedic, as in later times, not a region of primitive herdsmen but of great traders and scholars. It probably contained many foreign traders and their enclaves, as it did in later times. It was one of the most important centers for world culture in ancient times. At the time of the Greek visits to India, which followed Alexander, Gandhara was inhabited by traditional Aryan peoples. They were not displaced until the Muslim invasion. Afghanistan itself was called "the land of the Aryans" from ancient times.

Gandhara has also been the main area from which different peoples have invaded India throughout history. There may have been attempts to invade India from this region in Vedic as in later times. Hence though this region was very important, we must remember that it is still peripheral to the other and more central regions of India, like the Saraswati, which are more frequently delineated.

Along with Gandhara, we can trace the Vedic people into Central Asia. The Persians also called the Oxus or Amu Darya river 'the Indus' and considered it to be one river. The Oxus is the only real river in this area and the only one that could be compared to the streams of India. Oxus, we should note, is Greek for the Sanskrit Vakshas. One of the main northern tributaries of the Oxus is still called today the Vakhsh. Vakshana is one of the Vedic synonyms for river.[e]

The Persians had a sacred river like the Saraswati, the Ardvi Sura Anahita. Yet there are no real rivers in Persia. The river myth probably came from India. The Persians also worshipped Soma (Haoma) and sought it in their mountain regions, particularly those to the east in Afghanistan. Perhaps they were also looking back to some eastern sacred land of the Soma in the Himalayas.

THE RASA

Rivers in Central India

The rivers in the first half of this verse, Trishtama, Susartu, Shweta and Rasa, whose identities are quite disputed, must also mark some region of importance. They are said by modern scholars again to be minor affluents of the Indus. Yet where would they be? The hymn has already described the different tributaries of the Indus in the Punjab to the east and in the mountains to the west. We even have Sushoma, a special name for the Indus in the northern mountains, and also an unknown Marudvridha and Arjikiya in this region. This leaves no place for four other important rivers as tributaries of the Indus, one of which at least is well known as a large stream.

The Rasa is the most commonly mentioned river in the *Rig Veda* after the Saraswati and Indus. Like them, it can be a generic term for the world river or for the cosmic sea. Like the Saraswati it is worshipped as the Great Mother.

> With those aids by which you make the Rasa overflow with a flood of water, with those aids come to us, oh Ashwins (I.112.12).
>
> May the Rasa, the Mighty Mother, flow for us (V.41.15).[2]
>
> Clear-seeing Soma flow, fill great Heaven and Earth, like the dawn the Sun with his rays. Flow to us from all sides with your most peaceful current, like the river Rasa around the world (IX.41.6).[3]

The Rasa is associated with the Ashwins, and thus also with the myth of ocean travel and the cosmic ship. The Rasa is thus a great river, perhaps equal to the Indus, and as associated with the ocean.

> Your wide vehicle encompasses Heaven, when from the ocean it returns you. Let the Indus with the Rasa anoint your horses (IV.43.5-6).

The Rasa is said to flow into the ocean. It is compared in greatness as a river as the Himalayas are as mountains.

> Whose they say are the Himalayas with their majesty, and the ocean with the Rasa, whose are these five directions, whose are these two arms, to the unknown God may we give our offering (X.121.4).[4]

The Rasa appears here to mark one of the boundaries of India along with the Himalayas on the other side, and the five directions or lands of the five Vedic peoples between.

The ancient Persians in the *Vendidad*, one of their ancient scriptures, mention the sixteen known divisions of their world, most of which are found in Afghanistan. The fifteenth land is "the land of the Seven Rivers" (Hapta Hendu; Sapta Sindhu) or north India. The sixteenth is the region of the Rasa (Ragha).[f] Some have identified it with the Tigris, which however is nowhere near the land of the seven rivers or India. The Persians also have a Rasa that marks one of the divisions of the known world. It again appears to be a region of some size. As it is past the region of the seven rivers, perhaps it also marks one of the boundaries of that region, or India. Certainly it is not merely a minor mountain tributary of the Indus.

The Rasa is also the mythical river in the distance where the Panis, the enemies of Indra, reside (X.108.1-2), and which Indra has to cross to gain back the wealth they have stolen. In later mythology it separates the Earth from the infernal regions. We also know that the Panis raid the cattle from the Aryans and take them up into their hills. May these be the hills of central India?

There is an association of the Rasa with the Narmada, one of the important rivers in central India. Though we do not find the name Narmada mentioned in the *Rig Veda,* it is traditionally associated with some of the oldest Vedic kings. According to the *Puranas* (VP IV.3.7-13), Narmada married the great king Purukutsa, who defeated her enemies across the region of the Rasa, Rasatala, the nether world. She had a son by him called Trasadasyu. Purukutsa and Trasadasyu are two of the most renowned hero-kings in the *Rig Veda.* Trasadasyu is the only Vedic king who has a hymn to himself as a demi-god (IV.42.8), who is one with the Gods Indra and Varuna. The *Vishnu Purana* (II.3.10) also mentions a Surasa (good Rasa) river along with the Narmada. This may suggest that the Narmada itself was called the Rasa. If this is correct it would bring the Vedic Aryans into central India at an early period of the *Rig Veda.* The upper reaches of the Narmada, which go east and slightly north, are not far removed from the great eastern cities of India along the Ganges and Yamuna. The Narmada valley is the closest access of east India to the Arabian sea and the main trade route by sea from east India to the west. Hence much of Vedic culture and trade could have diffused from here. At the mouth of the Narmada was Bhrigukaccha, the famous city of the Bhrigus, one of the most ancient lines of Vedic seers, thus further identifying the *Vedas* with this area.

In the Puranic story the Narmada marked the entrance to Rasatala, the nether world or the world of the demons. Regions below the Rasa may have been those south of the Narmada. This suggests a time when the Vedic land ended at the Narmada. It is perhaps the king Trasadasyu who drove the Dasyus across the Narmada. Hence the Vedic Rasa may be the Narmada — but, wherever it is, it must have been a large stream of its own, not a minor tributary of the Indus.

THE MARUTS

Travels of the Vedic Sages

In the main text of the *Rig Veda* particular rivers are seldom mentioned. When they do occur it is mainly in the hymns to the Maruts. The Maruts are Gods of storm and rain and appear also as river Gods. They represent the wandering sages who travel throughout the known world and have a special knowledge of the world and its regions.

> The rivers and the mountains cannot obstruct you. Wherever you decide, oh Maruts, there you go; and you travel around Heaven and Earth (V.55.7).[5]

Parushni (Ravi) and Yamuna are mentioned (V.52.9, 17) in regard to these Gods. Scholars wonder why two rivers in different areas are mentioned. I believe it is to mark the boundaries of the Saraswati river region. They are mentioned as the two sites of the battle of King Sudas, who appears to have defended this region from attack (VII.18.8, 19). In fact, Sudas is mentioned in the following hymn to the Maruts which also mentions other great Vedic rivers:

> To what, Sudas, did you flow along with the rain and the nourishing waters?
>
> Come, oh Maruts, from Heaven and from the atmosphere and from here (the Earth). Do not stay in the distance. May the Rasa, Anitabha, Kubha, Krumu, and Sindhu not obstruct you, oh Maruts. May the Sarayu full of the heavenly waters (Purisha) not stop you (V.53, 2, 8-9).

These appear to be the rivers in the distance ruled by Sudas from his central Saraswati region. They appear to mark the boundaries of his greater kingdom. The Indus, Kubha, and Krumu have been identified as the rivers of western India and nearby Afghanistan. The others probably mark eastern or southern boundaries of the Vedic land.

It appears that the Sindhu, Sarayu, and Rasa are compared here to the rivers of Heaven, the atmosphere, and the Earth. Kubha and Krumu may be lumped with the more commonly mentioned Sindhu and Anitabha with the more commonly mentioned Rasa. The Sarayu is the river that holds the rains, as the rains come from the heavenly waters (Purisha). The Rasa is the river of the Earth or the southern region. Perhaps the Anitabha is the Tapi river south of the Narmada.

Keeping with the wide traveling of the Maruts and the cosmic symbolism here, we need not place these rivers next to each other. The travel of the Maruts was considered to be marvelous or magical.

> Oh skillful Maruts, when through the nights and the days, oh powerful ones, when through the atmosphere and the region, when through the level ground you drive like boats, across all difficulties you are not disturbed (V.54.4).

The Maruts are likened to ships. As rain Gods they are also Gods of the monsoon. This also identifies them with the rains, the Sarayu, and the sea.

> Oh Maruts, you raise up from the ocean the rain, and as carriers of the heavenly waters (Purisha) make it rain (V.54.5).[6]

These rivers appear to mark the main regions of the Vedic world. Indus and its tributaries mark the western boundary of the land of the Aryans. Rasa and its tributaries mark the southern boundary. Where then is the Sarayu?

THE SARAYU

Rivers to the East

Purisha or the heavenly ocean, mentioned with the Sarayu river, occurs a number of times in the *Rig Veda.*

> Come to us Indra from Heaven or Earth, quickly from the sea (Samudra) or the heavenly ocean (Purisha) (IV.21.3).[7]

Traditionally, the main Vedic dynasty was the solar dynasty founded by Manu at the city Ayodhya on the Sarayu river. This Sarayu is located in east India and identified with the Ghaghara or Gogra, the next major river of the east after Yamuna and Ganges. The Vedic Sarayu river is usually regarded by Western scholars as some minor affluent of the Indus (as it is mentioned with the Indus), though there is no Hindu tradition and the Vedic Sarayu is described as a great river in itself. The Persians named one of the main rivers of Afghanistan the Harirud from Sarayu. Yet even if a mountain river is named Sarayu, this does not prevent an eastern river from having the same name. It is hard to place a small mountain stream on a par with the great rivers of India or to make it the source of the rains.

The Purishas are the heavenly waters from which the rain comes. Actually, Purisha means a 'swamp' or 'jungle'. Probably Purisha referred to the marshy region of the Ganges and eastern Sarayu into the Bay of Bengal. This is in keeping with the idea that Samudra or the earthly (western) ocean is the Arabian Sea and Purisha or the heavenly (eastern) ocean may be the Bay of Bengal. In India the rains come from the east and go to the west and the country is wet to the east and dry to the west. The region most struck by the rains, the Purishas, is the east of India.

The Purishas are mentioned relative to all the Vedic rain Gods, including Parjanya, the main God of the rains.

> Parjanya and Vata, bulls of the Earth, you energize the heavenly waters (Purishas) (VI.49.6).

More specifically Parjanya is the God of the Indian monsoon. Dedicated to him is the sacred day when the monsoon begins (VII.103.7). Again this associates the Purisha with the east of India where it is wetter.

There is another reference in the *Rig Veda* to the Sarayu (IV.30.18). Indra is said to have destroyed two Aryans named Arnas and Chitraratha on the other side of the Sarayu. Now Arnas means 'flood' or 'ocean'. Chitraratha is also the name of an eastern river in the *Mahabharata.*[8]

These two Aryans appear to have been Aryan cultures who lived by the ocean on the other side of the Sarayu.

Sarayu is mentioned as a great river on a par with the Saraswati and the Indus.

> We invoke the great waters, the three times seven rivers, the forests, the mountains and the fire for grace. Saraswati, Sarayu and Sindhu with their waves: may the great rivers with their great favors come, the Divine Mother Waters (X.64.8-9).[8]

Both the Indus and Saraswati were indeed great and large river systems. What about the Sarayu? It must be the third of the three great Vedic river systems. We know that the Indus marks the rivers in western India and the Saraswati those in the center. We know that the Saraswati is the most central to the Vedic river system. We also have a Sarayu to the east associated with the oldest Vedic kings. Hence the Sarayu must stand for the Ganges river system of east India, which it is part of. The three great river systems of the *Rig Veda* are the Indus, Saraswati, and Ganges-Sarayu.

This last hymn is by Seer Gaya who in his previous hymn (X.63.1) refers directly to Manu, Yayati and Nahusha — the prime Vedic founding fathers — something only done a few times in all the hymns. According to the *Puranas,* Gaya was an early king in the solar dynasty of Manu (VP IV.1.12) and the region of Gaya in Bihar, just southeast of the confluence of the Ganges and Sarayu, is named after him.

Certainly we have confirmation in the *Rig Veda* for the Sarayu as one of the earliest sites of Aryan habitation. Yet why does the great River hymn not mention it? This is probably because of the importance it gives to the Ganges as the first river. It is close to the Sarayu and part of the same system. If we consider it farfetched for ancient people to have had such a wide knowledge of geography, we should again consider such statements about the Maruts:

> Of easy access for the Maruts is the Earth, of easy access is Heaven for their descent, of easy access are the paths of the atmosphere, of easy access are the mountains to those who move quickly (V.54.9).[9]

That the Hindus were not poor geographers is well-proved by the extensive lists of mountains, rivers, peoples and countries that we find in texts as old as the *Mahabharata.*

MORE ON THE GANGES

The River of the Dolphins

Since there are only two direct references to the Ganges in the *Rig Veda,* some have thought that Vedic culture did not include the Ganges until a later period. The most obvious reference to it is the one from the River hymn that mentions the Ganges as first of the rivers. The second reference speaks of the liberality of a king:

> Bribu of the Panis has ascended the greatest height with a wide girth (uru kaksha) like of the Ganges (VI.45.31).[10]

Some scholars have doubted that Gangya here has anything to do with the Ganges river. Yet if we examine these words carefully we find them to be highly suggestive of a great river. Kaksha means a zone or an enclosure but more specifically a marshy area or coastal region in later Sanskrit literature. From it arose the later Sanskrit term 'kaccha', the name of coastal regions below the Indus (i.e. the Rann of Kaccha or Kutch).

The Persian equivalent of Sanskrit Uru Kaksha is Vouru Kasha, meaning "wide coast," which is their name for the Caspian Sea,[h] particularly its coast in northern Persia. Hence this Vedic hymn is speaking of the wide shore of the Ganges — the Ganges by the ocean. This would place the Vedic people not only along the Ganges but by the Ganges to the sea. Certainly this idea of the wide coast by the Ganges makes perfect sense with the Ganges as the first river mentioned in the hymn to the Rivers.

Other names for the Ganges appear in the *Rig Veda* and confirm its early importance. Jahnavi appears twice in the *Rig Veda*. The same word, pronounced slightly differently, is a common name for the Ganges in later times. The Vedic Jahnavi has been regarded primarily as the name of a people but some have seen it as a river. Vedic peoples were commonly named after the river they lived along. It is said to the Ashwins

> Your ancient home, your auspicious friendship, your wealth is on the Jahnavi (III.59.6).[11]

This is a hymn of Vishwamitra, a seer and king whose kingdom was said to have been on the Ganges and who was a descendant of Jahnu, after whom the Ganges was named Jahnavi. It suggests the Ganges as an ancient home of the Vedic peoples.

The second reference is also validating:

> Ashwins, when you came speeding on your course to Divodasa-Bharadvaja, holding you, your splendid vehicle traveled, yoked by a bull and a dolphin. Carrying wealth, dominion, progeny, life and vigor, accordant you came to the Jahnavi with strength, where your offering is made three times a day (I.116.17-8).[12]

There is a special species of dolphin (Delphinus gangeticus), shimshumara, that lives in the lower Ganges region . Here it is associated with the Jahnavi, thus affirming the Jahnavi as the Ganges of the *Rig Veda.* The "river of the dolphins" is the Ganges. It cannot be some stream in Central Asia nor some minor affluent of the Indus in the Punjab. Divodasa-Bharadvaja is known in the *Puranas* as a king of Kashi or Benares, the great city on the Ganges.

The yoking of the bull and the dolphin suggests the Minoan culture and their art work, their acrobatics with bulls and dolphins. The Ashwins have boats and travel on the sea and thereby represent Vedic sea travel. This suggests some connection between the Minoans and Vedic India.

Other ancient Vedic names for rivers occur in eastern India, like the Gomati east of the Ganges and another Sindhu flowing into the Yamuna. The river on which the great city of Benares is founded is called the Varuna, after the great Vedic God of the sea, associated with both the eastern and western seas.

There is a famous story in the *Puranas* and *Itihasas* about the digging of the ocean and the bringing down of the heavenly Ganges. The sons of Sagara, searching for the sacrificial horse of their father, the King, that had been stolen, dug huge holes in the Earth to find it. Finally they found the horse at the center of the Earth with Kapila the sage. They attacked him and were destroyed by his mystic power and turned into a heap of ashes. One of their ancestors prayed for the descent of the heavenly Ganges through the grace of Shiva, which filled up the ocean (more specifically the Bay of Bengal, called Sagara). A great shrine of Kapila is located near the mouth of the Ganges. This story may refer mythologically to the time when the Ganges shifted its flow from west into the Saraswati to east into the Sarayu, as geological studies today suggest that it did in prehistoric times. If so, the later prominence of the Ganges over the Saraswati may have reflected these ancient changes of river beds. As previously the Ganges would have been part of the Saraswati system, the main river of eastern India would have then been the Sarayu.

MOUNT KAILAS
The World Mountain

In later Hindu literature, Mount Kailas in Tibet, also called Meru, is the most sacred mountain of the Aryans and their possible place of origin. It is identified with the north pole and is the mountain at the center of this world-continent (Jambudvipa; VP II.2.7).[1] The region around it is called Ila-vrita, the land of Ila (VP II.2.24), much like the central homeland of the Vedic people (RV III.23.4) and is said to be the region of Manu, the Vedic original man.

Meru is said to be the source of the four great rivers that go around the world. These are the divisions of the heavenly Ganges as it falls on the sacred mountain. The main branch of the Ganges river, the Alakananda, is said to be the southern branch. The other three rivers are the Sita to the east, identified with the Yellow River of China, the Chakshu to the west, identified with the Oxus of Central Asia, and the Bhadra to the north, identified with the Ob of Siberia. These are the main rivers of the Tibetan plateau in the four directions (VP II.2.32-6). The Meru region or Ila-vrita is also marked by four great lakes. The fourth which is the Manasa (VP II.2.25) is identified with Manasarovar lake at the base of Mount Kailas.

Kailas is the sacred mountain of Shiva and of his yogic sons (Vedic Indra and the Maruts). While we do not note any specific mention of Kailas-Meru in the *Rig Veda,* it does have its sacred mountains. Those beloved of the Gods go to the vast mountains.

> Savitar, those supreme in Indra you send to the vast mountains, to dwellings of the Pastyavats (IV.54.5).[13]

The Pastyavat or Pastya region, as already noted, is associated with mountain Soma lands like Sharyanavat, Arjika, and Sushoma (IX.65.23). It is also associated with Aditi (IV.55.3) and literally means the home region, the home of the Soma or the Aryans. These great mountains may be the Himalayas.

Meru appears in later Vedic literature, as in the *Taittiriya Aranyaka,* as the home of the Sun Gods or Adityas. The eighth Sun, Kashyapa, does not leave Mount Meru (TA I.7.20). Kashyapa is also the name of a famous Vedic seer, whose hymns are found in the Soma book (IX) of the *Rig Veda.* His hymns also mention such Soma lands as Sharyanavat and Arjika (IX.113.1-2) and speak of the existence of seven directions and seven Suns (IX.114.3).

If we examine the region of Kailas, we find that all the main rivers of north India originate nearby. The Indus, the main river of western India, and the Brahmaputra, the main river of the east, start to the west and east of Kailas less than a hundred and fifty miles from each other. They flow in opposite directions and then south and enter the ocean at the Arabian Sea and Bay of Bengal over fifteen hundred miles apart. These two rivers generally served to mark the boundaries of north India in later times. While we have no certain mention of the Brahmaputra in the *Rig Veda,* it may have been known to them.

Most importantly the lake below Kailas (Manasarovar) is the origin of the Sutlej (Vedic Shutudri), which now flows to the south and west and eventually into the Indus. However, in Vedic times the Sutlej was the largest tributary of the Saraswati. *Thus the real origin of the Saraswati may be the same as that of the Sutlej — Lake Manasarovar.* Vedic Saraswati is described as flowing through large mountains (VI.61.2), which would not be the case if the Saraswati was only the smaller stream arising from the Himalayan foothills. The smaller branch of the Saraswati rising from the Ambala hills in north India may have been chosen for habitation as it was less likely to flood than the larger Sutlej.

Lake Manasarovar is the great Manasa lake, to which the little Manasa lake in Kashmir is related. I think that Kailas is the Vedic region of Sharyanavat. The medieval commentator Sayana's idea that Sharyanavat is a lake along the Saraswati may be true but in its higher reaches and Himalayan source. The Vedic Aryans and their Soma may have derived primarily from these two sacred lakes of Kashmir and Kailas, along with the nearby rivers and mountains.

The Ganges and Yamuna also arise from the mountains south of Kailas on the other side of the Himalayas. The Ghaghara, which is identified with the Vedic Sarayu, through its affluent the Karnali, starts by Manasarovar also. In fact, through the upper regions of the Karnali are the main passes that go from north India across the Himalayas to Kailas. Manu was said to have founded the solar dynasty at the great city of Ayodhya on the Sarayu just south of the Himalayan foothills that lead to Kailas. Perhaps Manu came down from Kailas in this direction, which would have been the most direct route to the plains of India. The Vedic rivers are thus primarily the rivers of the Himalayas and these are centered in the Kailas/Manasarovar region and surrounding areas. This region marked by the Himalayan rivers is the land of Manu and Vivaswan, the land of the Aryans and land of Soma. The Himalayas are the Vedic home of the Soma.

This is not to say that Kailas was the center of Vedic civilization. It is a remote mountain region at the roof of the world. It is more likely the home of the Vedic sages, the great yogis and seers who guided the culture which grew up along the Saraswati river in the plains of north India. Yet it is possible that many of the original Vedic people, who are described as families of the seers, originated in such mountain regions.

Diffusion Along the Himalayan Rivers

The *Vedas* thus may look to Mount Kailas and Lake Manasarovar as their most sacred region, to the seers who lived there and served the Aryan kingdom on the Saraswati-Sutlej river below it. The upper reaches of the Indus west of Kailas may have also been important sites of early Aryan habitation. They were of easier access from Kailas than the direct routes over the Himalayas. Kashmir was a famous site of Vedic knowledge as its passes to the north and east go to Kailas. Perhaps even some of the Aryans went along the Brahmaputra to the east and through the plain of Tibet. Even the Chinese, who also have the myth of this sacred mountain with four rivers in the west, may have originated here. According to the *Puranas*, Manu ruled as many kingdoms north of Kailas-Meru as south. Perhaps this included the Tarim basin in western China, wherein Tocharian, an Indo-European language, was spoken until the Muslim invasion of the region.

We see a diffusion of Vedic culture and peoples from the seers centered in the Kailas area extending throughout the valleys of the Himalayas. Some went down the Saraswati and Sarayu into north India. Others came down from the upper Indus into Kashmir and Afghanistan. From there they went west into Persia or north, perhaps along the Amu Darya river into Central Asia and Europe. The Vedic mountain people could have followed the Persian plateau all the way into what is modern Turkey (Anatolia).

Going down the Indus and Saraswati, the Aryans extended into Gujarat and Sind on the Arabian Sea. From there they moved into the Persian Gulf and may have founded the civilizations of Sumeria and Babylonia. Going down the Ganges, Sarayu, and perhaps Brahmaputra, they extended into south India and east into Malaysia and Indonesia, probably founding cultures there in ancient times, as they did in later times. Some Vedic people may have gone north and east to China. The early Aryans were probably not limited to members of the Caucasian race, nor were they necessarily confined to speakers of Indo-European languages.

The mountain ranges in central India were probably difficult to tame and may have been inhabited by inimical peoples. Yet the Aryans did enter south India at an early period, if the Rasa/Narmada connection is accurate. They probably went around it by sea first, and colonized it via the coasts, establishing an important center in the Tamil Nadu region, from which Dravidian culture arose.

THE LAND OF THE SEVEN RIVERS

Based on the rivers mentioned and the prominence of both mountains and oceans we can divide the land of the *Vedas* into five regions:

> 1. The Saraswati region from the Ganges or Yamuna to the Ravi (Parushni), the central kingdom. It perhaps is the first region mentioned in the River hymn (X.75.5) demarcated by the rivers Ganga, Yamuna, Saraswati, Shutudri, and Parushni. Its identity is rather clear and we can be certain of its centrality in the *Rig Veda,* apparently from the beginning of Vedic culture.
>
> 2. The northern region, from the Ravi (Parushni) to the Indus, including the Asikni, Marudvridha, Vitasta, Arjikiya, and Sushoma. This consists of most of what is now the Punjab and the mountains of Kashmir.
>
> 3. The western region, marked by the Sindhu (Indus), Kubha, Krumu, Gomati, and Mehatnu. It would mainly be the region of Gandhara and western India extending into Afghanistan.
>
> 4. The southern region marked by the Arabian Sea and the ocean outlets of the Indus and Saraswati. It probably included the Rasa/Narmada.
>
> 5. The eastern region marked by the Bay of Bengal, including the lower regions of the Ganges and the Sarayu and their affluents.

The last two regions are marked more by the ocean than by rivers. These five regions were probably the basis of the five Vedic peoples and the five groups of Vedic Gods. This describes the region of north India as marked out by Manu as the land of the Aryans:

> But the tract between the two mountain ranges, the Himalayas and Vindhyas, which extends as far as the eastern and western oceans, the wise call the land of the Aryans.[j]

The Narmada is the main river that marks the Vindhya range. The three main river systems of the Vedic region are the Indus, Saraswati and Ganges, marking the west, center and east of the region. I think we can also identify the seven rivers, Sapta Sindhu:

1. The Indus (Sindhu)
2. Chenab (Asikni, including Vitasta)
3. Ravi (Parushni)
4. Saraswati
5. Yamuna
6. Ganges
7. Ghaghara (Sarayu)

The Saraswati marks the center with three rivers to its east and three to its west. This 'Land of the Seven Rivers' includes the whole region of north India from sea to sea but is more centrally marked by the area from the Indus to the confluence of the Sarayu and Ganges, or the area from Peshawar in the west to Patna in the east. It can be divided into smaller regions. According to *Manu Samhita*[k] the middle region, Madhya Desha, is from Prayag in the east, modern Allahabad where the Ganges and Yamuna come together, to the place where the Saraswati disappears in the west, which would be in the Bikaner district of Pakistan. This statement comes from a later period after the Saraswati ceased to flow into the sea and shows the extreme antiquity of Vedic culture even at the time of this ancient text. This western boundary was marked by the Ravi in the *Rig Veda* before the Saraswati went dry.

However, the Vedic land was larger than the seven river region, if we include its peripheral regions. References to Balkh place the Vedic people in the Amu Darya region in central Asia, as noted, beyond the Himalayas. That two other main rivers of Afghanistan have the same names as two of the most important Vedic streams — the Harirud (Sarayu) in northwestern Afghanistan and Haraquiti (originally Saraswati) in the southwest — brings all of Afghanistan into the greater field of Vedic culture. These last two rivers were no doubt named after original great streams in India by colonists to the west. As Afghanistan was not as inhabitable and was difficult to access, it was not always included in the Vedic land. In the same way, other regions, like south India, could have been included in the greater Vedic land.

The Vedic people came down from various valleys of the Himalayas in early ancient times. They moved down along the Himalayan rivers from the Amu Darya (Oxus) in the west to the Sarayu in the east and spread their influence throughout the world. But their main center was the Saraswati region, with the Himalayas as their spiritual homeland. North

India has the most extensive system of fertile river valleys on Earth and a warm climate as well. It was something like the garden of Eden in ancient times and a very suitable place for the development of civilization.

THE LAND OF THE GODS BETWEEN THE TWO OCEANS

'The Land of the Seven Rivers' was India. These rivers appear to flow into more than one ocean in the *Vedas*. This land is placed between two oceans — the eastern and western, or the heavenly and earthly. In the *Rig Veda,* it is said of the Keshin, a symbol for the Sun and for the ascetic:

> He nourishes both oceans, that which is eastern and that which is western (X.136.5).[14]

The Gods move from the east to the west and back again. Of Savitar, the Sun God, it is said:

> He surveys the all-encompassing richnesses between the eastern and the western mark (X.139.2).

Between the two oceans or Heaven and Earth is the land of the Gods or the land of the Aryans, symbolized by the atmosphere. The Vedic kings, performing the great horse sacrifice, Ashwamedha, let their horses loose to travel through this region from ocean to ocean to stake their claim as rulers of the world. The greatest of the *Upanishads,* the *Brihadaranyaka,* begins,

> The day is the greatness born to the east of the horse. His source is in the eastern ocean. The night is the greatness born to the west. His source is in the western ocean. These two greatnesses have come into being around the horse (BU I.1.2).

The *Upanishad* is only reflecting a Vedic idea. The Vedic horse also takes birth between the heavenly and earthly ocean.

> When you were first born, oh horse, you neighed, as you arose from the ocean or the heavenly waters (I.163.1).[15]

This again confirms the idea that the earthly and heavenly waters, samudra and purisha, are the western and eastern seas. The same hymn states further about the horse,

> Three, they say, in Heaven are your bonds, oh horse, three in the Waters, three in the ocean, and you appear to me as Varuna, where, they say, is your supreme birth (I.163.4).

The horse comes from the ocean and returns to the ocean. He is the Sun that travels between the lower and the higher seas. His supreme birth is as the God of the ocean, Varuna.

> And both oceans are Varuna's flanks (AV IV.16.3).[16]

The Vedic people thus encompass the Land of the Seven Rivers between two oceans.

If the Vedic people knew of north India from sea to sea it is quite possible they went by ship from one side of India to another. The magic vehicle of the Ashwins that encompasses the region may refer to this movement from the eastern to the western seas. Just as the Sun went from his western setting to his eastern rising, so could ships disappear in the west of India and magically appear in the east.

The *Rig Veda* thus portrays the land of India in its sacred geography, not any other. This could only have been possible if the *Rig Veda* grew up there, not if it was imported from the outside. The *Rig Veda* is the product of India from the Himalayan lands of the seers to the ocean.

PART II

THE THRONE OF INDRA
STORIES OF THE VEDIC KINGS

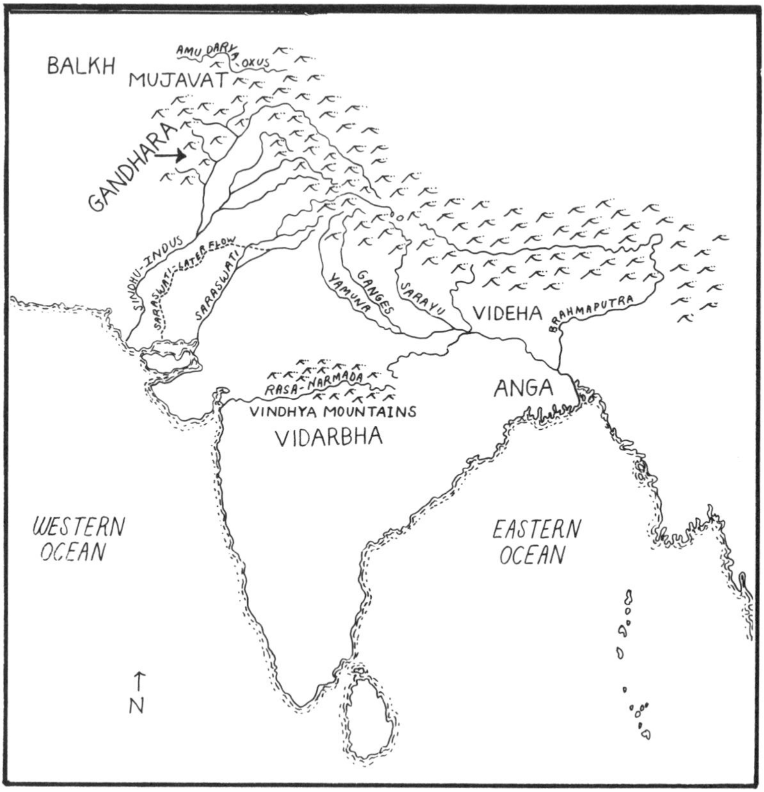

India at the Time of Vedic Culture (before 4000 BC) with Outlying Regions

Note that the Yamuna and the Ganges Rivers originally flowed west into the Saraswati in an earlier ancient period reflected in the *Vedas*.

1
STORIES OF VEDIC KINGS FROM THE *RIG VEDA*

May I be all-encompassing, possessed of all the Earth, possessed of all life, from the one end up to the further side of the Earth bounded by the ocean, sole ruler.
— Aitareya Brahmana VIII.15

With this great anointing of Indra, Vasishta the priest anointed Sudas Paijavana the king. Therefore, Sudas Paijavana went around the Earth completely, conquering on every side, and offered the horse in sacrifice.
— Aitareya Brahmana VIII.21

In these chapters on the Vedic kings, we will examine the nature of the Vedic kingdoms, their extent, and the types of wars that they fought. This reveals a series of great kingdoms and empires in India in Vedic times, if anything larger and more powerful than those of later times. To approach this we must first understand the Vedic ruling class.

THE VEDIC NOBILITY

There are two main classes of the Vedic people, the Aryans of the *Rig Veda;* the priestly or Brahmin class, whose main activity is the ritual and meditation, and the noble or Kshatriya class, whose main activity is warding off inimical peoples and protecting the ritual. The Vedic ritual or sacrifice can be symbolized as a battle, and war is regarded as a sacrifice that can only be won through the power of prayer. The Vedic kings followed the advice of their priests, who stayed outside of political affairs and gave only spiritual guidance.

> He dwells well-placed in his own home, to him the Goddess of wisdom gives abundance throughout the days. To him the people bow down of their own accord, in the King by whom the Brahmin is given precedence (IV.50.8).

The alliance between these two classes was the basis of Vedic society. Apart from them were the people in general, called the Vish, from which term the later Vaishya or merchant class developed. Originally it consisted of the entire general populace, including farmers and traders. The fourth class, the Shudra or servant class, evolved in time as those outside of the Vedic spiritual culture but under the rule of Vedic kings. We find similar social orders throughout the ancient world.

The Vedic nobility were powerful warriors. They protected the sacrifice and guarded the spiritual life of the Aryans. They sometimes fought with each other but under strict codes of honor. Many of these inter-Aryan struggles were no more than games, including horse races. Some were clashes between champions for leadership, sports of the nobility to test and sharpen their prowess. However, some in time became full fledged wars. Yet it is doubtful that these involved the masses of people.

Vedic warriors portrayed their battles as a struggle between good and evil, light and darkness, truth and falsehood. In this regard they appear more like the knighthood ideal of the Middle Ages. They allied themselves with their priests and used the power of prayer and mantra to protect them. Usually it was the mantras and rituals of the Brahmin priests that were the decisive factor in the battles. The priests often struggled with the prayers or curses of the priests of the enemy, as war was largely a magical affair. The Vedic warriors were often in the minority and overcame great odds, largely through the grace of the Gods. Often the great Brahmin priests stood with their kings as warriors without arms, using only their spiritual or mantric powers.

When Aryan warriors were defeated by other Aryans they submitted and accepted their defeat as the decision of the Gods. They accepted the rule of the victorious Aryans and the culture of the people continued with little change. However, when they fought with non-Aryans, with unspiritual people, the latter often did not submit and had to be deprived of their power. Some of these hostile people were assimilated into the Vedic culture. Others remained as outsiders, sometimes retaining their own culture, perhaps becoming some of the aboriginal peoples we find in India today. Others appear to have been driven out of the region altogether.

In the course of time, battles between the different Aryan peoples grew more fierce. Permanent differences arose among the Aryans themselves. Often it is hard to tell whether a battle is with non-Aryans or with fallen Aryans who had become power-seeking and unspiritual. Sometimes fallen Aryans were allied with non-Aryans. Sometimes non-Aryans were allied with Aryans in a positive way.

Vedic warriors only resorted to force of arms when no alternative existed. They would use force to oppose what they saw as evil, if that evil attacked them unrighteously. Their supplications for power and victory, not usually aesthetically rendered, can be made to appear primitive. They used a variety of weapons, like bow and arrow, sword, spear, axe and dagger, which the hymns reflect; yet they called on the Gods and used the power of prayer as their main support. They rejoiced in the wealth of their enemies which they conquered; yet this was not a mere plundering but a sharing of the wealth with all the peoples and using it for the sacrifice. The main wealth of the Vedic people was given to the priests and used for the ritual. It was not allowed to be hoarded for mere worldly purposes.

While later Indian philosophy, with its emphasis on non-violence, might have difficulty with the occasional Vedic glorification of force, we must remember that it is the force of truth that is meant, not any aggressive activity. Even in later times, Hindu and Buddhist monks accepted the use of force on the part of their kings to protect the social order. The *Bhagavad Gita* itself, given by Krishna on the battlefield to encourage Arjuna to fight, was in line with this old Vedic warrior spirit. This is to fight for the truth, not to fight with the thought of harming others.

From the standpoint of the nobility, the Vedic hymns can be interpreted as chants to the Gods for prowess, victory, and prosperity. A few hymns reflect the battles of kings and their victories, from which we may be able to gather something of a record of their activities. On this level, however, the deeper meaning of the hymns cannot be perceived and so we must not take it as the essence of the *Vedas*. It is a crude version of the warrior meaning of the hymns that has become the main interpretation by modern scholars, who have been unable to perceive the inner truth of the ritual.

Vedic kings, we should note, appear only as symbols of the teaching. The *Vedas* set forth primarily the ritual, which inwardly is the practice of Yoga. The *Vedas* do not just simply glorify kings but rather include the kings as one small but important aspect of their greater teaching. The greatest Vedic kings are those who follow the seers whose protection saves them and allows them to overcome all opposition. In this regard, the *Rig Veda* portrays non-violence and humility, surrender to the Gods and sages, as the right conduct for the nobility. As one verse states,

> Who of our own kin or those alien to us, or those among us who would assault us, may all the Gods prevent him. The Divine Word is my inner armor (VII.75.19).[1]

Vedic society consisted of different kingdoms which often vied with each other for imperial power. Most important of the kings was the king of the spiritual kingdom, the land of the Brahmins, the region of the

Saraswati river. The ruler of this kingdom was the natural leader of the Aryan kings. Some Vedic wars consisted of the attempts of aggressive kings to conquer the spiritual kingdom. Even great armies were defeated trying to conquer this land, which was protected by the Gods.

All kings had to follow the wisdom of their Brahmin priests. Each king had a ruling priest called a 'Purohit'. Yet the priestly and kingly classes were kept apart by Vedic law. The priest could not assume worldly power. The king had to propitiate the Gods but could not himself assume spiritual power by his kingship alone or represent himself as a God. This mistake was commonly made in many ancient cultures, including some Aryan ones. In them we see the worship of the king as a God. We find the nobility ruling the priests or the priests assuming secular power. Such conditions corrupted both classes. However, sometimes a great sage, like the avatar Rama, was born as a king to maintain the Dharma in the world. In such instances the worship of a king as a God was appropriate.

Conflicts between the Kshatriyas (nobility) and the Brahmins (priests) are mentioned in Vedic literature. Proud kings refused to accept the rule of spiritual knowledge (symbolically, they refused to give the gift of the cow to the Brahmins). However, in all phases of Vedic literature, down to the *Upanishads,* wise and spiritual kings are mentioned both as rulers and teachers along with great priests and seers. There are great king-sages throughout Vedic literature.

THE STORY OF SUDAS AND THE BATTLE OF THE TEN KINGS

Most central to the historical interpretation of the *Rig Veda* is the story of Sudas and the legendary Battle of the Ten Kings (Dasarajña). It is the most important and apparently the last major epic in the *Rig Veda.* Indeed, the *Rig Veda* appears to have been compiled by the dynasty of Sudas. His great victory is a recent occurrence relative to many of the hymns. The great war of his time was an event in early ancient Indian history probably as significant as the Mahabharata war was in later ancient times. It similarly may have involved most of India.

Some modern scholars have seen in the story of Sudas the Aryan conquest of India and its aboriginal peoples. Some consider that this Battle of the Ten Kings first opened up the plains of India to the invading Aryans. In this regard, the seer Vishwamitra (III.33) speaks of Sudas and his army crossing two rivers of the Punjab, the Vipas and Shutudri or modern Sutlej and Beas.

> They came from afar with their wagons, a warring army directed, impelled by Indra (III.33.9, 11).

This appears to be indicating an Aryan invasion into India from the northwest, through the Punjab.

However, on closer examination of the *Rig Veda,* this view is found to be without foundation. The enemies of Sudas are clearly described as Aryans or fallen Aryans — people of similar language and religion but who have turned away from the spiritual teachings. In the most significant hymn of the Battle of the Ten Kings (VII.18), his enemies are members of the five Aryan peoples, along with descendants of the famous Bhrigu Rishis.

> Turvasha was the leader, seeking gain, like hungry fish with an appetite for gain. The Bhrigus and the Druhyus followed his advice. Friend to friend crossed over from opposite regions (VII.18.6).[2]

Turvasha, the leader of the enemies of Sudas, is usually listed as the first of the five families of the Aryan people. With him side the Bhrigus, the most famous family of Vedic seers after the Angirasas, with whom they are related; and the Druhyus, another of the five Aryan peoples. The five Aryan peoples are mentioned a number of times in the *Rig Veda:*

> Indra-Agni, whether you are among the Yadus or Turvashas, whether among the Druhyus, Anus or Purus, come to us and drink of the Soma (I.108.8).

Among those Sudas defeated (VII.18.12) were the famous Kavashas, an old family of Rishis, who appear in later Vedic literature. The Druhyus are mentioned again in this same hymn (v.12, 14), as are the Anus (v.13, 14), another of the five Aryan peoples. The hymn calls them "people of harmful speech" (v.13).[3] Some have seen this term as "people of foreign language" — the so-called original non-Vedic people of India; yet the term is clearly applied to Aryans, and to the oldest families. Hence it does not mean those of a foreign language or indicate a war of invasion of a new race into India. It indicates those whose speech is harmful or untruthful, not necessarily those who speak a language unrelated to the Vedic. It indicates that some Vedic people fell from the original culture and became harmful to those who tried to preserve it. Puru is a name of another of the five families of the Aryans and is often generic for the Aryan peoples. Sudas, as the hymns indicate, thus defeats his own kinsmen.

> The king defeated the twenty-one famous peoples of both Vaikarnayas.
>
> Of the Anus and Druhyus sixty thousand, six thousand and sixty six warriors were put to sleep (VII.18, 11, 14).

The exact number of warriors defeated has been translated variously. Other Vedic wars mention sixty or a hundred thousand enemies conquered (i.e. VI.26.5-6), so the rendering here is not too high a number. The number may also mean sixty times six or three hundred and sixty thousand, standing mystically for the zodiac or the year, as the Vedic king is identified with the Sun who conquers time. By ancient standards these are large numbers and a major war is indicated with organized armies, something quite different than skirmishes of invading nomads. The organized armies on both sides were led by Aryans. This is a great civil war. More specific names of peoples are mentioned (v.7, 19): Pakthasas, Bhalanasas, Bhanantas, Alinasas, Vishaninanas, Shivasas, Ajasasas, Shigrus, Yakshus. No one appears to know exactly who these peoples were, but the names are predominantly Aryan. They are probably the different groups of the Turvashas etc. defeated. There is nothing that indicates a war of conquest of racially different peoples.

Another hymn describing the battle of Sudas affirms this information.

> Indra and Varuna, aid Sudas with grace and destroy his opponents both Dasa and Aryan.
>
> Where men who carry flags come together, in which battle there is nothing good, where all the worlds that see the light are afraid, there Indra and Varuna bless us. The ends of the Earth appeared full of dust. The noise rose up to Heaven.
>
> Both sides call upon you in the battle, Indra and Varuna, for victory (VII.83.1-3, 6).[4]

Sudas defeats both Dasas and Aryans in a great battle. Both sides in the battle not only had the same ancestors, they worshipped the same Gods.

In the *Rig Veda*, Dasas and Aryans are related. Fallen or inimical descendants of Aryan kings or peoples are sometimes called in the *Rig Veda* Vritra, Pani, or Dasyu; terms which may have also been given to those who never were part of the Vedic culture. Another related hymn of Vasishta describes a great victory of the Aryans over the Dasyus or Panis. They are described as:

> Unwise, binders, harmful in speech, traders (Panis), without faith, unholy, conquer those Dasyus, oh Agni (VII.7.3).[5]

Yet the same hymn also calls the Dasyus "Nahusha" (v.5), after Nahusha, the progenitor of the five Aryan peoples mentioned above, showing them to be of common ancestry with the Aryans. Inter-Aryan conflicts appear elsewhere in the *Rig Veda.*

> These your friends who have gone astray, once friendly they have become unfriendly. May he destroy himself with his words who attributes falsehood to the righteous. He who with reverence offers sacrifice to you, oh Fire, he protects the truth of the radiant spirit. Let him come to a wide and good dwelling, the offspring of far wandering Nahusha (V.15.5-6).

We have an original ancestor for both the Aryans and Dasyus — Nahusha — one of the early descendants of Manu and the ancestor of the five Vedic peoples. The Dasyus are thus largely fallen Aryans. The Aryans are those who maintain the original laws of Manu, the original man. The Dasyus are those who fall from the spiritual path. Even if the Aryans came into power in India at some point, the Dasyus were considered to be related to them in ancestry, language, and religion but fallen in terms of spiritual values. The Vedic Gods also have to defeat their inimical father (i.e. VI.59.1). Perhaps this is symbolic of an inimical older but related people the Vedic Aryans had to fight with.

The war of Sudas is everywhere portrayed as a defensive war. Sudas is said to have been attacked from the outside, to have been surrounded and pressed in upon by his enemies who were much larger in number:

> Pressed in by ten kings (VII.83.6);[6]
>
> Oppressed on all sides in the Battle of the Ten Kings (VII.83.8).[7]
>
> Ten united unholy kings could not defeat Sudas (VII.83.7).
>
> Like the stick for driving cattle, the Bharatas (the people of Sudas) were much smaller in number and surrounded (VII.33.6).[8, 9]

The victory of Sudas under such circumstances was a kind of miracle, brought about by the power of the Gods.

> With the weak, Indra did something unique, with the goat he killed the lion. He gave all the wealth to Sudas (VII.18.17).[10]

This great conquest was accomplished not by a large army but through the help of the priests, like Vasishta and Vishwamitra, who appeared as white-robed warriors without arms.

> By your chants you crossed the river. By them you defeated Bheda. Thus in the Battle of the Ten Kings, oh Vasishtas, Indra furthered your chants (VII.33.3).[11]

The priests helped Sudas cross the river in a flood. His enemies, however, are drowned in the flood.

> The floods extended for Sudas. Indra made them easy to cross. The hostile army, speakers of a new language, the unworthy gained the curse of the rivers. Of evil mind, trying to drain the Earth (Aditi), the unwise parted the Parushni river. They went to their goal, their defeat on the Parushni. Even the swift did not return. Indra for Sudas, for man, defeated the strong, unfriendly people of false speech (VII.18.5, 8-9).

Indra released his great weapon, the flood. He destroyed the fallen Aryans who had also become false in speech; who ceased to speak the truth.

Sudas is said to have defeated enemies, who are his kinsmen, who attacked him from both sides.

> King Sudas destroyed the enemy in the east, west and north and then gave worship at the best place on Earth (III.53.11).[12]

His battle is a defensive war around his homeland, not an invasion into new territory. Where was his homeland then? Sudas appears to be a ruler of the land around the Saraswati river. The war of Sudas occurred with battles at two points, the Parushni or Ravi in the west (VII.18.8) and the Yamuna in the east (VII.18.19). *These mark the boundaries of the Saraswati river region.*

Western scholars have assumed his army moved into India from the northwest, penetrating from the Parushni to the Yamuna, or that the Yamuna may here be another name for the Indus. This does not agree with the statements of the *Veda*. As Sudas was fighting a defensive war, the battles to the west and east are in perfect accord with his location. His army went from the Saraswati to the Parushni, crossing the Vipas and Shutudri along the way (as according to Vishwamitra's hymn, III.33, which celebrates the crossing of these two friendly rivers by Sudas). He was not moving into India from the northwest, but from within India to an attack by hostile forces from the northwest. His army crossed these rivers but was going opposite in direction to the so-called Aryan invasion. It similarly defeated an invasion from the east on the banks of the Yamuna.

The central region of the kingdom of Sudas was from the Parushni (Ravi) to the Yamuna, with the Saraswati and Drishadvati valleys in between.

> King Sudas defeated the enemy in the east, west and north and then gave sacrifice at the most holy place on the Earth (III.53.11).[13]

We have already encountered "the most holy place on Earth" as a definition of the Saraswati-Drishadvati region (III.23.4). Most of the great Aryan kings ruled from this region. Vasishta, the priest of Sudas, also describes the Saraswati as flowing to the sea (VII.95.2). Hence, the kingdom of Sudas probably extended down the Saraswati to the ocean.

The enemies Sudas defeated on the Parushni could have included many Aryan kings. In the *Rig Veda* we find the Aryans well-established all along the Indus, into the Gandhara region of Afghanistan and perhaps beyond. So a number of kings from these regions could have attacked Sudas on that side. Vasishta speaks of a great victory of the Aryans over the Dasyus where the Asikni people fled in fear.

> From fear of you, Agni, the Asikni people fled and abandoned their possessions (VII.5.3).

Asikni is the name for the Chenab, the next river in the Punjab west of the Parushni. This affirms the victories of Sudas to the west.

If Sudas was attacked by a large confederacy of mainly Aryan enemies east on the Yamuna, this further indicates that the Aryans had long been established there with several comparable kingdoms to that of Sudas. This confirms the idea that such Vedic rivers as Jahnavi (Ganges) and Sarayu are eastern rivers and that even in the *Rig Veda* the Aryans ruled north India from sea to sea.

The main battle, in fact, was in the east rather than the west. Bheda, whose name means 'division', is mentioned as the name of the enemy of Sudas (VII.86.4). He was defeated on the Yamuna river to the east.

> The Yamuna aided Indra and the Tritsus (the people of Sudas), there Bheda was completely defeated. The Ajas, Shigrus and Yakshus gave the offering of their horse's heads (VII.18.19).

Turvasha, the eldest of the five Aryan peoples and stated to be the leader of the enemies of Sudas, was said to be Yakshu, meaning "desirous of victory" (VII.18.6). The Yakshavas thus appear to be the Turvashas who dwelled east of the Yamuna. In the *Puranas,* the descendants of Turvasha are said to have inhabited the southeast of India, which can be thus identified with southeastern India to the Bay of Bengal. This means that the oldest of the Aryan peoples were located east of the Yamuna river even within the period of the *Rig Veda,* and shows the Vedic culture prominent in east India from the earliest era.

Turvasha, along with Yadu, the second of the Aryan peoples, is said to have been saved by the power of the Gods from across the sea in several of the hymns (I.174.9, V.31.8). If Turvasha was in the east it would have been the Bay of Bengal across which he was saved. This would indicate that some of the Vedic peoples may have come into India from this direction. Yadu and his kingdoms were traditionally located on the Arabian Sea, the western ocean.

Indra states:

> I am the destroyer of the seven. I am more like Nahusha than the Nahushas. I glorified with strength Turvasha and Yadu. I as a bull uphold seven rivers, wealth-giving streams on Earth. Of strong will, I cross the floods (X.49.8-9).

Yet though Turvasha and Yadu were great and probably the oldest and originally most powerful of the Aryan peoples, they were also at another time defeated, as here by Sudas.

As we will explain further in our section on the *Puranas,* the battle of Sudas and the five Aryan peoples explains their location and fate. The Turvashas were originally located in the southeast of India but were largely driven out. The Anus were located in the north and the Druhyus in the west and were also partly driven out of India. These fallen Aryans were said to have peopled regions outside of India. We should also note that the Bhrigu seers also thereby appear to be located originally in the west of India.The main enemies of Sudas appear to have been an alliance of far western (Anu and Druhyu) and far eastern (Turvasha) people, with the Yadus probably involved as well. This may explain why eastern regions of Bengal and Bihar (Anga and Magadha) were viewed with suspicion, as well as western regions of Gandhara and Balkh (Bactria), as in the *Atharva Veda* (V.22.7, 14). Their kings tried to overthrow the central Vedic kingdom and thereby fell from the Vedic Dharma for a time. In this regard the *Garuda Purana* (82.1–18) places a people called the Kikatas in Bihar (Magadha). The Kikatas are mentioned in the *Rig Veda* among the enemies of Sudas (III.53.14). They appear to have been among the Turvashas.

However, the Yadus continued on in India as did the Purus. Yet the Yadus were chastised. In fact, in the *Puranas* it is mainly the Yadus who have to be kept in check by various kings and seers (like King Sagara and Parashurama). The victory of Sudas is, moreover, said to have given him tribute from across the sea.

> Who bent down their plastered walls with his weapons, who made the dawns companions of the noble, having subdued the peoples of the Nahushas, the mighty fire made them tribute bearers by his strength. In whose peace all men stand according to their nature seeking his grace, the Universal Fire dwells at the most choice place on Earth, in the bosom of the parents. The Divine Universal Man gained the foundation treasures in the rising of the Sun, the Fire received them from the inferior and superior ocean, from Heaven and Earth (VII.6.5–7).[14]

Here the king is Agni Vaishwanara, the fire as the universal man or world-ruler, apparently Sudas. He has defeated his enemies, the Panis, Dasyus, and Nahushas, who are fallen Aryans — descendants of Puru, Turvasha, Druhyu and Anu. He is the great sage-king who brings peace to the world.

> The seer, the guiding ray, the foundation, the light of the mountain, they direct him as a kingdom of peace on Heaven and Earth (VII.6.2).[15]

He receives tribute from across the sea, perhaps from colonies of these defeated kings who also had naval forces. The inferior and superior ocean are not just Heaven and Earth but the eastern and western seas of India, the Bay of Bengal and the Arabian Sea, the lands of Turvasha and Yadu.

We read of the wealth that Sudas gained from across the sea elsewhere.

> Ashwins, bearing wealth on your vehicle, you brought treasures to Sudas. The wealth from the ocean and from Heaven, much to be wished for, give to us (I.46.6).

Sudas was aided by Varuna, the God of the Sea, affirming the extent of his power. Vasishta, the priest of Sudas and his battle, not only speaks of the Saraswati as flowing from the mountains to the sea, he speaks of Varuna and going out into the ocean in a ship with Varuna, travelling along the waves, as far as the heavens extend (VII.87.3-4).

This victory of Sudas is said to have been a conquering of seven cities.

> In an instant Indra destroyed all their firmnesses, he conquered with force seven cities (VII.18.13).[16]

These must have been the seven cities of the Aryans. Just as later India had seven sacred cities, so may have Vedic India. Some of these may have been the same and may have included prime sites throughout north India.

After the victory of Sudas the Aryan peoples were divided.

> Half the army of the warriors that did not worship Indra were driven out over the Earth. Indra reduced the wrath of the wrathful and as the ruler apportioned paths for them to travel (VII.18.16).[17]

This suggests that Sudas drove many of his defeated enemies and kinsmen out of north India.

> Indra established boundaries (VII.18.17)[18]

That is, Indra defined the land of the Aryans or the land of Bharata.

Bharata is another name for the people of Sudas (III.53.12). Indra, the ruling power or Divine grace behind Sudas, established the land of north India as a spiritual land or sacred space and drove out the fallen materialistic people who dared to try to conquer the central kingdom of the Saraswati, the land of the Brahmins. The boundaries of this land are probably defined by the rivers in the hymn to the Maruts that mentions Sudas (V.53.2, 9), referred to in the chapter on the Rivers. They are the

Indus in the west, Sarayu (Ghaghara) in the east, and Rasa (Narmada) in the south.

The defeated people were largely Kshatriyas or nobility and Vaishyas or traders that had ceased to pay homage to the seers. These Dasyus who had been in the east were driven to the west (VII.6.3). This may not be just a mythical statement of driving the powers of darkness away from the place of the light. Perhaps some were driven from the east of India, the land of Turvasha, to the west and out of India, possibly becoming some of the peoples of the Middle East.

The victory of Sudas is thus portrayed not as a minor clash among Aryan kings, much less an Aryan invasion of India from the Punjab, but as a victory in a great civil war establishing a large empire and era of peace. It was marked not only by war but by a great flood that no doubt brought many changes to the land and the people. It marks the end of one era and the beginning of another and appears to mark the end of the main Rig Vedic period. It marked the time when the Vedic culture began to contract, define its boundaries and become protective of itself. It appears to be the time wherein India or Bharata defined itself as a particular land.

The great seers Vasishta and Vishwamitra, famous in later Hindu literature, appear in the *Rig Veda* primarily as the priests of Sudas. Their books in the *Rig Veda* may thus be among the last to be finished. Their power increased through the ascendancy of Sudas and they became the main seer-families in India. The dynasties and cultures which exalt them are probably, therefore, later than Sudas. The conflict between Vishwamitra and Vasishta, which is prominent in later Vedic literature, must come after Sudas, though the origins of it may have occurred at his time. As the other Aryan peoples were defeated by Sudas, power went to Vishwamitra and Vasishta, whose families may have eventually clashed over it in time. In the *Rig Veda* itself we find no real conflict between them and the later stories of their conflict in the court of Sudas may reflect a later time. The story of Sudas shows the Aryans had been in India long before the end of the Rig Vedic period — that the *Rig Veda* was composed in India itself.

DIVODASA AND THE DEFEAT OF THE DASYUS

Divodasa is the great king who defeated Shambara, the primary non-Aryan or Dasyu enemy of the Vedic people. He is perhaps the archetypal Vedic king, the great destroyer of unspiritual cultures. His story is more mythical than that of Sudas but it appears to have something of an historical basis, though ancient even in the earlier hymns of the *Rig Veda.* While Sudas is the great king of the seventh, the third and parts of the fifth book of the *Rig Veda,* Divodasa is mentioned everywhere but most prominently in the sixth book, that of the Bharadwajas, who are said to be his Rishis. He is also a significant figure in the fourth book, that of Vamadeva.

Divodasa is stated to be a gift given by the river Saraswati.

> She gave the fierce, debt-removing Divodasa to the worshipper Vadhryashwa (VI.61.1).

Divodasa thus appears to have dwelled along the Saraswati. His kingdom was the central Vedic region of the Saraswati. The same hymn which mentions Divodasa glorifies the whole Saraswati basin to the sea (v.8). Divodasa was probably a king of the Saraswati river perhaps down to the sea, as was Sudas in later times. The legend of Divodasa defeating Shambara and conquering his hundred cities follows an earlier mythological event: Indra destroying Ahi or Vritra and allowing the seven rivers to flow to the sea — the image of a great flood.

> Indra destroyed the ninety-nine cities by the strength of his arms, and slew the serpent (VIII.93.2).[19]
>
> I was Manu and the Sun. I am the seer Kakshivan, the sage. I made Kutsa humble. I am the seer Ushanas, behold me. I gave the Earth to the Aryans. I gave the rain to the worshipping mortal. I led the roaring floods. The Gods moved according to my will. In ecstasy I destroyed at once the ninety-nine cities of Shambara, and the hundredth habitation completely when I aided Divodasa (IV.26.1-3).

Here we see the Flood and the destruction of the cities of Shambara together.

Divodasa appears as the king for whom Indra gave the Earth to the Aryans.

> Who broke open the hundred ancient stone cities of Shambara, who threw down the hundred thousand warriors of Varchin, bring the Soma to Indra (II.14.6).[20]
>
> For Divodasa, Indra destroyed the ninety-nine cities of Shambara (II.19.6).[21]
>
> Indra, with strength you accomplished that, when you, hero, you slew the hundred thousand. You struck down Shambara from the mountain, when you aided Divodasa with manifold aids (VI.26.5).[22]

Indra aids Divodasa in the destruction of the hundred cities of Shambara and his hundred thousand warriors, largely through a great flood. Shambara is finally defeated by throwing him down from his last and most glorious city or fortress described as a great mountain (IV.28.2). The implication is that Shambara had a number of mountain fortresses from which he oppressed the Aryan people, the foremost of which was situated on a high mountain.

MOUNT ABU AND ARBUDA

The Vedic culture was sometimes plagued by inimical people, often mountain or hill people, who raided their villages and stole their cattle, an image we find throughout the *Rig Veda*. They may have originally been remnants of the great and hostile civilization of Shambara and his hundred cities. Eventually they were reduced to smaller groups, often no more than thieves.

The most obvious place for these fortresses would be in the Vindhya and related mountains of central India. It was probably not from the Himalayas that the Aryans were attacked as this was their sacred land of the Soma. The mountains of central India are old stony mountains. Many of them naturally look like castles. Even up to recent times in the mountains of Rajasthan the kings had great castles and rocky fortresses. We find confirmation of this idea in the *Rig Veda*.

After the Himalayas, the mountains most famous for the Soma, according to the great Ayurvedic doctor Sushrut, are the Arbudas.[a] Arbuda is also the name of a demon slain by Indra, who appears related to Shambara and Vritra. Arbuda is also associated with Vala, the mountain fortress or cavern broken open by Indra and the Angirasas (II.11.20).

> Indra aided Kutsa in the destruction of Shushna. He defeated Shambara for Atithigva (Divodasa). He crushed great Arbuda with his feet (I.51.6).
>
> Indra with the greatness of the great flood broke off the summit of Arbuda. He slew the serpent and released the seven rivers (X.67.12).
>
> Indra threw the dragon from the vast shore. He drove the cows of Arbuda down from the mountain (VIII.3.19).
>
> Indra, you brought down the vast dwelling place, the summit of Arbuda (VIII.32.3).[23]

Arbuda is the ancient name for Mount Abu in Rajasthan, the highest and one of the most important mountains in this region. It would make sense as the prime fortress area for central and western India. It dominates the region around what was in Vedic times the mouth of the Saraswati river at the Rann of Kutch. From fortresses in this area the whole Saraswati region could be easily raided.

We should note that the demons defeated by Indra can all be symbolized by mountains, which are the regions that withhold the waters. These demons may refer to the mountain regions conquered or colonized by the Aryans.

The ninety-nine cities of Shambara destroyed in a flood, to the extent that they may have been actual cities rather than mythical cities of the demons, were most likely by the coasts and the river plains of India, possibly even in the Ganges region, where the Panis were said to dwell in one of the hymns of the Bharadwajas (VI.45.31). The spiritual Aryans appear have had their center in the Himalayas to the north. The materialistic Panis appear to have dwelled to the south of them with fortresses in the lower mountains to the south and possibly to the east. Yet just as it is the tendency of mountain people to remain more spiritual, it is also the tendency of people in populated areas to become more materialistic. The division between the Aryans and the Dasyus or Panis may have been originally this division between the spiritual people who prefer mountain regions and the materialistic people of the cities. We should note that the Naga people, the worshippers of serpents, dwelling in Assam in the east and related peoples in central India (Nagpur region) have periodically invaded and sometimes overthrown the various Indian kingdoms. Perhaps they are related to the serpent worshipping Dasyus and Panis of the *Vedas*. Before Divodasa they may have ruled much of India for a time, possibly from a central fortress in the region of Mount Abu.

This would indicate that Divodasa moved down from the Himalayas and defeated Shambara and his people, eventually taking over his final strongholds in the mountains of central India. Divodasa or his kingdom may have already been established in the Himalayan foothills and the upper regions of rivers like the Saraswati, the upper Indus or Kashmir, the lands of the Soma. Yet this was a movement of spiritual people from the Himalayas who conquered a materialistic culture in lower India that appears related to them. The northern or mountain culture appears to have preserved its spiritual values better, whereas the southern culture degenerated into materialism and had to be overcome. In this regard, the *Bhagavata Purana* (6.9.1-19) speaks of a battle betweent the Gods and the demons early in the Treta Yuga in which Indra defeated Shambara. It is said to have taken place on the Narmada river, the main river of central India.

There are some Vedic verses that show that the Vedic people may have been refugees from a materialistic Dasyu-Pani culture.

> When I was in the womb I learned all the births of the Gods. A hundred iron cities imprisoned me. Then I flew away with the speed of an eagle (IV.27.1).[24]

This gives the poetic image of the hundred cities of Shambara as places of confinement or imprisonment for the Aryans.

THE VICTORY OF DIVODASA

There is one hymn of the Bharadwajas (VI.47), the priests of Divodasa, that gives an account of the victory of his successors. The relevant verses are as follows:

> 15. He who worships him, who gives gifts and offers sacrifice to him, who is strong; Maghavan (Indra) furthers him always. Like moving the feet one after another, he makes the earlier later by his powers.
>
> 16. He is lauded as the hero who conquers each one that is strong, leading them down one after another. The knower of increase, the lord of both peoples, Indra gives gifts to the human peoples.
>
> 17. Renouncing the friendship of those earlier, favoring those later he moves on.
>
> 20. We have come to a land devoid of pasture, oh Gods. Though a wide land it has become narrow. Brihaspati, look forward in our struggle. Indra, find a path for your worshipper.
>
> 21. Day by day alike, to the other side he drove the dark peoples from their dwellings. The Bull slew the greedy destroyers in the confluence of the waters, both Varchin and Shambara.
>
> 22. Prastoka gave your treasures, oh Indra, ten chests of gems and ten stallions. We received the treasure of Atithigva, the wealth of Shambara from Divodasa.

These verses show a group of Aryans moving forward as aggressors, which is different than the defensive battle of Sudas. Yet the enemies are described as former friends of Indra. Divodasa's war appears as an attack by the Aryans against fallen Aryans in their own land. Brihaspati is the leading priest or Purohit of the king who is consulted to indicate a path to a new and better land.

This hymn celebrates the advance of the Aryans, along with a great gift to the seers who aided in the struggle. Varchin and Shambara are Panis, commercial people who had no respect for spiritual knowledge, and who apparently practiced black magic. A real battle is indicated here between the Aryans and the Panis. The Panis are portrayed as former friends of Indra. Hence Shambara can also represent fallen Aryans who lost the grace of Indra. The Panis are portrayed as having been very rich in gold, cattle and horses.

Atithigva appears to be a title which Divodasa possessed. Perhaps in some way it means king or emperor. Literally it means 'undivided light'. This hymn does not appear to celebrate the original victory of Divodasa but that of one of his successors, who modeled it after the legend of Divodasa.

Another hymn of the Bharadwajas mentions the victory of Sriñjaya and says Indra "gave Turvasha to Sriñjaya" (VI.25.7). This shows that Sriñjaya defeated Turvasha, one of the five Vedic peoples. Perhaps Divodasa's descendants in this hymn defeated some fallen Aryan descendants of Turvasha.

> Soma destroyed the ninety-nine cities and Shambara instantly for pious Divodasa and then Turvasha and Yadu (IX.61.2).[25]

This also shows the defeat of the Dasyus followed by an inter-Aryan conflict. Yet it even suggests that Shambara himself was perhaps originally a descendant of Yadu or Turvasha. This is also the implication of the Puranic view that makes their first King Divodasa defeat the Yadus. If Shambara was a Yadu, then his culture was not pre-Vedic but a fallen Vedic culture from an early era.

The Panis and Dasyus were thus originally defeated after a great flood. This was followed by their being thrown off a great mountain, perhaps Mount Abu in Rajasthan (or perhaps Sri Lanka which was said to be the home of the demons even before the time of Ravana). Both events may have followed a great earthquake. Their defeat became the archetypal or mythic image for the victories of the Aryan kings. The Panis and Dasyus became problems periodically in Vedic culture, as later in the time of Sudas. This is simply because they represent people of commercial and militaristic values. When a spiritual culture declines, such people naturally increase. In Vedic times the Aryan kings were able to defeat such unspiritual peoples. Though they periodically grew in strength, they were periodically defeated.

Divodasa represents an Aryan king who destroyed a large kingdom of Panis. The hundred stone cities of Shambara indicate a large civilization for that time (although we should remember the Aryans themselves were said to have a hundred cities of their own). Some centuries, perhaps more, must have occurred between the time when the Panis had a hundred cities in India at the time of Divodasa and the time of Sudas when it was the inimical Aryans that were defeated. The priest of Divodasa is Bharadwaja, closely related to Brihaspati, the first of the Vedic priests. This shows an earlier era than Vasishta and Vishwamitra, the priests of Sudas. A Divodasa is also said to be the father of Sudas (VII.18.25). Yet this may be a different Divodasa, of which Vedic literature records several, or only a metaphor. Their stories reflect greatly different epochs of Vedic history.

In the *Rig Veda* the Flood myth is allied with the myth of destroying the serpent in the mountains. The fortresses of the demons are said to be in the mountains, in which they withhold the waters and the cows (the symbols of wealth). This image has been compared with the rain clouds that withhold the waters and the sunlight (the cows), and are broken open by Indra (the God of the rain) and his thunderbolt. Some have seen in it the mountain snows melting in the spring, filling the rivers. Others have seen in it the image of the melting glaciers and the ending of the last Ice Age. Some have regarded it as a memory of a time when the Aryans dwelled in arctic regions and the image of arctic spring. Yet there remains the historical image of a culture with large, mountain-like cities, or at least with fortresses in the mountains, in which they hid their wealth and from which they raided the lands of the Aryans.

Before the time of Divodasa there appears to have been a great non-Aryan civilization in India, perhaps centered in the Vindhya mountains, which is also described as the fallen Aryans of an earlier era. We see, therefore, that there was an Aryan renovation of India but it was long before the time of Sudas, in the earliest era of the *Rig Veda.* It would have been also long before the Indus Valley culture. Still it was not an invasion of a different race but a shift in social values. It was a revolt of the spiritual people in the culture against the rule of materialistic kings.

The *Rig Veda* portrays a conflict of social values — spiritual and materialistic — but not a conflict of races. This conflict occurred largely in India and India was thereby established as a spiritual kingdom. However, this spiritual kingdom degenerated and had to be reestablished again. Divodasa established a great spiritual kingdom in India, though even he is not portrayed as the first to do so. Sudas reestablished it again some time later.

OTHER KINGS

References to wars among the Aryans occur elsewhere in the *Rig Veda.* There is the story of Turvayana, which resembles that of Sudas and

Divodasa put together. He destroys ninety-nine cities and twenty hostile kings.

> When twice ten kings of men came to fight with friendless Sushravas, with the hard step of the chariot wheel, you trod over sixty thousand famed heroes and ninety-nine cities. You helped Sushravas with your aids and, Indra, Turvayana by your protection. To him, the mighty young king, you subjected Kutsa, Atithigva, and Ayus (I.53.9, 10).
>
> This deed you have done today is praised. When you made subject Kutsa, Ayus and Atithigva to him and destroyed many thousands over the Earth, and with boldness guided Turvayana (VI.18.13).

Turvayana or Sushravas, like Sudas, wins a war against a great alliance of kings, including representatives of famous Aryans like Kutsa, one of the most famous Vedic seers, Atithigva, another name for Divodasa, and Ayus, one of the earliest Vedic kings. This also shows a defeat of older Aryan peoples by new favorites of Indra. Here the ninety-nine cities he conquers are those of the Aryans. Sushravas appears related to the Persian Husravah,[b] later called Khosrav, a friendless king like Sudas who was said to have united the Aryan nations into one kingdom.

Purukutsa is a great hero of the Purus. Purukutsa similarly wins the seven cities like Sudas. Purukutsa is the father or ancestor of another great king, Trasadasyu.

> Fighting for Purukutsa, Indra, you broke open seven cities. When you made the altar for Sudas, you created wideness for the Purus (I.63.7).
>
> Indra, you struck down the people of the evil word and broke open seven yearly cities. You released stainless floods and conquered Vritra for young Purukutsa (I.174.2).

The story of Sudas appears archetypal of the ideal Aryan king who holds to truth and the sacrifice even when all the other Aryan kings turn against him and try to defeat him. It does not just occur at the end of the *Rig Veda* but is part of its spirit and contained in the stories of other kings. The story of Divodasa is of the ideal Aryan king who defeats the Dasyus or non-Aryans. The stories of various other kings reflect these two themes and weave them together in different ways as non-Aryans are also fallen

Aryans. The Vedic kings are thus more story figures than historical entities, though they have an historical basis. Their names appear at times as epithets or titles that actual kings can take. They may also represent dynasties, particularly those that they founded. Hence, we find their names or stories connected with a number of kings.

2
STORIES OF VEDIC KINGS
FROM THE *BRAHMANAS* AND *PURANAS*

THE *BRAHMANAS:* Rituals of the Vedic Kings

The *Brahmanas* are books of ritual and reflect the ancient Vedic sacrifice. Some of them were compiled in the courts of great Vedic kings. The *Aitareya Brahmana* provides much information about these rulers of ancient India. It describes the great anointing (Mahabhisheka) wherein the great kings and emperors were empowered by their priests. All traditional cultures had this passing on of power or virtue from the priests or religious leaders to their kings and champions.

The *Brahmanas* define a great king or emperor as a world-ruler, one who conquers the world — the land of the Aryans in north India between the Himalaya and the Vindhya mountains, between the eastern and western oceans. The chief priest gives the king "the great anointing of Indra" and the king offers the horse in sacrifice to seal his great victory. Many such Vedic kings are recorded to have performed this ritual, including one named Sudas. This may indicate the extent of the victory of Sudas in the *Rig Veda,* though he appears neither as the first nor the last to achieve it.

THE GREAT ANOINTING OF INDRA

The *Aitareya Brahmana* describes the different regions of India, their Gods and the rulership ascribed to them. This is part of the great anointing of Indra, which is later transferred via the priest to the king so that he might obtain rulership of all these lands.

> Then the Vasus, the Gods in the eastern quarter, anointed Indra for six days with the Pañcavinsha rite, with this chant, this sacrificial formula and these exclamations, for overlordship. Therefore in this eastern quarter, whatever kings there are of the eastern peoples, they are anointed for overlordship; "Oh overlord" they call their kings when thus anointed in accordance with the action of the Gods.

Then in the southern quarter the Rudras, the Gods, anointed him for six days with the Pañcavinsha rite, with this chant, this sacrificial formula and these exclamations, for paramount rule. Therefore in this southern quarter, whatever kings there are of the Satvants, they are anointed for paramount rule; "Oh paramount ruler" they call their kings when thus anointed in accordance with the action of the Gods.

Then in the western quarter the Adityas, the Gods, anointed him for six days with the Pañcavinsha rite, with this chant and this sacrificial formula and these exclamations, for self rule. Therefore in this western quarter, whatever kings there are of the southern and western peoples, they are anointed for self rule; "Oh self ruler" they call their kings when thus anointed in accordance with the action of the Gods.

Then in the northern quarter the All-Gods anointed him for six days with the Pañcavinsha rite, with this chant, this sacrificial formula and these exclamations, for sovereignty. Therefore in this northern quarter, the lands of the Uttara Kurus and the Uttara Madras, beyond the Himalayas, their kings are anointed for sovereignty; "Oh sovereign" they call their kings when thus anointed in accordance with the action of the Gods.

Then in this firm middle established quarter the Sadhyas and the Aptyas, the Gods, anointed him for six days with the Pañcavinsha rite, with this chant, this sacrificial formula and these exclamations, for kingship. Therefore in this firm middle established quarter, whatever kings there are of the Kuru-Pañcalas along with the Vashas and Ushinaras, they are anointed for kingship; "Oh king" they call their kings when thus anointed in accordance with the action of the Gods.

Then in the upward quarter the Maruts and the Angirasas, the Gods, anointed him for six days with the Pañcavinsha rite, with this chant, this sacrificial formula and these exclamations, for supreme authority, for great kingship, for suzerainty, for supremacy, for preeminence. He became the supreme authority, as connected with Prajapati (the Lord of creation). Anointed with this great anointment, Indra won all victories, found all the worlds, attained the superiority, pre-eminence and supremacy over

> all the Gods, and having won the overlordship, paramount rule, self-rule, the sovereignty, the supreme authority, kingship, great kingship, the suzerainty in this world, self-existing, self-ruling, immortal, in yonder world of Heaven, having obtained all desires, he became immortal (AB VIII.14).[a]

Here we see India divided into four quarters and a central land. The central quarter or middle region is that of the Kurus and Pañcalas. It included the Vedic Saraswati region, along with the area between the Yamuna and the Ganges. The eastern quarter is thus east of the Ganges and probably the region of India to the Bay of Bengal. The southern quarter, that of the Satvants, is in central India south of Mathura and into Rajasthan and central India. The western quarter, also called southern and western, is probably the Punjab and the land of southwest India, Sind and Gujarat — the regions by the Arabian Sea. The northern quarter is said to be "beyond the Himalayas." This land of the Uttara Kurus, which became a mythical land in later times, is most likely the Tarim Basin in western China, which was home to Indo-Iranian peoples even in historical times. It indicates the presence of Aryans and perhaps the rulership of Aryan kings of India in this distant land. The upward quarter is the land of the Gods above (Heaven).

This shows the land of the Aryans as essentially the land of north India from the Vindhyas to the Himalayas, with additional regions in Tibet and to the north. It is similar to the Vedic idea of the five peoples and most likely developed from it. The Purus, of which the Kurus are well-known descendants, dwell in the central region of India, the Saraswati, Yamuna, and Ganges region. The Anus probably dwell in the north regions of northwest India or the Punjab (possibly into the Himalayas and beyond as well). The Druhyus probably dwell in the west, Gandhara or Afghanistan and perhaps Sind (the lower Indus region). The Yadus dwell in the south to the Arabian Sea. The Turvashas dwell in the east or southeast to the Bay of Bengal.

ANCIENT INDIAN EMPERORS

The *Brahmanas* also mention the great aspiration of the Vedic kings. The Vedic kings had this prayer:

> May I win all victories, find all worlds, attain the superiority, preeminence, and supremacy over all kings and overlordship, paramount rule, self-rule, sovereignty, supreme authority, kingship, great kingship and suzer-

> ainty; may I be all encompassing, possessed of all the Earth, possessed of all life, *from the one end up to the further side of the Earth bounded by the ocean sole ruler* (AB VIII.15).[b]

These remarks clearly show that Vedic kings were renowned to have conquered the land of India from sea to sea. To gain this possession of the Earth from ocean to ocean, the king is consecrated by his chief priest (Purohit) with the great anointing of Indra.

> With this great anointing of Indra, Tura Kavasheya anointed Janamejaya Parikshit. Therefore, Janamejaya Parikshit *went around the Earth completely, conquering on every side,* and offered the horse in sacrifice.
>
> With this great anointing of Indra, Chyavana Bhargava anointed Sharyata Manava. Therefore, Sharyata Manava *went around the Earth completely, conquering on every side,* and offered the horse in sacrifice.
>
> With this great anointing of Indra, Somasushman Vajaratnayana anointed Shatanika Satrajita. Therefore, Shatanika Satrajita *went around the Earth completely, conquering on every side,* and offered the horse in sacrifice.
>
> With this great anointing of Indra, Parvata and Narada anointed Ambasthya. Therefore, Ambasthya *went around the Earth completely, conquering on every side,* and offered the horse in sacrifice.
>
> With this great anointing of Indra, Parvata and Narada anointed Yudhamshraushti Augrasainya. Therefore, Yudhamshraushti Augrasainya *went around the Earth completely, conquering on every side,* and offered the horse in sacrifice.
>
> With this great anointing of Indra, Kashyapa anointed Vishwakarman Bhauvana. Therefore, Vishwakarman Bhauvana *went around the Earth completely, conquering on every side,* and offered the horse in sacrifice.
>
> With this great anointing of Indra, Vasishta anointed Sudas Paijavana. Therefore, Sudas Paijavana *went around the Earth completely, conquering on every side,* and offered the horse in sacrifice.
>
> With this great anointing of Indra, Samvarta Angirasa anointed Marutta Avikshita. Therefore, Marutta Avikshita

> *went around the Earth completely, conquering on every side,* and offered the horse in sacrifice.
>
> With this great anointing of Indra, Udamaya Atreya anointed Anga. Therefore, Anga *went around the Earth completely, conquering on every side,* and offered the horse in sacrifice.
>
> With this great anointing of Indra, Dirghatamas Mamateya anointed Bharata Dauhshanti. Therefore, Bharata Dauhshanti *went around the Earth completely, conquering on every side,* and offered the horse in sacrifice.
>
> This great anointing of Indra, Brihaduktha the seer proclaimed to Durmukha, the Pañcala. Therefore, Durmukha Pañcala, being a king, by this knowledge *went around the Earth completely, conquering on every side* (AB VIII.21).[c]

This passage lists eleven great kings or emperors said to have conquered the whole of North India from ocean to ocean. There is a similar list in the *Shatapatha Brahmana* (VIII.5.4). Several of the kings and their chief priests, like Vasishta and Sudas, occur in the *Rig Veda*. All are Vedic kings of the later Rig Vedic age and after. Several occur in classical Indian literature as great world rulers, like Bharata. Is this mere myth or imagination?

A.B. Keith, western translator of the *Aitareya Brahmana*, states, "The political references do not hint at any great kingdoms, but at a large number of petty princes, who despite their titles and claims to sovereignty were doubtless rulers of limited portions of territory."[d] In other words, he ignores these passages and assumes they were fictional. Yet the fact is that the *Aitareya Brahmana* does portray many emperors of the whole of north India. Whether it is truthful or not is another matter, but certainly the political references are clear and unequivocal about the existence of a large number of great empires in India in Vedic times. They show north India united as an empire more often in times before the Buddha than after. As several great kings of the *Rig Veda* are mentioned in this way, the implication is that the other great kings of the *Rig Veda* had the same accomplishment and that it may therefore reflect the original great victory of the first Vedic kings.

Reducing "great kingdoms" to petty princes is like reducing clear ocean references to the upper regions of the Indus river. We see that this is not what the texts themselves say but a very contracted interpretation of them. Such an interpretation assumes that the texts are not telling the truth — probably just boastings of kings who were mere rulers of local tribes claiming to have conquered all of north India. However, where would such texts get this idea if it never happened? If eleven kings of Europe were said to have ruled Europe from Spain to Germany, or from the Baltic to the Mediterranean — an area no larger than north India from sea to sea — would we reduce them to mere local rulers of the Netherlands? Would we say that a book which mentioned such rulers showed no hint at any great kingdoms in Europe but only petty princes? Yet this is what has been done here.

Many scholars have ignored ancient Hindu references to oceans, constellations, and empires alike, not crediting the Hindus with such major achievements of civilization — though the *Vedas* frequently mention these very things. The *Vedas* would not have mentioned them in the first place if they were without any basis. Nobody claims to be like Napoleon if there never was a Napoleon. At least one of these Hindu kings must have ruled enough of north India for the idea of such a world ruler to have arisen in the first place. Such kings are mentioned elsewhere in the *Brahmanas:*

> This food Rama Margaveya proclaimed to Vishwantara Saudasamana ... This also Tura Kavasheya proclaimed to Janamejaya Parikshit; this Parvata and Narada proclaimed to Somaka Sahadevaya, to Sahadeva Sarnjaya, to Babhru Divavridha, to Bhima of Vidarbha, to Nagnajit of Gandhara; this Agni proclaimed to Sanashruta Arimdama and to Kratuvid Janaki; this Vasishta proclaimed to Sudas Paijavana. All of them attained greatness having partaken of this food. *All of them were great kings; like the Sun, established in prosperity, they gave warmth, obtaining tribute from all the quarters* (AB VII.34).[e]

These kings, of which Sudas is one, ruled like the Sun, and as world rulers gained tribute from the four quarters of India. The regions these kings came from are quite diverse. Janamejaya was a king of the Kurus, whose central region is by the Ganges and Yamuna. Gandhara, where Nagnajit came from, is in the mountains of western India and eastern Afghanistan. Janaki came from Videha to the east of the Gandhak river or eastern Nepal. Yet most interesting is Bhima, a king of Vidarbha. Vidarbha is in central India south of the Narmada river, around modern Nagpur. Originally it appears to have been a large kingdom encompassing much of the modern state of Maharashtra. This places the Vedic people well into central India by the time of the *Brahmanas.* It takes them beyond the boundaries of north India (the Vindhya range or Narmada river). We should note also that the Chedis, a people of this region, are mentioned as early as the *Rig Veda* itself (VIII.5.39). Of the other kings already mentioned, Sharyata was traditionally a ruler of Gujarat (Anartta; VP IV.I.20) and Anga of Bengal. The native lands of these kings cover most of modern India, and are certainly in keeping with the idea that these kings ruled an area from sea to sea. How can we see in such references only petty princes who knew limited regions?

After their victories these kings offered great sacrifices, giving away vast numbers of horses and cows.

> Of the cows for which the Brahmin Udamaya Atreya gave at the middle of the offering, the Praiyamedha seers aided in sacrificing, two thousand of myriads day by day. Eighty-eight thousand white horses, side steeds, Vairochana loosing them, the king gave when his Brahmin was sacrificing. With these brought from each country, all daughters of wealthy men, ten thousands Atreya gave, with necklaces on their necks. By reason of the gift of King Anga, having given tens of thousands of elephants at Avachatnuka, the Brahmin Atreya, wearied sought for attendants. "A hundred to you, a hundred to you," so saying he grew weary; by saying "a thousand to you," he got back his breath (AB VII.22).[f]

This offering states that eighty-eight thousand horses, ten thousands of cows and elephants, and ten thousands of women as wives for his men were given, brought from each country, no doubt as tribute. There were so many that the priest, wearied of giving them away by the hundred, had to give them away by the thousand! Does this sound like a petty kingdom, or the riches from both seas? In the *Rig Veda* many such gifts of the kings are mentioned, like the 60,000 horses, 12,000 camels and 10,000 cattle given by Vasha Ashwya (VIII.46.22). These were probably given to celebrate victories of a similar nature. Other of these rulers like Bharata (AB VIII.21) and Marutta (VP IV.I.17) are credited with similar gifts.

The rulers mentioned here lived long before the time of Buddha or Krishna. Many are figures in the *Rig Veda* itself. The fact is, therefore, that the *Brahmanas* mention Rig Vedic kings like Sudas, Bharata, and Sharyata Manava as rulers of the whole of north India and Rig Vedic Rishis like Vasishta, Dirghatamas, and Parvata and Narada as the chief priests of such great emperors. The *Rig Veda* verifies this in stating that Sudas received tribute from both oceans (VII.6.7), as we have already noted. The *Brahmanas* thus give credence to the great victory of Sudas, and show a whole series of similar great rulers of empires in north India in Vedic times.

THE VICTORY OF INDRA

Indra and Varuna

When the *Brahmanas* identify the victory of Indra, his winning of the worlds, with the victory of the Vedic kings over all of north India from sea to sea, they appear to be following an earlier custom. It is most likely that the great victory of Indra celebrated throughout the *Rig Veda,* the winning of the seven rivers to flow into the sea, refers to this winning of north India from sea to sea by the Aryan kings.

> Who as the strong in common dwelling with the strong, the emperor of the Earth and great Heaven, the best of the warriors, to be invoked in the battles, may Indra Marutwan come to us with his grace.
>
> Rijrashwa with Ambarisha, Sahadeva, Bhayamana and Suradha, having struck the Dasyus and Shimyus, with the arrow threw them down. He won the field with his white-robed friends. He won the Sun and the Waters, who wields the thunderbolt (I.100.1, 18).

Sahadeva is one of the great kings mentioned above in the *Brahmanas* (AB VII.34) as a world-ruler. Ambarisha is mentioned in the *Puranas* as one of the early kings of the Vedic solar dynasty. These Vedic kings are associated with the great world victory of Indra.

The *Rig Veda* celebrates this great victory of Indra, his winning of the worlds, his winning of the land of the seven rivers to the sea, along with his ability to take men across these great rivers.

> I as the bull uphold seven streams as wealth-giving currents over the Earth. Of strong will I cross over the floods (X.49.8).

This mythological victory of Indra was the symbol or the prototype for the victory of the Vedic kings, even in the *Rig Veda,* as we see in the beginning of the hymn that proclaims the great victory of Sudas.

> In you, oh Indra, are all the delights that our fathers, the singers, extracted. In you are the good-yielding cattle,

> in you the horses. You give the wealth that is most desirable to your worshipper. As a King you rule with your wives, as through the days you are the knower and the seer (VII.18.1-2).

The victorious king Sudas worships at "the best place on Earth" (III.53.11),[1] which we have identified as the region of the Saraswati, the land of Ila (III.23.4). More specifically I would say that this area is the throne of Indra on which the kings of the central region sat. In fact, the Kurus named one of their main sites in this region Indraprastha, meaning "the throne of Indra." Indra states that he gave the Earth to the Aryans (IV.26.2).[2] What land is this? It is the land of the seven rivers to the sea, the land of north India between the higher and lower oceans. It is not just the land of the Punjab.

Indra is the 'Swarat', the self-ruler; Varuna, the God of the ocean, is the 'Samrat', the emperor or world-ruler.

> They call one the emperor, the other the self-ruler,
> Indra-Varuna you are great and great in light (VII.82.2).

Varuna is subordinated to Indra. Varuna is the ruler of the ocean. As the chief of the Adityas, he is also the God of the western direction, the Arabian Sea. Hence the Persians came to worship him as Ahura Mazda. Yet Varuna was also the ruler of the eastern ocean, the Bay of Bengal. The *Atharva Veda* says that both oceans are his flanks (AV IV.16.3).[3] The great and ancient city of east India, Kashi or Benares, is on the Varuna river.

Indra and Varuna as joint rulers rule the land of the Aryans. Varuna says:

> Mine is the kingdom, the rulership of all life, as all the immortals know. I am king Varuna. For me the original powers are upheld. The Gods follow the will of Varuna. I wield the supreme authority over the people.

Indra replies:

> I am Indra, by your power, Varuna, the two worlds are great, wide and beautiful (IV.42.1-3).

The hymn ends:

> The seven seers were our fathers when Durgaha was oppressed. For her they generated King Trasadasyu, a demigod like Indra (IV 42.1-3, 8).[4]

This indicates that Trasadasyu was such a world ruler, that the Vedic kings were Indra or the world ruler incarnate.

PURANIC AND VEDIC LISTS OF KINGS

To further understand the Vedic kings we must look to the *Puranas,* which give additional knowledge on the subject. The *Puranas* are traditionally looked to in India for the accounts of ancient history. Purana itself means 'ancient'. There are eighteen *Puranas,* each quite long, partly dealing with the dynasties of kings and the histories of peoples.

The *Puranas* follow the Ashwini listing of the lunar constellations and mark the vernal equinox at 0° Aries, which occurred around 400 AD according to the system of Hindu astronomy. It was about this time the *Puranas* reached their final form (though minor additions or alterations to them may have occurred later). However, much of their material is older than this. The *Puranas* are set in the court of kings who reigned after the time of the avatar Krishna, particularly during the reign of Janamejaya, the great grandson of Yudhishthira, Krishna's companion. Krishna's period marks the end of the Vedic era. The *Puranas* appear to have commenced about this time. They were, however, part of an oral tradition going on since Vedic times and preserve aspects of Vedic knowledge, perhaps some not found in the *Vedas* themselves.

The term Purana itself occurs in the *Upanishads* as a kind of teaching and is also found in the *Rig Veda.* Hence though the *Puranas* have a very ancient basis in Vedic literature, what we possess of them may come from a later date. The *Puranas* appear to have undergone more alterations than Vedic texts as the *Vedas*, being very old and no longer understood, were largely left as they were. Hence, the *Puranas* may reduce Vedic events by their distance from them. The *Vedas* are earlier and their events appear sometimes different than the Puranic view. There may have also been earlier *Puranas* that were lost. Even the *Rig Veda* can be interpreted, in some hymns at least, from a Puranic or mythic/legendary perspective. Indeed, as the source of all the *Vedas,* the *Rig Veda* can also be considered as the original Purana.

The most noteworthy proof that the *Puranas* may have forgetten the extent and antiquity of Vedic culture is that they take little note of the Saraswati river. They appear to know little of the era when it was a great river system of its own as the *Vedas* portray it. Though the *Rig Veda* and the *Manu Samhita* make the Saraswati the central site of Vedic culture, the *Puranas* explain the diffusion of the Hindu religion from Pratishthana, modern Prayag (Allahabad) at the confluence of the Ganges and Yamuna, on the eastern border of the Vedic central region. The *Puranas* do mention Kurukshetra, one of the great Saraswati sites as important, but do not specifically associate it with the Saraswati. They connect it with Pururavas (VP IV.6.33), one of the early kings of the lunar dynasty, said to have ruled in Pratishthana (VP IV.2.13). This emphasis on eastern regions suggests that the *Puranas* were done at a time after the Saraswati went dry and there was a shifting of the Vedic cultural center to the Ganges. The *Mahabharata (Sabhaparva* 85.90) makes Prayag the most holy site of the Kali Yuga or iron age. It makes Kurukshetra the most holy site of the Dwapara Yuga or bronze age. It makes Pushkara, a site in the mountains of Rajasthan above the earlier course of the Saraswati, the most holy site of the earlier Treta Yuga or silver age, thus showing the shift of Vedic culture from the Saraswati to the Ganges in later ages.

The *Puranas* contain elaborate lists of kings, including many related seers, going all the way back to the legendary first king and first man, Manu. Many of these figures occur in the *Vedas* as well. Some Vedic figures, or their names, occur under several different lineages in the *Puranas* and some great Vedic figures are hardly mentioned in the *Puranas*. There is more than one Divodasa and Sudas in the *Puranas,* but they are not as important figures as in the *Rig Veda*. While the seers Vasishta and Vishwamitra are important in the *Puranas* like the *Vedas,* they are not as closely connected with Sudas.[g] In short, while the *Puranas* preserve much ancient knowledge, their orientation is a little different from the *Vedas* and may require some readjustment. Therefore, correlating the *Puranas* and the *Vedas,* particularly on an historical level, is complicated. While we can use the *Puranas* to supplement the Vedas, we should not give them the same priority in understanding the most ancient culture, which, if anything, the *Puranas* underestimate. Even the ancient *Puranas* are modern relative to the *Vedas* and show us how old the *Vedas* must be.

Some scholars have tried to make a chronology out of the Puranic lists of kings.[h] They show about one hundred and thirty-five kings starting with the first king, Ikshwaku, to the time of Mahapadma Nanda (c. 400 BC). The Greek historian Arrian's *Indicka* (9.9), quoting Megasthenes, states that "from Dionysos (Shiva) to Sandracottus (Chandragupta Maurya) the Indians counted a hundred and fifty-three kings over six thousand and forty-three years." How many years we may give these kings is speculative. We may not want to afford them six thousand years, though this agrees quite well with the astronomical references in the *Vedas;* yet we must admit that there is nothing in the records of Hindu kings that suggests any Aryan invasion or late entrance of the Vedic people into India (like 1500 BC).

Such an extensive list of kings counters the idea that the Hindus have no history and that their records do not go back very far. Their records in this regard are more extensive and no less legendary than those of other ancient cultures like Egypt and Babylonia. They are much longer and more intricate than those of the *Bible.* We have just chosen to ignore them as they do not fit in with our ideas about the ancient world. While they are hardly perfect, accurate or complete from a modern historical perspective, this is no reason to ignore them altogether or to reduce them to a period of a few centuries before the Buddha. Certainly the ancient Greeks, whom we rely upon for much of our view of ancient history, respected them.

It should be noted that religious teachings often speak of teachers and kings far removed from each other in time. A modern Christian may talk of Abraham, Moses, David, Solomon and Jesus. This does not mean that all these are modern figures, like the person who mentions them, or that each is a contemporary of the other. Hence just because the *Vedas* or *Puranas* speak of great religious leaders or kings in the same text or same hymn does not mean that we have to place them all in the same time period. Yet this is the tendency of modern scholarship.

The *Puranas* speak of two main dynasties of Aryan kings — the solar and lunar — ruling simultaneously and both originating with Manu, the mythical founder of the human race. In the *Rig Veda* it is the kings of the lunar dynasty, though not specifically defined as such, who appear more prominent, while the distinction of two dynasties is not yet defined, though the seeds for it exist. The Vedic kings dwell mainly on the banks of the Saraswati river.

Ikshwaku, the founder of the solar dynasty, is mentioned in a hymn of the tenth book.

> In whose rule Ikshwaku glorious is increased for splendor, like the five peoples in Heaven.
>
> With the descendants of Agastya the king yokes his two stallions. He conquers all the materialistic Panis (X.60.4, 6).

Ikshwaku is associated with the descendants of Agastya, a contemporary of Vasishta (VII.33.10) famous for taking the Vedic Dharma to south India. Other kings related to the solar dynasty in the *Puranas,* however, like Trasadasyu, Purukutsa and Tryaruna are commonly mentioned in the *Rig Veda,* and the first figure is quite famous and perhaps the most archetypal of the solar dynasty kings of this earliest text. The solar dynasty is said in the *Puranas* to have ruled at Ayodhya on the Sarayu river. We do find the city Ayodhya mentioned in the *Atharva Veda* (X.2.31), so it is a very ancient city.

Rama, the great avatar, another king of the solar dynasty, appears to be mentioned in the *Rig Veda*. His name occurs as a great king or benefactor (X.93.14). The story of Indra and Vrishakapi, the male ape (X.86), resembles the story of Rama and Hanuman, as many scholars have noted. Rama's consort Sita appears as the Goddess of the Earth or of agriculture (IV.57). Rama thus appears to emerge towards the end of the Rig Vedic period.

THE GREAT DYNASTY OF NAHUSHA

MANU
|
ILA
|
PURURAVAS
|
AYUS
|
NAHUSHA
|
YAYATI
|
TURVASHA — YADU — PURU — DRUHYU — ANU

The dynasty of Nahusha is the most prominent line of kings mentioned in the *Rig Veda*, whose names relate to the earliest era. The *Puranas* place them in the lunar dynasty. Yet these original kings may not be individuals. They probably signify peoples or dynasties. The five sons of Yayati symbolize the five peoples of Man. These may be five social groups, or, as we have already seen, the five regions of India and their inhabitants.

Some hymns of the *Rig Veda* mention these kings by name and may come from their time period. Hiranyastupa (I.31) refers to Manu, Ila, Pururavas, Ayus, Nahusha, and Yayati, as well as to the early Vedic teacher Angiras. Gaya (X.63-64) mentions Manu, Nahusha and Yayati. His hymns sing of the Aryans spreading over the Earth, by sea and land.

> Those who wish to gain friendship from the beyond, delighted to Man, the generations of Vivaswan, the Gods who dwell on the sacred grass of Yayati, son of Nahusha, may they speak to us.
>
> Well-protecting Earth and ineffable Heaven, the Divine ship, with good oars, unfailing, not leaking, may we ascend to well-being.
>
> Auspicious be our paths among the shores, auspicious the paths in the waters where the heavenly light converges (X.63.1, 10, 15).

The Vedic people are called Manusha, as they derive from Manu. Their original homeland is Ilavarta, the region of the Saraswati, named after Ila, the son or daughter of Manu. Another name for human beings is Ayus, meaning 'living beings', from Ayus, the great-grandson of Manu through Ila. Men are also called Nahusha, from Nahusha, the son of Ayus. The names of the first descendants of Manu through the so-called lunar dynasty are thus also generic names for human beings. The five Vedic peoples take their names after the five sons of Yayati, the son of Nahusha: Turvasha, Yadu, Puru, Anu, and Druhyu. Puru becomes another name for people in general. The kings of the Puranic solar dynasty do not have this generic meaning, with the exception of Prithi Vainya, from whom the Earth, 'Prithivi', is said to be named. Even when the name of the early figure of the solar dynasty, Ambarisha, occurs in the *Rig Veda,* he is associated with the offspring of Nahusha (I.100.16–7).

Some of the descendants of Nahusha, though originally Aryan, lose their Aryan status during the period of the *Rig Veda.* Some of them are driven out of India, as in the story of Sudas. This causes a division of the human race arising between Manusha and Nahusha — between those who maintain the laws of Manu and those who follow a fallen culture derived from Nahusha or his fallen descendants. While Manusha is never used as a name for the Panis or Dasyus, Nahusha sometimes is (VII.6.5). Hence the dynasty of Nahusha in part falls and becomes unaryan. The term Nahusha which originally stood for a great Vedic king and family becomes associated with unaryans during the time of the *Rig Veda.* Sharyata, a son of Manu, states,

> The Sun and Moon who dwell in Heaven and revolve, by the thought, oh Shami and Nahushi, recognize that (X.92.12).

Here Nahushi may relate to the Moon or the lunar dynasty, while Shami may relate to the Sun and the solar dynasty.

THE FIVE VEDIC PEOPLES IN THE *PURANAS*

The five Vedic peoples — the Turvashas, Yadus, Purus, Druhyus, and Anus — are mentioned in the *Puranas*. Both the Yadus and Purus are prominent. The lines of the other three change.

There is an interesting story in the *Vishnu Purana* (IV.10) in this regard. King Yayati, who by the curse of the seer Ushanas, had become old and infirm before his time, went to his sons, asking them to give him their youth. First he asked Yadu, his eldest son, but Yadu refused. Then he went to Druhyu, Turvasha and Anu, but they each refused. Yayati therefore cursed all of them. Finally he went to his youngest son, Puru, who accepted. Yayati regained his youth and Puru became old. Yayati then had a long and glorious reign. After it he returned his youth to Puru and accepted old age, and Puru became young again and assumed rulership of the kingdom.

Yayati divided up his kingdom into five quarters (VP IV.10.17-8). To Turvasha he gave the southeast; to Druhyu the west; to Yadu the south; to Anu the north; and to Puru the center as the supreme king of the Earth. These are probably the parts of India where these people are known to have lived. Using the Vedic Saraswati region (rather than Pratishthana as the *Puranas* suggest) as the central region of the Purus, this would place Turvasha by the Bay of Bengal, the Yadus by the Arabian Sea, the Anus in the Punjab, and the Druhyus in Afghanistan (Gandhara). Turvasha and Yadu are frequently associated with the sea in the *Rig Veda,* as we have seen.

We can identify these regions with idea of the quarters of India and their Vedic Gods as referred to in the *Brahmanas* (AB VIII.14). The Turvashas relate to the Vasus in the east, the Yadus to the Rudras in the south, the Druhyus to the Adityas in the west, the Anus to the Maruts in the north, and the Purus to the Sadhyas in the center. While these two correspondences may not be exact they reflect a similar and very ancient Vedic concept, the geography of north India.

In the lineages of the *Puranas,* the Yadus and Purus continue on as prominent dynasties in India. The line of Turvasha continued for a short time but merged into Puru. "The *Vayu, Matsya, Agni* and *Brahma Puranas* enumerate several descendants in this line, for the purpose evidently of introducing, as the posterity of Turvasha, the nations of the south of India: the series is Varuttha, Andira; whose sons are Pandya, Karnata, Chola, and Kerala."[i] These are the Dravidian peoples of south India.

The lineage of Druhyu was similarly short. His sons included Gandhara, after whom that region (Afghanistan) is named. It ends with the hundred sons of Prachetas who were "the princes of the lawless Mlecchas or barbarians of the north," presumably Central Asia (VP IV.XVII.1-2).

The lineage of Anu was also broken up. The sons of one of them, Shivi, gave their names "to different provinces and tribes in the west and northwest of India."[j] Others, Anga, Banga, Suhma, Kalinga, and Pundra became the peoples of Bengal and Bihar to the southeast (VP IV.XVIII.1).

While the Battle of the Ten Kings is not specifically mentioned in the *Puranas,* the effects of this war may appear in this story. Sudas, who can be identified with Puru in the story, divided up the five peoples and had some leave the area. This explains the lineages of Turvasha, Druhyu and Anu, since these were the main peoples who opposed Sudas. It also gives us the reason for the battle against Sudas. The king of the Purus took over the central throne of India from Yayati. The dynasty of Yayati, probably founded by Nahusha, had degenerated and was purified by Puru, who tried to reestablish a more spiritual kingdom. The other, perhaps older, Aryan peoples of this dynasty, Turvasha and so on, who had probably become quite powerful in their own right, resented this and tried to take it back from the Purus; they formed an alliance and attacked Sudas.

The Aryans were already colonizing the world by the time of Yayati. After Sudas they were protective of their borders. Yet many of the people defeated by Sudas reformed themselves and became true Aryans again. We should not cast a stigma on any group that participated in the battle against him. In time the whole human race fell from the rule of spiritual knowledge to materialism and to religious sectarianism.

With Sudas, Brahmanical traditionalism appears to have begun. The Vedic land gained defined boundaries and looked at external areas with suspicion, perhaps fearing additional attacks. Later texts like the *Manu Samhita* (X.43-5) and *Aitareya Brahmana* (VII.18) look to the people outside of north India as fallen Aryans. They are regarded mainly as fallen Kshatriyas, some of them exiled in wars in which they opposed the spiritual rule of the Brahmins. The battle with Sudas was only one of these. Other rulers, like Sagara of the solar dynasty, were said to have cast out such inimical peoples (VP IV.3.18-21).

Sometimes these fallen Kshatriyas are said to be descendants of Vishwamitra, the great sage-king (AB VII.18). Vishwamitra cursed the half of his sons who refused to accept the boy Shunashepa into their family to become Dasyus. As Vishwamitra was a great priest of Sudas, this also shows a split among the Aryan peoples about the time of Sudas and perhaps contains the religious reason for it. It suggests that before Sudas the domain of Aryan culture was probably larger and areas outside of north India were considered part of it.

The *Rig Veda* itself appears to have been first compiled about the time of Sudas. Hence there may have been other Vedic or Aryan teachings preserved by the people defeated by Sudas, or by those Aryans outside of his sphere of influence. This may have included teachings of the western Aryans that gave rise to Zoroastrianism and those of the eastern Aryans that gave rise to Buddhism and Jainism. Other early Aryan teachings may have been preserved in south India and other areas that had perhaps been colonized by the earlier Aryan expansion before Sudas.

While the *Rig Veda* is our oldest and most authentic document of the early Aryan teaching, it also bears some mark of the division of the Aryan peoples in its later portions. It is more evident in later Vedic teachings, like the *Brahmanas* and *Manu Samhita,* in which the free spirit of the earlier *Veda* is lost and a narrow traditionalism is gradually emerging.

About the time of Sudas the *Rig Veda* was probably completed, except for minor additions and alterations. The dynasties of the Nahushas and earlier kings were replaced primarily by the Bharatas, descendants mainly of Puru. Then the Puru dynasty declined again. The power in north India shifted to the east and the solar dynasty. This may have followed the drying up of the Saraswati river or it may have had a political cause. The Brahmins that came to aid Sudas were mainly followers of Vasishta and Vishwamitra. Both were originally from the east of India; Vasishta from Ayodhya on the Sarayu river, and Vishwamitra from Kanouj (Kanyakubja) on the Ganges. They perhaps represented allies of Sudas from the solar dynasty and brought its influence. It is even possible that Sudas himself was originally related to the solar dynasty or was himself a solar dynasty king who inherited the line of Puru for some reason or another. Perhaps he came from the east of India, with his priests Vasishta and Vishwamitra, to assume the throne along the Saraswati. This may give us a further reason why his rule was rejected by the other kings. The enemies defeated by Sudas on the east may not have included kings of the solar dynasty.

THE SOLAR AND LUNAR DYNASTIES

The story of Yayati and his five sons contains other interesting information about the origins of the Vedic people. King Yayati had two wives; the first, Devayani, was a daughter of Bhrigu, from whom he had Turvasha and Yadu, the two older of the five Vedic peoples. This shows that the first Vedic kings were offspring of Kshatriyas and Bhrigu Brahmins. As Turvasha and Yadu were saved from across the sea, it suggests that the Bhrigus may have also come to India from overseas. Bhrigu himself is the son of Varuna or the God of the ocean.

The second wife of Yayati was Sharmishta, daughter of the Asura king Vrisha Parvan. With her he had Anu, Druhyu, and Puru. This shows an Asura kingdom existing concurrently with and intermarried with the oldest Vedic kings. It may be possible to identify these Asuras with Assyrians, Persians, or other worshippers of the Divine as Asura. It also links some Vedic kings, particularly the Nahushas, with the Asuras (and possibly Pani-Dasyus) as related peoples.

This has been the basis for some scholars developing the idea of "pre-Vedic Aryans," into which group they place figures like the Bhrigus or Nahushas. Yet these figures are found in the *Rig Veda* itself. They are spoken of as contemporaneous with the hymns, and many hymns are done by Bhrigus. We cannot consider members of Vedic seer families and kings of Vedic dynasties as pre-Vedic. They may be early Vedic figures but cannot therefore be placed as originally outside of or prior to Vedic culture. Other scholars have tried to see in such stories an Asuric or Assyrian India in pre-Vedic times, but these Asuras were originally part of Vedic culture, practiced the same rituals and descended from the same kings and sages. The negative meaning of Asura comes only in the late Vedic period. There is an Asuric side of Vedic culture but no pre-Vedic Asuric culture found in the *Vedas*. Moreover, as the Kshatriya or warrior class tends to seek power, it has an Asuric (violent) side of its nature. Again it is a matter of quality, not of race or ethnic group.

In later Indian thought, the lunar dynasty rulers were regarded as powerful kings but had certain character flaws. They tended toward gambling and drinking and were of a luxurious, artistic and free-spirited temperament. The Kurus, a later branch of the lunar dynasty, suffered from these same problems, which led to the Mahabharata War. The Rig Vedic kings attributed to this dynasty had similar characteristics. Nahusha himself, in later mythology, was said to have become drunk with power and was turned into a serpent. Pururavas in the *Rig Veda* was associated with the Gandharvas, celestial musicians, one of whom he married, and in the *Mahabharata* he had a similar fall as Nahusha.

The lunar dynasty, with its more expansive spirit, was also more aggressive and more likely to have colonized other areas and created empires. Perhaps the war of Sudas was the karma of the lunar dynasty for its empire building. These ancient Indian kingdoms also may have spread far across the sea to the east and the west, perhaps as far as Egypt and Indonesia. Such empires could have made them similarly arrogant and contentious and resulted in a war in their common homeland, like the two World Wars that followed in Europe after European imperialism.

The freedom and creativity of the lunar dynasty also had a positive side. The lunar dynasty carried the seed of life, which is why one of its earlier kings was named Ayus or 'life'. They were strongly connected to Soma. Because of their free spirit they, or their teachers, the Bhrigus, who are like them in many ways, are prominent in the inner or esoteric teachings, which emphasize ecstasy or direct perception and reject any narrow moralism or ritualism.

The solar dynasty kings did not suffer from such character flaws. They had great integrity, honor and self-discipline. Their only flaw was perhaps an excess traditionalism or asceticism. They were not usually interested in empire and many became yogis or sages. Hence they are not as prominent as the founders of culture or the builders of empire but may have preserved better the purity of the original teachings.

While Krishna, himself in the line of Yadu, represents the higher side of the lunar dynasty, Rama represents the higher solar side, as does Buddha. Krishna is a God of love, and the flute expresses the free spirit of the lunar kings, while Rama as a God of law and principle and Buddha as the ascetic show the high principles of the solar kings. Both types of dynasties were necessary to allow for the creative unfoldment of all human potentials. A certain amount of seeking of pleasure and power, as the lunar dynasty shows, is inherent in the warrior mentality and was usually allowed to the kings and nobility of all cultures. Yet in excess it becomes their downfall. Both the spread and fall of Vedic culture occurred mainly through the lunar dynasty of Nahusha. However, some lunar kings allied themselves with sages, like Sudas with Vasishta, and continued to renew the spiritual power of their line. Perhaps they allied themselves with kings of the solar dynasty, as Vasishta was historically the priest of the solar kings. These Vedic stories may, therefore, reflect the kings and sages of the solar dynasty chastising, correcting, or purifying those of the lunar dynasty. Yet we must remember the common origin of the two dynasties and their constant intermingling with each other. Probably both originally were based in the Saraswati region. The fall of the Nahushas may have included the split of the one original Vedic dynasty into solar and lunar branches.

After what may have been a long period of decline following Sudas, the Purus came to power again with the Kuru dynasty, of which Janamejaya of the *Brahmanas* was the great king. After a long period of Kuru rule came the great war of the *Mahabharata* and the ending of the Vedic period. The opposing armies met at the sacred site of Kurukshetra in the already dry Saraswati region and turned their ancient central homeland into a battlefield, thus burying the Vedic age.

Though it is difficult to give dates to these figures, we can at least establish a sequence. Manu, Ila, Ayus and Nahusha, the earliest Vedic rulers, probably represent peoples or dynasties of the earliest era, including Divodasa. Early solar figures like Prithi, Trasadasyu, Ikshwaku and Ambarisha may also come here. Yayati and his sons mark the later phases of this era, wherein the five Vedic peoples had come into existence and spread over the world. Sudas started another era. Between Manu and Sudas we have many kings of the lunar and solar dynasties. After Sudas, the power shifted to the east for a time and then back to the west with the Kurus. The Kuru era itself is said to have extended over a thousand years. The *Puranas* state that there are 1,050 years between Parikshit of the Kurus and the last Kuru king at the time of Mahapadama Nanda (c. 375 BC).[k] The other eras appear if anything to have been longer. Certainly this gives us a long history for the kings of India.

In Vedic times the seers empowered various kings to reestablish the spiritual culture of India. The Vedic kings are such figures. Some of them were raised and educated by the seers for this purpose, as in the story of Rama. The seers protected such kings through the power of their asceticism (tapas) and raised them to the throne. As the darker ages of humanity began it was no longer possible to produce such great spiritual kingdoms, though the influence of the great seers and yogis did have its effect on a number of later kings. The seers retired into seclusion in the Himalayas after the Mahabharata War. Only if there is some purity of heart in the world can they descend again to establish such spiritual cultures as the Vedic. We are still far from that today. Periodic renovation of the spiritual kingdom of India went on for millennia in the Vedic period. Perhaps it extended into previous World Ages.

THE SPLIT BETWEEN THE SEER FAMILIES

There are many versions in Vedic and Puranic lore about wars between the Devas and Asuras, the Gods and the demons. These are primarily symbolic but do reflect divisions or conflicts among peoples. In the *Rig Veda*, it is primarily the war between the Aryans and the Dasyus or Panis. The teacher of the Asuras is said to be Bhrigu or Shukra, the founder of one the two main families of Vedic seers, the Bhrigus. This by itself connects the Aryans and the Asuras, not only in terms of ancestry but also in terms of religion.

The *Puranas* (VP IV.6) speak of a war between the Gods, led by Brihaspati of the Angirasa line of seers, and the Asuras, led by Shukra of the Bhrigus. The *Rig Veda* culminates in the great civil war between the Aryans of India, the Battle of the Ten Kings. The defeated peoples are partly driven out of India. Among them are descendants of the Bhrigus

(VII.18.6). In this regard, Turvasha and Yadu, two of the five Vedic peoples, are said to be descendants of Devayani, a Bhrigu, and Turvasha was the leader of the war against Sudas. We must conclude, therefore, that the split between the Aryan peoples included a split between the Aryan seers.

Originally there was one line or family of seers, the Bhrigvangirasas. This divided into two groups, the Angirasas and the Bhrigus. The Angirasas were led by Brihaspati (Jupiter) and the Bhrigus by Shukra (Venus). With the diffusion and division of the Aryan peoples, some of the seers left with the migrating people.

As kings and peoples fell from the earlier ages of light, so did the seer families. Their main fall consisted in the practice of black magic or the negative use of the occult. It was not only the Bhrigus that were faulted for this; in the *Atharva Veda* the Angirasas, Kanwas and other seers are also often mentioned as sometimes having a destructive influence. Even Vedic Gods like Indra sometimes have to fight with the Gods or Devas (IV.30.1). Vedic Gods, particularly in the *Atharva Veda,* can represent cosmic forces, like time, which may obstruct us.

The Bhrigus appear related to many supposedly non-Aryan cultures of the ancient world whose calendars were based upon the cycles of Venus (Bhrigu) like the ancient Egyptians and American Indians, the Mayans. The Bhrigus thus show the connections between so-called Aryan and non-Aryan peoples. Yet the Angirasas also appear in other cultures of the world, as not only India but China used a calendar or sixty-year cycle based on Jupiter. We can find evidences of both groups of seers, who were originally one anyway, throughout the ancient world and looking back to an Indian or Himalayan homeland.

Vasishta, the priest of Sudas, who drove some of the Bhrigus out of India, was also a son of Mitra and Varuna and related to the Bhrigus, as Bhrigu himself is a son of Varuna. Vasishta was said to be born of the mind of Urvashi, the celestial nymph who was the wife of Pururavas who founded the lunar dynasty. Hence, the division was not simply between the Angirasas and the Bhrigus but between the seers and their fallen descendants. The split between the seers similarly reflects the fragmentation of humanity through the dark ages.

As the enemies of the Vedic Aryans, the Panis and Dasyus, are related to the Vedic people, their priests are also related. The priests of the Panis must be related to the priests of the Asuras, the Bhrigus. This is logical, for as Venus, which can function as a planet of illusion (Maya), becomes our guide, we tend to fall from truth, though on a higher level Venus can provide aspiration, love and Divine grace. Jupiter's influence creates more wisdom or love of truth, though on a lower level it can create an attachment to religious formality. That is why in some versions of this myth Jupiter represents the outer religion, while Venus defends the mystic tradition or way of ecstasy that rejects ceremonialism. Both Venus and Jupiter, we should note, are figured as Brahmins in Vedic symbolism.

The Angirasa Rishis may represent the more orthodox Brahmins of the *Rig Veda,* while the Bhrigus may represent the unorthodox trend in Vedic thought. Some Angirasas degenerated by a too rigid purity and orthodoxy, a too great attachment to the outer form of the teaching. Some Bhrigus fell by departing from purity and tradition and bringing magical and occult practices into the Vedic teaching, including consorting with kings and politics. As the Bhrigus were free spirits we find them not only falling from the tradition more easily but also more prominent as teachers of the inner or non-ritualistic teaching. Yet both families as one original great Vedic seer family represent the great sages that all ancient cultures look back to. The conflict between these two groups of seers occurs throughout human history. It is the archetypal duality between the various types of human sages and occurs on different levels through different periods of time.

PART III

VEDIC ASTRONOMY
THE TESTIMONY OF THE STARS

The Movement of the Precession

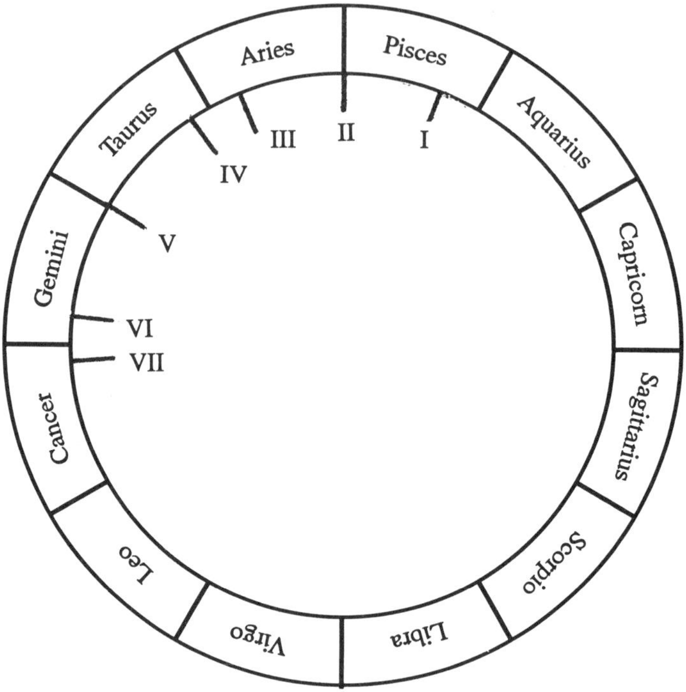

Positions of the Vernal Equinox

	DEGREE	NAKSHATRA	DATE
I.	07° 00′ Pisces	Uttarabhadra	c. 1991 AD, Today
II.	00° 00′ Aries	Ashwini	c. 400 AD, Puranic Era
III.	23° 20′ Aries	Bharani	c. 1280 BC, *Vedanga Jyotish*
IV.	06° 40′ Taurus	Krittika	c. 2250 BC, Late Vedic Age
V.	00° 00′ Gemini	Mrigrashira	c. 4000 BC, Middle Vedic Age
VI.	26° 20′ Gemini	Punarvasu	c. 6000 BC, Early Vedic Age
VII.	05° 00′ Cancer	Pushya	c. 6500 BC, Early Vedic Age

1
HINDU ASTRONOMY
THE KNOWLEDGE OF THE PRECESSION

The Krittikas (Pleiades) do not swerve from the eastern direction, all the other constellations do.
— *Shatapatha Brahmana II.1, 2, 3*

When ancient people observed the stars, they saw a different orientation than we do today. The seasonal points of the solstices and equinoxes fell among different stars than they do now. This is because of slow changes in the Earth's orientation to the constellations according to the precession of the equinoxes.

The *Vedas* present such ancient astronomical positions in many places. These have been largely ignored because they give dates much earlier than those conventionally ascribed to Vedic culture, and because there is a tendency among Western scholars not to trust any astronomical data from the Hindus, as they are believed to be unscientific people. However, such a calendar as the *Vedas* mention must have worked to some degree or it would not have been used. An obsolete calendar, like a bad clock, wouldn't have sufficed for such important things as agricultural plantings and sacred rituals.

Astrology moreover was the most cherished of Vedic sciences, called "the eye of the Veda." This is because it was the foundation for the timing of the rituals around which Vedic culture was based. Western scholars also tend to look down upon Indian astronomy because of its astrological orientation, but all ancient astronomy is mixed with astrology, even the Greek.

Today we hear of the dawning of the "Age of Aquarius." The point of the vernal equinox — the position of the Sun among the stars on the first day of spring — is approaching the sign of Aquarius. This phenomenon is caused by a backward tilting of the Earth on its axis, the precession, which changes at a rate of about 50″ (seconds) per year and completes a whole cycle of the zodiac in about 25,800 years.

The astrology of India has always been 'Sidereal' or based upon stellar positions. It determines the positions of the signs of the zodiac relative to the observable fixed stars. This is different from the astrology of the older Western world which employed a 'Tropical' zodiac, one that determines the signs of the zodiac relative to the equinoxes and solstices (the Tropics of Cancer and Capricorn). A Sidereal zodiac naturally must take the point of the precession into consideration, whereas the Tropical ignores it. The Tropical zodiac uses the seasonal points as its prime consideration, whereas the Sidereal zodiac uses specific stars. This means that if we know at what point in the Sidereal zodiac the equinox occurs, like the dawning of the Age of Aquarius today, we can determine the astronomical era and the date of the reference in question. This will be our main method of determining the time period of the *Vedas*. It uses the most universal of all clocks, the stars.

The exact amount of the precession today as figured by various Hindu astronomers is a matter of dispute, but the differences are minor, within one or two degrees. Now the vernal equinox is in early Pisces sidereally, approaching Aquarius. Most Indian astronomers place it around 23° from 0° Aries as of 1950, or at about 7° Pisces. While such precessional changes are not noticeable in an ordinary human lifetime, if cultures endure over a period of centuries, particularly over millennia, they become quite obvious if the culture is employing a Sidereal system of astronomy.

Some Greek astronomers and astrologers knew of the precession, though they did not know exactly what it was or how to calculate it. Hipparchus appears to have discovered it among the Greeks and calculated it at 36″ per year, which Ptolemy, the most famous Greek astrologer, adopted. The Hindus, in the *Surya Siddhanta* calculated the rate as 54″, much closer to what is observed today as 50.3″ per year.[a] While modern scholars consider this figure a lucky guess on the part of the Hindus it may reflect a better knowledge of the precession, perhaps arrived at by long term observations and necessary calendar shifts through time.

For this reason, it is hard to derive Hindu astrology from the Greeks, as most Western scholars do. The Hindus compute the zodiac differently and the precession more accurately than the Greeks. Yet we are told, based upon the appearance of minor Greek terms in later Hindu astrology, that any accuracy in Hindu astronomy comes from the Greeks. Hindu astronomy has a long history and an extensive literature following different methods than those of the Greeks. As Vedic astrology is Sidereal, we cannot discountenance the astronomical references we find commonly in Vedic literature relative to the precession. *Precessional changes are the hallmark of Hindu astronomy, the essence of the system. We cannot ignore them in ancient texts just because they give us dates too early for our conventional view of human history.* In Hindu astronomical and religious books we can trace the precession progressively back to early ancient periods. This does not mean that the nature of the precession was always understood astronomically but that an ongoing record of such changes was kept. Many such changes as the Age of Aquarius can be found in Vedic literature.

The Indian calendar has several types of time, including 'Sidereal time'. A Sidereal month is measured not from one full Moon to another but according to the Moon's return to the same place among the fixed stars. Hence a Sidereal month amounts to twenty-seven days. Hindu astrology divides this Sidereal month into thirty lunar days (tithis), each of which is a little shorter than the normal solar day. These lunar days, in fact, are the type of days used traditionally for Vedic rituals. A Sidereal month requires a clear observation of where the Moon is located among the stars. It cannot just be mechanically calculated from full Moon to full Moon like the ordinary month.

A Sidereal year is marked by the time the Sun returns to the same position in the fixed stars. A Sidereal day is four minutes shorter than a regular day and so there are 366 of them in a normal year. This orientation to a specific point in the sky causes the calendar to gradually slip backwards with the precession of the zodiac. In other words, the indication of the precession is built into the Hindu calendar through its usage of Sidereal time.

Any culture employing Sidereal time or a Sidereal zodiac will find the position of the equinoxes to move back a week or so every five hundred years or about seven degrees in the zodiac. This would be noticeable to people whether they knew anything about astronomy or not. For example, today the Hindus celebrate the Sun entering the sign of Capricorn on Jan. 14, as this is the observable or Sidereal position, whereas Western Tropical calendars use Dec. 21, the date of the winter solstice (which is now actually in the stars of Sagittarius).

Hindu Sidereal calculations are thus more complicated than Tropical ones. Hindu astronomy is a very specialized system that requires precise astronomical observations and shows an ongoing knowledge of the exact placement of the planets and equinoxes relative to the fixed stars. Such Sidereal measurements show how much the Hindus relied on actual stellar positions. On this basis it is hard to dismiss the positions of early Hindu astronomy as having no basis in observation. Even Vedic rituals are often described relative to Sidereal calendars in ancient texts like the *Nidana Sutra* and *Srauta Sutra.*

THE ANCIENT ZODIAC AND CALENDAR

For observational purposes, the ancient Hindu astrologers employed, as do the modern ones, a system of twenty-seven or twenty-eight lunar constellations called 'Nakshatras'. The Nakshatras provide the Moon with a different constellation for every day of the lunar month. It is a more scientific system and easier to compute than the twelve signs of the zodiac in which there is a change of sign for the Moon every two and a quarter days.

While each of the twelve signs of the zodiac consists of a thirty degree section of the heavens, the Nakshatras cover an area of thirteen degrees and twenty minutes. This means that about every thousand years the equinox would have to be moved back another lunar constellation to adjust for the precession. This compares with over two thousand years for the twelve signs. Hence the use of the lunar constellations involves a strict observation of planetary positions and reflects a culture that watched the stars closely. Changes in equinoctial positions in Hindu literature are relative to these lunar constellations (please note the Table of the Nakshatras in the Appendix as we discuss these changes in this chapter).

Each month of the year in the Hindu-Vedic calendar is named after one of the lunar constellations, that in which the full Moon normally occurs during the month. This makes sense also because the point of the full Moon is observable, not the point of the new Moon wherein the position of the Moon in the stars is hidden by its proximity to the Sun.

If we examine the lunar constellations chosen to rule the months, we find that they mark the beginning part of their respective sign. The constellation Ashwini, which marks the beginning of the sign Aries, becomes the constellation denoting that month. The constellation Krittika, marking the beginning of the sign Taurus, becomes the constellation denoting the next month. In other words, the Hindu months were devised according to a correspondence between the lunar constellations and the twelve signs and show that whoever invented the system knew of both ways of computing the zodiac. As this method of computing the months appears to be as old as that of the lunar constellations, it appears that whoever invented it knew of the twelve signs as well. The invention of twelve signs for the zodiac obviously follows the pattern of the twelve months of the year. Such factors indicate that at the beginnings of Hindu astrology, whenever it may have been, there was a system of twenty-seven lunar constellations and twelve solar signs and a system of correspondence between the two according to the months.

In Hindu reference books the lunar constellations are listed in order of their sequence starting with the constellation that marks the vernal equinox. Medieval lists begin their listing of the constellations with Ashwini, which marks the beginning of the sign Aries as the vernal equinox. Ancient lists started with Krittika (the Pleiades), showing the equinox at the beginning of Taurus and earlier reference points are also found.

This does not mean that the shift of the equinox was noticed only every two thousand years when it moved back an entire sign in the zodiac. However, when the equinox retreated back to a previous sign (and thereby to a previous month), a major reform of the calendar was required, not just a minor adjustment. Hence it is not surprising that we find such eras when the equinox came to the initial point of one of the twelve signs more prominently marked in Vedic texts than the intermediate changes, some of which, however, are also in evidence.

The Vedic year, for purposes of the sacrifice, began at the winter solstice. This computation makes sense as the ancient sacrifice followed a solar symbolism, identified with the Sun and the year, with the Sun being born or renewed at the time of the winter solstice. The lunar constellation marking the full Moon at the winter solstice is thus mentioned as the first month of the year. Vedic literature tells us some of the months named by these lunar constellations and the days within them in which the solstices occurred, affording us additional means of calculating these eras.

THE SUMMER SOLSTICE AT THE END OF CANCER OR 1280 BC

The *Puranas*, the religious literature of classical India, like Greek and Muslim astrology, place the vernal equinox at 0° Aries, which in the Hindu system would give a date of around 300–500 AD.

> The equinoxes occur in the seasons of spring and autumn, when the Sun enters the signs of Aries and Libra. When the Sun enters Capricorn, his northern course commences; and his southern when he enters Cancer (VP II.8.63).

The northern course of the Sun refers to when the Sun is moving northward or higher in the sky, which occurs between the winter and summer solstice. His southern course, when it is appearing progressively lower or more southward in the sky, is from the summer to the winter solstice. The idea of these two courses of the Sun is prominent in Vedic literature also, as we will see.

The *Puranas* begin their series of constellations with Ashwini, or the beginning of the sign Aries, as marking the vernal equinox. Today Hindu astrologers start the sequence with Uttarabhadra rather than Ashwini as the first constellation, since it is the real place of the vernal equinox today. However, the entrance of the Sun into 0° Aries (Ashwini) is no longer counted as the first day of spring, on March 21, but rather April 14, showing the adjustment of the calendar according to the precession.

Earlier systems occur in Vedic literature. Varaha Mihira, an Indian astrologer and astronomer of the classic period, states that in his time the summer solstice occurred in the lunar constellation Punarvasu, which marks 20° 00′ Gemini–03° 20′ Cancer. He states that previously the solstice was in the middle of Aslesha which marks the end of Cancer, 16° 40′ Cancer–00° 00′ Leo.[b]

> When the return of the Sun took place from the middle of Aslesha, the solstice was then right. It now takes place from Punarvasu.[1]

The middle of Aslesha is 23° 20′ Cancer. The beginning of Cancer by Hindu calculations marked the solstice around 400 AD which would have been in Punarvasu. The solstice in the middle of Aslesha would have occurred around 1280 BC. This is based upon a precessional cycle of 25,900 years, the modern figure. There are some variations in the precession, however, and the exact period is not known; hence these figures may vary slightly. In any case, this statement establishes a calendar and a knowledge of the constellations in Vedic and Hindu circles going back well into the second millenium BC.

This reference of Varaha Mihira corresponds to an old text, the *Vedanga Jyotish* (v.5), which places the beginning of the year with the new Moon located at the beginning of the constellation Shravishta.[2] The beginning of Shravishta is opposite the middle of Aslesha and marks 23° 20′ Capricorn, showing the same date of 1280 BC.

We find quotations from other ancient Vedic astronomers that afford us similar data. Garga, quoted by Somakara on *Vedanga Jyotish* (V.5) says:

> From the bright half of the month of Magha is the beginning of the northern course of the Sun. The Sun and the Moon begin their rise from Shravishta.

Here a calendar is employed placing the winter solstice at the beginning of the month of Magha. The new Moon of the Vedic months occurs in the lunar constellation previous to the one it will be full in, which the month is named after. Hence when the full Moon is in Magha, the new Moon of that month will be in Aslesha, the constellation before it in the zodiac.

Bhishma, a great warrior in the *Mahabharata* who possessed superhuman powers of choosing his time of death, waited to die until the Sun started its northern course, or the point of the winter solstice. This was said to have taken place in the bright half of the month of Magha, thus confirming this same calendar.[c] Yet whether this reflects the calendar used in his time or that employed by the poets who wrote the story is another issue.

THE SACRIFICE, THE YEAR, AND THE CONSTELLATIONS

In the *Brahmanas,* the Vedic ritual texts, a number of astronomical and calendar references occur. In the *Kaushitaki Brahmana,* the lunar months reflect such an earlier sequence when the new Moon of the month of Magha marked the winter solstice.

> On the new Moon of Magha he rests, being about to turn northwards: the priests also rest, being about to sacrifice with the introductory Atiratra chant; thus for the first time they obtain him (the Sun or the year); on him (the year) they lay hold with the Chaturvinsha rite; this is why the lay hold rite has its name. He goes north for six months; him they follow with six month rites in forward arrangement. Having gone north for six months he stands still, being about to turn southwards; the priests also rest, being about to sacrifice with the Vishuvat (solstice) day; thus for the second time they obtain him. He goes south for six months; him they follow with six month rites in reverse order. Having gone south for six months he stands still, being about to turn north; these also rest, being about to sacrifice with the Mahavrata day; thus for the third time they obtain him. In that they serve him (the year) three times, and the year is in three ways arranged, verily it serves to obtain the year. With regard to this the following sacrificial verse is sung,
>
> Ordaining the days and nights,
> Like a cunning spider,
> For six months south constantly,
> For six months north the Sun goes (KB XIX.3).[d]

We see here a clear knowledge of the solstices and the northern and southern courses of the Sun and the same stellar positions as *Vedanga Jyotish* or a date of 1280 BC. This is not presented incidentally but as central to the Vedic sacrifice and the means of its determination. The *Brahmanas*, the textbooks of the Vedic ritual, have many references to seasons and to new and full Moons in different constellations, showing an elaborate astronomical calendar for determining the times for the sacrifices. The sacrifice follows a yearly session marked by the seasons, the equinoxes and the solstices. Dr. Haug, in his introduction to the *Aitareya Brahmana,* has observed that: "The sattras (sacrificial sessions), which lasted for one year, were nothing but an imitation of the Sun's yearly course. They were divided into two distinct parts, each consisting of six months of thirty days each. In the midst of both was the Vishuvat, i.e. the equator or central day, cutting the whole sattra into two halves."[e]

The *Brahmanas* frequently relate their rituals to the year and the cycles of time within it.

> The year is a revolving wheel of the Gods; this is immortality (KB XX.1).
>
> Soma (the Moon), the king, is the year. Coming with the seasons he approaches (KB VII.10).
>
> The year is sixfold having six seasons; by this sixfold offering the Gods obtained the sixfold year with its six seasons, and by the year all desires, all immortality (KB XIV.1).
>
> Three hundred and sixty are the days of the year; so great is the year; the Lord of creation is the year; the sacrifice is the Lord of creation (AB II.167).

The *Yajur Veda* mentions the solstices:

> The Sun, therefore, goes by the south for six months and for six months by the north (TS VI.5.3).

The day of the solstice, the Vishuvat, was a very sacred day. It served to divide the year into two. According to the *Brahmanas,* sacrifices performed on that day had the power to win the year and were as good as a year-long sacrifice.

> The Vishuvat is like a man; the first half of the Vishuvat is like the right half of a man; the second half of the Vishuvat is like the left half (AB IV.22).
>
> The Vishuvat is the head of the sacrifice (KB XXVI.1).

The *Kaushitaki Brahmana* thus uses the same sequence as *Vedanga Jyotish* or a date of 1280 BC. Its accuracy is affirmed by the astronomical orientation of the Brahmanical sacrifice. This date in itself is extraordinary. Though by most accounts the Aryans were in India at this time, they were not thought to have advanced very far in the arts of civilization, nor were such later Vedic texts as these thought to have been completed. It shows a clear awareness of astronomical positions at least back to this period which far antedates any Greek influence. However, we find that there are a number of references to earlier dates than this, some in the same strata of Vedic literature. With the credibility of this date and this system established, we must take these earlier references seriously.

I have also found a late hymn from the *Atharva Veda* (XIX.49.2) to the Night that calls her Shravishta at her most extreme point,[3] which may indicate this constellation for the winter solstice as the longest night of the year and the midpoint of the dark half or night of the year. This suggests a similar date.

There are other Vedic references to the year beginning at other points in the month of Magha. This would make perfect sense if the culture was in its late phase with the Magha new Moon reference. The Ekashtaka, or eighth day after the full Moon, is said to be the wife of the year. Tilak states, "All writers on the Mimamsa or ritual, including Jaimini, the foremost, take this Ekashtaka to mean the eighth day of the dark half of the month of Magha."[f] This would be three weeks in advance of the new Moon date which would be about 1,500 years or a date about 2800 BC.

This Ekashtaka day is mentioned in the *Atharva Veda:*

> Who is the wife of the year, may she be auspicious to us. Who is the replica of the year, we worship you as that night (AV III.10.2-3).[4]

The *Tandya Mahabrahmana* (V.92) similarly states:

> The Ekashtaka day is the wife of the year. When this night comes the Lord of creation (Prajapati) resides with her. Immediately from the beginning of the year, the rites of initiation are observed.

Another ancient astronomer, Laughakshi, quoted by Somakara, places the beginning of the year in between these two positions.

> They sacrifice to the year, four days before the full Moon in Magha.[g]

This would show a time when the winter solstice occurred on the eleventh day of the month of Magha, a time of about 800 years before the new

Moon date or about 2000 BC. There is yet additional information to support these positions.

THE VERNAL EQUINOX IN EARLY TAURUS OR 2000 BC

Vedic literature in its later phases, as we have mentioned, begins its listing of the constellations not with Ashwini but with the Krittikas (26° 40′ Aries-10° 00′ Taurus). The Krittikas are the stars of the Pleiades, a well-known small cluster of stars. Along with this we also find references to the summer solstice (ayana) in the lunar constellation Magha (00° 00′-13° 20′ Leo). Both of these events would have occurred 2480-1760 BC. This shows the existence of an earlier calendar and that the 1280 BC date was not the first precessional point noted in Vedic literature. It confirms the references to the winter solstice later in the month of Magha. We have a clear indication of this position in a hymn of the *Atharva Veda,* which mentions all the lunar constellations.

> Easy to invoke, oh Agni, may the Krittikas and Rohini be, auspicious Mrigashira and peaceful Ardra. Graceful be Punarvasu, beautiful Pushya, bright Aslesha, with the solstice at Magha for me. Virtuous be Purva Phalguni and Uttara, Hasta and Chitra peaceful and may Swati give me joy. Bounteous Vishakha, easy to invoke, Anuradha, the best Nakshatra Jyeshta, I invoke, and Mula. May Purva Ashadha provide me nourishment and Divine Uttara Ashadha give me strength. May Abhijit provide virtue, as Shravana and Shravishta grant beauty. May Shatabhishak give me greatness for expansion, and the two Proshtapadas give protection. May Revati and Ashwayujaur give me fortune and Bharani grant me wealth (AV XIX.7.2-4).

The term 'ayana' specifically means solstice in later astronomical literature, so we cannot ignore such a meaning in its occurrence here. We find it in the northern and southern courses of the Sun as uttara-ayana and dakshina-ayana. Moreover, we see Agni, the God of the east and the vernal equinox, leading the list of the Nakshatras from the Krittikas, as Ashwini did in later times.

The *Taittiriya Brahmana* states:

> One should consecrate the (sacred) fire in the Krittikas; ... the Krittikas are the mouth of the Nakshatras (TB I.1.2.1).

Here the Krittikas also lead the list of the Nakshatras, not as a theoretical statement but as a practical timing for establishing the sacred fire. The same *Brahmana* also states:

> The Nakshatras are the houses of the Gods ... the Nakshatras of the Gods begin with the Krittikas and end with Vishakha, whereas the Nakshatras of Yama begin with Anuradha and end with the Apabharani (TB I.5.2.7).

The Gods are identified with the constellations. They are divided into two halves, those that relate to the Gods or the powers of life, and those that relate to Yama, the God of death (Yama, we should note, is the ruler of Apabharani or Bharani and Agni of Krittika). This suggests a division of the zodiac by Agni and the Krittikas as the point of the vernal equinox and the autumn equinox occurring between Vishakha and Anuradha (a position of 03° 20′ Scorpio).

The *Shatapatha Brahmana* similarly states,

> The Krittikas do not swerve from the eastern direction, all the other constellations do (SB II.1, 2, 3).[5]

This shows a time when the Krittikas marked the vernal equinox or eastern point in the zodiac, thus also confirming this order. Some scholars have objected to this reference, saying that the Nakshatras only referred to the Moon and should not be oriented to solar equinoctial positions. This is easily refuted by the importance of the twofold division of the Sun's path through the year, based upon the solstices, as the *Brahmanas* state so clearly. Vedic astronomical directions are based upon a solar orientation, with the east as the vernal equinox.

This gives us a number of references to a time in which the vernal equinox was in the Krittikas, along with the appropriate points of the summer solstice and autumn equinox. The winter solstice would have been in the later part, rather than the beginning of Shravishta. The Pleiades is a special constellation for the eye to note, a small cluster of stars like the Big Dipper. No doubt the equinox here would have made a strong impression upon anyone who observed it.

We find a similar position mentioned in the *Upanishads:*

> The Sun is the origin of time. His form, from the instant as the first division of time, is the twelvefold year. The year has two halves, one belonging to Agni (fire) and the other to Varuna (water). From Magha to the middle of

> Shravishta, step by step, belongs to Agni. From Sarpa at the beginning to the middle of Shravishta, step by step, belongs to Soma (MaiU VI.14).

Sarpa is another name for Aslesha. These positions would serve to mark the points of 0° Leo (the beginning of Magha) and 0° Aquarius (the middle of Shravishta) for the solstices or the northern and southern courses of the Sun into which the year was divided.

The *Puranas* show knowledge of a similar date:

> When the Sun is in the first part of the lunar mansion Krittika, and the Moon in the fourth of Vishakha; or when the Sun is in the third part of Vishakha, and the Moon is in the head of Krittika (these positions being contemporary with the equinoxes), that equinoctial season is holy and is styled the Mahavishubha, or great equinox (VP VIII.71-3).

Krittika marks 26° 40′ Aries-10° 00′ Taurus, Vishakha is opposite it at 20° 00′ Libra-03° 20′ Scorpio. The point between the first and second quarters of Krittika and between the third and fourth quarters of Vishakha would be 0° Taurus and 0° Scorpio. The vernal equinox at the Krittikas or 0° Taurus is obviously implied (with the autumn equinox opposite it). This is a date of around 1760 BC.

REACTION OF MODERN SCHOLARS

The western translator of the *Kaushitaki Brahmana,* A. B. Keith, notes the astronomical reference of the new Moon in Magha.

> Note should finally be made of the statement in the Kaushitaki (XIX.3) that the winter solstice took place at the new Moon of the month of Magha. This notion is, however, clearly nothing more or less than the datum of the Jyotish and thus yields us no date of any assured value for the period in question; Weber places the limits of the date of the initial fixing of the series of Nakshatras in the Jyotisha at 1820-860 BC and there is no reason to show for how long the order would be kept after it had ceased to represent the facts, apart altogether from any other considerations as to the origin of the Nakshatras. If, as is most probable, the Nakshatras were not an Indian invention at all, but were derived from some foreign, perhaps

> Semitic, source, it is clear that the date of their fixation would not have the slightest value, save as an upper date, for the Brahmanas.[h]

In other words, he dismisses this reference, and through it any others, as of no accuracy at all. First, as a datum of Jyotisha or astrology it is not to be relied on. Second, he states that the calendar was probably in use long after it ceased to correspond to the facts and third, that it was probably derived from a foreign source and could have even been adopted from them long after it ceased to represent the facts for those who invented it.

Yet the references to these positions are quite clear and numerous and show ongoing changes through time. The Nakshatras are repeatedly stated as a system used in observation. The Vedic priests did not rely on their positions in astronomical reference books. They had to look at the stars at night. How could they have instituted the Nakshatra system in the first place from a foreign source, at a time when it was already out of date, when they had to use it in a practical way for their sacred rites? One could argue that, once instituted, a calendar like this could have been kept going for some time, particularly when the ritualistic culture declined as it did in late ancient times, but one would have to admit that such positions were actual for the priests in the texts that first mention them.

This response of Keith is typical of the modern materialistic mind to Vedic and to ancient literature from all over the world: regard the ancients with a spirit of skepticism or treat them as unreliable and reduce their statements as much as possible. Western scholars, with a few exceptions, have simply ignored such astronomical references in the *Vedas*. They do not credit the ancient Hindus with enough scientific objectivity to be capable of accurate observations of the heavens. Or they have assumed that this system was adopted from outside of Vedic culture at a much later date than it originated. Both of these objections do not deal with the material but are means of explaining it away. To assume a lack of credibility is no explanation of data. As the ancient Hindus have a ritualistic calendar based upon the movement of the Sun and Moon and the constellations and show its periodic revisions, astronomical references for equinoctial positions cannot just be ignored when they are not convenient to our interpretations of history.

ORIGIN OF THE LUNAR CONSTELLATIONS

Where did the lunar constellations or Nakshatras first come from? The term Nakshatra occurs several times in the *Rig Veda*, referring to the Sun, stars and probably the lunar constellations. Some of the names of the lunar constellations occur in the *Rig Veda* but there is no specific listing of their entirety. However, they are listed completely in such old Vedic texts as the *Atharva Veda* and *Yajur Veda,* which puts them far back into the pre-Buddhist era.

The lunar constellations are employed not only by the Hindus but by the Chinese and the Arabs in slightly different forms; also starting with the Pleiades for the Chinese. The Arabs obviously did not invent them. A Middle Eastern origin appears unlikely as they did not become popular there until medieval times. They probably came to the Middle East via the Persians, who as relatives of the Hindus similarly had a highly developed system of astronomy. The Persians probably derived their system from the Hindus or a common Aryan culture.

The Chinese system, on the other hand, does not have a zodiacal basis. Its orientation is equatorial. As the lunar constellations appear to have originated as part of a zodiacal system, it is unlikely that the Chinese invented them. One could not imagine that they were originally non-zodiacal and then were adapted to the zodiac. It is far more logical to believe the zodiacal origin of the lunar constellations was forgotten by the Chinese. In the Indian system they have always been related to the zodiac, as they are by the Arabs. Hence, a Hindu origin or at least early usage appears without serious doubt.

In Hindu astronomy various Gods are made the rulers of these lunar constellations. Such Gods are not the later Hindu Gods we find in the classical pantheons, like Shiva and Kali, but the oldest Vedic Gods like Indra, Agni, Soma, and Rudra. We also find many of these constellations mythologized according to the stories of the Vedic Gods. This identifies them with the oldest strata of Vedic literature. It would be unlikely if they were introduced from a foreign source at a late date.

In fact, in most of the earlier texts the constellations are named according to the Vedic deities that rule them. Such ancient astronomical texts as the *Soma-siddhanta, Archa-jyotisha, Pitamaha-siddhanta,* and *Vriddhavasishtha-siddhanta* name the constellations according to their ruling deities. This suggests that originally they were referred to by their ruling deities and only later did they come to be known by special names of their own. If this is the case, their antiquity must go back to the earliest level of Vedic literature when these Gods were prominent. This correspondence of deity names and constellations caused one Vedic scholar to conclude, "Most of the asterisms (Nakshatras) at an early period were known by names assigned to what became their presiding deities."[i] As the Hindus or Aryans were intimate with this system at the core of their mythologies and probably invented it, it must have had an observable basis. The texts which mention positions relative to them are most likely stating the facts of their times.

ANCIENT OBSERVATION OF THE HEAVENS

Some argue that ancient peoples, particularly the Hindus who were not of a scientific bent, could not have had such precise astronomical calculations to note equinoctial positions. However, such calculations do not require great precision. A difference of one lunar constellation or about thirteen degrees in stellar positions is easily observable by the naked eye and requires no instruments or calculations, just a general delineation of constellations.

There is additional evidence that the Vedic people knew of the planets and stars and had a clear system of observing their positions. A hymn in the *Atharva Veda* states,

> Peaceful for us be the planets and the Moon, peaceful the Sun and Rahu (AV XIX.9.10).[6]

Graha is the Hindu astronomical term for the planets. The same hymn (V.7) says the Grahas "move in Heaven," should we have any doubt that it is the planets they refer to. Rahu is the north lunar node. Knowledge of the lunar nodes suggests the capacity to predict eclipses, as it is through them that knowledge of the nodes arises. The importance of eclipses as omens in ancient cultures is well known from literature all over the world and they were also probably used to help determine the calendar. So at least by the time of the *Atharva Veda,* these factors were known. This hymn occurs near the one that gives the Krittika-Magha data or a time of about 2000 BC, suggesting the Hindus had such knowledge by this period.

In the *Rig Veda,* an eclipse of the Sun is described (V.40). The Sun is pierced by darkness by Swarbhanu, a demon (V.5). Now 'Swar' means sunlight and 'bhanu' a ray. This suggests that the seers knew that the eclipse was caused by the reflected light of the Sun through the Moon.

The Vedic culture was based upon a ritual using the calendar via astronomical positions. Clocks and books were not in vogue. In fact, the priests and the ritualists were the timekeepers. This was largely done by noting the constellations in which the full Moon appeared during the months and seasonal points relative to these. We would have to consider that they kept up better with astronomical changes than we do today. How many of us know where the Moon is going to be full this month? The ancients had no choice; it was a necessity of time-keeping for them. In the time of the *Yajur Veda,* which speaks of the Krittika or Taurus era, when the ritual was the center of life for the Vedic people, an appropriate calendar must have been used.

Ancient people may have been primitive in some respects of modern technological standards but for that very reason they were much more aware of the stars. They did not have electric lights and frequently went out in the starlight and slept in the open. They were much more intimately aware of the heavens. All over the ancient world we find monuments and stones, like Stonehenge in Europe, that show a strong awareness of the heavens and the seasons. These were no doubt ritual centers which were the life of the culture. It is unlikely that the ancient Aryan Hindus lacked such knowledge when their whole life was ritualistic.

Such cultures were also very conservative. Ancient cultures kept up their customs for much longer periods than modern ones, not just for decades or centuries but for millennia, as we can see in ancient Egypt or even in India today where rituals of the Vedic age are still being performed today in many places. If such a culture endured for a thousand years, the equinox would occur in a different lunar constellation and the old point would be off by nearly two weeks. It does not take high scientific achievement or great mathematical skills to notice this. Mere common observation by anyone with a knowledge of the stars could note such a change.

The doubt would not be whether the ancients could observe such positions but whether their culture could maintain such a continuity to remember earlier positions. The Vedic culture has given us many different strata of literature from a pre-Buddhist era (before 500 BC), some of which are still being passed down today thousands of years later. Obviously, a strong culture has existed with a great continuity. Such references cannot be refuted on the grounds that such a continuity is not possible in earlier and more conservative times.

Hence, examining astronomical references in Vahara Mihira and *Vedanga Jyotish*, we arrive at the equinoctial positions of about 1280 BC. This is found as the latest reference in later Vedic texts like the *Brahmanas*, with the new Moon in Magha marking the winter solstice. Using the different points of Krittika as marking the vernal equinox and the lunar positions earlier in the month of Magha back to the eighth day of the waning Moon (Ekashtaka), we get a period of 2800–1760 BC. Vedic references show an ongoing adjustment of their solstice-oriented calendar, proving the existence of Vedic culture at this time along with the existence of a sophisticated system of astronomical observation.

However, such references occur late in Vedic literature. Krittika references do not occur in the *Rig Veda* at all. This suggests that the bulk of the Vedic age, like the bulk of Vedic literature, was before this era. Hence we see that the Vedic culture was in its later phases when the vernal equinox entered the Pleiades.

If we had no previous references to rely on, based on this information alone, we would have to put the Vedic era back over a thousand years earlier than the 1500-1000 BC date now given to the *Rig Veda*. This itself is enough to refute the modern interpretation of Indian history. Even if earlier astronomical references than these are not accepted, this information is sufficient to require an entire reorientation of our sense of Indian and world history. We cannot reject these clear astronomical references merely on the grounds that it is hard for us to place the Vedic people in India, by the sea, or at a high stage of civilization at such an early time. Our opinions are more likely to be wrong than are the stars. The calendar given in these texts marks the same time period as the Indus Valley culture (c. 2000 BC) and indicates its Vedic nature.

2

BREAKING THROUGH THE BARRIER OF TIME

ASTRONOMICAL REFERENCES IN THE *RIG VEDA*

The bridal train of the Sun Goddess comes, which the Sun God has set in motion. In Magha (Leo) the cows are slain, in the Phalgunis (Virgo) she is wed.
— Atharva Veda XIV.1.13

The full Moon night in the Phalgunis (Virgo) is the beginning of the year (the winter solstice).
— Kaushitaki Brahmana V.1

SAGES, PLANETS AND STARS

In this chapter we will explore the astronomical references in the earliest Vedic texts. They indicate that the Vedic people had a calendar allied with equinoctial and solstitial positions going back to at least 6000 BC. While such references would be difficult to substantiate in themselves, they are entirely consistent on the basis of what we have already established regarding Vedic astrology and astronomy. To approach them we must first examine the astronomical and astrological nature of these ancient texts.

Most modern scholars have said that astronomy was unknown in the period of the *Rig Veda* because this, the most ancient of the Vedic texts, does not appear to mention the planets by name, nor is there much evidence of the constellations or signs of the zodiac. Yet if we look deeper, we find that the names of the planets occur under the names of the Vedic seers. Most evident is Brihaspati Angirasa, the most ancient and foremost of the Vedic seers, who is identified in later literature with the planet Jupiter, which is named after him. His role as the original Brahmin priest is quite in keeping with the religious and ceremonial role given to Jupiter in astrological literature all over the world.

The Bhrigus, the second great Vedic seer family, are identified with the planet Venus. Venus is said to be Shukra, a Bhrigu, in all later literature. The name Venus itself may also appear as Vena Bhargava, a seer and God of beauty and light (X.123), who like Venus is born from the sea, and is related to the Moon (Soma; IX.120) and to the angels or Gods of music (Gandharvas).

The Vedic God Soma is identified with the Moon. He is also identified with the Vedic sage Soma Atri. Budha Atri (seer of V.1) is identified with Mercury. The seer Atri is said to be the Sun, as is Kashyapa. Vamadeva states,

> I was the father of the human race and I became the Sun (IV.26.1).

The Vedic seers and kings are identified with the Sun. The Vedic families descend from the Sun and the Moon.

Vedic names like Surya (the Sun), Soma (the Moon), Brihaspati (Jupiter), Shukra (Venus), and Budha (Mercury) are the classical Hindu names for the planets. Verses from the *Rig Veda* are still used for the worship of the planets today, as in the pujas (rituals) to the nine planets. The Greek name for Mars is traceable to the Vedic Marut, the martial storm Gods.

The legendary Seven Seers, Sapta Rishi, of the *Rig Veda* are identified with the seven stars of the Big Dipper, as is indicated in the *Brahmanas.*

> In silence, with closed eyes, the priests sit until the Nakshatras (lunar constellations) appear. When the Nakshatras appear, they open their eyes; the Nakshatras are light. They enter the two oblation holders by the western door; then the Adhvaryu approaching the pole of the northern oblation holder says, "May you sing prosperity to the sacrificial session." They creep beneath the axle of the northern oblation holder, muttering an Atichandas verse to Indra; verily by the Atichandas verse the sacrificers smite away evil under the axle. "We go around the oblation holders to the north," Kaushitaki used to say, "following the path of the sacrifice, *not being concealed from the Seven Rishis.*" (KB XXVII.6)[a]

The Vedic sacrificial area was often in the open, marked by various stakes. Here the rite involves looking at the constellations at night and going around these stakes to the north and looking at the stars of the Big Dipper, imitating the revolution of the heavens around the pole star. This shows that the priests knew of the constellations and used them in their rites.

In the *Rig Veda* another name for stars is the bears. In one hymn the stars or bears, riksha, are said to be high or in the north.

> Your bears placed high, which appear by night, where do they go by day? (I.24.10).[1]

The *Taittiriya Aranyaka* (II.11.49), before mentioning this same verse, speaks of the Rishis who dwell with the Nakshatras.

Late Vedic literature makes the pole star so important that the bridegroom shows it to his bride as a symbol of marital fidelity. It is called Dhruva, "the unmoving." We must note that the pole star also shifts with the precession. Presently the star Polaris marks the north pole but it did not do so in ancient times. The last major star to mark it was Alpha Draconis, which occurred around 3000 BC. The unmoving north pole star of the later Vedic era must have been Alpha Draconis and could not have been Polaris. When it marked the pole, the stars of the Big Dipper were also at their closest approach to the north pole. Hence the prominence of the Seven Seers as the seven stars of the Big Dipper may reflect this era. Occasionally there is an eighth seer, Kashyapa, who is said not to depart from Mount Meru (TA I.7.20). Mount Meru is also a name for the north pole. This eighth seer or pole star must therefore be Alpha Draconis.

Some Vedic seers are specifically identified with various stars. The great Vedic Rishi Agastya is identified with the star Canopus, though this is not specifically mentioned in the *Rig Veda*. Agastya is the Rishi who traditionally brought the Vedic teaching to south India and Canopus is a bright southern star. The idea that the seers relate to different stars or constellations is found in the *Rig Veda*.

> Indra, direct the men for the slaying of the dragon, even when hid among the peoples of the seers who have the power of the constellations (X.22.10).[2]

A hymn to Brihaspati or Jupiter states:

> The Fathers fashioned heaven with the constellations (Nakshatras), like a dark horse with pearls. They placed the darkness in the night and the light within the day. Brihaspati broke the mountain and found the rays (X.68.11).

The Vedic seers are frequently called the Fathers in Vedic literature. They are not simple human forefathers but ancestral cosmic creators, who even fashion the stars.

Brihaspati clearly meant Jupiter at the time of the *Brahmanas:*

> Brihaspati as he was born revealed Tishya Nakshatra (TB III.1.1.5).[3]

Tishya is the lunar constellation also called Pushya and marks the part of the sign Cancer where Jupiter, astrologically speaking, is exalted (has his best sign placement). It is in the Pushya part of Cancer (05° 00′ Cancer) that his exact exaltation occurs in Vedic astrology. In Vedic astrology Brihaspati is the deity who rules the Nakshatra Pushya or Tishya.

The constellation Tishya is mentioned several times in the *Rig Veda.*

> The Maruts who do not fail us with their grace like Tishya from the sky (V.54.13).[4]

Perhaps Tishya here means the planet Jupiter, which traditionally dispenses Divine grace.

The five visible planets appear in various fivefold symbolisms in the *Rig Veda.*

> The five bulls that stand in the middle of great Heaven (I.105.10).[5]

The five planets along with the Sun and Moon appear as the seven horses of the Sun, which are very commonly mentioned throughout the *Vedas.* Why else should the Sun have seven horses if the seven planets were not known?

> Seven yoke the chariot that has one wheel. One horse conveys it who has seven names (I.164.3).

This also suggests knowledge that the seven planets all shine with the light of the one Sun. In later Hindu astronomy, the Sun is shown as a horse with seven heads, representing the seven planets and the seven days of the week that they rule. The *Vedas* are filled with a sevenfold symbolism relating to the Sun. How can we separate the seven planets from this?

The Vedic Gods are all basically Sun Gods. The Vedic is a solar religion based upon a strong awareness of the Sun and its movement. All the Gods can be called Adityas or 'Sun Gods', born from Aditi who may be identified with the heavens or the zodiac. All the great Vedic Gods can be lauded as the Sun, including Agni, Indra, Soma and the many forms of Surya-Aditya, the Sun God, including Savitar, Mitra, Varuna, Bhaga, Aryaman, Vishnu, Twashtar, and Rudra. We read of seven or twelve Sun Gods (Adityas), the latter which become rulers of the months in later literature; the former may well be the planets. The groups of the Vedic Gods, like the Adityas, Maruts, Vasus, and Ribhus often appear as rays of the Sun, as stars or constellations.

> They yoke the red horse who moves around those who stand. The lights (or constellations) shine in Heaven (I.6.1).

Here the Maruts appear as the fixed stars or constellations around whom Indra travels as the Sun or red horse.

It is said of the Maruts, the companions of Indra,

> With the Maruts, Indra, let your friendship be. Then you will defeat all enemies. The three times sixty Maruts, increasing you, are holy like a mass of rays (or stars) (VIII.96.7-8).

The Maruts number one hundred and eighty, or half the days of the year. This may refer to the sacrifice, as the Brahmanical sacrifice had two sessions, one following each solstice. The Maruts may symbolize the heavens or constellations.

> The Maruts are visible from afar, like the heavenly ones with the stars (I.166.11).[6]

Other Vedic Gods are compared to Heaven with the stars.

> Like Heaven with the stars, Agni appears along both firmaments (II.2.5).[7]
>
> Agni is first established here by the ordainers, the holy invoker, to be worshipped in the sacrifices. The bearer of truth, most wise, he appears as Heaven with the stars (IV.7.1,3).[8]

The idea of the Milky Way or milky ocean is a Vedic idea.

> The seers of ten rays first thought out the sacrifice. May they direct us in the breaking of the dawn. The dawn opens up the night with her red horses, with the great light of the luminous sea of milk (II.34.12).[9]

STELLAR MYTHOLOGY AND THE IMAGE OF TIME

It was mainly at night, while looking at the stars, that mythology was first developed. Gazing at the heavens was not only man's way of communing with the cosmic forces, it also provided a background on which the force of his creative imagination could be released. Vedic mythology also has a stellar orientation to its symbolism. This heavenly mythology reflected the cycle of time, which in turn mirrors all possible processes of transformation of energy in the universe, both on spiritual and mundane levels.

The great Vedic War is for the cows which symbolize the rays of the Sun. It is for the dawns and the days, for extending the sunlight. It is for the Waters, which are those of Heaven or the Sun-world, as in the *Vedas,* rain comes from the Sun who draws up the earthly waters to him. The Vedic War, in fact, is for the Sun itself, who is the year. The sacrifice is carried on for the period of a year, in order through it to win the year, win the Sun, win the Light and gain immortality. The sacrifice must be guarded carefully throughout the year to assure this victory, and the demons or powers of darkness try to obstruct its performance. The critical points in this sacrifice-battle-year symbolism are the junctures of the seasons and the solstices. Eclipses are also important and dangerous times for the sacrifice. Also significant are intercalary months or other periods of adjustment between the different calendars used.

The main Vedic myth of Indra is of the winning of the seven rivers to flow to the sea and the release of the Sun out of darkness. The seven rivers also relate to the seven planets. This victory of Indra occurs at the end of the year.

> Our fathers who drove up the wealth made of light, by Indra at the end of the year they destroyed Vala. By the truth they made the Sun rise in Heaven (X.62.2–3).[10]

Indra wins the cities which are said to be "yearly," sharada. His conquering of seven or a hundred cities appears to reflect seven-year or hundred-year rituals. The hundred cities or years won by Indra may be a sacrifice lasting the full duration of human life, an apt ideal for a sacrificial culture.

In the *Puranas,* King Nimi is said to have instituted a sacrifice of a thousand years (VP IV.5.1).

The main Vedic ritual is the Soma ritual. Soma is the Moon and the sacrifices followed new and full Moon dates (as in the *Brahmanas*). Thus the observation of the Moon in the constellations was an important part of the timing of the sacrifices. The Soma rituals reflect the movement of the Moon and the cycle of the months.

The Vedic chants are well-known to have been done three times daily, at the rising and setting of the Sun and at noon. With this basis it would not be much to expect that the Brahmins noticed the seasonal points in early Vedic times, as they did later. That they performed special sacrifices at the corresponding points in the year, the solstices and equinoxes, is well-known in later literature, as we saw in the *Brahmanas.* Why should we ignore such possibilities in earlier texts which themselves are quoted as the source for the rituals and chants used in these later yearly sacrifices? The Brahmanical rituals for these periods are all based on chants from the *Rig Veda.* Yet modern translators and interpreters of the *Veda* have given the sacrifice a daily orientation but not accepted its monthly and yearly implications.

The seasons are commonly mentioned in the *Rig Veda* along with the rituals. The Gods drink the Soma according to the seasons, which are themselves worshipped as Gods (I.15, II.37). There are four seasonal cups and "in the fourth cup is immortality" (II.37.4).[11] The Gods part the seasons and perhaps thereby mark the seasonal points of the equinoxes and solstices.

> He arises from his rest and divides the seasons. The Divine holy Sun has come (II.38.4).[12]

In the *Rig Veda,* ritu, season, and rita, truth or ritual, are often equivalent. Agni several times is said to speak according to the seasons.

> He speaks according to the seasons the words that must be said (VII.9.3)[13]

The season is said to be the mother of Indra, the greatest of the Gods.

> The season was the Mother. From her work, instantly born, he entered into the plants in which he grew (II.13.1).[14]

The Vedic ritual followed the seasons, like the *Brahmanas,* related to the Moon's residency in various constellations.

Not only do the rituals have an astromomical symbolism, so do the metres of the chants.

> By the jagata meter he held up the heavenly river (the Milky Way), in the rathantara chant he saw around the Sun (I.164.25).
>
> Arranging the thirty-six and the four, they organize the chants according to the twelve. The wise seers, having measured the sacrifice, make the chariot of the Rig and Saman chants revolve (X.114.6).

The Vedic chants are organized according to the thirty-six ten-day sections of the year, the four seasons or cardinal points of the zodiac, and the twelve months. They set in motion the chariot of the Gods, the vehicle of the chants, which takes the sacrificer to Heaven.

All the mathematical terms of later astronomy and astrology occur in the *Rig Veda,* including the terms for the solstices and equinoxes (ayana and vishuvat). There are many references to a solar circle of twelve divisions or of 180, 360 or 720 portions.

The *Rig Veda* speaks of a lunar calendar with an intercalary month, which shows the existence of both solar and lunar years. The one additionally born or supplementary is the intercalary month.

> Varuna knows the twelvefold months and their progeny, and he knows the one additionally born (I.25.8).[15]

Later India used a calendar of six seasons or double months. This we find in the *Rig Veda* also:

> Six burdens, one unmoving bears (III.56.2).[16]
>
> The six Rishis born of the Gods are twins, the seventh they say is born alone (I.164.15).[16]

The six twin Rishis are the six Vedic seasons or dual months of the year, with the seventh born alone as the intercalary month.

The Vedic people followed a ritual that was based on a calendar cycle for the year, the month and the day. The word for night, aktu, sometimes means "star" and may refer to a constellation, as that ruling the equinox.

> The Sun Gods (Adityas) ordain in harmony the year, the month and the day, the sacrifice, the night and the chant (VII.66.11).[17]

In India, the rains come near the time of the summer solstice, the Brahmanical Vishuvat. We have a similar idea of the yearly sacrifices reaching their middle or place of rest at this time in the *Rig Veda*. The Brahmins who perform the observances are said to reside for a year (VII.103.1).[19]

> They guard the Divine order of the twelve months. The men do not violate the seasons. When the day of the rains comes in the year, having cooked the offerings, they gain their release (VII.103.9).[20]

According to the *Brahmanas* the Atiratra is an important solstice rite. It appears in the same way here in the *Rig Veda*.

> When the Brahmins, in the Atiratra rite of Soma, sing like a lake that is full, on that day the year ends; when the frogs become desirous of the commencement of the rains, the Soma-drinking Brahmins raise their voice, accomplishing the year-long rite (VII.103.7-8).[21]

Thus the end of the year wherein Indra destroys Vala and releases the cows and the Waters (X.62.3) is the day of the summer solstice when the rains come.

The twelve extra days of the year, the difference between the lunar year of 354 and the solar sidereal year of 366 days, are sacred to the Ribhus, who while sleeping during them renew the earth.

> When for twelve days, oh Ribhus, you delighted, sleeping in the house of him who cannot be hidden, you made the fields fertile, you led down the rivers. Plants stood in the deserts, the waters entered the depths (IV.33.7).[22]
>
> The house of him who cannot be hidden is that of the Sun God Savitar (I.110.2-3).

This shows the existence of both solar and lunar calendars in the *Rig Veda* and a sidereal year.

Dirghatamas in his hymns relates many astronomical references:

> The wheel of truth with twelve spokes does not age as it circles Heaven. Fire, I see your twin sons standing there, seven hundred and twenty. They call him the fivefold father, possessing twelve forms, who is full of water in the higher half of Heaven. Others call him the clear-seeing, placed in a sevenfold wheel with six spokes (I.164.11-12).[23]

The seven hundred and twenty twin sons are the days and nights of the year. The father is the Sun with five seasons and twelve months. The sevenfold wheel is the seven planets or days of the week, with the six spokes of the double months of the year.

> Who knows the one wheel with twelve fellies and three axles? Therein are set together the three hundred and sixty like spokes moving and nonmoving (I.164.48).[24]

Here again we have the twelve months and 360 days or the twelve signs and 360 degree division of the zodiac. Dirghatamas refers to the solstice, Vishuvat, as well.

> I saw the Shakadhuma by the solstice in the distance, dividing the superior from the inferior.[25] The heroes cooked the spotted bull. These were the first laws. Three horses with manes appear with the seasons: in the year one of them is shorn; one sees all with his powers; the movement of one is seen but not his form (I.164.43-4).

Vishuvat here as in later literature shows the point of the solstice that divides up the Sun's course. Shakadhuma means literally "the smoke of cow dung." It is identified with the Moon or Soma, or perhaps the Milky Way. Some consider it to be the name of a lunar constellation. The *Atharva Veda* has a whole hymn to it and calls it the "king of the Nakshatras" (AV VI.128.4). If we knew what lunar constellation it referred to, we would be able determine the time period involved. Unfortunately, no one seems to know which it is.

The three horses that appear with the seasons are Agni (fire), the Sun and the Wind. These verses show the knowledge of the solstice associated with the first laws, the foundation of the Vedic ritual order. It shows that the sacrifice was performed at the solstice, here the sacrifice of the bull, which must symbolize the Sun or Moon. These passages reveal the equation of the chant, ritual, year, Gods, and constellations.

Another hymn of Dirghatamas describes Vishnu, who in the *Rig Veda* is also a Sun God:

> With four times ninety names, like a turning wheel, he sets in motion fast energies (I.155.6).[26]

This also shows the use of a circle of 360 divisions or the zodiac, divided into four according to the cardinal points of the seasons and equinoxes.

Vedic numerical symbolism commonly uses the decimal system; one, ten, one hundred (shata), one thousand (sahasra) and ten thousand (ayuta) appear commonly. In fact, as we know, the decimal system originated in India. The Arabs brought this system to Europe in the Middle Ages, which still used cumbersome Roman numerals. The oldest Indian form of the decimal system is Vedic, thus showing a good sense of mathematics for the ancient sages and a good basis for astronomical calculations.

The duodecimal system is also very common, with multiples of twelve mentioned in the hymns as twenty-four, thirty-six, forty-eight, sixty and seventy-two. A hymn of Gotama, one of the Seven Seers according to later Vedic literature, states:

> With a thousand sing together, let twenty offer adoration, with a hundred sing to Indra the uprisen knowledge, lauding his Self-power (I.80.9).

The number meant here, taking into consideration the cryptic and poetic way of describing numbers in the *Veda,* is 120,000. These singers must be the rays, as Indra here is the Self-effulgent Sun.

The gifts of cows and horses given to the seers also use these mystic numbers and have a possible astronomical sense. A typical gift (V.27.2) is 120 cows. Elsewhere is mentioned 60,000 horses along with 12,000 camels (VIII.48.22), or the number 72,000. As we know from Vedic symbolism the horse is the Sun and the Sun is the year. There may be much occult knowledge hidden in such statements. One hymn (VIII.4.20) also mentions 60,000 cows, not of the herd. Another seer (VIII.2.41) receives a gift of 48,000. One hymn (VIII.55.2) calls such a gift "a hundred white bulls, like the stars that shine in heaven and by greatness uphold the sky."

The enemies slain by the Gods or the Vedic kings also follow these mystical numbers like 100,000 or 60,000. On an inner level they represent the powers of darkness slain by the Sun.

The numbers three and seven are found throughout the text. Seven in particular relates to the planets. The *Rig Veda* is filled with an extensive numerical symbolism that reveals a high sense of mathematics and music. This is quite evident in the meters of the hymns, which are said to reflect the cosmic order. As these numbers are correlated commonly with the Sun and Moon, the day, month and year, so astronomical, astrological and planetary values for them should be considered. Later Hindu astrology spoke of a kalpa of 4,320,000,000 years. Western scholars did not see such numbers in the *Rig Veda,* but we find them there symbolically.

> Four are his horns, three are his feet, two are his heads and seven are his hands (IV.58.3).

This is the cosmic bull who symbolizes time; 4, 3, 2, and 7 zeros, the great yuga of 4,320,000,000 years.

While not mentioning all the lunar constellations by name, the term for them, Nakshatra, is not uncommon.

> May the Earth, Heaven and the Waters hear our call, may the Sun with the Nakshatras and the wide atmosphere (III.54.19).

All the lunar constellations, however, may be contained in the numerical symbolism of the *Rig Veda.* Indra is lauded:

> Great is your nature, secret and touching all, through which you generated what has been and what will be. The five beloved have entered into the beloved light which you generated first. You filled Heaven and Earth and the middle region, the five Gods, seven by seven according to the seasons. With thirty-four lights of similar form but different law you see (X.55.2-3).

The beloved light is the Sun. The five which enter into it are the five planets, the five Gods. The thirty-four lights are said by the ancient commentators, who were not trying to justify any astronomical point, to be the twenty-seven lunar constellations, the five planets and the Sun and Moon. These are the lights of the world, of different law but the same underlying form. The German translator Ludwig says about this hymn, "It cannot be doubted that the original Gods were the constellations."[b]

THE PATHS OF THE GODS AND THE FATHERS

The Vedic Day and Night

The Vedic teaching is couched in the symbolism of the Sun's path through the year. In later literature, this was divided into two halves. First was the uttarayana or northern course of the Sun, also called Devayana or the 'Path of the Gods'. Second was the dakshinayana or southern course of the Sun, also called Pitriyana, the 'Path of the Fathers'. The northern course marks the time from the winter to the summer solstice when the days are increasing in length and the Sun is moving northwards in its position in the sky. The southern course marks the time from the summer to the winter solstice when the days are decreasing in length and the Sun is moving southward in the sky.

The prominence of the solstice or ayana, as marking transformation, pervades all Vedic and Upanishadic teachings. The great Vedic realization is, as the *Yajur Veda* states,

> I know that great Spirit, who has the effulgence of the Sun beyond darkness. Only knowing him can one go beyond death. There is no other path for the transition (SYV XXXI.18).

"The path for the transition" is literally that of the solstice, ayana. It refers to the return of the Sun at the winter solstice, the mythical resurrection of the Sun out of darkness, or the soul out of its bondage to the material world. As this solar-solstice myth is central in the *Vedas,* that it should be marked both astronomically and mythologically is not surprising, particularly when it was the basis for the ritual calendar followed by the Vedic people.

In the classical era of India the northern course of the Sun began with the Nakshatra or asterism of Uttarashada and ended with Punarvasu. The southern course began with Pushya and ended with Uttarashada. This shows the solstices at about 0° Capricorn and 0° Cancer, as already noted. In the *Vedanga Jyotish* era that we have discussed, the northern course began at the beginning of Shravistha and the southern in the middle of Aslesha, the points of 23° 20′ Capricorn and 23° 20′ Cancer. In the Vedic references to the vernal equinox in the Krittikas and the autumn equinox between Vishakha and Anuradha, the southern course began with Magha and ended with Shravistha as the solstice points. This shows the solstice at 03° 20′ Leo and 03° 20′ Aquarius. In this way we see the solstice points occuring yet further back in time.

The constellations that mark the equinoxes are important as they show the points at which the Sun goes over the celestial equator north or south. The point of the vernal equinox is thus central to the Path of the Gods and that of the autumn equinox to the Path of the Fathers. These are Ashwini and Chitra in the later system for 0° Aries and 0° Libra and Krittika and Vishakha for 0° Taurus and 0° Scorpio in the earlier system. The point of the vernal equinox is most important and is associated with Agni, the God of the Sun and of the east and the central power of the Path of the Gods. The autumn equinox was equated with Soma who was the God of the Moon and the western direction (or Varuna, God of the Waters).

If we can ascertain which constellations marked the beginning or middle of these two paths in yet earlier Vedic literature, we can determine what era the reference comes from and, most likely, the date of the hymn. The two paths are commonly mentioned in later Vedic teachings and occur a few times in the *Rig Veda.* The *Upanishads* (BU VI.2.2) quote a verse from the *Rig Veda* for their teaching of the two paths.

> I have heard of two paths of mortals, that of the Gods and that of the Fathers. By them all this moving world travels, what exists between the Father and the Mother (RV X.88.16).

These paths are an important teaching because at death the wise go by the Path of the Gods to regions of light and transcendence of rebirth, whereas others go by the Path of the Fathers to regions of half light and rebirth on Earth. The two paths are one of the key early Upanishadic teachings and one of the first to clearly outline the doctrine of rebirth.

A few direct references to these two paths exist in the hymns of the *Rig Veda.* Though astronomical in bearing, it is not easy to get a specific date from them, as for example:

> We have come to the path of the Gods. May we have the power to trasverse it. Let Agni make the offering, as he is the knower. He will arrange the sacrifice and the seasons. Who knows the path of the Fathers, may Agni, enkindled, shine bright for us (X.2.3, 7).[27]

Here the paths of the Gods and the Fathers are mentioned and associated with the arrangement of the seasons, along with Agni, the God of fire and the east, but no constellation reference point appears to be given.

There are other more prominent terms in the *Rig Veda* that may reflect the same meaning as the two paths. Day and Night, or Dawn and Night,

Ushasanakta, as dual Goddesses, are common throughout and occur regularly in the Apri hymns (i.e. II.3.6). The Path of the Gods is the day of the year and the Path of the Fathers is the night of the year. These two terms are also associated with Agni and his movement though time and the seasons. Vedic hymns show that this Day and Night is the day and night of the year.

> A day that is dark and a day that is bright, two regions turn by ways to be known. The universal Fire, like a king in this birth, dispels the darkness by the light.
>
> I know not the warp or the weft or that which they weave back and forth in their coming together. Whose son beyond will speak the words to be spoken here through his father below. He knows the warp and the weft. He will declare through the seasons the words to be said (VI.9.1-3).[28]

The son who is above or beyond is Agni and the Path of the Gods. The father who is inferior or below is the Path of the Fathers.

Another hymn shows the Vedic Day and Night as the two halves of the year:

> Two diverse in form (day and night) move to a common goal, one after the other they suckle the child. He appears golden in one, the Self-natured lord. In the other he is seen luminous and lustrous.
>
> Along the eastern direction of the Earth he is established and directs the seasons accordingly (I.95.1-3).[29]

This also equates Agni with the vernal equinox or eastern direction. We also read of the return of Agni from the west to the east.

> When by the path you are released from the parents, Agni, you who were in the west they lead back to the east (I.31.4).[30]
>
> Not to be neglected is your return, Agni, when being far, you are here again (III.9.2).

Another Vedic verse states,

> Two days diverse in form are yours, white is one, holy is the other, you are like heaven ... Pushan let your blessing be here (IV.58.4).

These two days of the Sun are explained in the *Taittiriya Aranyaka* as the northern and southern courses of the Sun as follows:

> The year has two halves, white and black; two sides, right and left. Hence is this verse (of the *Rig Veda*), "White is one, holy is the other, two days diverse in form are yours, you are like Heaven ... Pushan let your blessing be here" (TA I.1.7).

The two days of the Sun or the sacrifice in the *Rig Veda,* therefore, are the two sides of the year marked by the solstices.

Pushan is a well-known form of the Sun God who marks the path.

> Pushan was born in the start of the path, in the path of Heaven, in the path of the Earth. Both beloved stations he circles to and from with knowledge (X.17.6).[31]

He appears to mark the solstice, the dividing point of the Vedic day and night or the paths of the Gods and the Fathers.

Having established an astrological foundation for the earlier *Vedas,* let us see if we cannot discover some references that may help us date the text.

THE MARRIAGE OF THE SUN GODDESS
THE SUMMER SOLSTICE IN VIRGO, 4000 BC

Much has been made of the hymns to the Dawn in the *Rig Veda.* These were not merely poetic utterances. The *Rig Veda* is centered around a series of sacrifices. The Dawn hymns were for sacrifices at dawn. These special hymns, moreover, were probably not for any dawn. Even Western Vedic scholars like Bergaine have thought that the Vedic Dawn was not the dawn of any day but a solstice point, particularly the winter solstice, which marks the dawn of the year. We read of the Dawn beginning the Path of the Gods.

> The paths leading to the Gods have appeared to me. The ray of the Dawn appears in the east, she has come from the west through the houses of rest (VII.76.2).[32]

Do we have any constellations associated with the Dawn? A hymn found both in the *Atharva Veda* (XIII.14) and the *Rig Veda* (X.85) is to Surya Savitri, the female form of the Sun who is the Dawn. In Vedic lore, the Sun is the God and the Dawn is the Goddess. This hymn has much astronomical symbolism.

> The Moon (Soma) is placed in the midst of these constellations (v.2).[33]
>
> The bridal train of the Sun Goddess comes, which the Sun has set in motion. In the month of Agha the cows are slain, in Arjuni she is wed (v.13).[34]

The *Atharva Veda,* which has an almost exact version of the same hymn, reads:

> In the month of Magha the cows are slain, in Phalguni she is wed (AV XIV.1.13).

These names refer to the months ruled by the constellations, when the full Moon occurs in them.

Does this mentioning of two lunar constellations give us any point of reference to the two paths? I believe it does. The Sun Goddess would be wed at the beginning of the Path of the Gods or the winter solstice. She is wed to the Moon, whereby the light is renewed for another year. The cows are slain in the month of Magha. The cows, as a common Vedic symbol, stand for the rays of the Sun. The month before the solstice they are at their point of decline. Hence the month of Phalguni (Arjuni) would mark the winter solstice, the return of the light and the marriage of the Sun Goddess.

Soma, the Moon, is the father of the Brahmins, the chants and the Sun (IX.96.5). He marries the Sun Goddess at the winter solstice during the year and at the new Moon day of the month, thus renewing the light of the Sun. Constellational references to these points should not be disregarded. Other verses support this view.

> You have two wheels, oh Sun Goddess, that the priests by the seasons know (V.16).[35]

These two wheels of the Sun Goddess should be the northern and southern courses of the Sun which serve to mark the seasons.

> The Sun and Moon travel east and west by magic power. One views the whole world, the other ordaining the seasons is born again. Being born ever new, as the ray of the days you move at the front of the dawn. You ordain the portions for the Gods (i.e. the Path of the Gods), oh Moon, you extend our lives (V.18-19).

Such verses show the Moon ordaining the seasons and moving at the front of the dawn.

The Phalgunis are two lunar constellations and mark 13° 20′ Leo-10° 00′ Virgo. The month of Phalguni is marked by the full Moon in the latter or Uttara Phalguni, or about the beginning of Virgo, as it follows a month behind that of Magha, which marks early Leo. The full Moon in the middle of Uttara Phalguni would have marked the new year or winter solstice about 4000 BC. Showing the Virgo solstice, it would indicate the Gemini vernal equinox and take the constellations back another sign of the zodiac. There was one Western Vedic scholar around the turn of the century, H. Jacobi,[c] who also noted the astronomical meaning of this hymn. He used it to date the *Rig Veda* from 4500-2500 BC when the Phalguni solstice would have been used for the calendar. He places most of the Vedic hymns at the end of this period.

There is a passage in the *Gopatha Brahmana* that shows this same solstice position.

> Uttara Phalguni is the mouth of the year. Purva Phalguni is its tail, just as two ends of a thing meet so these two ends of the year meet together (GB I.19).

We find the same idea in the *Kaushitaki Brahmana:*

> The full Moon night in the Phalgunis is the beginning of the year; the latter Phalgunis are the beginning, the former the end. Just as the two ends of a circle unite, so these two ends of the year are connected. In that he sacrifices with the Vaishwadeva sacrifice on the full Moon night in the Phalgunis, verily at the beginning he delights the year. Again the four monthly sacrifices are sacrifices of healing; therefore are they performed in the joinings of the seasons, for in the joinings of the seasons, pain is born (KB V.1).

Should there be any doubt that the full Moon in the Phalgunis marked the solstice, the same passage tells us that it marked the joining of the seasons, as well as the beginning of the year. We see here the Vedic concept of the juncture points or 'Sandhis' being the main times for sacrifices. These during the day are sunrise and sunset; during the year they are the points of the solstices and equinoxes. To quote Tilak:[d]

> Several *Brahmanas* and *Sutras* take the full Moon night in the month of Phalguni to be the first night of the year. *Shatapatha Brahmana* (VI.2.2.18) says, "the Phalguni full Moon is the first night of the year."[36] The *Taittiriya* (I.1,2, 8) and *Sankyayana* (IV.4 and 4.1) have similar passages.

This provides us a whole series of references establishing this date. It shows dates in the *Brahmanas* between 4000 BC (Phalguni full Moon night as beginning of the year) and 1280 BC (Magha new Moon night as beginning of the year). The earlier date is also found in earlier Vedic literature like the *Rig Veda* and *Atharva Veda*. The later date occurs more in post-Vedic literature.

Does this mean that 4000 BC would date the *Rig Veda* or this hymn? It shows the institution of a calendar of this era within the time of Vedic culture. Such a calendar could have been used up to the time of its Krittika-Magha reform around 2000 BC and must have prevailed for some time before that era. Yet we should note that this hymn is more typical in style and symbolism to the *Atharva Veda* and appears to be a late addition to the *Rig Veda*. We could say, therefore, that it is more likely a transitional hymn between the two texts. Hence we would expect that the Rig Vedic era ended sometime in the Phalguni or Virgo solstice era and before the Krittika reform of the calendar in later Vedic texts.

The terms for these constellations, Magha and Phalguni, are different in the *Rig Veda* than the *Atharva Veda* and later texts. They are styled Agha and Arjuni. These may be variant names of the constellations, as some have more than one, but may be earlier names of them. Such a change of names through time would not be unexpected. It would also affirm that the Nakshatras are a Vedic system and Aryan invention. If we find these terms mentioned elsewhere in the *Rig Veda* they would suggest an astronomical meaning.

I have found one hymn in the *Rig Veda* that may reflect the Arjuni-Phalguni era. It is to the Dawn and calls her Arjuni.

> Your flying birds who have two feet and four feet, oh Arjuni, they direct the seasons, oh Dawn, from the ends of Heaven (I.49.3).[37]

The symbolism is highly suggestive. The birds with two or four feet may be the two solstice points or the four points of equinoxes and solstices. These direct the seasons from the ends or points of the sky that mark them. Hence this hymn tends to affirm the Arjuni era, as mentioned in the Surya-Savitri hymn. It occurs in the first book of the *Rig Veda*. Its language is typical of the *Rig Veda*, and suggests that typical Rig Vedic hymns were still written after the Phalguni solstice. It also suggests that the Vedic Dawn may be referred to or named by the month marking the winter solstice.

This then yields us a new orientation of the constellations. The summer solstice can be placed in Uttara Phalguni, the winter solstice in Purvabhadra, the vernal equinox in Mrigashira, and the autumn equinox in Jyeshta. These mark the initial points of the signs Gemini, Virgo, Sagittarius, and Pisces. They take us back to the Age of Gemini. Are there any other references to these constellations?

THE VERNAL EQUINOX IN ORION

There is an interesting story in the *Aitareya Brahmana* that has much astronomical symbolism.

> Prajapati (the lord of the year) felt love towards his own daughter, the sky some say, the dawn others. Having become a stag he approached her in the form of a doe. The Gods saw him. "A deed unknown Prajapati now does." They sought someone to punish him; they could not find anyone among them to do this. So they brought their most terrible forms together in one being. To him (Rudra) the Gods said, "Prajapati here has done a deed unknown; pierce him." Having aimed at him he pierced him; being pierced he flew upwards; him they call "the deer" (mriga). The piercer of the deer is he called by that name (mrigavyadha). The female deer is Rohini; the three-pointed arrow is the constellation of the three-pointed arrow.[e]

This is an astronomical myth with the names of several constellations near the zodiac. Rohini is the constellation at the end of Taurus, marked by the red giant star Aldebaran. The piercer of the deer (mrigavyadha) is the

Vedic God Rudra. It is the name in Vedic astronomy for the star Sirius. The three-pointed arrow is the name of the three stars in the belt of Orion. Mriga or Mrigashira is another zodiacal constellation marking 23° 20′ Taurus-06° 40′ Gemini, next to Rohini, mainly the constellation of Orion. Professor Whitney states, "There is the whole story illustrated in the sky; the innocent and lovely Rohini (Aldebaran); the infamous Prajapati (Orion) in full career after her, but laid sprawling by the three-pointed arrow (the belt of Orion), which shot from the the hand of the near avenger (Sirius) is even now to be seen sticking in his body. With this tale coming down to us from the first period of Nakshatras in India who could have the least doubt of its persistent identity from the earliest times to the latest?"[f]

What does this mean in terms of the equinoxes? It shows a time wherein the vernal equinox was moving from Mrigashiras to Rohini,[g] from Gemini (marked by Orion) into Taurus. No doubt this shifting position of the equinox was met with suspicion by the ancients, as they were always attached to the past and did not like to change. A moving back of the equinoxes was viewed as a violation. This shows that the Vedic people knew of a time when the vernal equinox was in Mrigashiras and then moved into Rohini.

The constellation Mrigashiras originally had another ancient name 'Agrahayana', which means literally "the beginning of the year." Hayana is a common word for "the year" in the *Atharva Veda* and agra means "first." This suggests that once, like the Krittikas, it marked the beginning of the constellations from the point of the vernal equinox. This would have also been around 4000 BC. The vernal equinox would have occurred in the constellation of Mrigashiras when the winter solstice occurred in the month of Phalguni. This gives additional confirmation to that sequence. Tilak, in his book *Orion*, explores the symbolism and mythology of this constellation and finds it reflected in much of Vedic lore. He even tries to show that the name Orion from the Greek derives from Agrahayana.[h] Through this Orion reference, the Virgo solstice is confirmed. Yet this is not the earliest date we find in the *Rig Veda.* We find that originally the Sun Goddess was married at a point relative to the beginning of Aries.

THE HORSE'S HEAD
THE WINTER SOLSTICE IN ARIES, 6000 BC

The constellation of Ashwini is described as a horse's head. It is associated with the Ashwins, the Vedic twin horsemen. There are a number of strange and mystic references to it in the *Rig Veda* that suggest a special importance for it.

> You brought the horse's head, oh Ashwins, to Dadhyak, son of Atharvan. He proclaimed the honey to you, the secret of Twashtar (I.117.22).[38]
>
> That great miracle I reveal to you, Ashwins, like the thunder the rain, when Dadhyak Atharvan spoke the honey to you by the horse's head (I.116.12).[39]
>
> Indra with the bones of Dadhyak destroyed ninety-nine unequalled dragons. Seeking the head of the horse, hidden in the mountains, he found it at Sharanyavat.[i] Then they thought out the secret name of Twashtar's bull in the mansion of the Moon (I.84.13-5).[40]

What is this honey that is proclaimed through the head of the horse?

> The spotted cows drink of the honey and sweetness of the solstice (I.84.10).[41]

The spotted cows stand for the stars, or for the rays of the Sun which they commonly relate to in the *Vedas.* Vishuvat, used here, is the term for the solstice from the *Brahmanas* and later astrology, as we have seen. Here it is related to the horse's head.

In Vedic astrology the Ashwins rule Ashwini, the horse's head, the lunar constellation marking 00° 00′-13° 20′ Aries. Here, by the horse's head, the honey of the solstice, the return of the Sun and the victory over the powers of darkness is achieved. The God Twashtar rules Chitra, the constellation opposite Ashwini in the zodiac, marking 23° 20′ Virgo-06° 40′ Libra. His name means the "Form fashioner." In the story of the Ribhus, they take his one cup and turn it fourfold, making him jealous or causing him to hide himself. This refers to the division of the one year into the four equinoctial points. His bull is probably the Moon. His secret name is probably according to the constellation marking the epoch.

Dadhyak, the seer, son of Atharvan, who takes upon himself the head of a horse to proclaim the honey-doctrine, is the old Sun, the Sun at the winter solstice. He appears the same as Dadhikravan, the sacred horse of the *Rig Veda,* and may also symbolize the horse sacrifice. He is one of the mythical ancestors of the Aryan peoples, like Manu (I.139.9), who are identified with the Sun. The bones of the sacred horse are identified with the Nakshatras in the *Upanishads* (BU I.1). Indra similarly with the bones of Dadhyak kills the dragon, Vritra, who among other things hides the Sun. Apparently the horse sacrifice relates to a time when the winter solstice was in Ashwini, marking the beginning of the Path of the Gods.

Ashwini, the constellation of the horse's head, is the head of the sacrificed horse.

The horse, the symbol of the Sun, is offered in sacrifice at the winter solstice. From there it goes by the Path of the Gods, being liberated from its body. Hence to die at the winter solstice is the most auspicious time to go. It takes us directly by the Path of the Gods.

The Vedic horse is the Sun, who is the year. We find this in the symbolism of the Vedic horse sacrifice.

> From the Sun, the Vasus fashioned the horse. You are Yama (the God of death), you are the Sun, oh horse (I.163.2–3).

The solar horse, or his sacrificed head which is the Sun, travels by the Path of the Gods. The horse is the year, whose various parts are divided up by the seasons.

> When men lead the sacred horse, who goes by the Path of the Gods, round three times by the seasons, there the goat, the portion of Pushan, precedes him, revealing the offering to the Gods. The thirty-four ribs of the swift horse, the friend of the Gods, the axe enters. Cut his limbs unbroken with wisdom, declaring them piece by piece, dissect them. Twashtar is the one dissector of the horse, two are his controllers, according to the season. The limbs of his by the seasons I cut. These in balls I offer into the fire (I.162.4, 18–9).

The thirty-four ribs of the solar horse are said by the commentators to be the twenty-seven lunar constellations, the five planets, the Sun and the Moon (as in X.55), showing a complete knowledge of these in the times of the *Rig Veda.* Twashtar cuts the horse of the year in two, perhaps by his constellation of Chitra marking the summer solstice. His two controllers may be the Paths of the Gods and the Fathers. The solar horse is naturally dissected by the seasons, as the being of light or time is divided up by the seasons of the year. The Vedic horse sacrifice is an imitation of the Sun's course through the year.

The honey, madhu, is also the sweetness of Soma, the Moon.

> Soma, your celestial Ashwinis, faster than thought, flow with milk in the upholding laws. Within the stable

> ones, the seers pour you, the ordainers who adorn you, ruler of the seers (IX.86.4).

The seers or Rishis may be the planets or the months. The stable or fixed ones, the Ashwinis, are the constellations, the stars that do not move, marking the solstice.

The Ashwins serve to divide Heaven and Earth. We can identify Heaven with the northern course of the Sun and the Path of the Gods, and the Earth with the southern course and the Path of the Fathers.

> Powerful Lords of magic power, you broke the two united worlds apart. When the two worlds were separated, the Gods were sad. They said to the Ashwins, bring them back together again. May my going away (para-ayana) be full of honey and full of honey be my return (punar-ayana). Oh Gods, through your Godhead, make us full of honey (X.24.4-6).[42]

Ayana means solstice, as we have seen both from later astronomical and from Vedic literature. This also suggests the constellation of the Ashwins marking the winter solstice. They dispense the honey of the new year and a new entrance on the Path of the Gods.

To return to the theme of the Dawn and the Sun Goddess, in the *Rig Veda* she mounts the car of the Ashwins as their wife.

> For glory, oh Ashwins, the daughter of the Sun mounted your chariot (VI.63.5).
>
> Your chariot that holds your wife pushes the ends of Heaven by its circuit, oh Ashwins. When the night was turning into the grey of morning, the maiden, the daughter of the Sun, chose your splendor (VII.69.3-4).

The Ashwins also mark the Path of the Gods, as does Ushas, the Dawn.

> We have crossed the limit of darkness, holding this praise to you, oh Ashwins. Come to us by the paths of the Gods (I.183.6; I.184.6).[43]
>
> We have crossed the limit of darkness, holding the praise to you, oh Ashwins. Choosing you, we have directed the sacrifice along the path (VII.73.1, 3).
>
> Come to us by the paths of the Gods, oh Ashwins, for you are these casks of honey (III.58.6).[44]

The Ashwins mark the point between the Dawn and Night, which as indicated are the dawn and night of the year.

> The Night retires before her sister the Dawn. The black relinquishes to the red her path, rich in energy and light we call you, oh Ashwins. May blissful horses turn your chariot at this most inferior breaking of the dawn (VII.71.1, 4).[45]

The most inferior breaking of the dawn is quite likely the winter solstice, when the days are darkest and the dawns are most welcome, the inferior point of the year or lowest point of the Sun in the sky. As the Ashwins are usually invoked at the beginning of the dawn, the dawn of the winter solstice would be the most appropriate time of the year for them. This is when we cross over the limit of darkness for both the day and the year. Hence the original story of Surya Savitri, the Sun Goddess, in the *Rig Veda* reflects the Ashwini era of the winter solstice, and thereby a date of at least 6000 BC when the winter solstice was in Aries, possibly as early as 7000 BC, when the solstice first entered Ashwini.

The Ashwins have many stories about them in the *Rig Veda,* a number of which have solar or astronomical symbolism. They save Bhujyu who has been thrown into the ocean by his evil father. It is said of them —

> You carried Bhujyu for three nights and three days with your fast birds, to the shore of the wet ocean, with three chariots, with a hundred feet and six horses (I.116.4).

Bhujyu, as the other Vedic texts note, is the Sun. He is cast in the ocean by his evil father. He is the Sun at the end of the Path of the Fathers, the Sun at its ebb at the winter solstice. He is renewed by the power of the Ashwins who take him on their chariot to the Path of the Gods. Three chariots with a hundred feet and six horses is symbolic for three hundred and sixty degrees or days of the year. He is saved by a horse or a boat symbolic of the sacrifice or the course of the year that brings order to the movement of the Sun.

Atri is a famous seer who discovers the Sun that had been hidden in darkness.

> When, oh Sun, Swarbhanu the demon had pierced you with darkness, as one confused who does not know the way, all creatures were bewildered. With the fourth Brahman (prayer) Atri found the Sun that was hidden in darkness. When Swarbhanu the demon pierced the Sun with

> darkness, the Atris found him. No one else had the power to do it (V.40.5, 6, 9).
>
> Ashwins, you saved Atri from distress and darkness (VII.71.5).[46]

Atri is another seer who is saved by the magic of the Ashwins. Atri in later literature is also identified as the Sun. It is by the grace of the Ashwins that he finds the Sun, or that as the Sun he himself is renewed. Atri himself is probably, like Bhujyu, the old Sun or Sun at the winter solstice. The fourth Brahman may be the chant given at the winter solstice, the fourth of the cardinal points of the year.

Perhaps many or all the miracles of the Ashwins can be explained under this symbolism. In another famous story, they bring the aged Chyavana back to youth.

> You released Chyavana from old age (VII.71.5).

This may also refer to the renewal of the Sun at the winter solstice or beginning of the year. They give a fast or white horse to Pedu. This horse must also be the Sun.

Most of the exploits of the Ashwins are listed in several hymns of the famous seer Kakshivan (I.116-120). His father called Dirghatamas, meaning "extended darkness," is also saved by the Ashwins and may refer to the Sun at the darkest point of the year. Dirghatamas thus appears like Bhujyu and in one of his hymns to the Ashwins (I.158) he is also saved from drowning and appears as the great teacher for coming World Ages. Bhujyu as a mythic ancestor of humanity shows the origin of the human race from the old, lost or dark Sun, which represents the spiritual consciousness darkened and lost in the material world. Even Christ, like most of the ancient Sun Gods and solar saviors, is born at the winter solstice.

Perhaps all the miracles of the Ashwins we find frequently mentioned in the *Rig Veda* can be be explained under this symbolism. Tilak states, "Taking their clue from this indication (i.e. the Ashwins as rescuing the Sun), many scholars, and among them Max Muller, have interpreted all the Ashwin legends as referring to the Sun in winter and the restoration of his power in spring or summer."[j]

None of these scholars, however, has given the Ashwins a solstice point of reference. With such a connection between the Ashwins and the winter sun, it is hard to believe that the Vedic priests and their ritualistic calendars would not have noticed the constellation point or related it in some way to the Ashwins. There is no doubt that the Ashwins are the earliest of the deities of light and start the Vedic Path of the Gods. That their constellation marked the winter solstice in Vedic times is not only evidenced, it is upheld by the entire symbolism and mythology of these Gods.

PUNARVASU, THE VERNAL EQUINOX IN CANCER

Revati is the name of the star that marks the beginning of the zodiac at 0° Aries. We note in this regard:

> May Mitra and Varuna be auspicious to us, auspicious be the Path of Revati, auspicious be Indra and Agni, may Aditi be auspicious to us. Auspicious may we travel the path like the Sun and Moon (VI.51.14-5).[47]

The path of the Sun and Moon is here called the path of Revati, one of the lunar constellations that marks the beginning of the zodiac (0° Aries). Revati thus appears as marking the beginning of the zodiac in Vedic times, even before the time the vernal equinox occured there, which did not happen until 400 AD. This suggests that Revati previously marked a cardinal point of the seasons, the most recent of which would have been around 6000 BC when it marked the winter solstice. The Vedic Dawn, which begins the Path of the Gods, is sometimes called Revati (III.61.6).

A hymn of the last book of the *Rig Veda* (X.19) mentions some of the lunar constellations. It may be the most specific of the astronomical references in the text. It speaks of the Revatis.

> Return, do not go further. Stay with us, Revatis. Agni-Soma, Punarvasu, hold our wealth for us (V.1).[48]

Revati marks 16° 40′ Pisces-00° 00′ degrees Aries, being next to Ashwini in the zodiac. The point exactly between Ashwini and Revati is the beginning of the zodiac at 0° Aries. Agni-Soma also means the Sun and Moon. These are related to Punarvasu, the constellation that marks 20° 00′ Gemini-03° 20′ Cancer. This is the only time that Punarvasu occurs in the *Rig Veda,* so it is difficult to give it a generic sense. It appears to indicate a time when Punarvasu marked the beginning of the list of constellations, the point of Agni or the vernal equinox.

The winter solstice in Revati and the vernal equinox in Punarvasu would have occurred together, as these constellations are ninety degrees apart. It would have happened from about 6000-5000 BC. Wealth may refer to the cosmic forces distributed by the year, as the light and rain. The hymn continues lauding this return of the light.

> Make these return again, make them return back. Indra, control them. Agni, drive them. Let them return again and flourish in their herdsman. Let Agni hold them here and let our wealth stand (V.2-3).

Indra is the God who wins back the Sun, the fire, the dawn, waters and cows. He controls the Path of the Gods. Agni is the main force of this path. The herdsman, as often in the *Rig Veda,* is the Sun, particularly in the form of Pushan, the Vedic God who rules the constellation Revati.

> Who knows their return course and their return path (ni-ayanam), and their path away (para-ayanam), their turn and return, that herdsman I call. Who upholds their path apart (vi-ayanam) and who upholds their path away (para-ayanam), their turn and return, let that herdsman return (V.4-5).[49]

Ayana is the traditional name for the solstice, particularly the summer solstice, as early as the *Atharva Veda* as we have seen (XIX.7). Ni-ayana, "return path," would indicate the winter solstice, the lower (ni) ayana. "Path away," para-ayana, would indicate the summer solstice. In the appendix to the *Rig Veda,* there is the following verse.

> Turn and return, seasons of the end of the year (RVP 29.28).[50]

The turn mentioned in both places, avarta, would be the autumn equinox and the return, nivarta, the vernal equinox.

> May the returner make them turn and return. Indra, give back our cows (rays of light), that we may experience them alive. On all sides I encompass you with sap, ghee and milk. May all the holy Gods unite us together with wealth. Returner, make them turn, returner, make them return. From the four directions of the world, by these make them return (V.6-7).

The emphasis is on the returner (nivarta) as the hymn is centered on Punarvasu as the vernal equinox or point of return. This is Agni's return,

> Not to be neglected is your return (nivartana), Agni, when being far, you are here again (III.9.2).

The four directions of the world are the four seasons and their points in the sky.

We see therefore in this hymn of the *Rig Veda* the terminology of the constellations, the seasons, the equinoxes and solstices. We cannot regard it a mere coincidence that the names of constellations and the names for the solstices occur together. It gives us a Punarvasu beginning for the constellation list and marks the Cancer equinox to affirm the Aries solstice.

This Punarvasu hymn is part of the Yama cycle of hymns of the tenth book of the *Rig Veda,* which some consider to be a late addition to the text. Like the Surya Savitri hymn they occur in a more expanded form in the *Atharva Veda.* They look upon and eulogize the families of the Rishis as those departed. The Yama hymns appear to mark the end of an era. The Rishis are treated as legendary figures, now in Heaven, rather than on Earth as in more typical hymns of the *Rig Veda.*[k] Yama himself is a figure of death and discipline. The Yama hymns introduce a spirit of contraction, and a looking with suspicion to coming ages.

> Further ages will come, where those who are kindred
> will do things that are not kind (X.10.10).

This suggests that at least some of the hymns of the *Rig Veda* come before the Yama hymns, perhaps including this one that marks a time of about 6000 BC. The idea of Yama as the original man appears to be a late addition to the *Rig Veda.* He is originally the God of the dead and departed but not commonly mentioned like Manu as a founder of the sacrifice or father of the peoples.

The seer of this hymn (X.19) is alternatively said to be Mathita Yamayana, Bhrigu Varuni or Bhargava Chyavana. The first would make him a descendent of Yama, the latter two are legendary seers of the earliest level of the Vedic teaching.

Punarvasu is also identified with Yama and called Yamakau, or Yama and Yami. This affirms its connection to Yama and the equinox here as marking his era. The ruler of Punarvasu is Aditi, the Mother of the Sun Gods or Adityas. That her constellation marks the vernal equinox would make much sense as the Vedic seers saw the eastern direction as the point of origin and the source of light.

Yama may therefore enter into the Rig Vedic literature as the original man around 6000 BC. Some ancient writers date Zoroaster to 6000 BC. Perhaps it was really the date or Yama, Persian Yima, the oldest figure to whom Zoroaster looks back, the Persian original man.

CHITRA, THE SUMMER SOLSTICE IN LIBRA

Chitra is a common term in the *Rig Veda,* meaning "bright." It is a common name or epithet for many Vedic Gods including the Sun.

> The luminous (chitra) presence of the Gods has arisen, the eye of Mitra, Varuna and Agni. He has filled Heaven and Earth and the atmosphere, the Sun, the Self of all that is stable and moving (I.115.1).

Surya is the bright Sun, the Sun at noon or the summer solstice. The Sun itself is called Nakshatra (VII.86.1). Was the Sun, like the Moon, sometimes named after the constellation of the solstice or equinox?

Indra is identified with the Sun as Chitra (IV.31.1, 15). Indra is well known as the Sun at noon. The noon of the year is the summer solstice, with which other scholars have identified him. This would be marked by the lunar constellation Chitra (which marks 23° 20′ Virgo–06° 40′ Libra) when either Ashwini or Revati marked the winter solstice. The great Aryan victory of the light or winning of the Sun that Indra brings would reach its high point at noon and the summer solstice. This is also the point at which the rains come in India and Indra is the God of the storm.

Indra also steals the Soma from Twashtar, the God who rules the constellation Chitra.

> Having transcended Twashtar by birth, Indra drank his Soma in the vessels (III.48.4).

We know that Indra drinks the Soma by season.

> Indra, who drink by the seasons, drink the Soma by the seasons (III.47.3).[51]

Indra is also associated with one of the Ribhus, one of the Gods of the seasons. He is associated with noon and with the summer solstice. He rules the Father or the Moon.

> Indra released the chariot of the Sun in the middle of Heaven. The Aryan found a countermeasure for the Dasyu. As the Sun, he takes the full light from the Moon. Divided by you, oh Indra, the Father bears the rim of the wheel, ordaining the months in Heaven (X.138.3, 4, 6).

These references affirm the Chitra summer solstice, of which there are many more. The problem is that Chitra is a common word, meaning "bright," so that it is hard to give it a necessary astronomical meaning as a constellation in these hymns. Chitra as a constellations is usually in the feminine tense, which is seldom found in the *Rig Veda*. We do, however, find at least one reference to Chitra that may be astronomical in its import.

> Oh Chitra, appear for us as Chitra, you whose rule is Chitra, most Chitra like, the ordainer of the age, oh Moon with the Moons grant to the singer the Moon, a vast and manifold splendor (VI.6.6).

This verse comes at the end of a hymn to Agni, an old hymn that mentions the Navagwas (V.3), the oldest sages at the core of the main Vedic myth of the return of the Sun.

Chitra here is directly invoked as a deity itself or as a form of Agni. It is not just an adjective meaning bright. We read of Chitra as a ruling power, Chitra-kshatram, Kshatra being the Vedic basis for Kshatriya, the ruling class. It is the ordainer of the age, vayodham, or the granter of life. In the second half of the verse Chandra is lauded. Chandra is the later name for the Moon. It does not appear to always mean the Moon in the *Rig Veda* but there are a number of passages where it does.

> Oh sage, that mortal is like the Moon (Chandra), the most glorious in Heaven (I.150.3).[53]
>
> Him increasing in the region, in his own home, brilliant like the Moon, the serpents have placed (II.2.4).[54]

The Moon is often compared to a serpent by its form and movement. This hymn speaks of Chandra (masculine) with the Chandras (feminine). In the Vedic system the Moon is masculine and the months or the lunar constellations are feminine, his wives. This, I believe, shows an astronomical meaning. What is it marking? As referring to the Moon and the months or constellations it likely refers to a time when the full Moon in Chitra marked the beginning of the year or the winter solstice. This would also be about 6000 BC like the previous indications.

The *Taittiriya Brahmana* also relates Chitra to the head of the constellations:

> Chitra is the head of Prajapati (the God of the sacrifice or the year), Swati the heart, Hasta the hand, Vishakha the thighs, and Anuradha the foot (TB I.5.2.2).[1]

Hasta, Chitra, Swati, Vishakha and Anuradha are sequential as lunar constellations. Chitra as the head of the year may indicate the summer solstice. The same text (VII.4.8) mentions the full Moon in Chitra as one of the options for the beginning of the year. This also reflects an era when the solstice would have been in Chitra. Yet while the *Brahmanas* relate these positions as traditional, the *Rig Veda* speaks of them as contemporaneous.

Pushan

We have already mentioned the God Pushan as marking the beginning of the Path, which appears to be the Path of the Gods or the solstice. A hymn of the first book of the *Rig Veda* relates the months to Pushan.

> Radiant Pushan, drive back like a lost cow him whose field is light, the support of Heaven. Radiant Pushan found the king, hidden in secret, whose field is light. And to me with the Moons he pours out the six conjoined, as one who ploughs with oxen the grain (I.23.13-15).[55]

Pushan is a name for the Sun God, the one he finds appears to be the Moon. The traditional commentators saw in these verses the six double months or six seasons of India. "Whose field is light," Chitrabarhisam, may also refer to the Moon whose field of months begins with Chitra, for the lunar constellation Chitra would mark the summer solstice when Revati, the constellation ruled by Pushan, would mark the winter solstice.

In Vedic mythology Pushan and the Ashwins both marry Surya Savitri, the Sun Goddess, whom we have identified with the Sun at the winter solstice.

> Pushan, the good friend of Heaven and Earth, whom the Gods gave the Sun Goddess (IV.58.4).[56]

Pushan rules the two days that are identified with the northern and southern course of the Sun. Hence, the marriage of the Sun Goddess to Pushan and the Ashwins should mark the point between Revati and Ashwini of 0° Aries, the constellations they rule.

To Pushan is also offered the goat, which precedes the sacrificed horse on its journey on the Path of the Gods. This may also refer to the constellation Revati, ruled by Pushan, being next to that of Ashwini or the horse's head.

Pushan as the Lord of the Path goes well with him ruling Revati that marks the beginning of the zodiac.

> Pushan was born in the juncture of the paths of both Heaven and Earth. He moves back and forth around both beloved dwellings with wisdom (X.17.6).

This also indicates his marking the beginning of the Path of the Gods or Devayana. In Vedic literature Pushan is the name of the Sun that the seers enter into at death to follow the northern course of the Sun to liberation.[m] As death was best at the time of the winter solstice so the soul could go along the Path of the Gods, naturally Pushan would be the God to invoke as marking that point in the heavens.

Tishya

Tishya, another name for the lunar constellation Pushya, is mentioned in the *Rig Veda,* as we have noted, in connection with Jupiter. It is mentioned as at the "station," perhaps indicating the equinoctial position (X.64.8). This hymn has another interesting verse (V.3) which speaks of "the Sun and Moon, the twins (Yama) in Heaven." When the winter solstice was in Ashwini, the vernal equinox would have been in Tishya (Pushya) or Punarvasu, the previous constellation. Both are close to the beginning of the sign Cancer as the point between Tishya and Punarvasu is 3° 20′ Cancer. It is also near to the point (5° 00′ Cancer), where Brihaspati or Jupiter, who is often regarded as the founder of the Vedic religion, was said to have been born. This also may indicate that the Vedic religion or the Vedic ritual, symbolized by Brihaspati, may have been instituted or reformed along with the Tishya equinox or near 6000 BC.

In this regard there is an interesting verse in the *Vishnu Purana:*

> When the Sun, Moon, Jupiter and the constellation Tishya are in the same sign, then the Golden Age will return (VP IV.23.30).

Here again we have the association of Jupiter with the Nakshatra Tishya. It is the Vedic name of the Nakshatra again which is used, not the usual Puranic name, which is Pushya. While this date is said to refer to the return of the mythical Golden Age, it may reflect an ancient observation. This position in itself can occur a few times a century, so it is obviously not its ordinary position that is meant but when these factors mark the equinox or solstice. They marked the summer solstice around 100–200 AD, or in the Puranic era, so this cannot be what was referred to. It may reflect the earlier Vedic calendar, and the age of light that it came from, when Tishya marked the vernal equinox.

CHRONOLOGY OF THE VEDAS

We can trace the lunar constellations marking the vernal equinox back through many layers in Hindu and Vedic literature: Ashwini, Krittika, Mrigashiras, Punarvasu, Tishya. In addition, the solstice points can similarly be taken back. This takes us from 400 AD to before 6000 BC. There are many indications of the early Taurus or Krittika point in later Vedic literature. There are indications of the early Gemini or Mrigashiras equinox era in Vedic literature of the middle period, and indications of early Cancer or the Punarvasu era in the earlier Vedic literature.

While the references before the Krittikas (Taurus vernal equinox) are less clear, that reference itself is definite. Its language is as clear as stating "now the vernal equinox is in early Taurus." It proves that whoever the Vedic people were and wherever they lived, their culture was in its later phase by 2000 BC. With this reference substantiated the others become hard to dismiss.

The *Vedas* look back to a time when the winter solstice, the Path of the Gods or northern course of the Sun, began near the beginning of the sign Aries. The myth of the marriage of the Sun Goddess, the legends of the Ashwins, Pushan, Indra and Twashtar, Brihaspati, Yama, Dadhyak and the horse sacrifice all reflect it. This does not mean that the hymns which use such symbolism were all composed during this era, or even used this symbolism with an astronomical meaning. It means that the *Rig Veda* looks back in its mythology to this era as determining much of the symbolism of its Gods and the order of its rituals.

With such astronomical references in all Vedic texts, on what grounds can we deny them? If the *Rig Veda* uses the same terms as later astronomy, we cannot say they are wrong or referred to something else because it does not agree with our theories. Our theories may be wrong but the stars are not. According to the stars then I would give these dates for Vedic texts:

1. Proto-Rig Vedic: before 6000 BC
2. Early Rig Vedic: 6000–4000 BC
3. Later Rig Vedic/Four Veda Period: 4000–2000 BC
4. Transitional: 2000–1000 BC

In the proto-Rig Vedic period much of the language and symbolism of the *Rig Veda* existed. This is the era of the early seers; the Dashagwas, Navagwas, Bhrigus, Angirasas, and Manu. In the early Rig Vedic period a mass of hymns was set down as a tradition but it was probably not fixed. The patterns of the rituals were established. In the later Rig Vedic period the text was fixed, with minor alterations and additions occurring to the end of it. At the same time the other *Vedas* were in their formative stage.

In the transitional era the Vedic culture declined and became antiquated. The other three *Vedas* and finally the *Brahmanas* and early *Upanishads* reached their final form.

The Vedic Aryans were probably in India by 6000 BC as the Land of the Seven Rivers is defined in the earliest hymns. While details remain uncertain, it is clear that the *Rig Veda* was already an ancient text by the time of the introduction of the Krittika-Taurus era in 2000 BC, which marked the ending of the Vedic age.

PART IV

VEDIC RELIGION

1

VEDIC RELIGION

THE YOGIC BASIS OF CIVILIZATION

Seers of the vast illumined seer yogically control their minds and their intelligence. One only, he ordains the invocation of the Gods. Great is the glory of the Divine creative Sun. — *Rig Veda V.81.1*

We have examined the geographical model of interpreting the *Rig Veda,* which reflects the sacred geography of north India, and the temporal model, which shows the sacred time of the ritual and the calendar. The third model is that of the practice of Yoga. In this interpretation, sacred geography becomes the inner landscape of the subtle body and its seven chakras. Sacred time becomes the process of spiritual transformation through yogic practice. The Vedic Gods become symbols for different aspects of enlightenment or spiritual illumination.

It is our habit to credit the ancients with little practical knowledge of the world around them. We find their ideas of time and history to be warped by mere mythical (fictitious) ideas. Yet it is clear that the ancients valued the religious life more than we do; their lives centered around the worship of the Gods and most of the objects of their daily activities had a ritualistic significance. However, even in the spiritual or philosophical realm we also regard our own culture as more developed. We think that the idea of monotheism, that there is only One God, was practically unknown to the ancients before the time of the Hebrews. From a pride in our monotheistic beliefs we look down upon the great abundance of deities and religious practices of the ancients, even though most of our pursuits and values in life today are purely secular. However, once we have studied Yoga and the science of meditation, we find many indications of higher states of consciousness in ancient texts like the *Rig Veda* and the *Egyptian Book of the Dead.* These make our idea of monotheism appear much less exalted or ultimate than we think.

We may have a more abstract philosophical idea as to Divinity, but the ancients had a living experience. The rawness or concreteness of their religious language reflects a direct contact with the Divine, whereas our abstract ideas only indicate our distance from it. Particularly in the religion of India, the worship of many Gods has always occurred along with a teaching of the identity of our deepest Self with God. This has produced a great stream of yogis, gurus, and avatars and a knowledge of the deeper workings of the mind and mystical states that we rarely find in Western monotheistic religions. The Vedic seers are the most renowned of these sages of India. The ancient multiplicity of Gods thereby reflects not a crude polytheism but an abundance of living approaches to the Divine, a vast living spirituality as opposed to our usually dead beliefs.

The Vedic teaching culminates in the great Upanishadic realization "I am Brahman (God)."

> All this in the beginning was Brahman. It knew itself as I am Brahman. Seeing this, the Rishi Vamadeva realized "I was the father of the human race and I became the Sun" (BU I.4.10; RV IV.26.1).[1]

This realization is much like what Moses heard at the burning bush in the Old Testament, of God as "I am that I am." Yet such knowledge in the *Vedas* is not the property of a rare prophet or messiah but the heritage and goal of each soul, our own ultimate destiny.

The existence of the practice of Yoga and the idea of Self-realization is recognized to be common in later Vedic texts like the *Upanishads,* and to have been hinted at here and there in earlier teachings, even in a few places in the *Rig Veda* itself. Yet many scholars, including Indian ones, consider that earlier Vedic texts were ritualistic, not philosophical, and could only reach this idea rarely at their most exalted level. This philosophical view sees a development in ancient Hindu culture from the primitive naturalistic religion of the *Vedas* to the great spiritual realizations of the *Upanishads* and their rational approach. It views the Upanishadic era, the late ancient age in the centuries before the Buddha, as the great spiritual era of the Hindu tradition. This overlooks the fact that the *Rig Veda* is traditionally regarded as the "Scripture" or "Revelation" (Shruti), to which even the *Upanishads* look back and quote as their authority. All ancient cultures look back to earlier spiritual ages. They do not place their great spiritual ages in the declining ritualistic cultures of late ancient times but much earlier.

There are some thinkers who consider that the same spiritual teaching of Yoga and the *Upanishads* is hidden in the symbolism of the *Rig Veda* — that the *Rig Veda* can be interpreted along spiritual lines. These include Sri Aurobindo and Ganapati Muni, the chief disciple of Ramana Maharshi. Even earlier Hindu ritualistic interpreters like Yaska and Sayana note that such a tradition existed. By this view the knowledge of the Self permeates the entire Vedic tradition and the culture which derived from it. Vedanta, the spiritual philosophy of Oneness, was not the last phase of the *Veda* but its essence all along, its very origin. The great spiritual ages of humanity came early in ancient history, before what we regard as "history" began, at some original Golden Age from which we have fallen. The philosophical rendering of these teachings, as we begin to find in the *Upanishads*, indicates not their summit but the beginning of their decline, the fall from the true realization into intellectual hair-splitting such as occurred throughout the Middle Ages.

THE ORIGINS OF YOGA

Yoga is a system for the development of consciousness from the ancient world. While there is some doubt as to how old it is, we can trace it back to at least the *Upanishads*. Yoga has gained some respect in the modern world by the power of physical and mental control it affords. Yet to trace the origins of Yoga according to the preconceived view of history of the modern intellect, as is the usual case in historical studies, may be inappropriate. Yoga comes from a different idea of man and the world than is espoused in modern culture. Modern culture is not the product of Yoga; that is, it is not the product of inner integration but of inner fragmentation. Therefore, modern cultural standards may not be adequate for understanding the origin or meaning of Yoga, even in historical terms.

The modern view of the development of human civilization is far removed from the evolution of man according to the system of Yoga. The modern idea of civilization developing gradually through the growth of technology and scientific thinking contradicts the yogic point of view which rather sees culture as having been originally formulated and passed down by the sages. The Yoga teaching itself is said to come from Ishwara, the Cosmic Guru, whose significator is Om.[a] It is this same Om that is said to be the origin of the *Vedas* and the Sanskrit language. The Yogic tradition also reflects a spiritual origin for humanity and a scriptural origin for human language.

In medieval India, the India of the philosophical systems, Yoga referred to one of the six systems of orthodox philosophy, those based upon and accepting the authority of the *Vedas*. Yoga presents itself as a Vedic system, one giving the right interpretation of Vedic texts. Its main text is the *Yoga Sutras* of the sage Patañjali. Yoga is paired with another of the six systems called 'Sankhya', attributed to the seer Kapila who is mentioned in many Vedic and Vedantic texts, including the *Rig Veda* itself (X.27.16). Both Sankhya and Yoga share many ideas, which in turn are found to a great extent in all the systems of philosophy in India, orthodox and unorthodox.

This Sankhya-Yoga system, however, was often opposed by Vedanta, another orthodox system. Vedanta claims to accurately reflect the meaning of the *Vedas* and particularly the *Upanishads,* which are thought to show the highest side of Vedic knowledge. Sankhya and Yoga also claim to represent the valid interpretation of the *Upanishads.* Because of this conflict between Sankhya-Yoga and Vedanta, some scholars have ascribed a non-Vedic origin to the Yoga system. Medieval Vedantins often call the Yoga system 'unorthodox'. Some scholars have gone as far as to relate Yoga to a pre-Vedic Dravidian Shaivite culture, such as the Indus Valley culture is thought by them to be, and relate Vedanta to the Aryan north and a later entry into India.

It should be noted, however, that it is difficult to read ancient history into the philosophical hair-splitting of medieval India. Shankara, the greatest defender of Vedanta in medieval times, who refutes aspects of Sankhya-Yoga in his commentaries, was a Dravidian Shaivite from south India. Many great Vedantic commentators, like Shankara and Ramanuja, came from south India. To attribute ancient cultural origins of over two thousand years earlier to such later philosophical disputes is a great presumption. We do not try to judge early Christian history by the differences between St. Thomas Aquinas and other medieval Christian philosophers. Why should we apply this standard to a culture like that of India which is so foreign to us?

Moreover, apart from a few philosophical differences, Vedanta has always included within itself the whole cosmology of Sankhya and the practice of Yoga and has never rejected or refuted these. The differences have centered around a few ideas about ultimate reality, mainly the status of the Purusha as 'one' or 'many'. All else is common to both systems, including vows, practices and the Vedic texts they look back to and study. Sankhya and Yoga have always referred to themselves as Vedic in origin. There is no verse in their literature that anyone has ever pointed out wherein they claim a non-Vedic or pre-Vedic origin for their knowledge.

We possess one clear ancient text which discusses Sankhya, Yoga, and Vedanta. This is the *Bhagavad Gita* of Sri Krishna. He speaks of Sankhya, Yoga, and Vedanta as aspects of the same truth and in no place refutes one in favor of the others. The conclusion from this is fairly clear. Any conflict between Sankhya, Yoga, and Vedanta comes after the time of Krishna. This conflict was the product of a later philosophical age and is no measure of the origin of these systems, which the *Gita* finds to be integral parts of one tradition. Medieval India produced a method of philosophical debate wherein each system had to refute all the others. This was true not only of Hindu but of Buddhist systems. Buddhist systems also called each other 'heretical'. Should we thereby divide Buddhism up into ethnic groups such as Aryan and non-Aryan?

We must, therefore, discriminate between Yoga as a classical system of philosophy and Yoga as a practical system of spiritual growth. The two, though related, are not the same. Yoga predates the philosophical systems, including the *Yoga Sutras,* by a considerable period of time. The classical philosophy is a reformulation of an ancient tradition. Yoga is mentioned in Vedic texts before the time of the Buddha, who himself is known to have studied with two Sankhya teachers.

Yoga is mentioned in the *Bhagavad Gita,* the *Katha* and the *Shwetasavatara Upanishads.* Sankhya ideas like the five elements, the five sense organs, the five organs of action, and five Pranas are also found in a number of places in the *Upanishads*[b] and appear related to the numerical symbolism of the *Rig Veda,* which is often threefold and fivefold. Krishna in the *Gita,* among the sages, identifies himself with Kapila, the founder of the Sankhya system.[c] If later Yoga or Sankhya philosophy ceased to reflect adequately the truth of Vedanta, which the dualistic turn of their philosophy in medieval times suggests, this does not mean that originally they were not part of Vedanta. The split between the systems merely reflects the excessive focus on intellectual ideas by the philosophical mind in the dark age or Kali Yuga. In terms of the literature, therefore, Yoga and Sankhya have their basis in older Vedantic texts, which mention them frequently and are permeated with their language.

Let us trace the idea of Yoga in Vedic literature and see where and when it arises. The crucial text for understanding the origins of Yoga is the *Shwetasavatara Upanishad* (II) which is the most extensive classical Upanishadic text to present in detail the practice of Yoga.

> 1. Yoking first the mind, having extended the intelligence, discerning the light of the fire, the Divine Sun (Savitar) bore it forth from the Earth.
>
> 2. With a yogically controlled mind, in the energy of the Divine Sun (Savitar), may we have the power to enter the world of light.
>
> 3. By the mind and the intelligence yogically controlled, the Gods who seek the light move to heaven and create the vast light; may the Divine Sun (Savitar) give impulse to them.
>
> 4. Seers of the vast illumined seer yogically control their minds and their intelligence. One only, he ordains the invocation of the Gods. Great is the glory of the Divine Sun (Savitar).

5. I unite to your ancient Brahman by prayers of surrender. May this praise go forth by the path of the Sun. May all the sons of immortality who dwell in celestial regions hear it.

6. Where the fire (Agni) is enkindled, where the wind (Vayu) is controlled, where the Soma overflows, there the Mind is born.

7. By the impulse of the Divine Sun (Savitar) enjoy the ancient Brahman. Make your source there, then your virtue will not decline.

8. With the three places erect, having stabilized in balance the body, having placed the senses in the heart by the mind, by the boat of Brahman the knower should cross over all the channels that give fear.

9. Controlling the Pranas here, balanced in motion, when the Prana comes to rest at the source of the nose, one should breathe out. As horses difficult to control on a journey, the knower should control the mind without distraction.

10. In a level and pure place devoid of fire and insects, with the sound of water, controlling the mind, closing the eyes, residing in secrecy, one should practice Yoga.

11. Mist, smoke, a ray of light, fire and wind, glimmerings in space, lightning, sparks and moonlight, these are the preliminary signs that indicate Brahman in the practice of Yoga.

12. Earth, water, fire, air, and ether manifest their qualities in order in the action of Yoga. No disease, old age or death overcomes him with a body composed of the fire of Yoga.

Yoga comes from the Sanskrit root 'yuj' meaning to yoke, harness, employ, set to work, coordinate, organize, and harmonize. It is based on a more basic root 'yu' meaning to unite and to separate; hence the idea of coordination. Many words derive from this root 'yuj' both in the Vedic and later Sanskrit. This *Upanishad* gives us many verses relating to Yoga, with different verbal and noun forms of this root. No one doubts that the practice of Yoga is indicated here. But where do these verses and ideas come from? Does Yoga appear as a new invention, the intrusion of an outside factor in the tradition? If Yoga was not originally part of the *Vedas* this would be expected. Yet the language employed here is entirely Vedic, with the main Vedic Gods like Savitar, Agni, Vayu and Soma specifically referred to. They are given a yogic rather than a ritualistic meaning but one that is quite in harmony with their character, not forced upon them.

The first five verses of this chapter are not new at all but taken from a recension of the *Yajur Veda* (SYV XI.1-5), to which the *Upanishad* belongs. Verses four and five come from the *Rig Veda* itself (X.13.1 & V.81.1). In other words, Vedic scripture is quoted as a background for presenting the idea of Yoga.

The process of Yoga is not only related to Vedic verses but it is described in terms of Vedic deities. The God Vayu, the wind God, relates to Prana, the breath, and to the practice of Pranayama or breath-control. Agni, the fire God, relates to the fire of the Mind or mindfulness. Soma relates to Samadhi, the bliss of Yoga. These are not presented as a higher meaning for what were originally lesser nature Gods in the Vedic religion. They are presented as indicating their real status and purpose in the *Vedas*. In other words, in what is the earliest extensive rendering of Yoga in late Vedic literature, the system of Yoga is presented in an early Vedic language, as perhaps giving the key to the inner meaning of the Vedic Gods. The *Vedas* are thereby presented as textbooks of Yoga. The origins of Yoga here show its identity with the Vedic tradition.

It is not of any mere coincidence or minor connection that the practice of Yoga is related to the God Savitar or the Creative Sun. The Divine Sun, Savitar, is the deity of the Gayatri mantra, the most important and most commonly chanted of the Vedic mantras, which the twice-born are required to repeat daily at the rising and setting of the Sun. The great mantra Om is the basis for the Gayatri, which evolves from it as its more complete form. Here Savitar is shown as the deity of Yoga, the archetype of spiritual evolution in the human mind. This whole *Upanishad* section is a kind of extended Gayatri. In other words, the Gayatri itself or the main Vedic chant can be seen as a prayer to direct us along the path of Yoga. It can be translated as:

> We meditate upon the Divine Creative Sun (Savitar)
> that he may give inspiration to our intelligence (III.62.10).

The *Yajur Veda* also begins with the impulse of Savitar.

> Om, you for vigor, you for energy, you are breaths,
> may the God Savitar propel you to the most glorious action
> (SYV I.1).

The eleventh chapter, which the *Shwetasavatara* quotes, is specifically to Savitar and refers to the bringing forth of Agni, the fire from the

Earth and making a cauldron for the sacrifice. There is an esoteric or yogic ritual here as well. The fire is the spiritual intelligence brought forth from the earth of our material nature. Hence, the *Upanishad* uses these verses from the *Yajur Veda* to show the Vedic origin of Yoga and Yoga as the inner aspect of the Vedic ritual. Om is the Gayatri, is Savitar, is the *Veda* and the power of Yoga. The Vedic Gods guide and direct us on the path of Yoga. They aid in the integration of ourselves with the cosmos and with the Divine Being.

In the *Rig Veda* itself the actual term 'Yoga' is not common. As in later Sanskrit, the term cannot always be associated with spiritual practice when it does occur (it appears in both the *Vedas* and the *Gita* as yoga-kshema — work and rest — meaning the ordinary activities of life). Yet several verses, like the two quoted in this *Upanishad,* show its meaning as meditational practices. In addition, the broader idea of Yoga as 'yoking' is very common in the *Rig Veda,* as the chants are compared to animals or vehicles yoked to lead us to the Gods. Moreover, the concept of Yoga or integration is the essence of the Vedic work, though it occurs under different names. Hence, though the actual use of the term Yoga in a spiritual sense can be found only occasionally in the *Rig Veda,* the concept of Yoga, that of uniting the human nature with the Divine, of men becoming Gods or attaining immortality through the use of mystic chants and meditations, is the essence of the Vedic teaching.

The whole idea of Yoga as control of the mind is in evidence from the main verse of the *Rig Veda* on Yoga.

> Seers of the vast illumined seer yogically control their minds and their intelligence (RV V.81.1).[2]

While we may consider that this is an exceptional statement for the *Rig Veda* (though it is not), we cannot deny that at least the seed of the entire Yoga teaching is contained in this most ancient Aryan text.

The Vedic sacrifice and ritual, yajña, was inwardly the practice of Yoga. The outer fire sacrifice reflects an inner sacrifice of the ego to the flame of Divine Consciousness. The most basic form of Yoga is Mantra Yoga, the Yoga of sound or the Divine Word. The *Rig Veda* with its mystic mantras is full of that. We can see in the Vedic hymns to Agni, the God of fire, the path of the Yoga of Knowledge, Jñana Yoga. We can see in the Vedic hymns to Indra the path of Prana Yoga or the Yoga of the life-force. We can see in the hymns to Soma the path of Bhakti Yoga. I have examined these things in detail in my other books on the *Vedas* and *Upanishads.*

Vedic knowledge and Yogic knowledge are thus identical. Yoga gives more the practical side, Veda or Vedanta the theoretical. The Vedic tradition is the Yogic tradition and the Yogic tradition is originally the Vedic tradition. *Veda* is the knowledge or the theory and Yoga is the practice or application.

PRANAYAMA

Pranayama or the practice of breath-control is one of the most important and distinguishing methods for the practice of Yoga. The *Upanishads* are filled with references to Prana. Prana is identified with the supreme reality, Brahman, with the inner Self, the Atman, and with Indra, the king of the Gods. The five different types of Prana (Prana, Udana, Samana, Vyana and Apana) are mentioned showing the existence of a subtle science of life-force.[d]

The *Upanishads* state:

> The Self carries himself twofold, as the life-force (Prana) and as the Sun. Two are his paths within and without by which he revolves by day and by night. The Sun is the outer Self; the life-force is the inner Self. Hence by the movement of the outer Self, the movement of the inner Self is measured. But according to the Knower, who is free of sin, whose eye is turned within, it is by the movement of the inner Self that the movement of the outer Self is measured (MaiU VI.1).

The ancient seers used the movements of the Sun to understand the movement of the life-force in the body. This became the basis for the practice of Yoga. Yet according to their deeper vision, by meditating on the life-force within the body they also came to understand the movements of the Sun. In this way the science of the breath permeated the ancient solar religion.

Prana is also very commonly mentioned in the *Brahmanas,* the ritualistic texts. Breath is combined with the sacrifice or is a sacrifice in itself.

> Savitar is the breath (AB I.19).
>
> Soma is the breath (KB IX.6).
>
> The kindling sticks for the sacred fire are the breaths ... The Divine invokers are expiration and inspiration (AB II.4).
>
> The Upamshu and Antaryama cups are expiration and inspiration (AB II.21).
>
> The cups for the two deities are the breaths (AB II.26).

> The offerings to the seasons are the breaths (AB II.29).
>
> The Prauga is a litany of the breaths; seven deities he celebrates; seven are the breaths in the head; thus he places the breaths in the head (AB III.3).

The Gods, the chants and the rituals are identified with the breath or made diversifications of the breaths, which are thereby stabilized by them.

> "Forward" is the breath, for all these creatures advance following after the breath; thus he creates the breath, he makes the breath perfect (AB II.40).
>
> Therefore they say, "the breath is Vayu (God of the wind), seed is breath; seed comes into being first when man comes into existence." In that he recites a triplet to Vishnu, thus he makes his breath perfect. A triplet to Indra and Vayu he recites. Where there is expiration, there is inspiration; in that he recites a triplet to Indra and Vayu, thus his expiration and inspiration he makes perfect (AB III.2).

Through chants the Brahmins make their breath perfect. In yogic literature mantras are also used to aid in Pranayama. Is this not a continuation of an ancient Vedic practice?

> Verily does the Invoker establish speech and expiration and inspiration in the self, with a full life, for fullness of life; a full life he lives who knows this (AB III.8).

Here we see breathing practices giving longevity.

> Breath is immortality, thus by immortality he crosses death (KB XIV.2).
>
> Each quarter verse of these chants he recites, taking it separately; thus each breath he places in himself. With the last he utters the Pranava (Om); thus he lets go of this breath: therefore all the breaths breathe along this breath (KB XV.4).

We see from these quotes that the Vedic ritual, chant and breathing practices were combined together. Some sort of Pranayama practice was the inner side of the ritual. Krishna in the *Gita* describes the practices of various yogis.

> Some offer inspiration into expiration and others offer expiration into inspiration, controlling the path of inspiration and expiration, they practice Pranayama (BG IV.29).

This is not some novel practice but an old Upanishadic and Brahmanical method going back to the *Vedas.* The whole Vedic ritual thereby mirrors the practice of Yoga and the movement of the breath through the chakras.

Many passages relating to the breath or Prana can be found in the *Yajur Veda* also.

> May you purify my speech. May you purify my breath. May you purify my eye. May you purify my ear ... May your mind be abundant. May your speech be abundant. May your breath be abundant (SYV III.14-5).
>
> May your mind unite with the mind, your breath with the breath ... May the ruling Prana be placed in all your faculties. May the ruling Udana (upward moving breath) be placed in all your faculties (SYV III.18-9).

The Vedic sacrifice is inwardly a purification of our faculties, including our breath, for the realization of truth, for putting back together the cosmic man (Indra) who is our true Self.

The God of the breath or wind, Vayu or Vata, is an important God as early as the *Rig Veda* and is often identified with Indra, the king of the Gods.

> Vayu, this 'shukra' is offered to you, the foremost of honeys, in the heavenly sacrifices. Indra and Vayu, you should drink of this Soma (RV IV.47.1-2).

If we take 'shukra' here, as in the later Sanskrit sense of the reproductive fluids, we have the idea of offering the sexual energy to the God of the Breath, to aid in the transmutation of our nature, again suggesting the practice of Pranayama.

> As far as extends the self, as far as vigor, as far as men meditate with their eye, Indra and Vayu drink the Soma in us (VII.91.4).

It is clear from such passages that the Vedic ritual had a psychological (adhyatmic) application from the beginning. Indra's two horses (haris) which bring him to the sacrifice, may be inhalation and exhalation, as the

Vedic horse is the symbol of Prana or the breath. Vayu is the God of the awakened life-force or Prana. Indra is the God of the awakened Self or Divine being, Atman. To align our life-energy with the Divine being has always been the essence of the path of Yoga.

The importance of the God Indra in the *Rig Veda* reflects the centrality of the practice of Yoga, including Pranayama, to the Vedic Rishis. Yoga is described in the *Upanishads* as the control of the senses.

> The wise consider Yoga to be steady control of the senses (KU II.3.11).[3]

Why are the senses called 'indriyas', which literally means "powers of Indra," if the Vedic God has no inner or psychological meaning? Indra is the power which controls the senses, the clear or illumined mind. The deity or spiritual principle representing the steady control of the senses is Indra, who thereby is also the God of Yoga as defined in this *Upanishad.*

THE PRACTICE OF YOGA IN THE *RIG VEDA*

The *Rig Veda* is filled with numerical symbolisms. The most common is that of the number seven. There are seven seers and seven rivers. The Gods themselves are often seven or in groups of seven. Manu himself states,

> The seven Gods have seven spears and seven lights. They hold seven glories (VIII.28.5).

We can relate these seven Vedic principles in the practice of Yoga to the seven chakras of the subtle body.

A Vedic hymn of Ayasya Angirasa, one of the oldest and most famous of the seers, states:

> This intelligence, possessing seven heads, vast and born from truth, our father found. This certain fourth that generates all things Ayasya declared as the hymn to Indra. Declaring the truth, meditating straight, the sons of Heaven, the heroes of the almighty, the Angirasa seers, holding the station of sages, meditated out the original nature of the sacrifice (X.67.1-2).[4]

The original nature of the sacrifice is the practice of meditation through the seven chakras of the subtle body and the four states of consciousness

— waking, dream, deep sleep and the ever conscious (turiya state). The "certain fourth" is thus the unity of the three.

THE SYMBOLISM OF THE SUN

Most of the symbolism of the Sun, the seasons and the year can be related to the practice of Yoga.

> Seven yoke the chariot that has one wheel. One horse bears it who has seven names. It has three spokes and is undecaying, not to be overcome, in which all these worlds abide. This chariot in which the seven stand has seven wheels and seven horses carry it. Seven sisters sing together, where are hidden the seven names of the cow. Who has seen the one born first, the boneless one whom those with bones carry, the spirit, the blood, the Self (Atman) of the world? Who knows it that we can approach and ask (I.164.2-4)?[5]

This mystical hymn speaks of the seven chakras and shows the spiritual vision of the world as abiding within the mind. The revelation of the seven brings us back to the one, the Self.

> Soma has given the dawns good husbands. He placed the light within the Sun. He found the threefold nature in the luminous regions of Heaven, the immortality that was hidden in the third. He upheld Heaven and Earth. He yoked the chariot that has seven rays (VI.44.22-3).

The chariot with seven rays, the chariot of Soma and the Gods, is the subtle body and its seven centers. The higher threefold nature is Being-Consciousness-Bliss, Sacchidananda, as it is called in later literature. In fact the Vedic chariot or ritual vehicle is inwardly the practice of Yoga.

> Six burdens, one unmoving bears (III.56.2).

The six are the lower six chakras. The seventh is the one in which there is freedom and immortality.

> Of those born together, the seventh, they say, is born alone. The six are twins, the Rishis born of the Gods (I.164.15).

Of the seven Rishis, six are dual. These are the six lower chakras which have a dualistic function. Unity and immortality is only in the seventh, the crown chakra. From this idea of the six chakras as dual and the seventh as single, we also have the six double months or seasons of the year and the odd seventh (or thirteenth) intercalary month. Here again we see the correspondence between the movement of the Sun in the heavens and the breath in the subtle body that the *Upanishads* speak of. This is not a new idea but the original Vedic vision.

We read that there are seven directions each with its own Sun:

> The seven directions have their different Suns. They have seven invokers according to the seasons. The Sun Gods are seven. With them, oh Soma protect us (IX.114.3).

On an inner level these seven directions relate to the subtle body and are the seven chakras, each of which has its own light. Soma is the current of bliss that flows through all of them, bringing them into full manifestation.

The twofold day and night or the two paths of the Gods and the Fathers represent the movement of the Prana or life-force up and down the spine. This imitates the movement of the Sun from the solstices. The base of the spine marks the winter solstice. The top of the head is the summer solstice. The equinoxes mark the midpoints of this journey. This is the movement of the sacrifice. *While the ritualists follow this practice outwardly with the Sun, the yogis follow it inwardly with the breath.*

The Sun Goddess who mounts the chariot and follows the path is the power of the chant, the prayer or the aspiration with which we practice. She moves along this same solar path up the spine to the Divine consciousness in the crown chakra.

The cyclical movement of the Divine days is also the movement of the soul from life to life. The daily and yearly return of the Sun reflects the return of the soul to a new life. Hence Vedic symbolism is imbued with the knowledge of karma and reincarnation. Such experiences were not expressed philosophically but are evident from the solar symbolism. The return of the Dawn after long periods of time is often the return of aspiration to the soul after a previous life. The resurrection of the Sun out of darkness is the resurrection of the soul out of the body, of the consciousness of the Self out of its attachment to the material world.

INDRA, AGNI, SOMA AND YOGA

The three main Vedic Gods of Indra, Agni and Soma — all have profound correspondences with the practice of Yoga. Indra destroys Ahi or Vritra, the serpent or dragon, who lies at the foot of the mountain and holds captive the waters of the seven rivers. The serpent is the Kundalini, the serpent fire that lies coiled at the base of the spine, the world mountain. It holds the waters of the seven chakras, the currents of Divine energy. Indra is the power of Yoga, Pranayama, and the control of the senses which gains mastery over the serpent force.

Indra pierces three times seven mountain ranges.

> For him the dawns extended their course, for Indra the stars at night were sweet in speech. For him the mother floods, the seven rivers stood still, easy to pass for men to cross. The wielder of the thunderbolt, though agitated, pierced the three times seven gathered ridges of the mountains. No God nor mortal could do what the bull, exalted, accomplished (VIII.96.1-2).

These are miraculous events. The dawns extend their course or the dawns become longer. The stars at night yield better light. The seven rivers are brought to a standstill for men to cross. With his thunderbolt Indra pierces three times seven ridges of the mountains.

We could look for a naturalistic interpretation to this. Yet a spiritual or yogic interpretation is quite relevant and sensible. The seven rivers are the life-streams of the seven chakras. They must be stilled for men to cross over from the darkness to the light, from the ignorance to the knowledge, from death to immortality. The Prana is guided by its awakened intelligence as Indra pierces the seven spinal centers, the ridges of the inner or world mountain. Each chakra has three currents that move through it, corresponding to the solar, lunar and central channels.

In another Vedic symbolism, Indra releases his chariot in the middle of the heavens and thereby defeats the Dasyus (X.138.3). This is a symbol for the state of Samadhi wherein the breath or life-force (Prana), the inner Sun, is released from the body. The Sun that is released out of darkness in the Vedic myth is the essence of Prana or the Soul (Atman) freed from the bondage to karma and embodied existence into the eternal day of pure consciousness.

> Agni and Indra pour from heaven a sea with seven foundations, whose opening is above (VIII.40.5).[6]

This is the sevenfold ocean of consciousness and a profound metaphor, not primitive imagination.

Agni, the sacred fire, symbolizes the fire of the mind, the flame of aspiration and intention, the practice of mindfulness and wakefulness.

> Who remains awake, him the chants love, who remains awake to him the mystic song comes, who remains awake to him the Soma speaks and says, "I have my home in your friendship." The fire remains awake, him the chants love. The fire remains awake, to him the mystic song comes. The fire remains awake, to him the Soma speaks and says, "I have my home in your friendship" (V.44.15).

Soma is inwardly the nectar of immortality, the ambrosia of bliss or ananda which flows from the head chakra and the enlightened mind.

> Three times seven milch cows have yielded for him the milk of truth in the original ether. Four other lovely realms of being for his raiment he made, when by the truths he grew (IX.70.1).[7]

Here again we have the seven chakras and their threefold current. The four realms of being are perhaps again the four states of waking, dream, deep sleep, and the ever conscious turiya state of later yogic and Vedantic philosophy.

> The ten maidens purify you when you are pressed, Soma, as you are held by the thoughts and insights of the seers. Through the atomic points and the invocations purified, held by men, reveal to us the energy for the realization (IX.68.7).

Soma is purified by the ten maidens, whom I believe stand for the five sense organs and five organs of action in their purified state. He travels through the purification filter or the fleece, which stands for the point of pure awareness.

> The guardian of truth, of good will, is not to be deceived. He has placed three purification filters within the heart. The knower, he sees all the worlds. Those who are unwelcome, who do not follow the observances, he throws into the pit (IX.73.8).[7]

The purification is of our own hearts and minds through the three states of waking, dream, and deep sleep.

The Vedic purification rituals reflected the processes of purifying the mind.

> With three purification filters he purified the Sun, foreknowing by the heart, the light according to the thought. He held the supreme ecstasy by the powers of the Self-nature, then he saw all around Heaven and Earth (III.26.8).[8]

It is the Sun of awareness that is to be purified; by that we are able to see all the worlds and find the entire universe dwelling within us.

The Vedic Gods thus symbolize the practice of Yoga. Agni is the Kundalini, the flame at the base of the spine. Soma is the immortal nectar or Ananda in the head. Surya as the Sun is the consciousness of the Self (Atman) in the heart. Indra is the awakened life-force or perceiver who facilitates the practice.

THE SARASWATI AND THE SPINAL CURRENT

The Saraswati is not only a real river that has been mythologized, it also has an inner meaning. The Saraswati, like the later Ganges, symbolizes the Sushumna, the river of spiritual knowledge, the current that flows through the seven chakras of the subtle body. She is not only the Milky Way or river of Heaven, inwardly she is the river of truth consciousness that flows into this world. Many religions have such a sacred river in their symbolism like the Jordan or Ganges.

The left, the western or lunar current (Ida nadi) in the *Rig Veda* is represented by the Parushni. The right, the eastern or solar current (Pingala nadi)is the Yamuna. Between these rivers is the central domain of the Aryans. Sometimes in the *Vedas* the right current is called the Bharati and the left the Ila.

The cosmic symbolism of the Saraswati refers to her higher status in this way. The Vedic or knowledge ritual should be done on the banks of the river of knowledge, the stream of consciousness, that is along the current of the awakened chakras.

> Whose infinite, unencompassed, brilliant and mobile flood impetuously continues to roar. Bearing truth, may she take us beyond all opposition, beyond her other sisters and extend the days like the Sun. Who has filled the earthly realms and the broad atmospheric region, Saraswati should be adored. Who has three stations and seven levels, who increases the five births of men, in all encounters she should be worshipped (VI.61.8, 9, 11, 12).

The seven levels of the Saraswati are the seven planes of consciousness. On each level she is threefold as the positive, negative and neutral current, or the solar, lunar and balanced ones. The five births of men she nourishes are the five senses.

THE SYMBOLISM OF THE KINGS

The good king Sudas represents the awakened intelligence (buddhi) that dwells on the Saraswati, the river of truth or Sushumna, the central nadi of the subtle body. The ten kings he has to fight are the five sense organs and the five organs of action. The former have a solar nature and dwell on the Yamuna. The latter have a lunar nature and dwell on the Parushni. They try to invade or control the domain of truth, the Saraswati region. The seven cities of the Aryans he conquers are the seven centers of the subtle body, the seven chakras.

Similarly, all the Vedic kings represent stages of spiritual transformation. Divodasa who throws Shambara down off the mountain is the awakened mind that throws the ego down off the mountain of the spine.

YOGA POSTURES

It is difficult to know when the postures of Yoga originated. The older Vedic texts are scriptural and ritualistic, not manuals of philosophy or practice. Their language is symbolic and mystical, not rational or descriptive. If Yoga postures were known to them, we could not expect them to be specifically described in the texts.

The practice of 'Namaskara', putting the palms together in the gesture of prayer, is commonly mentioned in the *Rig Veda.* In one hymn (VII.103) the Brahmins in their observances are likened to frogs. Is this perhaps owing to their sitting in the lotus posture? Most Yoga postures were originally named after different animals. Perhaps also some of the Vedic sacred animals also referred to such postures or practices. Hence while we cannot be sure that the same Yoga postures were used in Vedic times as today, we can be certain that the main elements of Yoga — meditation, mantra, and Pranayama — were well known.

GODS AND SAGES

Vedic Gods are sometimes spoken of in human forms or as having been ancient sacrificers. These include the Maruts and the Adityas. The Angirasas, a Vedic family of seers, are equated with Gods like the Adityas in the *Brahmanas.* The Ribhus, a group of three Gods in the *Rig Veda,* are said to have been mortals and to have attained immortality.

> By the power and skill of their work, the sages (Ribhus) who were mortal attained immortality (I.110.4).

Other Vedic Gods like the Ashwins take a human form or incarnation to aid their devotees.

Brihaspati, though a God, is also the oldest and the original of the seers and, as we have already noted, is identified with the planet Jupiter. Shukra, another seer, is similarly identified with the planet Venus. Manu, the original man, has both a kind of historical status and the status of a God, as does Yama, the God of death, who is sometimes seen as his twin. Even Indra is sometimes spoken of as if he were a man. The great king Trasadasyu is said to have been generated by the seven seers as "a demigod like Indra" (IV.42.8).

It appears, therefore, that the Vedic Gods can represent various human teachers mythologized. The Vedic Gods indicate various teachings or spiritual transmissions passed on through the various seer families. The seers become Gods and the Gods work through them. Dirghatamas appears to refer to himself (his higher Self) as Agni in one of his hymns to the God.

> Him they question, not all profoundly question, what by his own mind the sage has grasped (I.145.2).

Indeed to become a Vedic teacher, one has to be sacrificed to the Gods and let the Gods speak through oneself. It is Agni, the sacred fire, who is the real teacher.

Hidden in the symbolism of the Gods, therefore, is the knowledge and power of the seers. The powers of various Gods like the Maruts to travel all over the world, or of the Ashwins to heal the sick or raise the dead, may symbolize the powers of the seers. In instances of seers becoming Gods we see the origin of later ideas like that of the avatar or Divine incarnation.

Some of the powers of the seers can be explained by the magic of Soma. The Ayurvedic doctor Sushrut says of those who drink the Soma:

> The use of the Soma, the lord of all medicinal herbs, is followed by rejuvenation of the system of its user and enables him to witness ten thousand summers on earth in the full enjoyment of a new youthful body. Such a person bears a charmed life against fire, water, poison and weapons and develops a muscular energy in his limbs which would be in no way inferior to the combined strength of a

> thousand excited elephants. Equipped with such excellent physique, he can easily and without any opposition cross the ocean and go up to the abode of the king of the Gods and roam to the extreme confines of Uttara Kuru (the far north) or any other place he likes.[e]

Vishwamitra states in the *Rig Veda,*

> The Angirasa seers, the sons of Heaven, the heroes of the almighty, are beneficent. Bestowing gifts to Vishwamitra, through a thousand Soma pressings they extend his life (III.53.7).

This suggests some longevity for the seer, literally a thousand years. The Vedic seers were yogis with great occult and spiritual powers.

VEDIC SEERS IN OTHER RELIGIONS

We have traces of the Vedic seers in ancient European religions also. Greek 'Angelos', Latin 'Angelicus' and English 'Angel' are our equivalents of Sanskrit 'Angiras', the name of the oldest family of Vedic seers. Like the angels, the Angirasa seers symbolize the lights of the seven chakras or subtle centers of the astral body. They are born from the fire or Agni. It is said of them:

> Who anointed with discrimination and sacrifice, in communion with the Lord (Indra), have attained immortality; Who were born from Agni, from Heaven in manifold forms, Navagwa and Dashagwa, the best Angirasas, together among the Gods grow great (X.62.1, 6).

Archangel is Sanskrit Arhat Angiras, noble Angiras. The Buddhists also called their ancient sages the Arhats, a Vedic word meaning noble, often applied to Agni. The Christian word evangel derives from Greek eu-angelos, Sanskrit su-angiras. It means good message or the good tidings of the seers.

Christ is Greek Christos, the anointed one, cognate with Sanskrit ghrita, clarified butter or ghee, the symbol of the clear light. Agni, the Vedic fire, resides in an ocean of ghee (II.3.11; IV.58.1). One anointed with the ghee is one prepared for the sacrifice, the highest sacrifice being the Self-sacrifice, Atma-yajña wherein the ego is offered to the Divine, represented in Christianity by the crucifixion. Christ thus demonstrates the knowledge and the action of the Angirasa Rishis.

Eucharist, the Christian Greek for the holy sacrament, comes from eu-kharistos, Sanskrit su-haritas. Hari is also the name for Vishnu, of whom the avatars are said to be descendants. When Christ says at the last communion that "this is my body,"[f] the Greek term for body is Soma, the Vedic name for the God of the immortal wine and nectar. The last communion is the Christian Soma sacrifice. Even the medieval search for the Holy Grail reflects the search for the ancient Soma chalice, the vessel in which the immortal Soma was held and from which it could be drunk.

The name Flamen for the priests of the ancient Roman religion is cognate with Sanskrit Brahmin.[g] Druid, the name for the Keltic priests and magicians, can be traced to Vedic Dru-vid, knower of the wood.[h] Our English word elf, originally from the Keltic, appears cognate with Vedic Ribhu (l becoming r and bh becoming f), the artisans of the Gods and an important group of seers.[i] Eire for Irish and Ireland is traceable to Vedic Aryan, the name of the Vedic people and of the Persians (Aryan = Iran). English man and German mensh can be traced to Vedic Manu, the Vedic name of the first man.[j]

Buddha himself not only proclaims his religion the Arya Dharma or law of the Aryans, he is also a king or prince in the ancient solar dynasty of east India. He is called Gautama, as he is a descendant of Gotama, one of the seven Vedic seers. The name of Zoroaster, the founder of the ancient Persian religion, is traceable to Sanskrit Hari-dyut-astra, the beautiful light of the star. Hari as a name of Vishnu suggests that Zoroaster was also a form or aspect of Vishnu, like Krishna and Christ.

HINDU GODS AND THE *RIG VEDA*

The great Gods of later Hinduism are Shiva and Vishnu. Both are mentioned in the *Rig Veda*, Shiva as Rudra, and have a few hymns to them and many references. Yet they are not as commonly lauded as the main Vedic Gods Indra, Agni and Soma. They become more important in later Vedic literature, including the *Yajur Veda, Atharva Veda, Brahmanas,* and *Upanishads* and do not become predominant until the *Puranas,* where the Vedic Gods in turn fall into the background or are treated as cosmic principles, like Agni as the element of fire. This has caused some people to consider that Rudra-Shiva and Vishnu were not originally Vedic Gods — that they were Gods of the indigenous people of India and adopted by the invading Aryans. Again this idea does not come from the people of India or from any historical or literary records.

It is not possible to judge the importance of Vedic Gods merely by the number of references to them. This is a superficial approach that can breed much confusion. The ancient mystery religions have much that is hidden or unspoken. We must also judge the Gods by the functions they fulfill. In this regard, Rudra is the most important father figure in the *Rig Veda.* He is the great father of all the Gods. All the Gods can be called Rudras. Most specifically the Vedic storm Gods, the Maruts, are called Rudras and Rudra is their father.

> The Maruts are the sons of the compassionate Rudra (VI.66.3).

Indra, the king of the Gods, is the leader of the Maruts. Rudra is also another name for Agni (IV.3.1), the second of the great Vedic Gods.

INDRA AND SHIVA

We cannot judge a God merely by his name either. Vedic Indra is referred to in the hymns much like later Shiva. He is the king and ruler (raja, ishana). He is in fact called Shiva (II.20.3, VI.45.17, VIII.93.3, VIII.96.10). He is also called Ghora and Ugra, meaning terrible and fierce (also later used as names of Shiva) more than a hundred times in the *Rig Veda.*[k] He has such descriptions like Shiva as the dispeller of fear, as sat or satya (truth or reality), and as the lord of Maya. Most specifically, like Shiva he is the dancer (VIII.24.9, 12). Like Shiva, his wife or consort is called power, Shachi. His mother is also called power, Shavasi.

Some have claimed that Rudra-Shiva is not a Vedic God because he is often presented as an outcast. Yet it is Indra, the foremost of the Vedic Gods, who is also regarded as an outcast. He does things that appear to violate the cosmic order. All the Gods abandon Indra and he has to face the dragon alone. His mother regards him as a curse and hides him (IV.18.5). He slays his own father (IV.18.12). His consort he finds in degradation and has to eat of a dog's intestine before he can get the Soma (IV.18.13). He causes an eclipse of the Sun (V.33.4). He destroys the chariot of the Dawn (IV.30.9-10). He likes war and does not flee from sin (V.34.4). Like Shiva, he is beyond good and evil and destroys demons and enemies. Indra not only defeats the demons, sometimes he even has to defeat the Gods.

> All the Gods could not conquer you, oh Indra, when you crossed over the days by the night (IV.30.3).[9]

Indra also befriends the weak and oppressed, the blind, the lame and the outcast.

> Indra you lifted up the outcast who was oppressed, you glorified the blind and the lame (II.13.12).[10]

Part of the attempt to claim Shiva as non-Aryan is said to be the Puranic story of his destruction of the sacrifice of Daksha, thereby giving him the appearance of being an enemy of the sacrifice. Daksha refuses to worship Shiva because he is Vedabahya, "outside the *Vedas*."[l] This statement has been interpreted as a non-Vedic origin for Shiva worship. Yet Daksha's daughter, who is also Shiva's wife 'Sati', claims that Shiva is the sacrifice itself, the Yajña,[m] the *Veda* itself, which all the Gods recognize once more after the destruction of Daksha's sacrifice.

This story of Shiva is just another account of Indra's stealing of the Soma from Twashtar (III.48.4), his killing or laying low of his father (Twashtar), or Indra as Trita killing the son of Twashtar (X.8.7-9). The son of Twashtar with three heads and sevens rays is also another symbolism for the seven chakras and three bodies or states of consciousness of waking, dream and deep sleep. He also symbolizes the sacrifice. Daksha is another form of the demiurge or Prajapati, as is Twashtar. Indra disregards or destroys Twashtar, as he represents the Self who transcends the cosmic process.

Shiva's destruction of Daksha's sacrifice is also just another form of the Vedic story of Rudra's slaying of Prajapati (AB III.33). As the God of time or creation which is the sacrifice, Prajapati or Twashtar must himself be killed. This is the job of the highest Vedic Gods Indra and Rudra. The sacrifice itself must be sacrificed or destroyed.

> The Gods with the sacrifice, sacrificed the sacrifice.
> These were the first laws (I.164.50).[11]

The sacrifice is merely a symbol for the negation of all things into the Divine. The sacrifice has to be negated in order for it to be fulfilled. The sacrifice is the cosmic process or time that must be transcended for the understanding of the eternal.

Twashtar is the outer God of form, like Daksha, while Indra like Shiva represents the inner God of spiritual knowledge. Both stories reflect a conflict between the outer and the inner, the ritualistic and spiritual parts of the tradition. They show a religious tradition that values the spirit over the form. They do not show a conflict between different traditions. Indra and Shiva represent the sage who is above the outer laws, including those of caste and stage of life.

If we interpret such references to Indra's negative nature like those of Shiva, we could just as well claim that Indra was a non-Aryan deity as well. Yet this would leave us without the main God of the Aryans. In fact, in the *Vedas* the Aryan people themselves are often portrayed as outcasts, minorities, as oppressed, in a world filled with hostile people who would destroy them ("full of manifold evils are the people of men," III.18.1). Thus the myth of the outcast, whether Indra or Shiva, is the myth of the Aryan, the man who goes against the outer social and world order and appearance to affirm the truth of the Spirit. The Vedic seers were not orthodox priests of a petrified social order but daring innovators, creative spirits who established a new culture. Indra, like Shiva, represents the spirit or Self in man. This is the part of our nature that transcends the worlds and all the laws which govern it, even those laws of the subtle world or realms of the Gods. It is only the manifestation of this transcendent side of our nature that results in liberation. Indra-Shiva as the main God of the Aryans shows the spiritual orientation of the Vedic religion, its truth of monism and Self-realization, rather than a monotheistic or polytheistic religion in which the individual and the Divine are regarded as separate.

The Maruts, the sons of Rudra, are not just Gods; they are also seers.

> Who have spotted horses, whose mother is Prishni, who move in beauty, the Maruts who frequent the sessions of knowledge, men with eyes of the Sun, may all the Gods come here with their grace (I.89.7).

The Maruts are Vedic sages. They are like the yogis, sannyasis and ascetics of later times who wander freely pursuing spiritual knowledge. The Maruts move freely over Heaven and Earth and among all the peoples of men. They are said to be "like the wild silent sage" (VII.56.8);[12] "young seers who have the knowledge of truth" (V.58.8).[13]

Shiva as the God of the yogis and the wandering monks thus occurs in the *Rig Veda* as Rudra the father of the Maruts. Indra as the eldest of the Maruts is the son of Shiva. The Vedic Gods are forms of the Divine Son and in this regard are sons of the Divine Father, Rudra-Shiva. Skanda, the son of Shiva in later times, is well known to be identified with Agni; to be Mars or the God of fire, born from the semen of Shiva carried by Agni. The Divine Child is Agni-Skanda (i.e. RV V.2.1). Yet the father of all these Divine Sons — Indra, Agni, Soma and Surya — is Rudra-Shiva. In seeing the sons, we should not forget the importance of their father in the background. Just as the stories of Skanda do not serve to make Shiva unimportant, so do the hymns to the Vedic Gods not denigrate their father.

VISHNU

Vishnu appears in the *Rig Veda* as a form of the Sun God. He absorbs all the Sun Gods into himself as Surya-Narayana. Hence all the hymns to the different forms of the Sun God relate to Vishnu, particularly those to

Savitar, who of the other Vedic Gods most resembles him. Vishnu also appears as the leader of the Maruts, Evayamarut (VI.87), and the companion of Indra. Again it is not simply by how often his name appears that we should judge the deity. Vishnu as the pervader absorbs all the Gods into himself. Vishnu as the deity encompassing all the numerous Vedic Sun Gods thereby has much importance in the *Rig Veda* itself.

THE GODDESSES

As Goddesses are not overtly mentioned in many Vedic hymns, the Vedic religion has been regarded by most modern scholars as male oriented. Yet we should note that the Vedic Gods are more commonly powers of nature, like Fire and the Sun, than any human forms. Their animal forms, like the cow and the horse, are more common than their human forms. Moreover, the *Vedas* are filled with many female terms and Goddesses are mentioned everywhere. The *Veda* itself as speech (Vak) is lauded as a Goddess and the Mother from the earliest period. Hence to judge the *Veda* superficially by the names of the deities to whom the hymns are given may be incorrect. As the hymn or word which invokes the Gods is itself the Goddess, She is everywhere in the *Vedas* and without her nothing is possible. Hence, the worship of the Goddess is important in the *Vedas* as it has been throughout the Hindu tradition.

Today it is in the worship of the Goddesses in India that the forms of the Vedic religion most survive. The Vedic ideas of the spiritual life as a sacrifice, a battle and a chant, are most found in Goddess worship. The Goddess as Durga is the main demon slayer in the war between the Devas and Asuras. The mantra is most associated with the Goddess, whose garland consists of the syllables of the Sanskrit language. In the later *Upanishads* addressed to different deities, Vedic verses and mantras appear most commonly in those to the Goddess (like the *Vanadurga Upanishad*). Hence in the later traditions of Hinduism the worship of the Goddess is closely associated with Vedic mantras.

THE DEITIES AS PERSONIFICATIONS OF THE SACRIFICE

Hindu Goddesses arise out of Vedic symbolism. The great Goddess Kali first arises in the *Upanishads* (MuU II.4) as the name of the first tongue or flame of the sacred fire, Agni. While these tongues are mentioned in the *Rig Veda,* and have a feminine nature, their names are not given. Kali represents the darkness of Agni, the ashes and embers he produces. She is the dark blue flame in which is the greatest heat. She is also traditionally lauded as Swaha and Swadha (DM I.73), the two main chants of offering to Agni. She is the mantra which conveys the offerings into the fire. She is clearly a personification of the feminine aspect of the fire sacrifice. Her sacrificial nature is evident by the garland of skulls she wears and the cut-off head she holds. She represents the highest Vedic sacrifice, the Self-sacrifice or Atma-yajña, wherein the ego is offered to the Divine. The worship of Kali therefore is essentially the worship of the sacrifice, emphasizing its feminine side. It is nowhere more prevalent than in the *Vedas.*

The great God Shiva, similarly, is related to the bhasma or ashes of the sacred fire. Whereas Kali represents the tongue of the fire that consumes the offering or the sacrificial victim, Shiva is the residue, the purified essence that comes forth through the sacrifice.[n] The worship of both Shiva and his consort is permeated with the symbols of the Vedic sacrifice and is intimately related from its very beginning with the worship of the sacred fire, which the great Shaivite yogis strictly observe.

Shiva is also a Himalayan God. He is the God of the land of the Rishis. His home is Kailas and the Manasarovar lake, which is also the origin of the Vedic Saraswati river. He is also prominent in Kashmir, the land of the little Manasa lake where the Somas grow that are named after the Vedic meters. The worship of Shiva comes from the homeland of the *Vedas.* The Sanskrit language, the Vedic language, is said to have been created by the sounds issuing forth from Shiva's drum.

That Shiva and his consort are unaryan Gods is thus incorrect, as they are everywhere the deities which most personify the Vedic sacrifice itself, particularly in its inner meaning. It is not only the fire sacrifice that we see in them, it is also the Soma sacrifice. Shiva is the greatest drinker of the Soma, which is the crescent Moon he wears upon his head. He is the God of ecstasy, intoxication and abandonment. The Shaivite and Vedantic values of austerity, tapas, renunciation and purity are also nothing but the same Vedic values of the sacrifice, specifically in its internal or adhyatmic nature. That Shiva or Kali are not prominent names in the *Rig Veda* does not matter. They symbolize or summarize its teaching. They contain within themselves the whole Vedic teaching.

Vishnu is also a deity who symbolizes the sacrifice. It is well known in the *Bhagavad Gita* that Yajña, sacrifice, is Vishnu. Vishnu is the light of the sacrifice. His consort Lakshmi is originally worshipped through the sacred fire.[o] She is the abundance that comes forth through it, the prosperity that arises when our offerings bring the flow of Divine Grace.

VEDA AND TANTRA

There has also been the tendency of scholars to divide the ritualistic Tantric tradition from the philosophic Vedantic tradition and to make the former pre-Aryan and the latter Aryan. Yet the chief features of Tantra are also that of the *Veda,* which is highly ritualistic. These include the importance of mantra, myth, the fire-sacrifice and the worship of terrible forms of the Divine. All Tantric mantras are based on Sanskrit and many derive from Vedic verses. For example. the great mantra 'Hum', used in both Hinduism and Buddhism, is the bija mantra or seed syllable for Agni. Agni is called Hotar, from this root, meaning "the invoker." The Vedic Gods are usually invoked with verbal forms of the root 'hu'.

Tantric rituals use fire and are patterned after Vedic fire rituals. Tantric deities with their power and sometimes violence are much like the Vedic. In fact, more of the outer side of the Vedic religion can be found in Tantra than in the philosophical texts. The Vedic horse sacrifice resembles some strange Tantric ritual more than Vedantic philosophy, though if we look deeply, we see its connection with the latter as well. In fact, the oldest and longest *Upanishad,* the *Brihadaranyaka,* begins with the Tantric-like image of the horse sacrifice, not with a philosophical dialogue.

In Tantric philosophy, Vedic Gods like Agni, Soma, and Surya appear as powers of Yoga and are related to different chakras of the subtle body, as we have noted. Kashmir Shaivism, the most exalted of Tantric philosophies wherein perhaps the mantra achieved its greatest power and articulation, came from a famous homeland of the Vedic chants.

THE UNIVERSAL FIRE RITUAL

All the Gods of the ancient world relate to the fire sacrifice, as this was the most universal custom of the ancient peoples. We find the fire sacrifice everywhere — among the Greeks and Romans, the Kelts and Germans, the Persians, the Israelites, Babylonian, Egyptians, Chinese, and American Indians. All ancient religions used the fire offering and their Gods reflect its cosmic meaning. Fire is the most natural symbol of the Spirit hidden in matter and so fire offerings provide our most natural way of communication with the Gods or inner realities. All ancient or traditional cultures have their sacred fires. In this respect, all ancient cultures were Aryan as the Aryan religion is that of the sacred fire.

The fire ritual is part the solar religion or religion of light we find all over the ancient world. The fire on Earth represents the Sun in Heaven, as the immanent presence of the transcendent Divine.

OM AND THE *RIG VEDA*

We are told by some modern scholars of the *Vedas* that the sacred syllable 'Om' was not known or used in the time of the *Rig Veda* because it is not found anywhere in it. We are told it only became important at the later time of the *Brahmanas* and *Upanishads,* wherein it first appears in the literature. This is typical of an approach to the *Veda* that only recognizes what is evident or superficial. Yet the *Veda* is a mystic text and was not intended to give every aspect of the knowledge of the seers in an evident form. While we do not find Om mentioned specifically in the *Rig Veda,* there is throughout the book an emphasis on the sacred word or chant, the mantra as the power whereby the Gods are revealed. This sacred word could very well have been Om. Let us see how later texts indicate that it was.

The *Upanishads* state,

> Who is the bull of the chants, possessing all forms, who from the immortal chants was born, may that Indra deliver me with wisdom (TU I.3.1).

The "bull of the chants" is Om. It is identified with Indra, the foremost of the Vedic Gods. Indra in the *Rig Veda* conquers the power of darkness with the Divine Word or Brahman. Om is also called Brahman.

A famous verse of Vamadeva from the *Rig Veda* describes the bull of the chants as:

> Four are his horns, three are his feet, two are his heads and seven are his hands. Bound threefold the bull roars, the mighty God has entered into mortals (IV.58.2 and MnU IX.1).

This is said by the various commentators like Sayana to be an explication of Om.

Om in the *Upanishads* is said to have four quarters, referring to the four states of waking, dream, deep sleep, and pure consciousness. The various mathematical versions of the chant and the sacrifice in the *Rig Veda* are the various levels of vibration of Om. The seven seers are the seven energies of Om. Indra is the power of Om. The Sun is the light of Om. The *Sama Veda* is the song of the Sun or equality which is Om. Om is the prime mantra of the *Vedas* from the beginning, middle and end. Through it the essence of Vedic knowledge can be gained. Om is the Vedic Brahman or Divine Word that is the Upanishadic Brahman or cosmic reality. Through Om the Soma bliss of immortality flows.

According to the *Upanishads* (CU I.4.1) the Sun chants Om. The prime legend of the *Rig Veda* is the resurrection of the Sun out of darkness by the seers and the Gods in unison. It occurs by the power of the fourth Brahman.

> By the fourth Brahman, the sage Atri found the secret Sun that was hidden by darkness (V.40.6).[15]

This Sun is Om and its fourth quarter in which the Divine is delivered out of darkness is its fourth state, the state of pure consciousness transcending the three lower states of waking, dream and deep sleep. The Sun that the Vedic seers make rise in heaven is the Sun of Truth, the Divine syllable Om.

Dirghatamas states in the *Rig Veda,*

> The sacred syllable of the chant in the supreme ether in which all the Gods reside, he who does not know that, what can he do with the *Veda?* (I.164.39).

That sacred syllable on which the *Vedas* rest is Om.

Other names of Om occur in the *Rig Veda.* Om in the *Upanishads* is also called 'udgitha'. It is composed of the root 'ga' meaning "to move" or "to sing," to which the preface 'ut', meaning "up" has been added. Hence it means the higher singing or upward movement, the highest point of the chant. This term occurs first in the *Rig Veda* in a verse which states,

> Brihaspati roared forth the light and he gave the prior affirmation and as the knower he moved upwards (X.67.3).[16]

This comes from a hymn of Ayasya Angirasa. Both this seer and Brihaspati are associated in the *Upanishads* (CU I.2.10-11) with Om and Udgitha. Hence the *Upanishads* refer to the *Rig Veda* as the basis of Om.

The same Vedic hymn states,

> This thought, possessing seven heads, vast and born from truth, our father found. This certain fourth that generates all things Ayasya declared as the hymn to Indra. Declaring the truth, meditating straight, the sons of Heaven, the heroes of the almighty, the Angirasa seers, holding the station of sages, meditated out the original nature of the sacrifice (X.67.1-2).

This thought which measures out the sacrifice is obviously Om. The central Vedic chant is the Gayatri mantra to the Sun God as Savitar, the Divine power of aspiration. This chant comes from three Vedic verses. Around it is formed the chants to the worlds with the chant Om as the basis (Om Bhur Bhuvar Suvar Om). It probably occurs even in the *Rig Veda* behind this chant as its seed syllable.

If Om is the central mantra of the *Vedas* from the beginning, why is it not mentioned in the earlier literature? For one thing, no seed syllables or bija mantras occur in the Vedic hymns. They are, however, quite in evidence from the nature of Vedic words which remain closely related to their original roots. Such a seed language was the basis of the Vedic language and is implicit in its form. Certainly a language which everywhere espouses the mantra and looks back to prime roots had its seed syllables also. These were part of the background of the hymns.

THE USE OF IMAGES IN THE *RIG VEDA*

We read by some accounts that images were not used in the Vedic era. The rituals, they note, mainly involved fire, sometimes water, and the symbolism was more naturalistic than anthropomorphic. Some scholars consider that the culture was probably too crude artistically to produce images anyway. They emphasize that Vedic customs were similar to the Zoroastrian, which was strongly aniconic. Yet while images and idols may not appear as obvious in the *Rig Veda* as in later Hinduism and Buddhism, we do have evidence of them.

Vedic language is poetic and highly imagistic. While anthropomorphic symbolism is not dominant, it is still common and Vedic Gods have a human aspect. They are often described in human form, holding weapons in their hands or dressed with certain ornaments, especially the Maruts and Indra. An old hymn of Manu (VIII.29) describes the Gods not too differently from the iconography of later times:

> 1. One (Soma) is a youth, brown, active and wise, who adorns himself with gold.
> 2. Another (Agni) radiant is stationed at the origin, wise among the Gods.
> 3. Another (Twashtar), firm among the Gods, carries an iron sword in his hand.
> 4. Another (Indra) holds the thunderbolt steady in his hand, by which he slays the dragons.
> 5. Another (Rudra) bears a sharp weapon in his hand, luminous and fierce, with healing powers.
> 6. One (Pushan) guards over the path, like a thief. He knows the treasures.
> 7. Another (Vishnu), wide in movement, has measured out three steps, where the Gods abide.
> 8. The twins (Ashwins) travel with a single wife and dwell far away like travelers.

> 9. Two (Mitra and Varuna) have fashioned the supreme seat in Heaven, like emperors anointed with ghee.
> 10. These, while chanting, meditated out the great song, by which they caused the Sun to rise.

While such hymns do not provide a detailed meditation on the form of each deity, the forms appear implicitly in the manner of what is said. As the hymns were only core texts, such more detailed information was probably available within the oral tradition.

It should be noted that human language was originally imagistic in nature and the concrete and abstract meanings of words were first blended together, as the word for milch cow in the Vedas, dhenu, meant "nourisher" in general. The Vedic language is of the same imagistic nature that we see in more visible form in Egyptian hieroglyphs. Hence the Vedic language clearly indicates that images were often in the minds of the worshippers of Vedic Gods as part of the prayer or meditation practices.

Some of these images appear in later times. The Vedic Sun God Savitar, with golden face, golden arms and hands, appears as the Golden Person, Hiranmaya Purusha, of the *Upanishads.*[p] The *Upanishads* contain other meditation images or visualizations which have a basis in the *Rig Veda.* The *Brahma Sutras,* the main and oldest commentary on the *Upanishads,* examines the place of symbols in worship.

Animal images and symbols are also very common in the *Rig Veda,* such as the cow, bull, horse, eagle and so on. The Gods have their respective animals or mounts; Indra and his two haris or bay stallions, Pushan and his goat, the Ashwins and their donkeys, the Maruts and their spotted deer. Here we see the origin of the 'vahanas', the animal vehicles of the Gods in later Hinduism, like Shiva and his bull.

These Vedic animals, however, often exist as symbols in their own right, sometimes presented in fantastic or mythic forms, like the bull with "four horns, three legs, two heads and seven hands."

The Vedic horse has,

> Wings of an eagle, limbs of a deer, golden horns and bronze feet, he moves faster than thought (I.163.1,9).[17]

We could almost imagine a metal cast of this mythic horse.

We see in the use of such fantastic animal forms that the ancients did not just worship animals. They used animals as symbols for the Divine and the deeper powers of the psyche. Sometimes the names of the animals reflect a secret meaning. The goat is called Aja, which also means "unborn," a-ja. "The one being who upholds the six regions in the form of a goat" (I.164.6) and "the goat that upholds Heaven" (VIII.41.10) is the unborn Self. Such imagery is comparable with the iconic approach used in ancient Egypt and Mesopotamia.

As in the later Hindu religion, the Vedic use of images and statues was not a form of crude idolatry. It was part of a science of Yoga. Images were used as aids in concentration and for devotional worship. Even the *Bible* and *Koran* have many imagistic metaphors, as does the mystical poetry of the Sufis. *The Revelation of St. John* uses the animal symbols of the ancient religions like the bull, eagle and serpent, as well as fantastic animal figures (the lamb with eyes all over his body). Christ himself is the Lamb who takes away the sins of the world, a similar idea of the gentle spirit like the Vedic Cow. Islam and Protestant Christianity banished these verbal images from formal representation but did not eliminate them as ideas because they are part of the natural language of the soul, which is more poetic than abstract.

There is no idolatry inherent in formal representation. Just as verbal expression can be used to aid us in understanding, so can formal representation. After all, a picture is worth a thousand words. Nor is there any lack of idolatry inherent in purely verbal expression. To reduce the Word of God to only one book may also be a form of idolatry, as it limits truth which is infinite to a particular form.

The *Rig Veda* also contains many abstract symbols like the chariot (ratha) and chariot wheel (chakra). They appear as mystical symbols like the chariot that took Elijah to Heaven in the *Bible*. They suggest geometrical designs like the yantras used in later Hinduism and a knowledge of the mystic centers, the chakras of the subtle body. The wheel of the Sun is an important Vedic symbol and shows the head chakra in which the spiritual Sun dwells. Vedic meditation involved the use of both concrete and abstract forms, as it did in later Tantric practices.

Whether statues or concrete images were actually made from these symbols, or what their prominence was in Vedic times, is more difficult to tell. Certainly many great artists and craftsmen are mentioned in the *Rig Veda*, like the Ribhus, working in gold, bronze, stone, and wood. This shows that the craftsmanship to do such work existed.

Just as images are generally not thought to be part of the Vedic religion, so are temples. Many Vedic rituals are still done outdoors today. Yet the *Rig Veda* does, not uncommonly, mention houses of worship and places of public assembly (sabha, samiti). Vasishta, the most well known of the Vedic sages, enters the vast mansion, the thousand-doored house of the God Varuna (VII.88.5).[18] Is this just a symbol or does it indicate large temples for worshipping the Gods? Other hymns to Mitra and Varuna indicate a temple of a thousand pillars made of bronze or gold (II.41.5;

V.62.6-8). Later Hindu temples were often made in the form of chariots (rathas). As the chariot is very prominent in Vedic texts, perhaps even in these it may have referred to temples of that form.

In Aryan culture each house was meant to be a place of worship. In this regard, the most important site was the central fire altar in the house, not a central image. Agni, the Vedic fire God, is the lord of the house. The house fire was not just for cooking but had a ritualistic function. Each city had a central communal fire, which was probably in a temple, along with a ritual bathing site for the Vedic water purification rituals, as we see in Indus Valley archaeological sites.

Pillars are common Vedic objects of worship and are the basis for the Shiva lingas of later times. The ancient Egyptians and other ancient peoples similarly had their pillars, standing stones and obelisks that they worshipped. The mortar and pestle have a sacred nature (note I.28), as do the stones for pressing out the Soma (X.76, 94, 175). The trees and the posts used for the sacrifice have a similar sacred value (note III.8). Yet this does not necessarily preclude the use of images, idols or seals. Various sacred artifacts were used along with the fire altar. These could have included some images, animal or human.

To whatever the degree they may have been used, temples and icons were not outside the mentality of the Vedic religion. They were probably used as much in ancient India as in ancient Egypt, whose culture also had a formless solar side and monistic cast to its apparent polytheism. Along with the cities mentioned as places of habitation for the Vedic people some temples must have existed. These at first may not have been highly decorated but were certainly not left bare. If the *Rig Veda* is as old as suggested here, such temples and images would have been among the earliest in the world.

The Vedic religion in its symbolism has much in common with the earlier iconic religions of ancient Egypt and Babylonia and their human and animal symbols that deserves further study. It is part of the non-dogmatic, holistic nature of the Vedic mind that it can contain both imagistic and non-imagistic approaches to the Divine. The use of images is part of the more open polytheism-monism of the Vedic religion, like the Egyptian, which sees all creation as the word and form of the deity.

The *Vedas* were not written, like the Biblical books of the Prophets, or the *Gathas* of Zoroaster, in reaction to an older religion that had degenerated into a crude form of idolatry. On the contrary, they show an earlier phase of human culture from which an imagistic religion could have easily arisen. They do not proclaim a single exclusive God opposed to any images of him. They proclaim a Divine Unity that embraces all multiplicity and encompasses all nature, which therefore has many symbolic forms that could easily be made into visual representations. As such, the religion of the *Rig Veda* derives from an era prior to the ornate imagistic religions of the Middle East and the monotheistic reaction against them. The *Rig Veda* reveals a religion from which both iconic and aniconic approaches could evolve in time and in which both are accepted.

PART V

PEOPLES OF THE ANCIENT WORLD
THE FALL FROM GRACE

1

ANCIENT ARYAN CULTURE

Indra speaks: I was Manu and I became the Sun. I gave the Earth to the Aryans. I led the roaring floods.
— *Rig Veda IV.26.1–2*

If the foregoing examination of Vedic culture is correct, it has many ramifications in terms of world history. In this section we will explore these implications. While much of this material is speculative, it does give a Vedic perspective, which as the view of one of the largest and oldest cultures in the world is worthy of some consideration and may provide us with new keys of looking at the ancient world. This can lead us to a rediscovery of our lost spiritual unity, which was present in our most ancient origins. We must return to this unity in order to establish the world culture that is necessary to deal with our present global crisis.

In the beginning there was one culture — that of the Spirit — and one language — that of the Truth. This culture was outwardly one of worship and inwardly one of meditation. The language was one of mantra and communication was from the heart. The outer life was simple. There were small cities and villages, mainly along the rivers. Agriculture was practiced with the use of domesticated animals. Boats and wagons were used for travel. The emphasis was on the inner life and the outer life was not considered important, nor was there any great effort or need to improve it. Nature was abundant. This culture did not come from the outside but came from within and was guided by sages, who generally lived in retreat in the mountains, who visited the peoples periodically and gave them instruction. From it later cultures diversified, along with divisions of language and religion, as we gradually fell from truth and our connection to the Divine to pursue outward and sensate values.

In time, the outer culture became more complicated and the intellect more cunning and refined. Larger cities, different languages and beliefs arose, along with conflict and misunderstanding between peoples. The apparent advance in civilization was also a spiritual decline, with outer complexity and display substituting for inner feeling and understanding.

Such briefly is the universal ancient myth of the origins of civilization. Hopefully we are at the end of this process of outer expansion and can begin our journey back within. Some of the tools and resources we have developed in our fall may even be helpful in making a stronger ascent, but we must recognize how far we have fallen before we can make our return.

This story is the basis for 'the spiritual model' of interpreting history. This model differentiates humanity into certain groups; yet it is not a division based upon race, language, politics, economics, or religion — the standard outer ways that we categorize people and cultures. It is a classification based upon spiritual values — how we perceive reality and where we see the true worth in things to be.

The most simple presentation of this spiritual differentiation of culture, though it has been in a rigid and often degenerate form since the time of the Buddha, is the class structure of ancient Hindu society. Such a society, based upon the rule of the sages, appears to have been followed by all the ancient world. Everywhere we see the model of the priests, nobility, and the common people. We find it in the ancient cultures of the Middle East, India, China, America, the Kelts of Europe, and in Christian cultures up through the Middle Ages.

By modern political and humanitarian standards we can only see the corrupt side of this cultural idea. Our negative reaction to it is quite understandable as this is what our recent history has shown us. The form this type of culture assumed in late ancient and medieval times could become brutal and inhumane. Yet we cannot judge a thing by its distortion, and many things turn into their opposite in the course of their decline. Let us clear our minds and see if this ancient idea of society had originally another meaning and deeper value which may still be relevant, in fact may be universal.

This spiritual differentiation of society is based on the main values we follow in life. These are defined by the Vedic sages as pleasure (kama), wealth (artha), fame (dharma), and liberation (moksha). These values create four classes and four mental natures. If we pursue pleasure we develop a servile mentality, as we become dependent upon external sources of enjoyment and stimulation. If we pursue wealth we develop a commercial mentality and judge the world in terms of property and prices. If we pursue fame or power we develop a political or militaristic mentality and its distinctions of ranks and status. If we pursue liberation we develop a spiritual mentality and seek the higher knowledge. We then perceive people by their freedom of mind and spirit.

Such a fourfold division of society is not artificial. Our values in life determine how we see the world and how we act within it. We cannot pursue commercial values as the most important thing in life, for example, and yet find the knowledge that liberates our soul. Our commercial preconceptions will color our knowledge and distort it. They will cause us to use religion for commercial ends. We may pursue wealth as a secondary goal, but if it is our primary goal we cannot expect to understand the truth of things, which requires freedom from investments — meaning that we do not invest things with our need to gain materially from them.

All cultures have these four groups. Though each culture may not have a specific system for regulating them, they still appear as classes within society. We too have our labor, commercial, political, and religious classes; divisions of society with their own laws and territory, particular needs and spokespersons. This is not to say that each group appears in its true form, however. In our culture, even religion is dominated by political and commercial interests. We do not have a real religious or spiritual class within our social order.

Pleasure, wealth and power are outer goals — the things of the external world bound by time. Liberation is the inner goal that alone takes us beyond time. Hence we can divide human cultures into two basic groups: those pursuing outer and those pursuing inner goals. In this regard there are only spiritual or materialistic cultures.

However, in life the outer goals commonly mask themselves as the inner. This is the great tragedy of society from which the greatest confusion and illusion arises. We veil our seeking of wealth and power as a pursuit of truth or as serving our religion. We use religion as a mask for promoting commercial and political goals. This is not something we necessarily do consciously. Most of the time we are victims of our own desires, which we blindly transfer into the religious realm where they have no place.

We like to feel that what we are doing has some greater value, that it is for some higher good, even when it is not. This has been the cause of the violence done in the name of religion. It is not the religions themselves in their true spirit that promote conflict but those of non-religious values who mask their greed in religious terms, not only deceiving others but deceiving themselves. Hence the modern mind has revolted against religion as a form of corruption and domination, as a perverted form of materialism, which it often has been.

It is wrong to blame the religion as such for this corruption. It is caused by worldly people who use the protection and sanction of religion to further their personal aims. All religions have a core of spiritual truth, but most of what has been done in their name has come not from this inner truth but from those who project their selfish needs through the name of their religion, while missing its true spirit altogether. Hence religion, the spirit of unity and compassion, has been continually corrupted by the forces of ignorance and made into a servant of violence and oppression.

This happened in the ancient world as well. Ancient cultures degenerated from spiritual into materialistic cultures masked in a religious form. Ambitious kings used religion to expand their empires. Ambitious priests used religion to gain political power and control the masses. All this has nothing to do with the real spirit of religion and is no measure of what the heart of these teachings stands for. In this regard, the movement from these pseudo-spiritual cultures to modern secular ones was inevitable, as the latter merely openly express what the former did covertly. Today we unquestioningly pursue outer goals of wealth and power as the true good in life. We no longer need to clothe them in some religious sanction. This however has not freed us from greed and corruption and has not brought peace to the world either.

Similarly the revival of religious fundamentalism that we see in the world today is generally not a return to true spirituality. While on the positive side it tries to reorient humanity toward a religious life which our modern materialistic life has deprived us of, it tends to do so in narrow and sectarian terms that cause further divisions and misunderstandings to arise. It is based on the religious divisions of the Middle Ages, not a creative or integrating force of love or wisdom. The true spirit of religion, which is unity, is quite different than promoting the interests of a particular group or belief. There is only one religion in truth. No one religion exists apart from the others or apart from the spirit of religion which is universal and infinite. It is this spirit of religion that we must revive, not any particular religion.

Hence we can divide religious cultures into two groups; the truly religious or spiritual, and the outwardly religious, which are really worldly cultures in disguise. False religious cultures try to impose their beliefs on others by force and propaganda and use them as a basis for political and commercial exploitation and oppression. They really deny the truth of the religion they claim to represent, though they may receive the favor of political and commercial powers.

True spiritual cultures are cultures of peace and humility and do not try to dominate or impose their ideas on anyone. They give reverence to the spirit of truth, which is universal, and do not sacrifice human beings at the altar of name and form, even that of God. It is the spirit of religion they further, not superficial adherence to a belief. They emphasize openness of the heart and the sacred nature of the individual. They do not emphasize differences or fuel collective conflicts. These are the truly religious people and they are not limited by the religions they are part of. They do not make excuses for the oppression or injustice done in the name of their religion, nor do they fail to honor the true spirit of religion represented by those in other religious groups.

We see in early ancient times, at the dawn of human history, that a culture existed based upon spiritual values and ruled by the sages. We find this in the myths of Vedic India, in the myths of the ancient Middle East, in Plato's idea of Atlantis ruled by philosopher-kings, and in the Taoist idea of an earlier age of truth. All ancient cultures had a similar idea. It was not just an idealistic imagination of later thinkers. This culture appears to have been centered in the Himalayan region of India. However, it probably existed in different forms throughout the world and by people of different languages, races, or cultures. Truth has never been the property of any one group of people or any geographical part of the globe, though the Earth does have her sacred areas wherein spiritual cultures are more likely to occur.

As humanity fell from this spiritual age, militaristic and commercial people gained ascendancy and took control. While such people were originally subordinated to a rule of spiritual or religious guides, they separated from them, revolted against them, and created or remade the religions in their own image. Hence from spiritual awareness humanity degenerated into rival religions that were excuses for developing or maintaining various power structures. The ascendancy of these outer values made society more complex and materialistic and moved people away from the simple culture of worship that prevailed in earlier ages. This created an artificial society based upon appearances, in which the true feeling of the heart was lost. We and our cultural type are their descendants.

There was an early unity of ancient religion throughout the world based upon the worship of the Divine or Truth as the real goal of human life. This was not like our modern creeds and their sectarian divisions. It was a religion of the heart and essence, not one of names and institutions. It did not seek to convert others but to worship the Divine in all. This unity of ancient culture broke down in the course of ancient history. There was a growing division of peoples, languages, and cultures (as in the Biblical story of the Tower of Babel). Each group began to view the others with suspicion, often seeing in them some force of evil. The religions became divided and began condemning each other, sometimes calling the other religions works of demons, heathens, heretics or barbarians.

No one group can be blamed for this fragmentation of humanity and the problems it caused. No culture was free of this degeneration. All the great civilizations of the ancient world fell in this process. In the course of time truly spiritual people became the minority in all of them. Similarly, each culture had smaller groups, sometimes in a traditional garb, sometimes in a reformist one, who tried to preserve or recreate the earlier spirit of truth and piety. These movements sometimes created religious revivals which tried to point out the deeper meaning of the traditions. Sometimes they founded new religions, which condemned the corrupt forms that the older religions had assumed. Yet these new religious movements themselves degenerated quickly under political, commercial and social pressures and soon became the very thing they came into being to oppose.

Today we have different religions in the world, each with a core of truth, but none that has a culture or state which truly represents it. The political and social establishments built around our religions have usually become their perversion. While through history there have occasionally been kings or leaders who tried to recreate true spiritual cultures, their influence has been transitory. It is doubtful whether the true spirit of religion can ever be organized. As a thing of the heart, it is beyond manipulation.

VEDIC AND ARYAN CULTURE

There is much confusion as to what the term 'Aryan' originally meant. It has gained many erroneous associations and become charged in the minds of people with negative connotations. In the Sanskrit language, Aryan primarily means "noble" or "pure" — people with high minds and good hearts, spiritual values. This is the sense behind its usage in Vedic culture. Aryan is a culture based upon the rule of the seers, men of spiritual realization. In this regard any spiritual culture is Aryan and any non-spiritual culture unaryan.

Nineteenth century European scholars adapted this term and redefined it to stand for some noble, primitive type they thought was the ancient prototype of European and Indo-Iranian peoples. This is totally apart from any original Sanskrit usage or meaning of the term which never had a racial connotation. The Nazis distorted the term further and brought their racial and political bias into it. These ideas were superimposed upon this originally Sanskrit term as part of the misinterpretation of Vedic culture. Unfortunately the common mind still associates the term Aryan with these negative associations that have nothing to do with the Vedic, Persian or Buddhist usage of it. Though we will use the term Aryan here in the Vedic sense, it is important not to let such wrong associations cloud its real import.

Modern historians have tried to understand the ancient world in simplistic racial or linguistic patterns and have cast the Aryans in that mold. They have tried to see the Aryan as a pure racial type speaking only one language. If we examine the cultures of the ancient world, we see as much diversity in physical types as in the modern world. We do not see several pure racial types each existing in a compartmentalized region of the globe, holding to their own distinct language. This is a convenient but simplistic generality of the intellect. Ancient cultures we know better, like Mesopotamia, had a bewildering array of languages and peoples, though a common religious culture. We find the same thing in India today where Hindu and Aryan culture is found among a great diversity of ethnic and linguistic groups.

Modern historians regard Aryan as a language, going back to some supposed proto-Indo-European tongue. According to the *Vedas,* Sanskrit is the original human language. It does not go back to an earlier one but does have earlier forms. Vedic culture is based upon the Sanskrit language as the language of the Gods, yet it would be simplistic to reduce it to that. Sanskrit is the inner or spiritual language of the culture (like Latin in medieval Europe). Common dialects also must have existed in Vedic times and some of these, like many of those in India today, may not have been directly or easily traceable to Sanskrit.

The Vedic Aryan is a culture of spiritual or yogic values. In this regard Buddhist culture is also Aryan, and the Buddha also used this term. Like the Vedic seers he named his teaching the law of the Aryans, Arya Dharma. Certainly there was no racial connotation in the term Aryan in his time of 2,500 years ago, which affirms that in Sanskrit it never had such a meaning.

The distorted use of the term Aryan by the Nazis is like their adoption of the swastika, the ancient Indian emblem of peace and harmony. The swastika and similar symbols of truth were used all over the ancient world. In India the swastika was used by Buddhists and Jains as well as by Hindus. We see in the modern perverted usage of it an inversion of terms that shows the mentality of the Asuras or the negative forces in the world.

A verse of the *Rig Veda* describes the Aryan victory as the victory of the powers of conscious evolution. It speaks of the action of the Gods as,

> ... generating the Divine Word (Brahman), the cow, the horse, the plants, the trees, the Earth, the mountains and the Waters, raising the Sun in Heaven, and releasing the Aryan laws over the world (X.65.11).[1]

Aryan is thus the noble or evolved state of things. As such, a beautiful tree is Aryan, the order of the cosmos is Aryan. It is not necessarily a human term, much less a racial one. Similarly the enemies of the Aryans like the Dasyus and Panis represent any force that obstructs cosmic evolution. They generally refer to cosmic or superhuman forces and only in some instances refer to human beings who are allied with the powers of darkness.

Vedic religion, like most ancient religions, is not a religion in the modern sense. In ancient times, religions grew up organically as part of life. They were not beliefs assumed by a choice of the mind. The Vedic religion is not a sectarian belief, nor is it a belief that one can adopt or graft onto the rest of one's life, which is left unchanged. It is a broad culture encompassing all of life, not a creed seeking converts. It is an entire way of life, which reflects the nature of the soul and the universality of creation. The Vedic teaching contains many different religions, many different names and forms of the Divine. There is much in the Vedic religion which can be regarded as not only proto-Hindu but also proto-Buddhist. Some of its teachings resemble Christianity, Judaism or Islam, as, for example, the cult of Varuna, the father figure of sin and redemption. The Vedic is much like the other solar religions of the ancient world from Egypt to Mexico. It also has factors in common with Shamanism, the occult religion of circumpolar regions.

The Vedic teaching contains monotheism and non-theistic approaches. It contains polytheism, as well as pantheism and monism. It recognizes the Divine as One, as Many, as the All, and as beyond all form. It is not a crude polytheism, its names of Gods are epithets. Indra means 'the Lord', Agni means 'the Knower', Soma means 'the Joyous one'. The Vedic Gods are truth principles and do not serve to cause divisions in the minds of those who worship them. For this reason any one of the Vedic Gods can become all of them. The Vedic Gods often become human or display human traits. Its sages often become Gods. Aryan culture, therefore, represents primarily the spiritual values that have motivated all great religions and all men of wisdom. These values have always had a special hold in India.

This universal religion is the basis of the Vedic Aryan culture. It is the legacy of the great solar religion of enlightenment that prevailed throughout the ancient world, which set up ritualistic cultures ruled by priests and seer-kings. The Vedic peoples reflect this culture and its development. In it all religious approaches and experiences are accepted and each is given its proper place.

ORIGINS OF THE VEDIC PEOPLE

There are a number of opinions as to where the Vedic people originated. According to Western scholars they came from Central Asia as part of a dispersion of Indo-European peoples (Aryans) sometime in the second millennium BC. This is based on the idea that the Indus Valley culture of ancient India in the third millennium BC is not Aryan, which is quite open to question.

It is presumptuous to believe that the Aryans entered India last, coming there only in 1500 BC or later, while entering Greece and Mesopotamia by 2000 BC, or as early as 6000 BC, which is the more recent view as through Colin Renfrew.[a] The Vedic Aryans have been the most spiritual, the largest in terms of population, the most traditional, and most continuously enduring branch of the Aryan peoples. Hence they appear as the main branch, not the last and least of this great group of people. As perhaps the most self-sufficient of all cultures who remained centered in the Sanskrit language, the best preserved of the ancient Aryan tongues, they were most likely the central group of the Aryans.

There is an additional theory of some scholars, primarily Tilak in India, that the Aryans came from Arctic regions in early ancient times. According to this view they traveled through Central Asia and into India, with other branches of the Aryans moving to Europe and Iran. The basis for this theory is that the symbolism of the Vedic hymns reflects the return of the Sun or the Dawn after long periods, after many months of darkness. However, the symbolism of the hymns can be explained otherwise,[b] and making the Arctic inhabitable during the period of the Ice Age is rather difficult.

The idea adapted here is that the Vedic people came down from the Himalayas as one of the periodic spiritual renovations of humanity. This perhaps occurred after a great flood that marked the end of the last Ice Age, as a part of great shifts of peoples and civilizations that occurred at this time. The Himalayas have always been the homeland of the sages and the Rishis, like those who founded Vedic culture. It would appear to make sense to place the origins of such a spiritual culture there. According to the Vedic teaching human beings derive from Manu, the original man. In some Vedic teachings, similar to the legend of the Biblical Noah, he is the survivor and spiritual father of humanity after a great flood. He is said to have established the Vedic religion on the banks of the Saraswati river in north India. The *Rig Veda* confirms this geographical location as its central region.

In the *Rig Veda,* human beings are called the descendants of Manu or of his descendant, Nahusha, whose name, we might add, resembles the Biblical Noah. It is the five grandsons of Nahusha who gave their names to the five divisions of the Aryan peoples; Turvasha, Yadu, Puru, Druhyu, and Anu. These we have related to the five regions of north India, though they may be related to other peoples of the globe as they extended beyond India. As we saw in our chapter on the ocean, the *Rig Veda* relates the origin of Vedic peoples from across the sea, as Turvasha and Yadu or

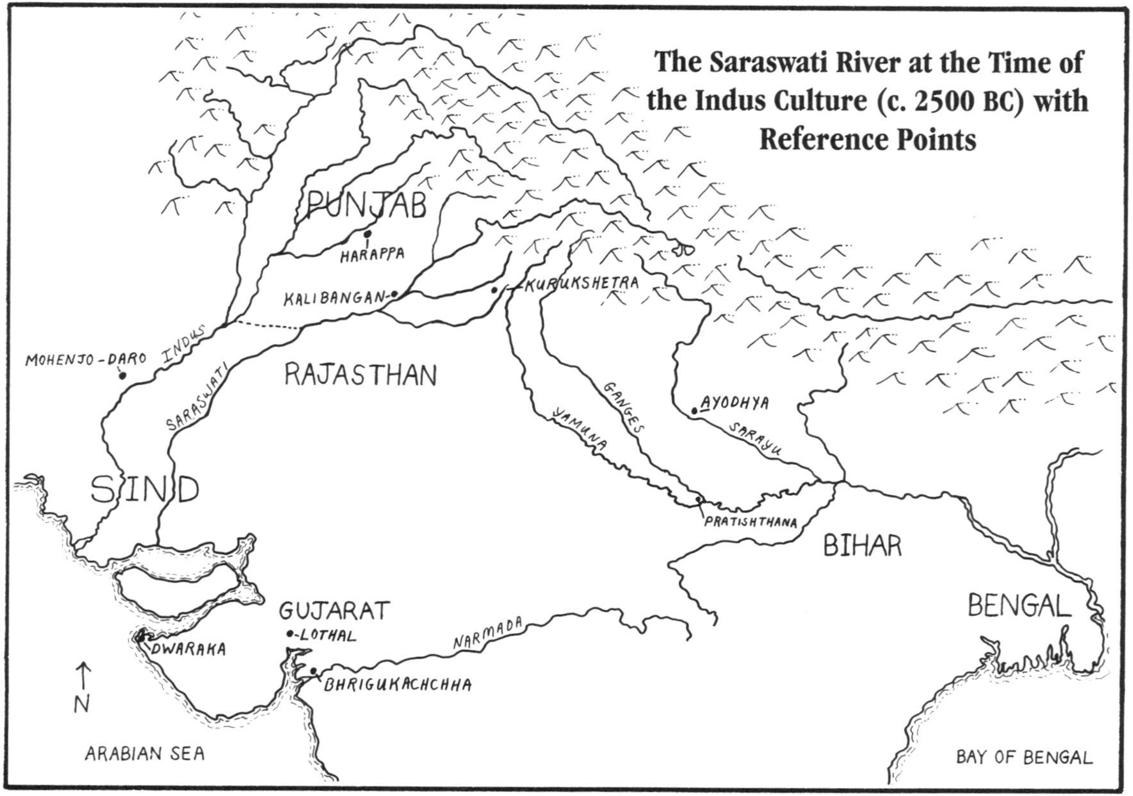
The Saraswati River at the Time of the Indus Culture (c. 2500 BC) with Reference Points
PUNJAB
HARAPPA
KALIBANGAN
KURUKSHETRA
MOHENJO-DARO
INDUS
SARASWATI
RAJASTHAN
SIND
GANGES
YAMUNA
AYODHYA
SARAYU
PRATISHTHANA
BIHAR
BENGAL
GUJARAT
LOTHAL
DWARAKA
NARMADA
BHRIGUKACHCHHA
N
ARABIAN SEA
BAY OF BENGAL

Bhujyu. Vamadeva relates the image, like Bhujyu, of having been imprisoned in a hundred bronze cities (IV.27.1). This suggests that some Vedic ancestors were confined or imprisoned, perhaps used as slaves in an urban but unspiritual culture, and escaped across the sea. Perhaps the Aryans, or some of them, escaped by sea to India, up the rivers to the Himalayas and then down again at safer times.

It is not possible to present firm conclusions on these issues yet. Much is hidden in myth and symbol. What our study proposes is that the *Vedas* possess a much greater antiquity than imagined by modern scholars, and that the Aryans were in India at a very early point in history (by 6000 BC). Vedic India was a point of diffusion of culture, perhaps the central point of diffusion for ancient civilization, particularly ancient religion and spirituality.

Our history would have the Hindus receive their culture from the ancient Middle East but that may only be our bias. While we would have them get their alphabet from the West, we should remember that it was their numerals, through the Arabs, that we adopted. Why should we assume they got their writing from our region? According to the Hindus, writing came through them. While the Vedic tradition emphasized the oral transmission, all ancient cultures did this. This does not mean that the Hindus had no writing. We find writing mentioned as early as the *Atharva Veda.*

> From which case we have taken the *Veda,* within that
> we place it (AV XIX.72.1).[2]

Books in India were collections of pages, made from banana leaves or birch bark, and kept in cases or boxes.

Civilization in ancient times moved from east to west. India, the great land of the rivers, is much larger and more fertile than the Mesopotamian region and thereby able to support much larger numbers of people. It was a more favorable region for civilization than the Middle East in ancient times also. It is more likely to be the homeland of the original great river cultures and their inventions of agriculture and so on.

THE INDUS-SARASWATI CULTURE

The Myth of the Aryan Invasion

The view of nineteenth century Western scholars, as we have mentioned briefly, was that the Vedic people were primarily a light-skinned, perhaps blond, alpine or nordic type like the Europeans. They were supposed to have invaded India around 1500 BC and fought the aboriginal peoples of India who were darker skinned and spoke a different kind of language. The *Rig Veda* was interpreted as referring to this conflict in terms of its war between light and darkness.

In the early twentieth century the remains of an older urban civilization were found in India. It has proved to be the largest of the ancient civilizations, being larger than the whole Middle Eastern realm of Egypt, Syria and Mesopotamia combined. It was called "the Indus Valley culture" as its first sites were found along the Indus river. It was also called "Harappa and Mohenjodaro" after its two largest urban sites. Today new discoveries are extending its domain yet further and the great majority of its sites are found east of the Indus. It included most of Gujarat to the south and now sites have been found across the Yamuna to the east.[c] It extended along the coast as far as what is now the coast of Iran to the west and nearly to the place of modern Bombay in the south and east. To the north, Indus sites have been found along the Amu Darya river in Afghanistan, and these appear closely related to cultures of ancient Central Asia.[d] Many of its sites, as we have mentioned, have been found along the now dry banks of the Saraswati river, the most holy of the rivers of the Vedic Aryans. Some scholars are now calling it the "Indus-Saraswati culture" for this reason.

The Indus culture was dated from 3000–1500 BC. As it was already presumed that the Vedic people entered India no earlier than 1500 BC, the view was then modified to regard the Vedic Aryans as barbarians from the steppes who destroyed this glorious ancient culture. The Indus Valley culture was hastily pronounced pre-Vedic and probably Dravidian in language, though proof of such things was quite lacking. This turned the *Rig Veda* into "the record of the destruction of one of the great civilizations of the ancient world." This cast a great shadow on the *Rig Veda* and its claim to be the scripture of the Hindus and the secret wisdom of the seers. It was reinterpreted as a crude statement of nomadic invaders who destroyed the true homeland of Hindu civilization.

However, this so-called pre-Vedic Indus Valley civilization, through an examination of skeletal remains, now shows the same racial types in existence there in the third millennium BC as in modern India today.

> Anthropologists have observed that the present population of Gujarat is composed of more or less the same ethnic groups as are noticed at Lothal in 2000 BC. Similarly, the present population of the Punjab is said to be ethnically the same as the population of Harappa and Rupar four thousand years ago. Linguistically the present day population of Gujarat and Punjab belongs to the

> Indo-Aryan language speaking group. The only inference that can be drawn from the anthropological and linguistic evidences adduced above is that the Harappan population in the Indus Valley and Gujarat in 2000 BC was composed of two or more groups, the more dominant among them having very close ethnic affinities with the present day Indo-Aryan speaking population of India.[e]

If the Aryans were a racial type, they were already predominant in India by 2000 BC or they had no real impact upon the physical types of India. This latter view has been the conclusion of modern scholars who believe in the Aryan invasion theory. Who were these invading Aryans if they left no mark on the racial types of India? How did they manage to change the language and religion of a subcontinent and leave no traces of their physical type among the people? It is hard to imagine that an invasion of a foreign race could change the language and laws of a culture and leave it with a respect for its sages as the greatest teachers of humanity, near Gods in status, and yet have no impact racially. Moreover, there was no memory left of any such invasion, even in the very ancient lore of the Dravidian people said to have been conquered and displaced.

To prove the idea of a racial war in the *Rig Veda,* a few Vedic verses are pointed out that appear to describe the Dasyus in a racial slur as "snub-nosed"(anasa; V.29.10). However, the term itself does not mean snub-nosed but "without nose." It should also be noted that the Dravidians whom the Aryans were supposed to have fought against are not a low-nosed race as any examination of their features clearly reveals. Nor was the Indus Valley culture one of more low-nosed peoples than those of modern India as the previous quote indicates. Moreover, the Dasyus are also described in similar verses of the *Rig Veda* as "without feet" (apada; V.32.8). Hence, it is a noseless, footless demon or a snake that is being referred to, not a snub-nosed, club-footed race of people. We are reminded of Vritra, the inimical dragon himself, who is said to be "without hand or foot" (apadahasto; I.32.7).

The Dasyus as "worshippers of the phallus" (shishnadeva; VII.21.5) have also been identified with the Shiva linga worshipping Dravidians. However, the Shiva linga is not phallus worship and the Aryans, like all ancient cultures, worshipped standing-stones, which is the real origin of the worship of Shiva lingas. Moreover, the Indian spiritual tradition has emphasized Brahmacharya or celibacy, which is all such a passage indicates. The Shiva linga, which is not limited to the Dravidians, is just another form of Vedic pillar worship. We should also note that the Dravidians are as much worshippers of Vishnu as of Shiva and that Shiva is also worshipped in many areas of north India, particularly the Himalayas, which are said to be his home. There has never been any simplistic division of a Dravidian Shaivite and Aryan non-Shaivite culture in India.

The early idea that the Indus Valley culture was destroyed by invaders has also been disproved. There is no evidence of destruction by war, or any radical end to the culture. The culture appears to have suffered damage mainly by flood and earthquakes but otherwise there is a continuity of culture through ancient history in India, with the forms of the Indus Valley culture gradually developing into those of later Hinduism.

Early investigators also based the non-Vedic claim for the Indus Valley culture on the absence of horses and chariots at the sites, such as are prominently mentioned in the *Vedas.* However, horses have been found, as well as wheeled toys that suggest the use of carts and chariots much as in the *Vedas.* In the *Rig Veda* itself the enemies of the Vedic peoples are also stated to have horses. The enemies of Sudas, after their defeat, offer him their horse's heads as a tribute (VII.18.19). Horses are in fact one of the objects that the Aryans win from the Dasyus (III.34.9). Hence there is nothing in the *Vedas* making the horse or the chariot a special possession of the Vedic people. They are rather part of the general culture of the region. We should also note that chariots are not the vehicles of nomadic people, nor do they function well in mountain or desert terrain from which the so-called Aryan invasion occurred. One cannot imagine anyone going over the rocky passes of Afghanistan in chariots. Chariots are the vehicles of an urban culture with much flat ground as is the case in north India. The Vedic emphasis on the chariot alone disproves any nomadic basis for the hymns.

Another point made is that the *Rig Veda* mentions a spoked-wheel, which does not occur until the middle of the second millenium BC in Mesopotamia. While this does not prove the earlier inhabitants of India were not Indo-Aryan, it would suggest that the *Rig Veda* was not finished before this period or that the spoked wheel existed in India at a much earlier period than its discovery elsewhere. It is the later view that we are suggesting here, based upon the earlier references of Vedic geography and astronomy.

The Vedic Aryans have also been identified as an iron-based culture, such as did not begin in India until after 1500 BC, and iron is not found in Indus Valley sites. Yet Vedic 'ayas', translated as "iron" by some scholars, is probably bronze or copper, as the equivalent term means in Old Latin (see Appendix). There is certainly nothing that proves it meant anything more than ore or metal in general, and not specifically iron. In any case, the enemies of the Vedic people in the *Rig Veda,* the Dasyus, also have 'ayas' and use it to make their cities (i.e. II.20.8). Hence the

Aryan-Dasyu conflict in the *Vedas* does not support the idea of a battle between iron-using Vedic people and non-iron using Indus Valley people. Both cultures used the same metal, whatever it was.

Another proof of the difference between the Indus Valley culture and later Hinduism was the lack of any urban archaeological sites in India from the time of the Indus cities to that of the urban age of later ancient India as found by the Greeks. The Greeks found massive cities in India and a highly developed culture based on the *Vedas,* but the cities were largely made of wood. Scholars thereby imagined that the urban culture found by the Greeks had arisen only shortly before their visits and was preceded by a long dark age after the Indus Valley culture, in which space the *Vedas* were placed. However, another type of city has now been found to have existed between the last Indus sites and later cities. New findings at Dwaraka and Bet Dwaraka show large stone port cities that flourished about 1500 BC, after the Indus Valley culture and presenting a culture intermediate between the Indus Valley and later India.[f, g]

At the end of the story of the *Mahabharata,* which is repeated in the *Puranas,* Dwaraka, the city of Krishna, was said to be submerged by the rising ocean. While this appeared to be a poetic fantasy to end a great tale, remnants of that city have now been found, and right at the traditional place of Krishna's Dwaraka. The Dwaraka site also relates to the same time that Puranic records appear to date Krishna, about a thousand years before Nanda, a king thought to have ruled around 400 BC, or a date of about 1400 BC.[h] The wall of Bet Dwaraka, a nearby city and identified with Krishna's summer palace, is larger than the pier at Lothal, an Indus Valley site, previously the largest port city found in ancient India, and one of the largest in the ancient world. The Dwaraka sites thus represent an urban development intermediate between the Indus Valley sites and the time of the Buddha and show a continuous urban civilization in India throughout historical times. If the site is Krishna's Dwaraka, it is as Aryan as his India was, and relates to the late Vedic period in which all Indian literary sources place Krishna. It shows that the Vedic Aryans were building great stone cities, and were engaged in maritime trade at the furthest tip of Gujarat at the time when they were supposed to be just entering India as primitive nomads.

Dwaraka also had trade relations, evidenced by pottery remains, with the Indo-Aryan Kassites who ruled Babylonia at that time (1500 BC). The appearance of Indo-Aryans in the Middle East of that era may not have been by a northern invasion but by a maritime interchange or colonization from India.

If we look at the location of Dwaraka we see that it is the furthest port on the Gulf of Kutch at the end of the Kathiawar peninsula. As Kutch was originally the outlet of the Saraswati river, the Dwaraka area was thereby the gateway to the Saraswati also and could have dominated trade into that region. According to many ancient sources like the *Puranas*, Dwaraka was built on the site of an earlier Vedic city called Kusasthali, founded by Sharyati, one of the sons of Manu.

> Anartta was the religious son of Sharyati. His son was named Revata who ruled over the region called Anartta after his father and dwelled in a city named Kusasthali (VP IV.1.20).

Anartta is the Vedic name for Gujarat, the region of India wherein Dwaraka is located. Perhaps Dwaraka was the greatest of the Vedic ports into the Saraswati delta. This connection of Dwaraka with the Saraswati region and with earlier Vedic cities also affirms its Vedic nature.

As Dwaraka reveals, India has had a continuous urban population since the Indus Valley culture which gradually developed into later cultures. The dark age said to have been caused by a barbaric Aryan invasion is also being disproved by archaeology. The ancient civilization of India is unbroken, and hence its literary records are also likely to go back to these early eras.

Though this idea of an Aryan invasion has dominated the whole Western interpretation of Indian history, there is no archaeological evidence to support any such invasion. It was placed in a dark period where no data was available on what happened, as if a lack of other data could prove a theory. Even the 'Painted Gray Ware', a kind of pottery often regarded as Aryan, is now found to be an organic development of the pottery of the region and not that of new invaders.[1] A modern scholar has noted:

> Current archaeological data do not support the existence of an Indo-Aryan or European invasion into South Asia at any time in the pre- or protohistoric periods. Instead, it is possible to document archaeologically a series of cultural changes reflecting indigenous cultural development from prehistoric to historic periods. The early Vedic literature describes not a human invasion into the area, but a fundamental restructuring of indigenous society ... The Indo-Aryan invasion as an academic concept in eighteenth and nineteenth century Europe reflected the cultural milieu of the period. Linguistic data were used to validate the

> concept that in turn was used to interpret archaeological and anthropological data.[j]

A number of archaeologists today, both Indian and Western, believe that Indo-Aryans were present in India before 2000 BC.[k] While the Indus Valley script was first thought to be of a Dravidian language, most evidence now is that it was Indo-European and that Brahmi, the later script of India, developed from it.[l] There is much resemblance between the most common Indus signs and the most common letters of the Brahmi alphabet which shows an organic development between the two, and the case endings of the Indus signs appear to be Indo-European, not Dravidian. The Indus script was used in parts of India as late as 500 BC thus showing its continuity and usage with probably Indo-Aryan languages. Moreover, a symbol appearing to mean "the Land of the Seven Rivers" is commonly found in the Indus Script. There is also much resemblance between the Indus Script and the ancient Semitic scripts, which could show a possible Vedic or Indian origin for our own alphabet, just as for our numerals.[m] In addition to a continuity of the script, the weights and measures used in the Indus Valley culture are related to those used in later India, as are many of the tools of trade, arts and crafts.

Western scholars first regarded the Indus Valley culture to be an offshoot from the Middle Eastern, probably Sumerian, though it was much larger in size and better organized. Recent excavations at Mehrgarh[n] show that the antecedents of the Indus Valley culture go back earlier than 6000 BC in India itself, and that it did not develop from an outside influence. If the Indus Valley culture is late Vedic, as the *Vedas* suggest, such sites as Mehrgarh would reflect the earlier Vedic age in India. The date of Mehrgarh is quite in keeping with the astronomical references we have uncovered in the *Vedas*. The Mehrgarh site also reveals the use of barley as a grain and the extensive use of cattle as domesticated animals which is characteristic of Vedic culture. Mehrgarh may have been a village of the Vedic age.

We are thus left with an Aryan invasion that was not remembered, even by the people they supposedly conquered, which had no effect on the racial types of the people, which occurred without any special war, and did not disturb the indigenous organic development of the culture. The next and logical step is to dispense with it altogether. Had there been an Indo-Aryan invasion and conquest of the subcontinent of India, an area larger than western Europe, there would have been evidences of it. We would find cities destroyed by the invasion, differences in racial types between earlier and later people of the regions, radical changes in the culture, shifts in the language or alphabet, the existence of pre-Vedic and non-Aryan place or river names, memories of such an invasion among the conquered peoples or something of the sort. While scholars have proposed such things, not only have they not been proved, the evidence is gradually but consistently refuting them. *For all the emphasis on an Aryan invasion of India, which remains the common view in historical books today, no solid evidence can be shown for it and the so-called literary evidence, the misinterpretation of the Vedas as a record of nomadic invaders, is the least credible.* Not only were the Vedic people not nomadic invaders, their very holy land, the Saraswati region, is described in the *Vedas* as it was during and prior to the Indus Valley culture, but not after, when the so-called invasion occurred.

One of the most progressive Western scholars in this area, Colin Renfrew, not only argues for an Indo-European movement into Europe by 6000 BC, he also suggests the same possibility for India. He notes that the literary interpretation of the *Rig Veda* does not prove any Aryan invasion.

> As far as I can see there is nothing in the *Hymns of the Rig Veda* which demonstrates that the Vedic-speaking population were intrusive to the area: this comes rather from a historical assumption of the 'coming of the Indo-Europeans'.[o]
>
> When Wheeler speaks of 'the Aryan invasion of the Land of the Seven Rivers, the Punjab', he has no warranty at all, so far as I can see. If one checks the dozen references in the *Rig Veda* to the Seven Rivers, there is nothing in them that to me implies an invasion: the land of the Seven Rivers is the land of the *Rig Veda*, the scene of action.[p]
>
> Despite Wheeler's comments, it is difficult to see what is particularly non-Aryan about the Indus Valley civilization.[q]

Hence, Renfrew suggests that the Indus Valley civilization was in fact Indo-Aryan even prior to the Indus Valley era.

> This hypothesis that early Indo-European languages were spoken in north India with Pakistan and on the Iranian plateau at the sixth millenium BC has the merit of harmonizing symmetrically with the the theory for the origin of the Indo-European languages in Europe. It also emphasizes the continuity in the Indus Valley and adjacent areas

from the early neolithic through to the floruit of the Indus Valley civilization.[r]

However, Renfrew does not know of the Saraswati River or of Vedic astronomy, much less of the Vedic Yoga. He still ascribes the *Rig Veda* to a late date, though he suggests that the culture before it was also Indo-Aryan. While his work is a movement in the right direction, it still is not sufficient for our understanding here.

This takes us to the view that the Indus Valley culture was a product of pre-Vedic Aryans. According to this idea the Indus Valley culture was a creation of Indo-Aryans, but a group different from the Vedic people, who are still regarded as having come later, around the 1500 BC date usually given the *Rig Veda*. The Vedic people are thought to have taken over this earlier Aryan culture, either by internal changes in the culture, or by an invasion from outside. As we noted in our section on the Vedic kings, some scholars identify the pre-Vedic Aryans with early Vedic figures like Nahusha, Yayati, and the Bhrigus. Such prominent figures in the *Rig Veda* and descendants of Vedic Manu cannot be pre-Vedic. This theory also does not explain the prominence of the Saraswati river as the ancient homeland of the *Rig Veda*, or the astronomical references. It merely appeases the opinion that the *Vedas* are of a late date, which has become treated as an unquestioned truth though it is nothing of the sort.

Many of these scholars also date the Mahabharata War or Krishna's Dwaraka around 1400 BC. As this period traditionally marked the end of Vedic culture, it leaves no time for earlier Vedic literature to be composed, which is very extensive and of many layers; nor is there any time for the many Vedic kings and dynasties said to have ruled before Krishna (a line of around a hundred). Such views which place the Mahabharata War in the early period of the *Rig Veda*, when it is everywhere stated to have come at a much later period, must ignore all the literary evidence. However, if we adjust the idea of pre-Vedic Aryans and instead divide the Vedic era into earlier and later periods, there may be much information in the idea of pre-Vedic Aryans that is important. We have shown the distinction between early and later Aryans, and how later reforms, like that of Sudas, occurred in relation to earlier peoples who had fallen in time from the spiritual practices originally given to them. These events are entirely within the time period of the *Rig Veda*. They are not before. While the idea of pre-Vedic Aryans is a move in the right direction, it still fails to explain the geography, calendar, and spiritual practices of the *Vedas* and can be still used to turn the Vedic into a late ancient culture without much worth or originality. The decipherment of the Indus Script, however, may be the only thing that will finally prove this issue.

ARYAN AND NON-ARYAN PEOPLES

The modern Western mind has identified the Indian Aryan with the European Aryan type by affinities of language, but there is no objective basis for regarding culture, race, or language as identical. In terms of religious practices, for example, the Vedic has many affinities not only with the European like the Keltic but also with the Egyptian, as, for example, their solar religion and the cult of the falcon, the spotted cow and the lotus. It also resembles the Babylonian religion with their Sun God, thunder God (Indra), sacred plant (Soma), sacred fire (Agni), and temple worship. The great Sumerian and Babylonian hero Gilgamesh goes to the eastern land of Dilmun to get the sacred plant. Is this not going to India to get the Soma, the Vedic plant of immortality? Why should we not regard the Hindus as related to their ancient Middle Eastern neighbors based on these affinities? Language is not the sole or even primary criterion of cultural affinity. The main factor is the customs and culture of a people.

The *Rig Veda* does describe a battle between light and darkness, truth and falsehood, spirituality and materialism. To make this into a battle between light and dark skinned people, however, is rather superficial. Such an idea is found in many religions, including the Zoroastrian and the Christian idea of God and Satan. Why not give these religions a similar political interpretation? As the Persian religion is even more dominated by the idea of a war between the powers of light and darkness than the Vedic, and has many of the same demon and hero-kings, it is clear that this idea is a common Aryan heritage and is not the product of a so-called Aryan invasion of India.

Some interpretations have gone so far as to suggest that great Vedic figures like Krishna were not Aryan. Because their names mean dark or black, they are said to have probably been dark skinned aborigines or Dravidians. However, there is a sage called Krishna in the *Rig Veda* (seer of VIII.85-87 and X.42-44), as well as others called Shyava or Rama, which also mean dark. Hence having a name meaning dark was never a ban on someone becoming a Vedic seer, if such terms ever had a racial meaning. Moreover, Krishna as a deity is dark blue, while his consort, Radha, is red or pink in color. Such colors have nothing to do with race but with the qualities these figures represent, or the conclusions we must draw will be quite absurd.

The Vedic war is a question of values and life-style, not a racial issue. It is the conflict between spiritual and materialistic values that occurs in all societies. Sometimes Aryan people in the *Vedas* become unaryan by a change in values, as indicated in the battle of Sudas. Sometimes unaryan people become Aryan, as in various Dasas supporting or donating to the Aryan seers. One hymn, for example, speaks of the great gifts and generosity of Dasa Balbutha (VIII.46.32). Even names of Vedic kings like Su-das and Divo-dasa, have the ending of Das or Dasa, meaning servant.

The Aryans are described as children of the light, children of the Sun, adorned with gold. Its people and its kings are said to be descended from the Sun God. But all the religious cultures of the ancient world from the Mayans to the Egyptians refer to themselves in this language. They similarly speak of a war between truth and falsehood, darkness and light. Were they Aryans also? It may well be so, at least in origin, if we go back to the real meaning of the term.

Even later texts from *Manu Samhita* to the *Brahmanas* and *Puranas* regard the foreign people around them as fallen descendants of earlier Vedic kings and peoples. They describe the people of the known world as fallen Kshatriya or Vedic nobility. The *Manu Samhita* states:

> But in consequence of the omission of sacred rites, and of their not consulting the sages, the following peoples of the noble class have gradually sunk in this world to the condition of servants — The Paundrakas, Chods, Dravidas, Kambojas, Yavanas, Shakas, Paradas, Pahlavas, Chinas, Kiratas, and Daradas. All those peoples in this world, who are excluded from the community of those born from the mouth, arms, thighs and feet of Brahman (the four Vedic classes), *are called Dasyus, whether they speak the language of the barbarians or that of the Aryans* (MS X.43-45).[5]

The Paundrakas are peoples of Bengal and Bihar, particularly in the coastal regions, while the Dravidas are the Dravidians of southernmost India. The Daradas are a people of the mountains of west India or Afghanistan, as are the Paradas and the Kambojas. The Kiratas are the mountain people, mainly to the east. These mountain peoples were regarded as impure for their hunting and meat-eating life-styles. Some of the coastal people were similarly regarded for fishing and trapping. The others are foreign peoples, some of whom invaded India at some point. The Yavanas (Ionians) are well known as the Greeks. The Shakas are the Scythians who dominated Central Asia in late ancient times. The Pahlavas are the Persians. The Chinas are the Chinese. These diverse peoples both in terms of race and language are said to be fallen descendants of the Vedic nobility, not alien peoples.

Manu states quite clearly that it is the failure to practice the Vedic teaching that turns people into Dasyus, not the language they speak. Hence even in the *Manu Samhita,* the traditional law book of the Hindus, Aryan does not refer to race or language. What makes a person Aryan in the Vedic teaching is a matter of practices, not appearance.

In the *Brahmanas* Vishwamitra curses his fifty sons that refuse to accept the young boy Shunashepa into their family,

> "Your offspring shall inherit the ends of the Earth." There are the people, the Andhras, Pundras, Shabaras, Pulindas, and Mutibas, who live in large numbers beyond the borders; *most of the Dasyus are descendants of Vishwamitra* (AB VII.18).[t]

The Pundras are the same as the Paundrakas, peoples of southern Bengal. The Andhras relate to modern Andhra Pradesh. The Shabaras, Pulindas and Mutibas are various uncivilized tribes in the Deccan. These people are also said to be descendants from Vedic kings.[u]

Modern scholars have said that such passages reflect a time before these regions of India came under the rule of the Vedic Aryans. Yet this is not what the texts say. They do not say that unrelated peoples inhabit the world around them. They place their own descendants in these regions. We would not say that someone who equates his neighbors with estranged kinsmen indicates that he does not know them or that he has just arrived in the area. By the later predominance of Hinduism in these regions we can only consider that such an estrangement was temporary. There is nothing in such passages which shows that these people were unrelated to the Vedic people, or were the original inhabitants of India displaced by them. They may show some Brahmanical prejudice in accepting their spiritual worth but they do not show any division of peoples in terms of race or language.

The main enemies of the Vedic Gods and peoples in the *Rig Veda* are the Dasyus or Dasas, Panis, and later, the Asuras. They are usually demons or negative cosmic forces — powers of darkness, evil, drought, disease, and death. They can at times represent people who ally themselves with the powers of darkness but we should always remember that the human side of these negative forces is secondary and only to the extent that these human groups have departed from their true humanity. The Dasyus appear as the oldest and most hostile, yet, as we have already seen, they are sometimes described as fallen Aryans.

The Panis, the other name for the inimical peoples in the *Vedas,* appear as commercially minded people without any sense of the Divine, who practice black magic and hoard wealth for themselves. They appear to be fallen Vaishyas, those of the merchant class who have strayed from the Vedic Dharma and established a culture devoid of Brahman or spiritual knowledge. There is some mention, however, in the *Rig Veda* of Panis who follow the Aryan path and give their wealth to the seers. One of the Bharadwajas, for example, lauds the gifts of Bribu, one of the Panis.

> Bribu of the Panis stands on the supreme summit, a wide extent like that of the Ganges, who, fast like the wind, quickly gives a thousandfold auspicious gift (VI.45.31-2).

The Asuras, the inimical peoples of the later Vedic age, derive from fallen Kshatriyas or warriors, those of the noble class who similarly establish a non-spiritual culture. The Dasas or Dasyus appear as those of the Shudra or servant class, those seeking pleasure who similarly establish a non-spiritual culture. They appear to have been those who turned the Aryan or spiritual people into servants or slaves.

The Dasyus and Panis are those who do not sacrifice to the Gods, who are not generous in giving but selfishly hoard their wealth. They attack and steal from the Aryans. They are of an alien law but not necessarily of a different physical type.

> Who have no will, binders, whose speech is harmful, traffickers, who have no faith, who give no increase, who do not sacrifice, Agni attacked those Dasyus, from the east he drove the unholy ones to the west (VII.6.3).

They are evil men allied with the forces of darkness, but not simply men of dark skin. This is not a racial image but a metaphor of truth and falsehood.

The division between Aryan and non-Aryan peoples therefore is a division between cultures following spiritual and those following materialistic values. Such a view accords with the Puranic idea that regards the Vedic as prototypal of all human culture, including earlier and later World Ages. Any human beings can only be Aryans or fallen Aryans, as each cycle begins with a Golden Age in which truth is natural to human beings and ends with a dark age in which people come under falsehood and ignorance.

The term that later meant class or caste, Sanskrit 'varna', occurs in the *Rig Veda*. It does not mean color in the racial sense, as some have thought. It means the quality of energy belonging to a person. A Brahmin is white because of the energy of purity (sattva), not because of the color of the skin. A Kshatriya is red as the quality of energy, will and action. Yellow indicates trade, the quality of the Vaishya. Black indicates ignorance and servility, the quality of the Shudra. Skin color, on the other hand, often reflects little more than climate. But even in this regard the Vedic Aryans are said to have the skin of the Sun or a golden color, which is another metaphor for the light of truth.

The Aryan varna is the quality of the spiritual classes; the quality of light, truth, and friendliness. The Dasyu varna is the quality of the unspiritual classes; the quality of darkness, falsehood, and enmity. Varna hence originally meant social value, not hereditary caste but the principles followed by the social group. The Vedic conflict, to the extent that it is a human conflict, is between people of spiritual values or temperament — Aryan varna — and those of materialistic values or temperament — Dasyu varna.

In the *Rig Veda,* Aryans and unaryan peoples cannot be distinguished in terms of race or location. It is simply the division between spiritual and materialistic people that is found everywhere and in all times. Only in Vedic times spiritual people gained predominance and overthrew a previous materialistic culture, which in turn had fallen from Divine grace.

Similarly, Sanskrit is prototypal of the language of truth, the language of the Gods, or Word of God. All human language must start out from this spiritual or mantric language as it is the natural language of the soul or the spiritual part of our nature. Different versions of this mantric language may exist and the Sanskrit we have may represent a later form of it, with traces of it visible in other ancient languages. People of harmful speech or false tongue mentioned in the *Rig Veda* are not merely those who do not speak Sanskrit or an Aryan language. They are those who do not speak the truth, who do not convey in their speech the language of the Gods. Again it is not a linguistic but a spiritual division that is meant.

2
PEOPLES OF THE MIDDLE EAST

Having established the nature of the Vedic Aryans and their antiquity in India, we can now explore how the different peoples of the world relate to or possibly derive from them. We will start with their Middle Eastern neighbors in Mesopotamia and Iran, as this is where we tend to see the oldest civilizations.

THE ASURAS
The Great Warrior Peoples

Asura is one of the main names of the Divine in the *Rig Veda,* second only to Deva in frequency and importance of usage. Asura derives from the root 'as' which means to sit, to be, to exist, to have power. Later it came to be derived as 'a-sura', or not divine, namely demonic. In the *Rig Veda* its original meaning is intact.

> The almighty power (Asuratvam) of the great Gods is only One (III.55).

Even when Asura is used in reference to the undivine in a few passages it is still an attribution of power rather than an indication of an undivine trait.

The term Asura in the *Rig Veda* means something like 'the Almighty', as in the Christian Almighty God. It can be applied to any of the Vedic Gods and can possess a general or almost monotheistic sense for the Divine. It is more specifically used for the Adityas, the solar Godheads, and especially for Varuna, the God of the cosmic and solar ocean, who is also the God of Divine Judgment responsible for the determination of sin or karma.

The Adityas, the foremost of whom is Varuna, are the kings or the military power of the Gods. Varuna is Samrat, the emperor or the world-ruler, the ruler of kings. The Adityas relate specifically to the western region of India and hence to other regions to the west. The worship of the

Asuras, therefore, appears more as part of the Kshatriya side of the Vedic religion, its religion for the warrior or noble class.

Varuna as lord of the ocean appears also as the symbol of the Vedic naval power concentrated in Vedic lands bordering the sea. He may also indicate the colonizing activity of the Vedic culture over the sea. The religion of Asura Varuna may, therefore, have been one of the more widely disseminated aspects of the Vedic culture, at least to cultures nearby open to trade by sea, particularly to the west.

In the Vedic era when the Brahmins and the Kshatriyas, the priests and warriors, remained primarily in harmony, Asura was equal with Deva as meaning the Divine. Later, when the Brahmins and Kshatriyas quarreled, which conflicts begin in the *Rig Veda* itself, Asura came to mean demon. Hence the Asura people may have been originally powerful Kshatriyas or warrior peoples, some of whom broke away from the rule of the Brahmins and at times warred against them, yet still under the banner of their Asuric, Vedic Gods like Varuna and Mitra (as we noted in some of the battles in the *Rig Veda*). The Asuras as descendants of Aryan kings were Aryans in origin. Their Gods were originally Vedic Gods. Their differences with the Vedic people similarly did not reflect a simple division of right and wrong but the gradual division of humanity as materialistic values developed. In this conflict it was not only the Kshatriyas that fell but also the Brahmins. We not only had the conflicts between spiritually-minded priests and worldly-minded kings but also between spiritually-minded kings and worldly-minded priests, not to mention conflicts between spiritual and worldly-minded kings or between spiritual and worldly-minded priests.

In this division of the Vedic people, some of the peoples may have gradually developed different religions, languages and customs. They may have come to live in different areas or even moved out of India either through a process of colonization or by defeat in wars. In later Vedic texts like the *Brahmanas* and *Puranas,* the Asuras first defeat the Devas and are only later defeated by them. This is said to occur in the third age or Treta Yuga, which refers to a very early era of Vedic history.

THE PERSIANS

Ancient Persia in its broadest extent included the entire Persian plateau from the Indus river in the east to the Tigris in the west, to the Amu Darya in the northeast and the Araxes in the northwest. The Persians ruled along the Indus at times. Vedic and Hindu culture similarly included eastern and northern Afghanistan and sometimes penetrated further west. Thus Afghanistan had both a Persian and Hindu influence. By the many references to this region in the *Avesta,* the ancient Persian scriptures, it appears that the Persians first came from Afghanistan, a region of Vedic influence. Zoroaster had as his first and greatest patron King Vishtaspa of Bactria (Balkh), and he also died in this region. He may have been born there as well.[a]

The ancient Persian religion, language and culture called itself 'Aryan' and is very close to the Vedic, so much so that a common origin is necessary for both. In the Persian Zoroastrian religion, the term Asura, changed by a sound shift into Ahura, becomes the main name for God as Ahura Mazda. Deva as Daeva comes to mean "undivine" or "demonic." This is opposite to the shift of meanings in the development of the *Vedas*, wherein Asura comes to mean demonic and Deva retains the sense of Divinity.

The supreme deity of the Persians, Ahura Mazda, is equivalent to Vedic Varuna, the greatest of the Asuras. Ahura Mazda is associated with Mithra, as is Varuna with Mitra. He is Varuna as the supreme God. The Persian religion is thus more a religion of monotheism, yet it still reflects much of the universality of the *Vedas*. It appears based upon an earlier teaching closer in nature to the *Rig Veda*, which like the *Veda* had a greater diversity of teachings. Zoroaster was said to have reformed the earlier religion that had degenerated into polytheism and idolatry. No doubt by his time the Vedic religion had declined in his area and perhaps had become the opposite of its original spiritual basis. Zoroastrians practice a fire worship like the Vedic with chants to deities equivalent to Indra (Vrethragna), Agni (Atar) and Soma (Haoma).

Most Western scholars first assumed that the Vedic and Persian Aryans separated in Central Asia, the Persians moving to the west and the Vedic to the east and south, that the two groups lost contact with each other and independently developed different religions, forgetting their common origin. The change of names of Deva and Asura was thus merely coincidental.

New evidence is challenging this view. It has now been found that the Persians, as they moved into Iran and the Middle East, encountered and displaced earlier Aryan peoples who spoke a language and worshipped Gods closer to the Vedic. The early Aryan peoples of the Middle East, like the Mittani of Syria, were Indo-Aryans, not Iranian.[b] This means that any split between the Indo-Aryans and Iranians occurred within a realm of Indo-Aryan or Vedic culture. The Iranians were related invaders or a reform movement taking over a Vedic culture which previously dominated the region from Iran to Syria by 1500 BC.

The Zoroastrian religion apparently arose in Afghanistan and spread west, displacing Vedic Aryans in Iran. When the Persians under Cyrus conquered Babylonia they already had a large empire stretching to the borders of India in the east. Yet the Persians did not defeat the Deva worshipping Vedic people within their region quickly. As late as the Persian emperor Xerxes mention is made of destruction of the lands of the Daeva worshippers in Persia, in the Mazandaran region south of the Caspian Sea.[c]

The Persians appear originally primarily as Vedic warriors or Kshatriyas who broke off from the main Vedic culture at some point of the Deva-Asura or Brahmin-Kshatriya conflict. The opposite meaning these terms gained was not an accident but reflects this division between the Aryan peoples. Yet while the two terms Deva and Asura were used in opposite senses by the Persians and Hindus, the duality of these terms reflects a common idea of a conflict between truth and falsehood, and between spiritual and worldly people. After the split the terms Deva and Asura gained a mythological meaning and their historical basis was forgotten. Hence while the terms came to refer to a mythical division of good and evil, they do have an historical basis. The original unified Deva-Asura idea of God found in the *Rig Veda* later became a God-demon idea as the conflicts between the priestly and warrior classes grew, along with the general corruption of society.

We should note that language in origin has a dualistic nature. The root 'div' for Deva or God also means "to play" and in the Persian came to mean "to deceive." Even in Sanskrit div also means a game of dice. The root 'as' for Asura means "power" and in the later *Vedas* stood for power in the lower sense of brute force and violence. Divisions of people are reflected in such divisions of language.

Both the *Vedas* and the Persian *Avesta* mention Aryan enemies who were guilty of a negative use of magic and power. There may have been located somewhere between them a fallen Aryan culture that caused each to be mistrustful of the Aryan influence in that direction. Or there may have been among each of them a group of fallen Aryans that caused similar difficulties. One of the five Vedic peoples is called the Druhyus. They are well known in the *Puranas* to have moved out of India to the west, the direction of the Persians. They were one of the peoples defeated by Sudas. They may have been the ancestors of the Persians or of the Indo-Aryan peoples that the Persians displaced. The Vedic-Persian division probably occurred fairly late in ancient times as the Persians preserved so much of a similar teaching and language. Yet an earlier Deva-Asura split may have happened as well (as we will see in our examination of the Assyrians).

The Persian religion reflects a later date than the *Rig Veda* in a number of ways. It does not appear in the form of earlier imagistic ancient religions like the Vedic or the Egyptian but has a strong aniconic form like the later Judaic, Christian and Islamic. These religions arose in reaction to the idolatry of the earlier ones, which shows their later date (though we should note that these ancient religions were not polytheistic in origin either, nor overly formalized). The Persian religion resembles in some ways the Assyrian, which also worshiped Asura (Ashur).

The Persian religion looks back to Yima, equivalent to the Vedic God of the dead Yama, as the original man and does not mention Manu.[d] Yama as the original man appears late and peripherally in Vedic literature. Zoroaster commonly mentions Atar, Vedic Atharva, and this suggests his teaching came after the period of the *Atharva Veda.*

The Persian religion also appears to know of Rama, the Hindu avatar. They have a God named Ram, to whom sacrifices are offered. He is identified with Vayu, the God of the wind. Most scholars have regarded the Persian God and the Hindu avatar as unrelated. However, his connection with Vayu shows a definite relationship. Rama's main companion is Hanuman, the monkey God, who is a form of Vayu called Maruti or Vatatmaja, the Son of the wind. The *Zend Avesta* describes Vayu like Hanuman as being able to assume any size or shape or go anywhere.

> Oh great Vayu! you are high up-girded, firm, swift-moving, high-footed, wide-thighed, with untrembling eyes.[e]

The date of the Persian religion is another matter of dispute. Zoroaster, its founder, is usually dated around 600 BC by modern scholars. Yet the ancient Greeks, like Aristotle, date him to 6000 BC, showing that he was already a figure of great legendary antiquity by their era. Hence the late date for Zoroaster, like that of the *Vedas*, may be questionable. The Persians do not appear in Assyrian historical records until the ninth century BC, though these records are fragmentary and limited. Even conservatively one could date Zoroaster at the latest along with the late ancient reform teachings of around 1500 BC like those of the Hebrews, Akhenaton in Egypt, and the *Upanishads.* While the *Upanishads* brought a monistic philosophy out of the ancient symbolic religion of India, the Hebrews and Persians brought a monotheistic religion out of the symbolic religions around them.

The 6000 BC date may relate more to the Vedic religion from which the Persian came. However, if Zoroaster came from this early period, it would only serve to make the *Vedas* yet earlier, as they show an earlier stage of the Aryan religion. In any case, the ancient Greeks, whom we admire so much for their scientific bent of mind, had no qualms in dating such Aryan prophets to many millennia before their time.

Hence the Persians and the Hindus come from a common Vedic religious and cultural matrix. Each reformed the Vedic religion in different ways as the original ancient teaching of the *Rig Veda* degenerated through time. We should note that the main enemies of the Persians were the Turanians, the Turks to the northeast, not the Hindus who eventually provided them a refuge after the Muslim conquest of their country. Fleeing Persia to India to escape the Muslims, the Zoroastrians may have been returning to their original homeland.

THE ASSYRIANS

The ancient Assyrians also worshipped Asura. In fact they derived the name of their main city and their whole culture from that of their main God Ashur. Assyrian Ashur, like the Vedic Asura, was a Sun God and a militaristic God of great power and victory. Like the Persian Ahura and Egyptian Sun God he was symbolized by the winged disc. The Assyrians were more typically a Kshatriya dominated culture, a militaristic culture of war, conquest and empire. Certainly the terrible reputation of Assyrian military power fits very well with the Vedic idea of the aggressive and violent Asuric nature that came to be associated with this name. Hence there can be little doubt that the terrible Asuras we read of in the *Vedas*, insofar as they have an historical counterpart, were not the Persians, who were close to the Vedic culture, but the Assyrians.

However, we must again be careful in giving mythological ideas too literal an historical basis. The Assyrians were not simple demons like the Asuras portrayed in later Vedic and Hindu literature. The Vedic account of wars between the Gods and demons reflects the conflict of truth and falsehood in the mind and does not have a simple historical meaning. The Assyrians had violent traits and confrontations with the Hindus that caused them to be associated with a negative appellation, but they had their positive side as well, and we read of Asuric people having alliances and intermarriages with the Vedic people.

The Assyrians, though perhaps only in their negative periods, appear to have founded a religious cult of empire that later cultures adapted and which has been the source of much of the violence and destruction in the world over the past millennia. It is the assumption of Brahmanical (spiritual) right by Kshatriya (military) power. We should note that it is not the power of the sword that spreads the truth or the good religion, but, to use the Vedic metaphor, the power of the cow, the power of the receptive and non-violent mind.

The Persians were in proximity to the Assyrians. They may have been ruled by them at certain times and may have been influenced by them. Yet the Persian religion, as it is closer to the Vedic, may better represent the

Asuric (and thereby Assyrian) religion before its split with the Vedic culture. The Assyrians in northwest Mesopotamia were also close to the Indo-Aryan peoples of this area, like the Hittites and Mittani, and may have descended from them. So perhaps the older form of the Assyrian religion was closer to the Persian and the Vedic. In this regard, the Vedic would also be the original form of the Assyrian religion.

As in most of the period of the *Rig Veda* the Devas and Asuras were on good terms with each other, it appears that at the time of the *Rig Veda* the Vedic and Assyrian people lived together in harmony. Some scholars have thought that the Vedic Aryans were associated temporarily with the Assyrians in their journey to India, that they passed through the Assyrian region of the world and took into their religion some of the Assyrian Gods. Certainly Aryan peoples, like the Hittites and Persians, lived in proximity to the Assyrians in ancient times. Others scholars have thought India was originally inhabited by Assyrians, who were pre-Vedic. Yet it appears more likely that the Assyrians were also Aryans and India was the home of the Aryans from prehistoric times. Perhaps the early Aryans included people speaking non-Indo-European languages like the Assyrian, or perhaps the Assyrian language was an early diversification of Sanskrit along different lines.

The Assyrians must have originally been powerful military (Kshatriya) people within the realm of Vedic culture. This may have been in India but could also have been further west, according to a greater idea of the extent of Vedic culture. There must have been major wars between India and Assyria at some point, though there were also periods of peace and trade between them. The Assyrians, or at least some portion of them, were probably first defeated in India and then continued the battle from their new homeland in Mesopotamia. The Assyrians not only attacked cultures to the west as far as Egypt but must have assaulted India to the east as well, to account for their reputation.

This leads us to believe that the Assyrians were a mighty people in the ancient world much earlier than modern archaeologists believe. They were well known to have been powerful after 1500 BC and particularly from 1100–700 BC. Yet Assyrian settlements are found in Asia Minor before 2000 BC, which scholars regard as trading settlements. However, as the Assyrians were not traders, they must have been present as conquerors. The Akkadians, who had a great empire in the Middle East around 2300 BC, are regarded by the Assyrians as their ancestors and they count Akkadian kings, like Sargon, as their rulers. The Akkadians may indeed have been Assyrians. The Assyrians appear as the prime power the Vedic Aryans encountered in opposition to them. Their influence must have often spread into Persia, Central Asia, and India itself by the time of the

Brahmanical texts (which largely employ the Taurus equinox of 2000 BC) which speak of them in a negative light.

THE HITTITES, MITTANI AND KASSITES
Indo-Aryan Peoples of the Ancient Middle East

Even today, Aryan peoples like the Kurds, Armenians, and Persians are predominant in the mountain regions of the Middle East. In the middle of the second millennium BC, various Aryan peoples like the Hittites, Mittani, and Kassites lived in these regions and ruled Mesopotamia. The Hittites had a great empire — one of the first that we know of in the ancient world — that included much of Anatolia (modern Turkey) and Mesopotamia, where they were predominant for over five centuries.

The Hittites have been found in northern Mesopotamia by 2200 BC. Their script is based upon the Sumerian of the third dynasty of Ur. Their art and physical features resemble the Sumerians. As the Sumerians are one of the oldest cultures in the Middle East this shows some antiquity for the Hittites also. Aryan peoples thus appear to be earlier, more advanced in culture and more intimate in association with the earliest ancient cultures of the Middle East than previously thought.

A treaty of the Mittani king Mattiwaza and Hittite king Subiluliuma that has been dated around 1380 BC mentions the Vedic Gods Mitra, Varuna, Indra, and the Ashwins. Among the Hittite tablets is a treatise using chariot-racing terms in virtually pure Sanskrit.[f] It is interesting to note that Vedic Gods first appear in our recorded history of the world not in India but in Syria. This reflects their influence from India; it does not mean that the Aryans were not yet in India.

The Mittani, who dominated northern Syria for a number of centuries and had intermarriages with the Egyptian pharaohs, had the closest language to Sanskrit of the Aryans of the ancient Middle East. The Kassites, who ruled Babylonia for six centuries, also worshipped Vedic Gods like Surya and the Maruts. In a Kassite record of 1750 BC a God named "Himalaya" occurs, which shows that the Indo-Aryans were in India prior to coming to the Middle East.[g] The Kassites may have passed on knowledge of astrology and other ancient sciences from Vedic India to Babylonia where Western astrology gradually emerged. The Hittites, like the Persians and Egyptians, also used the winged disc as the symbol of their religion or Sun God. They appear intermediate between the Persians and Assyrians in terms of their culture and religion, perhaps even between the Persians and Sumerians.

A modern scholar writes,

> It is now generally agreed by most authorities on the subject that the Aryan linguistic vestiges in the Near East are to be connected specifically with Indo-Aryan, and not with the Iranian, and also that they do not represent a third, independent group, and are not to be ascribed to the hypothetically reconstructed Proto-Aryan.[h]

Hence, prior to the Persians, the Middle East was dominated by Vedic Aryans. Perhaps these Indo-Aryans were also prior to the Assyrians, who like the Persians may have developed from them. Or perhaps they were part of an Indian conquest of the region to keep the Assyrians (Asuras) in check. In this way much of ancient Middle Eastern culture may have originated with the Indo-Aryans or at least have been strongly influenced by them.

THE EGYPTIANS

The name Asura for the Divine appears in ancient Egypt as well. The Egyptians worshipped the Divine as 'Asar', the Egyptian name of Osiris. Asar was symbolized by a throne, and meant to sit, to be, to have power, just as in the Sanskrit root 'as'. The Egyptians, like the Persians and Assyrians, used the winged disc as a symbol of their Sun God.

The Egyptians, like the ancient Indo-Aryans and Assyrians, also had a solar dynasty of kings, symbolized by the hawk or falcon. They had many common symbols with the Vedic like the lotus, the spotted cow and the bull. The oldest pharaohs, much like the Vedic Indra, were named destroyers of cities, or destroyers of the seven cities (for example, Narmer, identified as Menes, the first of the pharaohs).

Osiris, the Egyptian God of the Dead, appears very much like Yama, the Vedic God of the Dead. Yama is called 'Asu-niti', the guide of the spirit who conducts the soul after death much like Osiris. The Egyptian God Osiris is 'Asar-netar'. Netar is the Egyptian name for the Divine, which appears to be represented by a flag.[i] In the *Rig Veda,* after Deva and Asura, 'Netar', meaning "guide," is perhaps the most common Vedic name for the Divine.

> All mortals should choose the companionship of a Divine Netar (V.50.1).[1]

Some Vedic hymns sound like hymns to Osiris:

> Oh guide of the spirit (Asuniti), give us back our soul, return our breath and give us back our enjoyment. May we

> ever see the Sun rising. Guide of the spirit, give us compassion for our well-being (X.59.6).

This sounds much like the returning of life, breath and sight to the dead soul symbolized by Osiris in the *Egyptian Book Of The Dead.*

Yama is a solar resurrection figure like Osiris, the Divine Son who is sacrificed to establish a path to truth for humanity. Yama is especially associated with Varuna (X.14.7); together they are called the two kings. In this respect Yama represents Mitra, with whom Varuna is also commonly associated. There is much in the Yama hymns of the *Rig Veda* similar to the religion of ancient Egypt, including symbolism that suggests the attempt to preserve the body after death. In this regard note the hymns to Yama (X.14-6) and of Bandhu (X.59-60). These show a point of contact between Vedic and Egyptian religious thought. Perhaps the Egyptian religion comes from the solar dynasty of India and is a diversification of its worship of Yama. The Egyptians called the western land of the setting Sun where the dead go "the land of Manu," and the mountain where they buried their kings in Thebes "the mountain of Manu," suggesting some ancestry to Vedic Manu.[J]

Nimi, one of the early kings of the Vedic solar dynasty and said to have conducted a thousand-year-long sacrifice, is described in the *Puranas* as being mummified like the Egyptian pharaohs.

> The corpse of Nimi was preserved from decay by being embalmed with fragrant oils and resins, and it remained as entire as if it were immortal (VP IV.5.7).

The translator states,

> This shows that the Hindus were not unacquainted with the Egyptian art of embalming dead bodies. In the Kashi Khanda, s.30, an account is given of a Brahman who carries his mother's bones, or rather her corpse, from Setubandha or Rameswara to Kashi (Benares). For this purpose he first washes it with the five excretions of a cow, and the five pure fluids, or milk, curds, ghee, honey and sugar. He then embalms it with Yakshakardama, a composition of agaru, camphor, musk, saffron, sandalwood, and a resin called Kakkola; and envelopes it severally with Netravastra, flowered muslin; Pattamvara, silk; Surasavastra, coarse cotton; Manjishta, cloth dyed with madder; and Nepal blanketing. He then covers it with pure clay,

> and puts the whole into a coffin of copper. These practices are not only unknown but would be thought impure in the present day.[k]

The Egyptians attribute their culture as having come from across the sea, from a mythical tropical holy land/paradise of the rising Sun called Punt. Such an eastern land cannot be Somalia, as Western scholars have thought, since Somalia is to the south. Punt was a land where monkeys were worshipped. Ra, the Sun God of Egypt, appears very similar to Rama, also a form of the Sun God. Egyptian Amen-Re may be Vedic Om-Ram. The Egyptian pharaohs appear to have been related to the solar dynasty of eastern India.

The great pharaoh Akhenaton in the New Kingdom tried to restore the purity of the ancient solar religion. His hymns to the Sun God are much like the Vedic hymns to the Sun God. The art work of his era portrays the Sun's rays as culminating in hands. This is an old Vedic idea, the golden-handed Sun God Savitar (I.35.9). Egypt of his time was allied to the Indo-Aryan Mittani of Syria. Perhaps Akhenaton was also influenced by the Vedic solar religion of the Mittani.

We cannot regard the Egyptians, like the Assyrians, as a predominantly militaristic people. They were more of a religious (Brahmin) orientation and only pursued conquest in their later period. The Egyptian religion appears to reflect much of the worship of the Devas and its development appears to have been prior to, though related to, that of the Deva-Asura split. The Egyptians were more like Vedic colonists who conquered a distant land and preserved well the ancient teaching. Their religion was like the Asuric side of the Vedic religion, Varuna and Yama, but it remained open and not tied to any exclusive cult of only one God. Horus, the son of Osiris, also resembles the Vedic God Indra. Both are hawk Gods and demon slayers. The *Yajur Veda* is concerned with putting back together the cosmic man, Indra, for the purposes of going beyond death (see SYV XX). This is much like the Egyptian restoration of Osiris, who is also the cosmic man. The *Yajur Veda* dates astronomically to the same era as ancient Egypt, and reflects the common religious practices of the time.

THE SUMERIANS

The Sumerians are now regarded by historians as the oldest civilization in the world, the place where the rudiments of civilization like writing or the wheel were invented. Their language was neither Semitic nor Indo-European. It was an agglutinative language perhaps related to the Dravidian. Racially the Sumerians appear to be of the same Mediterranean or Armenian type as the rest of the people of the region. They also had an eastern holy land called Dilmun, a land of the rising Sun, to which they attributed their origins, and where their flood hero, Ziusudra, was said to have lived. It was also an actual land with whom the Sumerians traded throughout their history.

Some archaeologists have identified Dilmun with the island of Bahrain. However this island was too small and too close to Sumeria to have been a mythical paradise. Others (Samuel Noah Kramer) have identified Dilmun with India.[1] This would be in line with our ideas here. The standard units of measurement used in Bahrain have been found to be those of the Indus Valley culture (some of which were still used in India in later times), which shows that the Indus culture dominated the island. This would also tend to place Dilmun further east.

The Sumerians were also connected with a city called Aratta, thought to have been located in Iran. In the *Puranas,* Aratta (or Aradvat) is a name of one of the regions of Afghanistan, and one of the descendants of Druhyu who ruled it (VP IV.27.1). This further affirms the idea that the Druhyus of ancient India spread to the Middle East.

ELAM

Dravidians of the Ancient Middle East

East of Sumeria towards the foothills of Persia was the powerful and enduring culture of Elam. It dominated the trade routes from central Asia and India. It was prominent from the time of the Sumerians, with whom it was sometimes an ally and sometimes an enemy. By recent accounts (David McAlpin of the University of London) the ancient Elamite language appears to be related to Dravidian, the language of south India.[m] The main city of Elam was called 'Susa'. A 'Susha' is mentioned in the *Matsya Purana* "as the name of the beautiful city of wise Varuna."[2, n]

Vasishta in the *Rig Veda* is said to visit by sea a great thousand-gated temple of Varuna (VII.88.5),[3] perhaps Susa. Elam may, therefore, be the prime center of Mesopotamian culture and the diffusion of culture from India by both land and sea. Perhaps through Elam the Vedic culture seeded or at least strongly influenced the Middle East. Elam may have been an ancient Vedic colony or point of dispersion connected to the Vedic land of Ila or the Saraswati region.

Just as we find Indo-Aryans and Dravidians residing in the ancient Middle East, so too ancient India probably had, besides these two groups, peoples related to the Assyrians and Sumerians. Apparently the different peoples lived together, perhaps as different classes within the same society, and only in time did they settle down in distinctly different areas.

THE PHOENICIANS

The names given to the Phoenicians, like 'Poeni' by the Romans and 'Phoinike' by the Greeks, resemble the Vedic terms Pani, Vani and Vanik, meaning "trader." Some Vedic scholars have thereby identified the Vedic Panis with the Phoenicians. While this correspondence may not be exact, certainly the Phoenicians appear as members of the commercial class. The Vedic Panis, as noted, appear as fallen Vaishyas, fallen merchants, just as later the Asuras appear as fallen warriors or Kshatriyas. The Panis were probably merchants in India, perhaps largely sea traveling. Some of them may have strayed from the spiritual law of the land and been driven out.

Again we should be careful of taking the mythological metaphor too literally. The Phoenicians, though commercial in nature, cannot be simply regarded as demons, any more than the Assyrians. Yet we cannot ignore these terms as without historical basis either. The Phoenicians were a commercial people. They did appear to practice occultism and even human sacrifice more than other ancient people, and the *Bible* mentions them among the Philistines as having a dark side. Yet in their positive side they may have been like the good merchants of the *Vedas*. We should also note that the hostility between religious and commercial people would be exaggerated by both sides, particularly in ages of growing darkness and division. Hence we should not regard the Phoenicians simply as the demonic Panis but as Vedic merchants with both spiritual and materialistic types among them, though tending to the excesses of the commercial class.

The Phoenician navy is known to have traveled all the way around Africa (and to the Americas as well, it appears). A trade connection with India or even possible colonies in that region would also be possible. This was the natural traveling tendency of the merchant class.

The Phoenicians also worshiped Il. Perhaps they got their religion from Elam or perhaps the Elamites were their ancestors or relatives (such was the view of the Greek historian Herodotus). Hence a connection with India in terms of religion is suggested.

The Panis in the *Rig Veda* appear to be early inhabitants of India, perhaps the remnants of a fallen Aryan culture in the region. The demon Shambara, who had a hundred cities, is said to be a Pani. The Panis are the main enemies of Indra, sometimes said to live across the ocean or the world river. They would not just be the Phoenicians but an earlier and unspiritual commercial culture. The extent to which we may identify them with the Phoenicians is thus questionable but a connection is definite. The conflict between spiritual and commercial people is perhaps the central issue in humanity, even today. That it was so in the times of the *Rig Veda* is not surprising.

THE GOD IL AND THE GODDESS ILA

It is perhaps in the ancient names for God that the most original and universal words of the ancient languages are preserved. The most important Mesopotamian name for the Divine is 'Il'. It is common to the Elamites, Phoenicians, Syrians, Hebrews, and Arabs and may be the most common name for the Divine among the Semitic peoples, though it is not limited to them. A very late and short Upanishad called the *Allopanishad*, probably from the time of the Mogul emperor Akbar (sixteenth century), equates the Semitic Il with the 'Ila' of the *Rig Veda* and with the worship of Varuna-Mitra. It has such chants as "Ilam Varuna," "Mitra Ilam" (v.1), and "Ilela Akabarho" (v.3). These combine the main Islamic chant to Allah with old Vedic verses to Mitra, Varuna, and Ila. Other parts of the Upanishad are chants to Indra and the seven seers.[o]

The Vedic land of Manu is called 'Ilavarta', "the region of Ila," originally the Saraswati region of India.

> Oh sacred fire (Agni), we put you down at the best place on Earth, at the place of Ila in the clear brightness of the days. On the Drishadvati, Apaya and Saraswati rivers, shine out brilliantly for men (III.23.4).

Ila is called "the teacher of men," showing that great sages came from this region.

> You, Agni, were the first living one for living men. The Gods made you the ruler of the peoples of Nahusha. They made Ila the instructress of men (I.31.11).[4]

Elam as the name for the Susa region of Mesopotamia suggests that this region was named after the Ilavarta of India, perhaps by colonizers from it. Thus the Middle Eastern children of Ila may have also been descendants of Manu, from Ilavarta in India. The Vedic root 'il' means to pray, worship or energize. Indeed the *Rig Veda* begins, "I worship the sacred fire" (agnim ile; I.1.1). The same root also exists in other Indo-European tongues, as in the English word 'elegy.' The Goddess Ila is also closely associated with Agni. Agni is enkindled in the place of Ila:

> Agni, the son of Ila, is born.[5]
> We enkindle you at the place of Ila, the navel center of the Earth (III.29.3-4).[6]

The land of Ila is thus the land of worship or prayer, the land where the sacred fire rituals are practiced. Ila as a Goddess is akin to Saraswati, Goddess of the Divine Word, as two of the three Goddesses in the Apri hymns of the *Rig Veda.*

> May the Goddess Bharati in accord with the Bharatis, Ila with the Gods and Agni with men, may Saraswati with the Saraswatis come here, the three Goddesses to sit at this altar seat (III.4.8; VII.2.8).

The ten Apri hymns of the *Rig Veda* are very ancient ritualistic hymns. These three Goddesses, the three Vedic muses — Bharati, Ila and Saraswati — are one set of deities they invoke. Another verse of the Apri hymns refers ila (neuter tense) as the place where Agni, the sacred fire, is worshipped. My feeling is that the Apri hymns reflect the original Vedic seasonal rituals done at the temples on the Saraswati river that were established by Manu.[P]

I would suggest further that Il (masculine tense) was originally a name of Varuna, and Ila (feminine tense) is his consort. Ila may be another form of Aditi, the Mother of the Adityas, and the main Vedic Mother Goddess. Both Aditi and Ila are Vedic names for the Earth. Il-Ila would then be the Vedic forms of the Divine Father and Mother and all the Gods would be their children.

In the *Puranas* Ila (feminine) is the eldest child of Manu. Originally she was a man, the eldest son of Manu. In the Puranic story (VP IV.1), Ila was turned into a woman. This story may also suggest that an earlier culture, worshipping the Divine as Ila, fell through some lack of spiritual knowledge. Il-Ila may thus also be interpreted as Adam and Eve. Taking this idea yet further, Il-Ila as the progenitors of humanity may be names for Manu and his wife/daughter or Adam and Eve before their fall. The land of Ila, the river paradise of humanity, may be the Vedic equivalent of the Eden of the *Bible*. It is the paradise of prayer, worship or Yoga, from which we are cast out by our materialistic seeking.

Ila is also the name of the heavenly waters, particularly the heavenly source of the rains, and may be another general name for the sea. Varuna is the God of the sea and the rains. Ila is thereby a Goddess of inspiration, devotion and Divine joy, of the grace that falls from Heaven. She, like the Saraswati, is the Divine river that yields milk and honey.

> May the noble two kings, the great guardians of truth, lords of the river, come here. Mitra and Varuna, quick to give, send down from Heaven to us Ila, the rain (VII.64.2).

Varuna is the Divine Father, Mitra the Divine Son and Ila the Mother. Mitra is also commonly a name for Agni (i.e., III.5.4), who is the Divine Child and savior. In fact, all the main Vedic Gods — Indra, Agni and Soma — are forms of this Divine Son and savior.

VARUNA AND INDRA
The Divine Father and Divine Son

Varuna-Il, as both a solar and an ocean God, would therefore be the main God of the ancient Persians, Assyrians, Egyptians, Phoenicians, Elamites, Israelites, and Arabs, as well as the Aryans. Ila would be the land that he ruled, particularly by the ocean or a great river region flowing into the sea, the Vedic Saraswati region.

Indra or the storm God is also prominent, not only in India and ancient Europe, but as the many storm and thunder Gods of Mesopotamia, who like Indra destroy the primordial dragon (Tiamat) and bring on the flood. Yet the story appears to be that Varuna-Il is an older God. His son is Saturn (Chronos), whose son in turn is Jupiter (Zeus or Indra), the storm God, Semitic Adad, Hadad or Marduk. A book on mythology notes:

> *A History of the Uranides,* a war between the generations of deities relates: in the beginning was Elyun, the Most High, succeeded by Uranus. He is dethroned and emasculated by his son Cronus, who is Elos, but he has an avenger in the person of Zeus, who is Adados, now king of the Gods. There too we find the names of Semitic deities: Elyun is Elyon, who is named in an Aramean inscription and his is the title of the God of Israel in the Psalms; Cronus-Elos is El; Zeus-Adados is Hadad, the name of the Aramean storm God coupled with Zeus in the Hellenic period.[q]

The first God is succeeded by Uranus/Varuna (to equate the Greek and the Sanskrit) who establishes the cosmic order. He is overthrown by his son Chronos or Saturn, who is the God of time and death, the demiurge (Vedic Vritra) who eats his own children. Varuna's rule is reestablished by Jupiter (Zeus-Indra), whose wisdom brings immortality and returns us to the eternal Father. This is a common ancient myth, Aryan and Semitic.

Varuna is an old God in the *Rig Veda* and some scholars consider that his rule was usurped by Indra. The correct interpretation we see here is that Indra reestablishes the rule of his true father, Varuna, the God of Heaven, which was lost to his false or evil father, the serpent or demiurge,

Vritra. Sometimes the Vedic God Twashtar, the form-fashioner or artisan, appears as a lesser, though not evil father figure, whose rule Indra takes over or whose law he breaks. Hence there is both a lower and higher father in the *Rig Veda* and Varuna is the higher. In the *Rig Veda,* Indra and Varuna are often invoked together as a dual deity (i.e. VII.82, 84 & 85), as are Mitra and Varuna. Indra thus is also Mitra; they are both Gods of the day, as Varuna rules the night. Mitra-Varuna, Indra-Varuna or Agni-Varuna are all forms of the Divine Son and Divine Father.

Indra-Mitra as the Divine Son is the immanent Divine. He shows the spirit of the teaching, how man can realize the truth. Varuna as the Divine Father can represent the outer or more formal law of the religion, much like the duality of Christ and the older Hebrew father God. (Note that "our Heavenly Father" of the *New Testament* in the Greek is "Patar Ouranos," Vedic "Pitar Varuna"). Just as in the *New Testament,* the Vedic way to the Father is through the Son; the rule of Indra over Varuna is the Divine Son taking over the kingdom of the Father and perfecting his place on Earth and in the human being. It is Christ showing the rule of compassion beyond the rule of the law.

Indra's dominance over Varuna also represents the rule of a monistic over a monotheistic religion. Hence in some respects Varuna is the outer God of the Vedic religion and Indra-Mitra the inner God. Outwardly monotheism, the religion of One God, is inwardly monism, the religion that All is God and the Self is God. Varuna is thus the world-ruler and Indra the Self-ruler (VII.82.2). Varuna, the God of the old testament of the law, must give way to Indra, the God of the new testament of knowledge. These two aspects of religion are not simply sequential in time. Varuna is often the exoteric teaching and Indra the esoteric. One naturally leads to and finds its culmination in the other. This issue though is a matter of degree and Varuna in the *Rig Veda* can represent the inner teaching also, just as in later (Puranic) times, Indra came to represent the outer teaching (with Shiva and Vishnu coming to represent the inner). Indra is also the drinker of the Soma and Varuna is often identified with Soma, the God of ecstasy, as the God of the Waters. Mitra-Varuna is also Indra-Soma.

Varuna also can resemble Rudra-Shiva as the terrible father of the Gods. It is not only the wrath of Rudra that the ancients pray to be saved from but the wrath of Varuna.

> Oh Fire (Agni), knower of Varuna, remove from us the wrath of this God (IV.1.4).
>
> Do not slay us, Oh Rudra, or give us away. May we not be in the net of your wrath (VII.46.4).

In this way, the Middle Eastern El-Allah may be an old relative of the Hindu Shiva. Varuna-Rudra is one with his son, Mitra-Indra.

These dual Gods can be related to the Sun and Moon; though we should note that the Vedic Gods cannot be reduced to a single symbol as they are principles, not phenomena. Mitra, Agni and Indra appear more under the symbolism of the Sun, while Varuna, Soma and Twashtar are more under that of the Moon. The Divine Son relates to the Sun and the Divine Father to the Moon. The symbol of Allah, the Arabic Father God, is also the crescent Moon, which Shiva, the Hindu Father God, wears on his head. The later Hindu duality of Vishnu-Shiva also follows the somewhat analogy of the Sun and the Moon. The avatars, Divine incarnations, are forms of Vishnu, who is the Sun, Surya Narayana.

Between these two Gods, Indra-Varuna or the Divine Son and Father, we can see an underlying unity at the origin of the main religious concepts of humanity. Even Manu and Yama, the twin Vedic fathers of the human race, are the Sun and the Moon. The Sun Gods represent the Vedic Path of the Gods (Devayana), ruled by Agni and Manu. The Vedic Path of the Fathers (Pitriyana) is ruled by Soma, Varuna and Yama. These are the paths of the ascent of the light of the Divine Son and the descent of the grace of the Divine Father.

The Vedic Divine Sons are all aspects of the Divine Son or Christ consciousness. This Divine Son is the Sun. He is born at the winter solstice and travels by the path of light (the northern course of the Sun) to the Divine Father (the point of the summer solstice). The immortal Son is sacrificed to the Divine Father to redeem the sins of his mortal father, our human nature or conditioned mind.

However, we should not forget the role of the Divine Mother and Word Goddess. She is the virgin (pure) mind who gives birth to the Divine child of Self-knowledge. Vedic Ila-Saraswati, the Christian Madonna and the Buddhist noble wisdom (Arya Prajña) are all related to these original aspirations of humanity.

JUDAISM, CHRISTIANITY AND ISLAM

The Hebrew El or Elohim, God the Father, may therefore be another form of the same deity as Vedic Il-Varuna. Elohim is actually a plural and neutral term and suggests that the Hebrews originally worshipped the Divine in the form of many Gods and Goddesses much like the ancient Hindus and Egyptians. The *Old Testament* was compiled after the Persians released the Israelites from their Babylonian captivity. Several books of the *Bible* thereby have Persian (and perhaps indirect Vedic) influence, like the books of *Job* and *Esther.* The Hebrew idea of the Messiah comes from books like *Daniel* and *Ezekiel* which were written during the Babylonian captivity and may reflect further Persian influence.

Possible Vedic influence can be found prior to the time of the Persians as well. Abraham, along with his father Terah, went to the city of Haran (Charrhan) before going to Palestine. According to the Biblical story his father died there after two hundred and five years, and then Abraham left.[r] Haran was in northwest Mesopotamia, the region of the Mittani, an Indo-Aryan people worshipping Vedic Gods like Indra and Varuna and by some accounts may have been the capital of the Mittani. Perhaps Abraham took some of the Vedic and yogic knowledge of the Mittani with him. The Levites, one of the twelve Jewish tribes, have been related to the Luvian people of Anatolia, who also appear to have been Indo-European.

The Biblical Garden of Eden, like the sacred lands of Dilmun of the Sumerians and Punt of the Egyptians, was located in the east, toward India. Like the Hindu Mount Meru, it is the source of the four great world rivers.[s] Noah, whose three sons were said to have fathered the different peoples of humanity, resembles the Vedic Yayati, whose five sons have the same role. Both figures have a split with their children and end up protected by their youngest son (Vedic Puru and Biblical Japheth), whom they bless.[t]

The Israelites were a religious reform movement. On one hand, they tried to get back to the more simple form of the ancient religions of the Middle East, like those of Egypt and Babylonia before their fall and corruption. On the other hand, they appear to have rejected them altogether and formed a new religion of their own. The idolatry they complained of in their neighbors was not the true spirit of the ancient religions but their degenerate form. The *Old Testament* resembles, in several respects, the *Puranas* of India, books of ancient religious records and genealogies.[u]

The true spirit of the ancient religions, like that of Moses, was a worship of the Divine as "I am that I am," the Divine Self symbolized by the Sun that we find in the *Vedas* and *Upanishads*. Behind all the ancient solar religions was this sense of the solar Divinity, the Divine Self of pure light. In this regard we can identify the serpent in the Biblical Garden of Eden with the serpent of the *Vedas*. The Biblical serpent (Greek ophis) is Vedic Ahi-Vritra, the enemy of Indra. The great Vedic victory of Indra is the destruction of the serpent, which is also the winning of the Soma. The Soma-nectar of immortality is the fruit of the sacred tree, the tree of knowledge, that also grows in the Garden of Eden. The victory of Indra is thus the restoration of the soul of man to the Biblical Garden of Eden, which stands for the pure state of the soul before its identification with the physical body.

Some of the Vedic hymns to Varuna sound like Biblical psalms.

> King Varuna, may I not go to the house of clay. Be compassionate, great lord, grant me your grace. Oh Thunderer, when I go trembling, like a wind-blown skin, be compassionate, great Lord, grant me your grace. When through lack of will, oh great light, I have gone contrary to truth, be compassionate, great Lord, grant me your grace. Standing in the middle of the waters, your singer was afflicted with thirst, be compassionate, great Lord, grant me your grace (VII.89.1-4).

Christ is the Divine Son-Sun like Vedic Mitra, the counterpart of Varuna and also resembles other ancient Divine solar resurrection figures like Yama and Osiris. The Greeks call him Lord, Kyrios, which is the Greek equivalent of the Vedic Shura, Lord or Hero, a major Vedic name for Indra. Christ is one of the great ancient solar savior Gods, which is why he is born on the winter solstice. There is some Persian connection to Christianity as the three Magi that visited the Christ child were Persian priests. Christianity and the Persian-born Mithraism were thus not only two conflicting religions in Roman times but two related ones, and many of their myths overlap.

There are many trinities and threefold Gods and Goddesses in the *Rig Veda*. Later Hinduism has the trinity of Brahma, Vishnu and Shiva or God as the creator, preserver and destroyer. The Christian trinity most reflects the Vedic trinity of Varuna, Mitra and Agni — the Divine Father, the Divine Son and the Holy Spirit — the latter which is symbolized by the flame of Agni, the sacred fire.

The region of northern Syria, the land of the Indo-Aryan Mittani, remained an important center of learning and spiritual teaching into later times. It became a neutral zone between the Byzantine Christians and the Muslims. Much of the alchemy, astrology and magic that went to both of these cultures came through this region.

Islam began as another attempt to return to a true and genuine spirit of peace and surrender to the Divine, according to the simple yet exalted message of the prophet Mohammed. It also followed the ancient religions of Il and Varuna. It countered the Christian emphasis on the Divine Son with an emphasis on the Divine Father. The *Koran* begins with Alm, which may be Vedic Aum or Om (the Arabic 'l' being pronounced like a 'u' when it appears before a consonant). The sacred rock at Mecca may be an old Shiva linga (sacred stone for worshipping Shiva). The place Mecca (Arabic Makkah) appears to derive from the Sanskrit word Makha meaning sacrifice or ritual, which we find commonly in the *Vedas* (i.e. SYV XXXVII).

Unfortunately, a militaristic spirit arose in the western religions of Christianity and Islam and fueled various conquests, crusades, inquisitions, and holy wars including against India itself. Even in Hindu and Buddhist countries religion has often become a pretext for worldly forces, though more of social domination than military conquest. Today the world is still encased by creeds that imprison spiritual truth in political, social, commercial, and personal interests. Religion, the savior of humanity, has thereby become its curse. This has nothing to do with the real spirit of religion but merely reflects the confusion in the human mind as religion is perverted for worldly purposes.

ANCIENT WORLD UNITY

It appears therefore that at the time of the *Rig Veda* the people from India in the east to Egypt in the west were part of the same great culture. Their conflict and division became pronounced through time as human beings fell from spiritual into militaristic and commercial values.

Some of the Middle Eastern people were predominantly of the Vedic warrior class (Kshatriyas), like the Assyrians; others like the Phoenicians were of the merchant class (Vaishyas); and others like the Egyptians were priests (Brahmins). All four classes existed in these cultures, as in India, but to different degrees. The predominant religion was worship of the Sun through various temple rites and yogic practices. Middle Eastern religions arose mainly from the worship of the Asura Gods of the *Vedas* like Il-Varuna, who became their Divine Father. Vedic Mitra-Yama became the prototype of the Divine Son and savior, like Osiris and Christ.

Other Vedic Gods like Indra, Agni, and Soma were also worshipped as forms of the Divine Son, but in time these Gods were gradually rejected for a more exclusive monotheism, which paralleled the monistic development in Vedic and Hindu culture. They were absorbed into the Divine Father (Allah, Jehovah) or the Divine Son (Christ). Yet we should note that even in the *Rig Veda,* all the Gods are really names of the same Divine Unity. They are not separate entities but interrelated universal truth principles.

In this light, the *Rig Veda* may be the oldest document or scripture of all the peoples of the Middle East. In it can be traced the origins of the religions of this area including Islam, Christianity, Judaism, the religions of Egypt, Assyria and Babylonia, as well as those of the Persians and the Hittites. Yet we can trace its connection to the other peoples of the world beyond these regions.

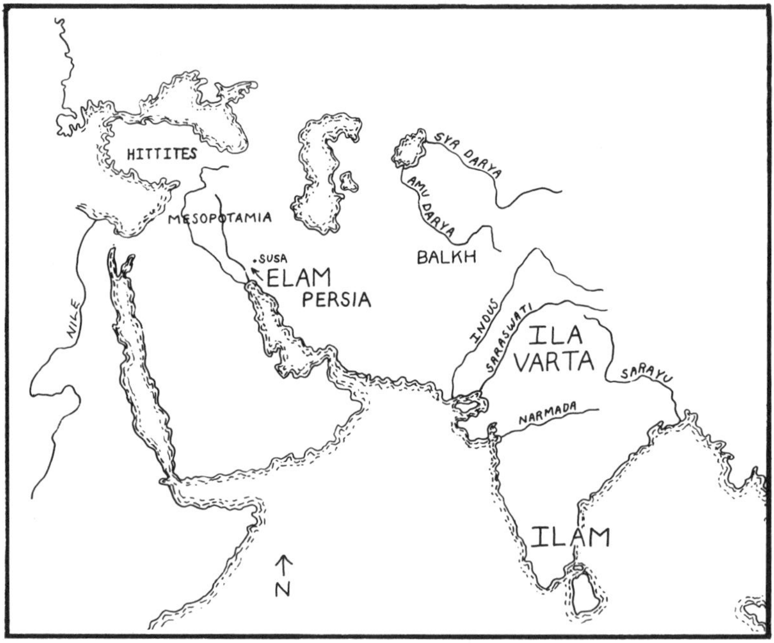

The Three Lands of Ila: The Source Lands of Ancient Civilization

3
THE GREATER WORLD CULTURE

THE DRAVIDIANS
The Third Land of Ila

The Dravidians of south India are held by some modern accounts to have been the original inhabitants of north India and the Indus Valley culture. Others consider that even though the Indus Valley culture was probably Aryan, that the Dravidians were present in India and had their own culture which did not derive from the Vedic. Yet by the traditional accounts of the Dravidians themselves their culture originated from Vedic Aryans who migrated from north India. They trace their culture back to the great Rig Vedic Rishi Agastya, whose representation is found in all the temples of south India. They consider themselves to be Aryans and to have better preserved the Vedic teaching than north India which was more subject to foreign invasions.

According to some *Brahmanas,* the Dravidians are regarded as fallen Aryans, as we have noted, descendants of the Vedic Rishi Vishwamitra or of the Turvashas, the eastern Vedic people. There is some temporary reluctance to place them fully into the spiritual fold of the Vedic culture but there is nowhere the idea that they are an older or unrelated people. In the *Ramayana,* however, the south Indians appear as supporters of Rama in his battle against the demon king Ravana. The Dravidians may therefore be followers or descendants of Rama or Rama may have brought them back into the mainstream of Vedic culture.

The Dravidians were probably an early Aryan people who created their own language but maintained an Aryan culture. At certain periods they may have departed from Vedic practices, as did even peoples of north India at times, with shifting religious values through history. It should be noted that they attribute the invention of their language to the same Vedic sage Agastya. They became a strong maritime culture and spread Aryan culture to southeast Asia and perhaps further east and to the west. They have an old and massive literature and appear to be among the earliest people of the ancient world.

In the *Puranas,* Manu, who took refuge in the Himalayas to escape the Flood, is regarded originally as a south Indian or Dravidian king (named Satyavrata). This shows an intimate connection of the Vedic teaching with south India from the beginning. Hence the Vedic people may have been, at least in part, refugees from south India in the first place.

It is interesting to note that the Dravidians even today name their land the land of Ila, just like the Vedic land. Some modern scholars have traced the language of Elam of Mesopotamia to a Dravidian origin, as we have noted. This suggests that the Dravidians named their homeland after the Vedic Ila. Ila also means "language" in Sanskrit. Many Dravidian sounds appear in the Vedic language. Hence the Dravidian language has an Aryan basis and may have been another early spiritual language of the Aryans.

This gives us three ancient Ilams, that of the north Indian Saraswati region, that of south India, and that of Mesopotamia. These three cultures were probably closely related, not only by trade but by culture and religion since the earliest period. They were probably the main points of diffusion of world culture from the central Vedic Ila-Saraswati region. The Dravidian language also appears intermediate between the Semitic and Indo-Aryan in terms of sounds and word formation (its preference for 'l' sounds like the Semitic, for example). These three languages dominated the ancient world. Perhaps they all originated from the sages along the Saraswati river. It may be possible to discover between them some original proto-language, perhaps best represented by the language of the *Rig Veda*.

OTHER ARYAN RELIGIONS

The Buddhists, Jains and Sikhs

We have referred to the Aryan nature of the Buddhist teaching. The main differences between Hinduism and Buddhism are a few philosophical points, which are largely semantical. The main teachings of Yoga, mantra and meditation are the same. Buddhism also employs Sanskrit as its main scriptural language. The central teaching of Buddhism, that of mindfulness, is the same as the Vedic cultivation of Agni, the sacred fire of awareness. The Buddhist Goddess of Wisdom, Prajña, is similar to Vedic Saraswati, who is also a Buddhist Goddess (the consort of Mañjusri). Particularly in Tantric teachings, both Hinduism and Buddhism are remarkably close. Buddhist culture employed Ayurveda (Vedic medicine) and Vedic astrology, which became the bases of Tibetan medicine and Tibetan astrology. Not only did Buddhism grow up on a Hindu foundation, it added much to Hindu culture, religion and philosophy with its own great insights.

According to the Buddhist *Jatakas,* our main source of ancient history through the Buddhists, Buddha himself was a descendant of the Vedic seer

Gotama, and hence called Gautama. According to the *Jatakas* also, the great Vedic King Nimi was also an enlightened one or Pratyeka Buddha. This also shows the early Buddhist regard for the ancient Aryan kings. The *Jatakas* link Buddhism closely to Vedic and Aryan culture both through its sages and kings.

The Jains also regard theirs as an Aryan teaching. They are older than the Buddhists by at least a few centuries, and much of what we associate with Buddhism — a religion based on karma, without God or a creator — began with them. Both religions philosophically are offshoots of early Sankhya and Vedantic teachings. The Jains, like the Buddhists, were once prominent throughout India and at times into Indonesia. Groups of them remain in India today. The Jains relate themselves to Mahavira, generally regarded as a contemporary of the Buddha, said to be a descendant of the Vedic seer Kashyapa. Through Mahavira they relate their tradition back some centuries to Parshwa, who was said to be the son of the Aryan king of Kashi or Benares. There is no mention of non-Aryan kings or peoples in either early Buddhist or Jain lore, including that going back supposedly to previous World Ages. The split between them and the Hindus appears entirely within an earlier field of Aryan culture and history that all these groups shared.

The Sikh religion, a great universalist movement in modern India, also has much in common with the Vedic. It was born in the same region as the Vedic — the Punjab area between the Yamuna and the Ravi (Delhi and Lahore), the old Vedic Saraswati area. The Sikh language, Gurumukhi, has much in common with the Sanskrit and the Sikh scripture is largely a paraphrase of Vedic and Hindu teachings. The Sikh religion in its synthetic approach has much in common with the universalist Vedic approach. The Sikh religion was not the first to be born in that region of north India. It may not be the last.

THE EUROPEANS

Most ancient European languages resemble Sanskrit. The religions of the ancient Europeans like those of the Keltic Druids or ancient Greeks also appear akin to the Vedic. They worship the Divine primarily under variations of the Sanskrit term Deva, as 'deus', 'theos', etc. but not so much as Asura or Il. They recognize human beings as 'men' (German 'mensh'), sons of Manu.[a] The Germanic name from which we derive our English word God appears to be related to the Vedic 'hotar', the Vedic fire priest or fire itself (from the root 'hu', meaning "to invoke").[b] The ancient Europeans thus had a closer religion to the Vedic than to the Iranian. They were not limited to one great God like Ahura Mazda but preserved the early multiplicity of Vedic Gods, though with slightly different forms and functions. Later the Europeans gradually gave up their own native religious traditions and adapted the religions of the Near East, particularly Christianity.

The religions of our so-called pagan European ancestors may not have been as primitive as we have thought. They may have reflected the same spirituality that developed into the *Upanishads* of India. The solar religions of ancient Europe were related not only to the Vedic, but to others of the ancient world and had similar ideas of illumination and enlightenment. Much of the spiritual roots of these ancient European teachings may therefore have become hidden by a veil of misunderstandings that came through the Christian conversion. No doubt many of the criticisms by the early Christians were justified by the fallen state of the solar religion in Europe at that time, as elsewhere in the late ancient world, but this did not necessarily reflect the real meaning of the earlier traditions.

Some of these ancient European teachings persisted into a late period. Christianity did not triumph in northern Europe, Scandinavia and the Baltic region until after 1000 AD, and in some areas until as late as 1400 AD. We still have records of the ancient fire rituals practiced in these lands, some still practiced today, and they may help us understand the European connection with the Vedic religion. The Vedic religion can provide us with a deeper appreciation of their spiritual value. In this regard, the division between Western and Eastern religions is rather superficial. Our ancient European ancestors followed a religion like the *Vedas* of India to the East, just as they spoke a similar language to Vedic Sanskrit.

This same fire-Sun religion was related to Christianity as a religion of the Divine Son-Sun. Perhaps some of the Druids and fire-priests saw this connection and accepted the new religion as a reformation of the old. In this way, aspects of the older religions of Europe were integrated into Christianity. Christmas itself, the festival of the birth of Christ or the Divine Son-Sun at the winter solstice, was present in these ancient solar religions of Europe and the Middle East long before the Christian conversion. It was the ancient Vedic winter solstice celebration, the birth of the sacred fire or Agni as the Divine Child to travel the Path of the Gods to the realm of light. European Christianity not only assimilated some of the spiritual teachings of pre-Christian Europe, but also made use of their philosophy as transmitted through Plato, Aristotle and Plotinus, who in turn reflected the Vedantic philosophies of India.

According to the *Vedas,* there are no pagans or heathens; there are only spiritual or worldly people. This division cuts across all religions, languages, races, and times. In what we know of as history there has been no social group, and certainly no religion, in which spiritual people were a majority, and no group in which they were entirely absent either. The ancient European "pagans" also had their saints and sages, perhaps more of them than later Europe because the earlier age was more spiritual.

The further we trace the European languages back, the more they resemble Sanskrit. In fact it appears that the further back we go in time, the more ancient European and Vedic culture coalesce. The Rig Veda in this way may also be the oldest scripture of the European peoples. Since the early inhabitants of Europe, including the Kelts, Germans, Slavs, and Scythians spoke Indo-European languages, probably the people who preceded them down to prehistoric times were of a similar stock, language and culture. This similarity between the Vedic and ancient European has caused Western scholars to assume a Central Asian or central European homeland for all Indo-European peoples, a proto-Indo-European culture and language, from around 3000 BC. Yet if the antiquity of the *Rig Veda* and its location in India as indicated here are correct, the date of such a culture would have to have been much earlier and the location closer to India, perhaps India itself.

A number of possibilities of diffusion for Vedic culture existed. As Vedic culture extended into the Amu Darya (Oxus) region of Central Asia, from there Vedic peoples could spread through the plains of Central Asia to Europe, particularly as they had horses. Some European peoples, perhaps the Greeks and Romans, may have been Vedic warriors (Kshatriya) who went west in the Vedic wars with the Asuras (Assyrians).

Another possibility is that some of the Aryan seers migrated west from their hermitages in the Himalayas with various groups of people to establish new cultures. The seers appear in history as guardians of humanity and culture makers. Perhaps even in later ancient times, like the time of the founding of Rome (c. 750 BC), they led such migrations to form the cultures which were to become prominent later. This is substantiated by the myths behind most ancient cultures of having been founded by Gods and sages.

The Kelts were an old European people who appear very spiritually evolved, with a strong sense of the Divine Word. Their fire priests and bards resemble the Vedic Brahmins and seer-poets. It was probably their ancestors who built the megaliths and stone monuments of Europe like Stonehenge. These were built, no doubt, as part of the ritual, to help fix the appropriate times for the sacrifices, whose form was probably similar to the Vedic. If we want to know the kinds of rituals done at these places we should study the Vedic *Brahmanas.*

By Roman accounts the Kelts possessed a large navy and were good sailors. They traded in the Mediterranean as far as Egypt and possibly also reached the Americas as well. In the third century BC the Kelts moved into Asia Minor and established the kingdom of Galatia in what was in ancient times the land of the Hittites. Their influence prevailed there some centuries into the Christian era. As ancient peoples had many migrations, the Kelts may have been in such eastern areas at earlier times as well.

The Greeks are also very ancient European peoples and were probably in Greece before 3000 BC. While we have made much of the scientific and intellectual side of Greek culture, from which modern technological culture has evolved, there was also a mystical side of Greek culture much like the Vedic, evident in their mystery religions and at Delphi. This tradition was no doubt stronger in more ancient times. Certainly the old Greek Gods and Goddesses — like Zeus and Apollo as Vedic Indra and Savitar — have their Hindu equivalents.

Much of the work of reclaiming the ancient Western spiritual heritage may therefore consist in rediscovering the mystical side of the Greeks. Even through their later history in the Middle Ages, the Greeks were a strongly religious people and preserved ancient Christianity in the face of repeated Islamic invasions. The side of their culture that seeded the modern world was not their dominant strain even in historical periods. In many respects, the Greeks are as much an Eastern as a Western people. After Alexander they ruled in Bactria and in parts of India for a time and much knowledge was exchanged between India and Greece.

The languages of the Greeks and Romans have much affinity with the Kelts, and are considered to be of one family with them. Yet Greek and Latin are closer yet to Sanskrit, with Latin being very similar to it.

We find a Brahmanical influence among the Romans as well. Their Gods and Goddesses have usually Hindu or Vedic equivalents. Jupiter (Dyaus Pitar) is Indra; Venus (Vena) is Lakshmi; Mars (Marut) is Skanda, etc. The Roman vestal virgins and their cult of the sacred fire is similar to the Vedic fire established by the three muses (Saraswati, Ila and Bharati) who were probably represented by three virgins in the Vedic ritual as well. The Roman term Flamen, the name for their priestly class, appears to derive from Vedic Brahman (B for F and R for L, which are not uncommon changes in Indo-European languages).[c] The Romans thus appear closely related to the Hindus. The Romans also had an extensive trade with India.

The Baltic people, particularly the Lithuanians, have many Vedic-like myths in their culture (like that of the marriage of the Sun Goddess), as well as a Sanskrit-like language. They were among the last of the Indo-European peoples to become Christianized. Lithuanian is regarded as the closest modern language to Sanskrit, perhaps more so than modern Indian dialects like Hindi.

Slav is Sanskrit Shrav, "one who hears the truth." The Slavic tongues, similar to the Baltic, are close to Sanskrit. The Slavs may be descendants of the Indo-Iranian Scythians (Sanskrit 'Shakas'), who were prominent in

Central Asia from the seventh century BC to some centuries AD. According to Greek accounts of ancient history the Scythians once defeated the Assyrians. They plagued the Greeks and the Persians who had large wars with them. The Scythians entered into India as the great horsemen of the steppes. They may have been powerful in earlier times as well, as the steppes of Central Asia appear to have been dominated by Indo-Iranian people in early ancient times. Perhaps many Europeans derived from or were related to them. Some consider that the Scythians were among the earlier people in Ireland. Probably all these peoples were interrelated.

The Germanic peoples, particularly the Scandinavians, were great sailors in ancient times and have left many runes and stone monuments. They appear related to the Kelts and were also fire worshippers. The Scandinavians even today have fire rituals much like the Vedic.

In short, the European peoples are of common stock and culture with the Vedic. Their fire worship, rituals, elaborate myths and legends, and multiplicity of Gods and Goddesses parallel the Hindu. It may be appropriate to write a new view of ancient European history under the title 'Hindu Europe'. The Vedas and Hinduism may not be as foreign to us as we think but may reflect our true spirituality.

However, because the Indo-Europeans preserved a similar language to Sanskrit does not mean that the Vedic culture must be limited to what we see as the achievements of the ancient Europeans. The original Aryan culture may not have been a composite of those factors which are common between all speakers of Indo-European languages, as many scholars have suggested. This is to reduce it to its lowest common denominator. Taking such linguistic affinities too literally, it could prove, as A. B. Keith once remarked, that the original Indo-European speakers knew butter but not milk, snow and feet but not rain and hands. It is not surprising, therefore, that such linguistic approaches have placed the original Indo-European homeland everywhere from the plain of Hungary in Europe to the west to the Altai mountains in China to the east. As the majority of languages they have chosen to analyze are European, it is also not surprising that they mainly place the early Aryans in Europe.

Moreover, we do not always find that an older form of a language is necessarily a sign of a higher or more advanced culture. Often people in outlying areas preserve older linguistic forms better than the main urban and populated areas which go through more changes of language in their frequent human contacts. For example, an earlier form of French is spoken among the French Canadians than among the people of Paris today. We cannot for that reason assume that the French Canadians are an older form of the French people who must have therefore migrated from Canada to France. The French Canadians in their isolation in a new area were able to preserve an older form of their language. Preservation of an older form of a language does not necessarily equate with an older location for the culture.

The Europeans in their isolation in the colder north may have preserved a form of the Vedic language but may not have developed or retained all the attainments of Vedic civilization. It is also very possible that the attainments of ancient European culture were higher than what we have regarded them to be.

The usual scholarly view today is that the Europeans were part of an Aryan migration, largely an invasion by horse people (the Kurgan people), into Europe in the third and second millennia BC. This is an idea of conquest or military force as the source of culture and language. Some new theories (Colin Renfrew) hold that the Aryans spread slowly via agriculture into Europe and were present there by 6000 BC.[d] Their original location according to his view is placed as Catal Huyuk, the seventh millenium BC city in Turkey. This would be more in the direction of the Vedic view suggested here, but does not go far enough east in its Aryan origins and remains dominated by an economic idea of humanity.

According to the ancients, culture did not come from agriculture or conquest. It originated from religion. Language also came from religion. Religion and scripture are the source of most languages that we know of. We can see how such languages were shaped from their scriptures as Hebrew from the *Bible,* Arabic from the *Koran,* Persian from the *Avesta,* and Sanskrit from the *Vedas.* Even the ancient European languages came from their bards and priests, two occupations which were always intimately linked together. We cannot explain human civilization in mere agricultural or political terms. These are commercial or militaristic ideas of history, based on outer or materialistic values. The true origin of history is in inner or spiritual values, arising from our contact with the Divine through our sages and seers.

No simple rule of diffusion of language or culture can be formulated. While ancient Europe had a language close to Sanskrit, ancient Babylonia and its temple worship had a ritualistic religion close to the Vedic and Puranic. Even today, though we see similarities between the languages of India and Europe, it is the religions of India and China (through Buddhism) that are related, though their language is not. While Aryan languages have been preserved more in the West, Aryan religions have been preserved more in the East, with their homeland of India and the Himalayas in the center between both linguistic and religious groups.

The ancient Europeans appear as an extension of Vedic culture, which they moved away from in time. Hence we should also look to the *Rig Veda* for the origins of Western and European civilization. In this regard, the next and more spiritual stage of Western civilization may be mirrored in the ancient *Vedas*. The Vedic heritage thus also belongs to Western and European culture and may be its secret origin, as well as its point of transformation and integration.

THE PLACE OF EUROPE IN THE ANCIENT WORLD

In our examination of the cultures of ancient India, Persia and Europe, we have seen a common background of Indo-European languages and Aryan culture. To this we can add the Indo-European linguistic groups of Mesopotamia, like the ancient Hittites, Mittani and Kassites or the modern Armenians and Kurds. We find in these groups many common names, places, and peoples. However, boundaries are not rigidly defined between these and other apparently non-Aryan cultures. Many common Gods also exist between the Indo-European groups, the Mesopotamian, the Egyptian, and the Dravidian, like the great Sun and storm Gods. We have evidence of a massive cultural nexus from India to Europe. Languages, religions, cultures and social structures are intertwined. Attempts to divide ancient people by such outer factors as race or language fail in the end and we discover a single ancient spiritual teaching and cultural force.

Ancient Europe was part of this whole system of ancient world culture. We cannot divide off the European from the Hindu or either one of them from the Middle Eastern. Our ancient European ancestors were much in the spiritual mold of the ancient Egyptians or Hindus. Their religions were of a similar order and may not have been less evolved. The spiritual practices of our European ancestors may thereby resemble more those of the modern Hindus than modern Western religious practices. The mystical side of the European mind may yet reemerge but probably with a universal approach like the Vedic. The study of its Vedic parallels may aid in this.

PEOPLES OF THE EAST

We have explained the origins and developments of the peoples to the west of India; what about those to the east? Certainly there is much in the ancient indigenous religions of China and Japan, Taoism and Shintoism, that reflects a similar solar and sacrificial religion to the *Vedas*. There is much in common between the Vedic religion and the Shamanism of Siberia and North America. Indeed, one could argue that Shamanism is a remnant of this ancient world-wide solar religion. There are also the religions of the American Indians which display a religion of Sun worship and sacrifice remarkably close to both the Vedic and the ancient Egyptian. We see something like a universal religion in the early ancient world and there are similar stories of floods and sages.

The main Vedic culture extended through north India from sea to sea with extensions into Afghanistan, from which a dispersion north and east in Asia would have been possible, as along the silk trail in historical times. Vedic lands in Tibet also had access to China.

THE CHINESE

The Chinese relate their spiritual tradition to Seven Sages, identified with the stars of the Big Dipper, just as the Seven Rishis of the *Rig Veda.* Similar to the Hindu *Puranas,* they have a cosmology based upon the rule of the pole star. They employ twenty-eight lunar constellations as in Vedic astrology. Since they start their list from the Pleiades (Krittika),[e] this system was most likely in use by them by 2000 BC when the Pleiades marked the vernal equinox. For their calendar they employ a sixty-year time cycle like the Vedic, which dates back to 2698 BC.

The Chinese not only adopted Buddhism, a religion from India in later times, their own older religion of Taoism has much in common with those of India previously and may be evidence of a common religious and cultural background between ancient India and China. Taoism has many practices like Hindu Yoga. Like Hinduism it is an organic religion, a religion of nature marked by tolerance and respect for all beliefs.

Taoism also speaks of a Golden Age and the fall of humanity, much like the *Vedas,* and looks back to earlier ages of light. According to the Taoist view of Lao-Tzu and Chuang-Tzu, human beings first had a simple spiritual culture in harmony with nature. What we see as the beginning of history, for them the first emperors of China, they saw as a fall from this earlier spiritual culture and the beginning of materialistic ages wherein appearance and ceremony took the place of genuine expression, and the natural virtue of the soul was lost.[f] This Taoist view sees the intellect, with its cunning, as a fall from our true natural intelligence, and the complexity of materialistic civilization as the indication of a fall into artificiality. This is the same view as the *Vedas* and most of the religions of the ancient world, which see history largely as a fall from grace.

The Chinese also have a sacred mountain to the west in the Himalayan area called 'Kun-lun'. It is the earthly capital of the Lord of the sky. It is the source of the Yellow River, which is, like the Hindu Ganges, said to flow in four directions. It thus appears as the Chinese counterpart of the Hindu Kailas or Meru. Yet it is hard to say if this myth, usually of a Taoist nature, came from later contact with India or from earlier times. With the connection of Kailas to the place of origins or spiritual guidance, perhaps the Chinese were connected with this region as well. Perhaps they were also early Aryans. The Chinese language is quite distinct from the Indo-Aryan, but we do not know what it was in such ancient times, nor is language, as we have noted, the prime factor in making a culture Aryan. Hence the ancient Chinese were probably closely related to the Vedic peoples in terms of culture and also had some communication with them or the sages they revered.

THE TIBETANS

The Tibetans are racially related to the Chinese but have a different language. They also possess an indigenous religion, the Bon, predating the arrival of Buddhism, that has not only Shamanistic but also some yogic knowledge.

According to the Tibetan Buddhists, there was an earlier Buddhist kingdom in Central Asia from which their teaching derives, called Shamballa, which appears to have been in the Tarim basin northwest of Tibet. This may have been at the time of the previous Buddha, said to be 5,000 years earlier than the historical Buddha. This earlier Buddhist culture in Central Asia was, by Tibetan accounts, also a culture in which Sanskrit, 'the Language of the Gods', was spoken. So it could not have been far removed from the Vedic culture. It may be the same as the land of the Uttara Kurus, mentioned in the *Brahmanas* as a sacred Vedic land beyond the Himalayas, which also appears to have been in the Tarim basin. This region had an Indo-European language, Tocharian, until the eighth century AD, as we have noted.

Shamballa appears to have been an earlier Aryan kingdom from which Tibetan Buddhism was derived. Perhaps the Chinese also had connection with it and it was behind much of their culture. The Tibetans similarly worship Mount Kailas as their most sacred and spiritual mountain and possible place of origins.

Like the Hindus, the Tibetans worship images, do pujas (devotional rituals), and chant mantras. Tibetan Buddhism, through its Indian Tantric roots, resembles Hinduism more than it does the Buddhism of southern Asia, which is less imagistic and devotional, and also less concerned with the practice of Yoga techniques. Tibetan Buddhism is highly ritualistic and many of its rituals resemble the Vedic. The abhishekas (anointings), sand-painted mandalas, the offerings of clarified butter and barley, the burning of ghee lamps, the use of the sacred grass (kusha) and other aspects of Tibetan rituals have their counterparts in the ancient *Vedas* and *Brahmanas* that date from before the Buddha.

INDONESIA AND POLYNESIA

Hinduism and Buddhism extended into Indonesia in historic times and were the basis of its culture. If a great culture did exist in the east of India in earlier times, like the empire of Rama, it is likely that its influence spread into these areas at an earlier period also. India contains people of the same stock as the Indonesian in its tropical areas, who grow the same foods and follow the same lifestyle. Certainly India has been the strongest cultural force in Indonesia in historic times, mainly through the Dravidians of south India.

Many of the aborigines of India are related racially to the people of Indonesia and Polynesia. The Hindus themselves also have some physical resemblances to these island people. Perhaps the Hindu Aryan type diversified in two ways, one as the Western Caucasian, the other as the island people of Asia. Or the Indo-Aryans may have been an earlier diversification of the older island peoples.

The aboriginal people of India may to some extent be the remnants in India of the Vedic Dasyus. We must remember, however, that many Dasyus accepted the rule of Vedic kings and sages and became part of Vedic culture and were a cultural, not a racial division. The Vedic people, moreover, originally appear at least in part as refugees from across the sea (as in the myths of Turvasha and Yadu), which may make them descendants from the island people. As such, southeast Asian people may be early Aryans. Hence the Himalayan and the tropical peoples probably have a common ancestry and religion going back to prehistoric times.

The Polynesian people possess a mantric language much like Sanskrit. The Hawaiian language itself appears to have many roots in common with Sanskrit. These cultures were probably based on that of east and south India. Polynesians relate their culture to Lemuria or Mu, a Pacific continent said to have been the culture of a previous World Age, like Atlantis destroyed by a flood. India appears to have been part of Lemuria as well.

AFRICA

Much of ancient African culture may be represented by the Egyptians, or by the Ethiopians who were culturally related to them. Like the Vedic people, the Ethiopians came from mountain regions and maintained a high level of both civilization and religion. They also traded with India and had an accessible coast for sea travel to India. They appear to be part of this same great nexus of ancient civilization. While the details of their early or ancient teachings are not certain, they appear to have been like the Vedic. Many of the tribal religions of Africa are also similar to Hinduism. They use images and mantric sounds and are organic religions, related to nature. In this way they also preserve much of the original ancient teaching.

THE AMERICAN INDIANS

The similarities between the solar religion of sacrifice of the *Vedas* and the religions of the great American Indian cultures like the Mayans and the Incas are so great as to be hardly coincidental. The temple worship, the rule of the priests, the rituals that follow the calendar and the stars, and many of the forms of the Gods and Goddesses are similar. The Mayans and the Incas and their predecessors had a sacrificial culture much like the Vedic Aryan, as have other Indians like the Hopis of the American Southwest. While some American Indian cultures, like the Aztec and Mayan, have been accused of a cruder form of sacrificial religion, like the practice of human sacrifice, it remains to be seen how much of this was wrongly attributed to them by the Spanish who had little understanding of their culture.

We should note that the languages of Mexico and Central America, including those of the Aztecs, are called Nahuatl, which suggests the Vedic ancestor Nahusha. Perhaps the American Indians were also offspring of Nahusha, as many of the early Vedic people are said to be. The Mayans were also regarded as great astronomers and astrologers. They use a calendar dating from about the same 3100 BC era found among the Hindus. In this regard we should note that Vedic astrology was originally taught by Asura Maya,[g] who is the same as Shukra of the line of the Bhrigu seers, the Vedic teacher of the Asuras. Shukra is the planet Venus and the Mayans used a calendar based upon the cycles of Venus thus confirming the connection. The American Indians, therefore, may relate to early Aryan peoples including the Bhrigus, Nahushas, and possibly the Turvashas or eastern people of India. They may be part of the early migrations of the Vedic people.

The American Indians may have been colonists from India; or they may have been a related people who had a similar evolution on the other side of the globe. Perhaps all the peoples of this World Age started their wanderings from a central point in north India or Mount Kailas, or perhaps there were several such centers throughout the world, one for each continent or major geographical region. The Andes are the southern and western counterpart of the Himalayas. Lake Titicaca in the Andes may be the western counterpart of Lake Manasarovar in Tibet. Perhaps it served as a similar spiritual center or place of origins for the peoples of the Americas.

Racially, the American Indians are related to the Tibetans. They share with them a Shamanistic teaching and many customs, like the wearing of turquoise and coral. The people of Nepal, relatives of the Tibetans, along with other peoples of eastern India and Assam, have similar practices. The origin of the American Indians from Asia has been a widely accepted idea. Perhaps at least one major group of them was derived in this way. While details are uncertain, the American Indians appear to be an integral part of an ancient world culture and solar religion that included the Vedic people of India. There is thus much in the *Vedas* that can also help us understand the religions of the American Indians.

Older Mexican civilizations also appear to have had contact with China and employ similar human and jade animal figures. Contacts with Polynesia and India appear to have existed as well. There is much similarity between the temples of south India and those of Mexico. Perhaps some navigators from India made the journey to America and vice versa. Even the Catholic religion of Mexico today, which reflects some of the pre-Christian beliefs of the region, with its strong devotion to images and its many festivals, has much in common with the Hindu.

ANTEDILUVIAN PEOPLES

The *Vedas* speak of periodic renovations of humanity, with the power of the Gods passed on to new peoples who return culture to its spiritual roots. The Vedic people appear as a spiritual reform of an older humanity marking a new age. There was a conflict between spiritual and materialistic people from the beginning of the *Rig Veda,* as we have seen in the battles between the Aryans and the Panis. Some of the Panis resided in India; some of whom were driven out in time, others assimilated. According to the Vedic myth, their main power was destroyed by a great Flood by the will of the Gods (Indra), but remnants remained and some resisted the Aryans. We can see in this the common Flood myth of ancient cultures from Greece and Egypt to China, the Biblical Flood and the myth of the destruction of Atlantis.

Here we approach one of the original and core myths of the *Rig Veda* that may show great cataclysms and major changes of land and climate on Earth possibly related to the end of the last Ice Age. The melting of large amounts of ice caused sea levels to rise several hundred feet. Most coastal and low-lying river regions would have been submerged by the rising waters.

The Panis referred to in the *Veda* were probably not only Phoenicians, though the two appear to have been related. They may have originally been members and survivors of such a fallen antediluvian culture. In this regard the Phoenicians and the pre-Flood Atlanteans have been commonly connected. When this earlier culture degenerated, the spiritual people within it retreated to various mountain regions like the Himalayas or the Andes. After the Flood they descended and took control of the Earth according to a higher law and new harmony with the Divine will. These were the true Aryans or people of spiritual values. Many mountain areas may have had such people, though they were probably most numerous in the Himalayas, the world's greatest mountains. Yet after an additional period of time, at least a few thousand years, the Aryans themselves fell, partly under remaining influences of the older culture, as well as by the usual decline that occurs in the process of time.

The degenerated antediluvian peoples would thus be represented in the *Rig Veda* by the powerful Dasyus dethroned by Indra, the God of the flood. The Aryans would be the people of the new World Age, the post-Flood humanity, which probably included several racial types. The Dasyus may have originally been the declining culture of an earlier World Age. Hence they were previously favored by the Gods but lost their grace. They are the evil father of the Vedic Gods and peoples in Vedic stories. The Vedic people may therefore have originally been spiritual refugees from this fallen antediluvian culture. This explains the myths of the ancestors of the Aryan peoples being delivered from across the sea, as well as the Aryans fleeing imprisonment from "the hundred cities of Shambara."

According to Plato, Atlantis, the center of the antediluvian culture, was destroyed in a cataclysm more than 9,300 years before him. This would be about the time of the ending of the last Ice Age. This cataclysm was said to have been preceded by a war in which the Atlanteans tried to conquer the Mediterranean region and were defeated by ancestors of the Greeks (Aryans?). If this correlation is correct, we could date the original great Vedic defeat of the Dasyus and Panis at the time Plato states, about 9600 BC. Though this is highly speculative, if our misinterpretation of the *Vedas* and ancient history is as great as it appears to be, we may have to consider such possibilities. It is strange that though we know human beings have been on the planet for hundreds of thousands of years, it is only in the last few thousand years that civilization appears to have arisen. Perhaps we have just not discovered these earlier World Ages or cycles of civilization. Certainly the ancients had many myths of such earlier humanities.

In the *Puranas* and *Brahmanas,* Manu is said to have taken refuge in a ship in the Himalayas, much like Noah's ark on Mount Ararat in Armenia. While we do not find specific mention of this story in the *Vedas,* there are indications of it in the *Atharva Veda.*

> At the place of the ship's descent at the top of the Himalayas, there resides the vision of immortality from which the Kushta plant was born; which the Ikshwakus previously knew (AV XIX.39.8-9).

The sacred plant Kushta, which is related to Soma, grows in the Himalayas. This plant is said to be known by the Ikshwakus, the early descendants of Manu. The most famous Vedic Himalayan mountain is called Trikakut, and is mentioned in the *Atharva Veda* along with another Himalayan mountain called 'Yamuna', deriving from the Yamuna river (AV IV.9.10). This suggests the Himalayan region of the Yamuna as the homeland of Manu, which takes us in the direction of Mount Kailas.

The myth of the boat or ark in which Manu or Noah was saved in the mountains may be only a metaphor. This boat is said in the *Atharva Veda* (XIX.39.7) to have been 'golden'. The word for ship, 'nau', also means the Divine Word. It was the ship of prayer or mantra that saved Manu and his people. The Flood as a metaphor may not only refer to a physical deluge but to a major change of conditions on Earth and the birth of a new cycle of civilization in harmony with the Divine will. Manu is said to have taken various things in his boat including the river Narmada. This suggests that Manu's boat is symbolic of the land of India itself, which is shaped like a ship and placed between two seas. India has been a land of refuge for religious groups throughout history. Perhaps this reflects its mystical role as the ark for humanity.

The Vedic kings subsequently recreated the original victory of Indra and hence placed their enemies in the image of the Dasyus and Panis. They were reestablishing the rule of the Gods and the powers of Light over the forces of darkness in the new World Age. They were perhaps reenacting the myth of the Flood.

While such Flood myths and antediluvian cultures may not be a necessary idea to appreciate the antiquity of the *Vedas,* we do find compelling evidence in the *Vedas* that tends to support them. Why have we not found remains of such cultures? No doubt the cataclysmic events and the influence of time is a great factor. This is compounded by our own unwillingness to accept them, as it would lead us to radically question our view of human history. Yet we do have a reliable record of them in the universal testimony of ancient humanity and, above all, the scriptures of the world.

In closing, it is important not to turn this story of the spiritual fall of humanity into a political issue. All the cultures of the world degenerated in time, and in all of them spiritual people became a minority. It is essential today that these spiritual traditions again become united, recognizing their common heritage. In this regard, all the spiritual traditions of the world are related. We find great and worthy teachings in all traditions, including those more obscure to us today like the ancient European or the American Indian. Similarly in all traditions we find much corruption and distortion has taken place.

While the outer spiritual homeland of this World Age may have originally been the Himalayas and its rivers like the Vedic Saraswati, inwardly it is the Divine Word and the stream of Divine grace, the inner river of truth that perpetually flows from the great mountains of Truth consciousness. It is there that we must return to find our true and spiritual humanity.

APPENDIX A

BACKGROUND MATERIAL

1
VEDIC COSMOLOGY

Sons of the infinite, may we be infinite, perfect, oh beings of light, in the Godhead and in humanity. Winning, Divine Lord and Friend, may we win you, becoming, oh Heaven and Earth, may we become you.

— Rig Veda VII.52.1

To understand the Vedic view of humanity and the scope of Vedic culture it is helpful to examine Vedic cosmology. While we can only deal with this issue in secondary way, owing to its complexity, we can present at least enough to confirm our other assertions on the sophisticated nature of Vedic culture. The Vedic view of the universe is of a vast cosmos with many different levels. It is a sacred view of the world and not meant to simply reflect outer actualities. Yet it does reveal a wide scope of vision and the idea of a complex and interrelated cosmic existence encompassing man, nature and the Divine in a common law. We see in it not a world view of barbaric nomads but a culture led by seers and yogis with a vast experience not only of the Earth but also of subtle planes of consciousness.

We have already seen much of Vedic cosmology in our study of the ocean and the rivers. The heavenly ocean and heavenly rivers accompany the earthly and the atmospheric. Everything in the *Veda* occurs on these three levels — the Earth corresponding to the body, the atmosphere to the life-force or breath, and Heaven to the mind.

THE VEDIC VIEW OF THE WORLDS

Heaven and Earth, Dyaus and Prithivi, are the Father and the Mother.

> Heaven is our father, Earth is our mother. The fire is our brother. May the Gods be compassionate to us. May all the Sun Gods along with the Divine Mother grant us an abundant peace (VI.51.5).

Heaven and Earth are also a dual or twin world, Rodasi. Between them is the atmosphere, Antariksha, where the Gods and the demons battle for the supremacy. Beyond them is the celestial Waters, Apas. Along with the waters is the world of light or the Sun world, Swar, as the transcendent fourth. This is related to the luminous heavens, Rochana, the great heavens of the Gods.

The Vedic vision is also quite aware of the unity of all the worlds.

> Indivisible is Heaven, indivisible is the atmosphere, indivisible is the mother, the father and the son. Indivisible are all the Gods and the five peoples of man. The indivisible is what has been born and what will be born (I.89.10).[1]

The indivisible, Aditi, is personified as a Goddess, the infinite Mother. Heaven and Earth become a dual Goddess, who in turn is addressed as the infinite and indivisible One.

> Oh Sublime Heaven-Earth, Indivisible, protect us, who were born for the perfect birth (VII.62.4).

The main goal of the Vedic ritual and meditation is to transcend Heaven and Earth, to go beyond the world.

> Slaying the obstructor they crossed over Heaven and Earth and made the vast for their dwelling (I.36.8).[2]

This is the same thing as going beyond the duality of phenomenal existence as sought in later Hindu and Buddhist texts, the duality of body and mind.

All the worlds are dwelling places for the Gods, in which they are free to travel. The vehicles of the Gods encompass the worlds. Such ideas are found in many passages:

> Of easy travel is the Earth for the Maruts, of easy travel is Heaven with its slopes, of easy travel are the paths of the atmosphere, of easy travel are the mountains (V.54.9).
>
> Your chariot comes that encompasses Heaven and Earth, which golden moves with powerful horses, whose path is clarity. Extending over five worlds with three seats it goes yoked by the mind, by which you visit godly people. It binds the ends of Heaven on your path (VII.69.1-3).[3]
>
> In one common yoke your chariot encompasses seven rivers (VII.67.8).[4]

> Endless wide paths encompass Heaven and Earth from all sides (V.47.2).[5]
>
> Whether you are in a distant habitation, or in the luminous realm of Heaven or in a house made on the sea, come to us oh Ashwins (VIII.10.1).

Vedic cosmology includes the worlds of the Gods and men together:

> Indra and Agni, whether you rejoice in your own home, whether in the Brahmin or in the king, whether in the Yadus, Turvashas, Druhyus, Anus or Purus, whether in the lower, the middle or the higher Earth, whether the higher, the middle or the lower Earth, whether in Heaven or on Earth or in the mountains, plants or waters, thus, oh powerful ones, come to us and drink of the Soma (I.108.7-11).

The Brahmins and the kings are the two higher classes of men. The Yadus, etc., are the five Aryan peoples.

The Gods also have their secret abodes beyond the known worlds:

> Three stations of the Ashwins are revealed, one transcendent is in secrecy (VIII.8.23).[6]

This is like the transcendent fourth, Turiya, of the *Upanishads,* which represents the state of pure consciousness beyond the three lower states of waking, dream and deep sleep.

Vishnu also has a secret third state:

> The mortal trembles at the vision of the two stations of Vishnu who sees the light. No one can dare to look at his third step, not even the flying birds (I.155.5).

The secret third may be the non-dual state, the unity that includes and transcends duality.

The one unmoving carries all the worlds:

> One unmoving bears six burdens. The rays approach him who is the supreme truth. Three mighty transcendent Goddesses stand near. Two are hidden, one is visible (III.56.2).[7]

The Gods transcend the worlds. They are not just naturalistic symbols but indicate aspects or ways of approaching the Absolute or the uncreate.

> Indra has grown yet greater for vigor. The one undecaying divides the treasures. Indra has transcended Heaven and Earth, half of him is equal to both the worlds (VI.30.1).[8]
>
> Indra, the vast axle of your wheel by greatness transcends Heaven and Earth (VI.24.3).
>
> Indra, if there were a hundred Heavens and a hundred Earths, not even if there were a thousand Suns could the world equal your effulgence at birth (VIII.70.5).

While such passages are more poetic or symbolic rather than philosophical utterances, they reflect the same truth of the Absolute or the pure Self, Atman.

The worlds have different levels and are sometimes divided in different ways. Savitar is the Sun God as the Divine Father and creator. He rules five realms divided threefold. Mitra and Varuna rule four realms divided threefold.

> Savitar by greatness has encompassed three atmospheres, three regions and three luminous heavens. Three Heavens and three Earths he has directed, may he guard us through his nature by his threefold law (IV.53.5).
>
> Mitra and Varuna, three luminous realms and three Heavens, you uphold three realms. Adityas, you are the upholders of the region, of the luminous heaven, of Heaven and Earth (V.69.1, 4).

The higher realm of light or higher Heaven of Swar beyond the two worlds thus has three realms, in which the seers attain immortality.

> All worlds and all creatures exist eternally in the presence of Savitar. Three heavens are his with two in his presence. One in the realm of Yama (the God of the dead) is the abode of heroes (I.35.5-6).

The Divine creator rules all these worlds and directs the beings within them toward the fulfillment of their aspirations.

> Not to be diminished is the truth of Divine Savitar, that he will uphold the entire universe. Whatever on the summit of the Earth or on the ridge of Heaven he creates with his beautiful hands, that is his truth. Those who are supreme in Indra he directs to vast mountains and gives dwellings for them to abide. However, they may move in different ways, even so, Savitar, they stand according to your will (IV.54.4–5).

The three higher Heavens correspondent to the Vedantic trinity of Sacchidananda, Being-Consciousness-Bliss, which are the great abodes of the Gods.

> Three supreme hard to attain luminous heavens three heroes of the almighty rule (III.56.8).

Men can also go to these regions of the Gods and become one with them.

> May I attain that beloved abode of his, where godly men rejoice, where there is kinship with him of wide stride, a fountain of bliss in the supreme abode of Vishnu (I.154.5).
>
> That supreme abode of Vishnu like an eye extended in Heaven, the seers ever see (I.22.20).

Heaven and Earth also relate to the day and the night, which in turn are the two paths of the sacrifice: the Path of the Gods and the Path of the Fathers. By the heavenly path, the way of light, creatures go beyond the lower realms and become immortal. By the earthly path, the way of darkness, they must be reborn again and must fight the serpent of ignorance again. The truth of karma is clearly stated in the *Rig Veda:*

> Savitar, for the holy Gods you first generated the highest gift of immortality. Then as a bondage for mortals you opened out successive lives (IV.54.2).[9]

Mortals represent the Sun that is hidden in darkness, the consciousness bound by karma to cycle through repeated births.

> With seven sons the infinite Mother went to the earlier eon. For birth and death, she bore Martanda (the mortal egg) again (X.72.9).

The Dawn or Sun Goddess who returns to the Gods is our mortal soul returning to the Godhead. One part of the Divine takes birth or becomes the creation, the greater part remains in the uncreate.

> Three quarters of the Spirit ascended, his fourth part took repeated birth here (X.90.4).

Manu, the legendary Vedic law giver, speaks of the unity between men and Gods in the *Rig Veda,* an idea that occurs in several places in the text:

> The Gods who have a common spirit with men, who all together are beneficent (VIII.27.14).
>
> Auspicious Indra, Vishnu, Maruts and Ashwins, we bear in the mother's womb a brotherhood, indeed a common nature with you (VIII.83.7-8).
>
> Ashwins, with you we have an ancestral friendship and common bond, recognize that (VII.72.2).

Mortals by this common inner nature with the Gods can become like them, immortal:

> Sons of the infinite, may we be infinite, perfect, oh beings of light, in the Godhead and in humanity. Winning, Divine Lord and Friend, may we win you, becoming, oh Heaven and Earth, may we become you (VII.52.1).[10]

This verse sums up the Vedic aspiration. It shows a creation in which men can win the nature of the Gods and become Heaven and Earth, in which we can become perfect both in our divinity and in our humanity.

THE VEDIC VIEW OF THE EARTH

The Earth itself is recognized to be a vast world with oceans, rivers, mountains, forests and deserts:

> May Heaven and Earth be peaceful to us in our invocation. May the atmosphere be peaceful to our vision. May the plants and the trees be peaceful to us. May the victori-

ous lord of the atmosphere give us peace. May the firm mountains be peaceful to us; peaceful be the rivers and the waters. May the infinite be peaceful to us with its laws (VII.35.5, 9).

Savitar (the Sun God) has illumined the eight peaks of the Earth, three desert regions and seven rivers (I.35.8).[11]

We are not given any specific data about these regions of the Earth. Yet with what we have learned about the rivers and seas we can surmise it. The Land of the Seven Rivers is India itself. The eight mountains around it are the Himalayas, Vindhyas, and other mountain ranges of India. The three desert or shore regions would be the Arabian Sea, the Bay of Bengal and the west Indian desert.

Because the term Himavat or Himalayas is mentioned only once (X.121.4) in the *Rig Veda* some have considered that the Vedic people had no knowledge of these mountains until a later period. With the knowledge we have gathered about the ocean and rivers we must consider that the generic Vedic terms for mountains apply primarily to the Himalayas. The main Vedic myth is the release of the seven rivers from the mountains to flow to the seas. If the Vedic mountains are lower mountains of Afghanistan or Central Asia the whole myth of the seven rivers flowing to the sea makes no sense. The myth of Indra, the rain or thunder God, releasing the rivers to flow into the Sea, is the great Himalayan myth. It is the myth of the great mountains, rivers, oceans and monsoon of India.

Many Vedic Gods are associated with the mountains. Vishnu is a God "who dwells in the mountains and lives in a cave" (I.154.2). The idea of the Himalayas as the home of the Gods is a Vedic idea. Indra is sometimes lauded with Parvata, the mountain, as a dual God (III.53.), and the mountain or mountains are often listed among the Vishwedevas, the Universal Gods. The Maruts are commonly associated with the mountains.

Yet the mountains are also the demons destroyed by the Vedic Gods or their enemies who come down from the mountains and steal their cows. These, however, may be the mountains of central India, not the Himalayas where the Vedic Soma lands were. Mountains also symbolize the spinal mountain, the subtle body, where the yogic work of purification goes on. The mountain myth is also a yogic meditation myth.

Rain is commonly mentioned in the *Rig Veda* and many of the great Vedic Gods are rain Gods. These include Indra, the foremost of the Gods, his companions, the Maruts, and water Gods like Varuna and Parjanya. Indra, the greatest Vedic God, is very much the personification of the monsoon. Such great rain symbolism shows a specific and pronounced rainy season. It indicates the great summer monsoon of north India. Vedic mythology reflects great rains giving rise to rivers, not cold winters, ice or snow, nor predominantly dry or desert regions. Instances of cold are occasionally mentioned in the hymns and a metaphor of leaves falling from a tree (X.68.10). Snow is nowhere explicitly described. Yet some of the mountain demons destroyed by Indra have been regarded by scholars as glaciers or mountain snows. This may reflect summer in the Himalayas and the melting of snow that goes with it.

A six-season calendar is mentioned a few times (I.22., VII.103, VIII.63.11), as is unique to India, with the last hymn celebrating the coming of the rains in north India. A fourfold division of the year is sometimes found (i.e. I.155.6), though it may just refer to the equinoxes and solstices.

The three main terms in the *Rig Veda* used for the seasons are 'sharad', autumn, 'hima' or 'hemanta', winter, and 'gharma', summer. The year is called sharad, after the autumn, or hima, after winter. The summer season was probably divided in half into a hot and a rainy season.[12] The Vedic people pray to live for a hundred winters, showing that something of a winter season was known but it is rain and heat that are mainly referred to. North India does have some winter cold, though much of it seldom experiences frost.

North India has a hot season that starts abruptly after the mild winter. It turns into the rains followed by a long fall season. Hence a three-season climate makes more sense in subtropical north India than in temperate regions. In short, north India appears to be the main site climatically and geographically. No other region has the great rivers, oceans, mountains and monsoon, as well as nearby deserts.

The Gods win for mortals all these worlds and the regions of the Earth.

> The supreme ever conqueror, who gives victory, Indra, who won the Sun-world and the Divine Waters, who conquered Earth and Heaven, the wise exult according to him. He won those who go beyond and he won the Sun. Indra won the cow who gives nourishment to all. He won gold and enjoyment. Having slain the Dasyu he furthered the power of the Aryans. Indra won the plants and won the days. He won the trees and the atmosphere (III.34.8–10).

This shows a power of conscious evolution working its way through different births on Earth towards its full unfoldment in humanity.

The Vedic world view therefore is quite vast. It shows both an extensive outer knowledge and a profound inner knowledge. It shows the view of an ancient people that had explored not only most of the physical world but who also went more deeply into the inner realms than modern man.

ANCIENT CATACLYSMS

The symbolism of the *Rig Veda,* like that of many ancient scriptures, including the Judeo-Christian *Bible,* is often cataclysmic. We read of great floods and great rivers being released to the sea. We read of great earthquakes, of mountains trembling, of great fires, even meteors. These are generally judgments rendered against humanity by the Gods for a life out of harmony with cosmic law. They are miraculous events and often miraculous actions by the sages go along with them.

The Vedic myth, as indicated, can go well with the end of the Ice Age. Indra destroys the serpent who lays at the foot of a mountain encompassing the waters, and thereby frees the seven rivers to flow into the sea.

> Indra with the greatness of the great flood split the head of the serpent. He destroyed the dragon who withheld the seven rivers. May Heaven and Earth protect us (X.67.12).
>
> Indra, you released the watery flood along with the rivers (III.32.5).[13]

The coiled serpent at the mountain, to the extent it reflects a physical reality, may symbolize the glaciers or the snow and ice in the Himalayas.

Slaying the dragon, Indra not only releases the waters but the light.

> Indra cast out the dragon who possessed of magic power lay over the great river. Heaven and Earth trembled in fear (II.11.9).
>
> He slew the serpent that lay at the foot of the mountain. As cows bellowing, flowing the rivers entered directly into the ocean. When Indra slew the first born of the serpents, then he dissolved the magic power of the magicians. Then he generated the Sun, Heaven and the Dawn (I.32.2.4).

Indra not only brings on cataclysms, he calms them.

> Who made firm the quaking Earth, who quieted the shaking mountains, who in his movement made the atmosphere wider, who upheld Heaven, he, oh men, is Indra (II.12.2).

> He by strength made firm the mountains to the east and made the downward flow of the waters. He upheld the Earth that gives support to all. By magic power he up pillared Heaven from shaking (II.17.5).

These images suggest the action of Indra as an earthquake causing floods and bringing about great geological changes. These hymns may reflect great earth changes that occurred in the Himalayan region at the end of the Ice Age.

> Indra, you are great, for you the Earth and Heaven consent to your power and follow your greatness. With strength you slew the dragon and released the rivers consumed by the serpent. Heaven trembled at the brilliance of your birth. The Earth trembled in fear at your wrath. The stable mountains shook; the deserts were flooded as the waters flowed. With strength you broke open the mountain with your thunderbolt, as with power you revealed your vigor (IV.17.1-3).

This myth of Indra is the core myth of the *Rig Veda* and relates to the Angirasa seers, the oldest Vedic seer family.

> Lauded by the Angirasa seers, Indra broke open the enclosure, he burst the firmnesses of the mountains. He broke their artificial embankments (II.15.8).

Indra destroys the mountain-like cities or fortresses of the Dasyus. He lays low a hundred of them, often throwing at them his thunderbolt or the Sun wheel.

Agni also can have a cataclysmic affect. He is symbolized as a great conflagration:

> Luminous Agni, your wind driven rays, luminous move to every side. Your powerfully destructive celestial rays disport themselves breaking the forests. Your luminous, pure, freely moving horses shear the Earth. Then your ember shines wide, reaching to the summit of the Earth (VI.6.3-4).

Is this a mere forest fire or some great conflagration that a major warming of the climate at the end of the Ice Age may have brought about?

The Maruts, the Vedic Gods of power and the storm, also have cataclysmic effects:

> The islands fly apart, evil is halted, both Heaven and Earth are united. You spread out the shores, you who wear luminous rings, as you drive forth self-effulgent. Things immovable, the mountains and trees, shake and roar upon your course, and the Earth quakes as you move (VIII.20.4-5).[14]
>
> The Earth trembles in fear at their wrath, like a full ship that shakes and lets the water in (V.59.2).

Such passages said to reflect the monsoon in India may have originally referred to much more than that.

A number of Biblical myths and stories occur in the *Rig Veda.* These include the Flood, the Tower of Babel, and the parting of the waters, as well as the general idea of the chosen people. Just as Moses parts the Red Sea for his people to cross, Vasistha, Vishwamitra, and other seers part the rivers of India for the Vedic people to cross. This parting of the waters is a common Vedic occurrence.

> The great seer, God-born, God-impelled, Divine in vision, stopped the flooding river. When Vishwamitra carried Sudas across, Indra was delighted with the Kushikas (III.52.9).
>
> The floods extended wide for Sudas, Indra you made them shallow and easy to cross (VII.19.5).

Indra parts the waters of the river for Sudas to cross. Yet when his enemies follow him, like pharaoh the Israelites, they are drowned.

> Those who are unworthy gained the curse of the rivers (VII.19.5.).

A number of other instances of the Gods controlling the waters occur in the *Rig Veda,* as mentioned in the chapter on the Ocean.

> Indra, the river Vibalyam, flooding over the Earth, you stopped with your magic power (IV.30.12).
>
> The great stream that nourishes all, flowing to Turviti and Vaya, Indra by prayers you calmed the flood. You made the rivers easy to cross (IV.19.6).

Indra releases the flood to destroy the Dasyus, the evil people allied to demonic powers:

> I gave the Earth to the Aryans, the rain to the mortal worshipper. I led the roaring floods. The Gods moved according to my will. In ecstasy I destroyed the ninety-nine cities of Shambara (IV.26.1).
>
> United with you and in your friendship, oh Soma, Indra made the floods to flow for man. He destroyed the serpent who held the seven rivers. He opened out their covered channels. United with you, oh Soma, he broke off the wheel of the Sun suddenly with force. As it revolved through the great mountain, the great evil was removed from all life (IV.28.1).

This is the image of a solar force coming to Earth and throwing the powers of darkness off of a great mountain, this along with the image of the flood.

The Dasyus, the enemies of the Aryans, commit several sins against the Gods. They lose the power of the word and become speakers of evil or harm. They try to ascend Heaven in their pride. This resembles the Tower of Babel story:

> Indra, those who were cunning with magical powers, who wished to ascend Heaven, you threw the Dasyus down (VIII.14.14).
>
> Who threw down the demon Rahuhina, as he tried to ascend to Heaven, he, oh men, is Indra (II.12.12).

The Vedic people are the chosen people of the Gods. The Gods have given over the Earth to them to build a culture of spirituality and compassion. The Vedic people are descendants of seers, with a Divine mission. They are a spiritual culture guided by sages and seers who are men of Divine wisdom and yogic power. Such similarities between the *Bible* and the *Vedas* reflect a common ancient mythos.

2
VEDIC CIVILIZATION

With these, oh sacred Fire, your unlimited strengths,
protect us with a hundred cities of bronze.
— *Rig Veda VII.3.7*

The *Rig Veda* is primarily a book of ritual and meditation. It records the exploits of kings but secondarily or insofar as they become spiritual symbols. Aspects of the outer life of the people and the nature of the culture appear but only incidentally and in a general manner. It almost appears as if anything extraneous to the ritual is avoided in the hymns as perhaps inappropriate to a sacred literature. We must not forget that the *Rig Veda* is a manual of the priests or Brahmins and does not represent the common life of the general populace.

We cannot assume that all aspects of the culture will be found in the *Rig Veda.* A modern book of ritual or meditation would not tell us all aspects of modern culture, nor would a book of poetry. If we have only one book as the record for an entire culture a certain one-sidedness of view will develop if we cannot see what may have been left out. We cannot rigidly limit all of Vedic culture to what appears in the hymns. There must have been other teachings giving social laws and customs, such as we find in later Hindu literature. These customs were not as sacred or as unchanging as the religious ones and were thus less likely to have been preserved. The purpose in this chapter is not to explore the outer culture in detail. It is to point out enough of its complexity to confirm the sophisticated nature of Vedic civilization to support the rest of the book.

FOOD SOURCES AND PLANTS

The most common food source mentioned in the *Rig Veda* is dairy products. Milk and various milk preparations are very common. Different kinds of milk are mentioned, from different animals or from cows of different types. 'Dadhi' is yogurt. 'Piyusha' is probably cream. 'Ghrita', ghee or clarified butter, is very common, not only as a food or cooking oil, but also as oil for lamps.

Barley, 'yava', is commonly mentioned and is the generic term for grain or bread. Perhaps other grains are meant by it also, though barley must have been the most important. While the most common name for rice, vrihi, is not specifically mentioned until the *Atharva Veda,* the term 'dhanya', which later referred to several different types of rice including vrihi, also occurs in the *Rig Veda.* The emphasis on barley also caused scholars to propose a northern or non-Indian origin for the *Vedas,* as barley was thought to be primarily a cold climate grain. Now we know from archaeology that barley was one of the oldest grains in the world and traces of it have been found in ancient Egypt and in the Indus Valley culture, as well as in the earliest agricultural sites in India. Barley is still grown in India, even in the tropical parts, and several wild varieties exist. Hence the use of barley as a grain affirms the early date of the *Vedas* and does not require a non-Indian location for them.

Breads, cakes and gruels are also mentioned (dhana, karambha), indicating that a variety of baked goods were made including pastries with honey. There was a collective storing of grain, as grain storehouses are mentioned.

> Who is the king of heavenly, earthly and treasures of the land, priests, fill him like a grainery with grain (II.14.11).[1]

A kind of cucumber is mentioned (urvaruka; VII.59.12). Note is made of taking fruit from a tree.

> Indra, shake out the gathered treasure, like the ripe fruit of a tree with a hook (III.45.4).[2]

References to particular food types are, however, rare.

For sweeteners honey (madhu) is used. Sugar (svadhu) is recognized but it is not certain whether it means sugar cane or just sweet taste. A honey wine or mead was made. A kind of of wine or fermented drink called 'sura' was used more rarely and under prohibitions. The main elixir drink, however, is Soma.

Cane or bamboo (vamsha) is commonly mentioned and was used at least for building, as in later India. Reed (venu) was used for making flutes. Flax (atasi) is also commonly mentioned and may have been a source of fiber as well. Cotton is not yet identifiable. Sesame seeds, tila, are not mentioned but a golden pillar is said to be erected in an auspicious field that perhaps means "abundant with sesame" (tivile; V.59.7).

Plants and herbs are commonly mentioned but also generically (oshadhi and virudh). The lotus (pushkara) occurs a few times.

> You, oh fire, Atharva pressed from out of the lotus, from the head of every sage (VI.16.13).

The Vedic Gods, the Ashwins, are particularly associated with the lotus. Another word for lotus, 'pundarika', is found also (V.78.7, X.142.8). As in later yogic literature, the lotus appears to stand for centers or chakras of the subtle body, particularly the crown chakra.

Trees are mentioned generically also as 'vana', 'vriksha', and 'vanaspati', and many implements and tools were made out of wood. The ashwattha or pippal (Ficus religiosa), the tropical fig tree, is important (I.135.8, I.164.22, V.54.12). It is said to be the home of the herbs and plants (X.97.5). There is a long hymn to plants and healing herbs (X.97). The only plants we can really identify are mainly those of the Indian subcontinent, though specific plants are not commonly mentioned in the hymns.

ANIMALS

The Vedic people had a wealth of domesticated animals — horses, cows, bulls, buffaloes, sheep, goats, dogs, camels, and donkeys. In fact, the *Vedas* mention almost all the known domesticated animals of the ancient world. Many different names for different varieties of horses are found (vaji, arvan, sapti, haya, ashva, hari, harit, hita). Horses were used for riding or to pull chariots. Cows were used for dairy products and leather. Sheep were used for wool. Oxen were used to carry wagons or to plow the fields. Herds of horses, up to sixty thousand, enter the symbolism of some hymns, herds of cattle of up to one hundred thousand are not uncommonly mentioned. These are given as gifts to the seers.

> Playoga's son has thus surpassed all others in giving with cattle in tens of thousands (VIII.1.33).[3]
>
> Vibhindu has given aid to him with cattle four times ten thousand and eight thousand extra (VIII.2.41).[4]
>
> Sixty thousand cattle have I, a seer, driven away from the herd (VIII.4.20).[5]
>
> Thus Kashu Chaidya has given one hundred of camels and ten thousand of cattle (VIII.5.37).[6]
>
> Three hundred horses and ten thousand of cattle, they gave for the powerful chant (VIII.6.47).[7]

> Chitra is the king, all others are like kings who dwell along the Saraswati river. Like the rain God extending with the rain, he has given cattle a thousand times ten thousand cattle (VIII.21.18).[8]
>
> Sixty thousand horses I won and ten thousand and twenty hundred of camels (VIII.46.22).[9]
>
> Trivrishna shines with tens of thousands of cattle (V.27.1).[10]
>
> Four thousand of cattle I have received among the Rushamas (V.30.15).
>
> Sixty thousand cattle followed. Kakshivan won them at the close of the days (I.126.3).[11]

Compared to these gifts to the seers in the *Rig Veda* the Upanishadic gifts of a thousand cows, as we find in later ancient India, appear meager. Surely these great Vedic gifts are not the gifts of a poor people or mere nomads. In some instances a golden chariot was included (VIII.46.24). Such a culture appears more affluent than ancient India of the late Vedic and early classical era. These great herds of animals suggest a rich pasture area, not a desert or high mountain homeland.

Animal Sacrifice

Animal sacrifice in the *Vedas* is symbolic in nature and actual victims were rarely used. Just as the Vedic human sacrifice is a symbol for the offering of the ego to the Divine, so the animal sacrific symbolizes offering our vital nature to the Divine.

> The rice cake which is offered is the victim which is killed; its chaff is the hair, the husks the skin, the polishings the blood, the pounded grains and fragments the flesh, whatever is substantial the bone. With the sap of all animals he sacrifices who sacrifices with the rice cake (AB II.9).

Animal sacrifices were not looked upon with favor.

> The Rakshasas (demons) have the blood as their share (KB X.4).

Yet in late Vedic times, when the culture had fallen and come under the influence of the warrior class, animal sacrifice became common in India as it did elsewhere in the ancient world. Originally animal sacrifice of a limited nature was only allowed as a means to teach the people of lower classes, who were inclined to eat meat indiscriminately, that animals were sacred and could not be eaten except as an offering to the Divine done with the strictest formality and ceremony. In this way such restricted animal sacrifices directed the people to eventually give up meat-eating altogether. The eating of meat was also allowed in difficult conditions like famine or the eating of wild game during travels when no other food was available.

There are references to the Vedic Gods eating animal flesh, mainly Indra. This appears, along with Indra's nature as a transcendent God beyond good and evil to do something forbidden, like the slaying of his own father. It does not indicate widespread meat-eating.

> When he ate three hundred buffaloes and drank three lakes of Soma, all the Gods invoked a prayer, an offering, as Indra slew the serpent (V.29.8).

The main ritual offerings are ghee and Soma, the medicinal plant.

> Pour the drink from all sides, Soma the supreme offering (IX.107.1).[12]

The female cow is called "aghnya," meaning "not to be killed," and "aditi" meaning "not to be cut or divided." This shows a non-killing of cows in the time of the *Rig Veda*. The cow is a very sacred animal in the hymns from the beginning and is everywhere glorified and revered. The Vedic culture is the culture of the cow.

Wild Animals

Many wild animals are mentioned in the *Vedas*. The lion and falcon are very common in Vedic symbolism as in that of the ancient Middle East. The great God Indra speaks as the falcon (IV.26). The lion even today is a resident of the Kathiawar peninsula in Gujarat, near the mouth of the ancient Saraswati river central to Vedic culture. This is probably the home of the Vedic lion which was set to dwell by the waters (III.9.4). The swan, 'hamsa', the bird of the soul, is the most famous Vedic bird (IV.40.5). The sacred Hamsa bird is said in later literature to migrate to Manasa Lake by Mount Kailas in Tibet. This may be the home of the Vedic swan also. A number of other birds are mentioned in the hymns as well. Serpents are mentioned and deified, and protection against the scorpion is sought in one hymn (I.191). Elephants are mentioned with kings (ibha; I.65.7) and elsewhere (IV.16.14). Boars (varaha) occur and fish are noted, including the dolphin (I.116.18).

METALS, STONES AND IMPLEMENTS

Gold

The most common metal mentioned is gold, which is alluded to hundreds of times and under various names (hiranya, suvarna, rajata, rukma). The Vedic religion is the religion of the Sun and its culture is the culture of gold. No wonder the Vedic age was called the Golden Age. The Himalayan region has many sources of gold and the love of gold has remained constant throughout Indian history. All types of gold articles are mentioned in the *Vedas.*

> Prithushravas gave as a gift a golden chariot (VIII.46.21).[13]
>
> Pushan your golden ships that are within the sea (VI.58.2).[14]
>
> On the heads of the Maruts are extended golden helmets (V.54.12).[15]
>
> There are no others like unto these Maruts, who shine with golden weapons on their bodies (VII.57.3).[16]

Gold lumps or gold coins (pinda) occur and measurements of money (shulka) up to ten thousand units are related.

> I would not give you away, Indra, for a great amount of money, not for a thousand, ten thousand, or a hundred thousand (VIII.1.5).[17]
>
> I gained ten lumps of gold from Divodasa (VI.47.23).[18]

Silver is also mentioned, as a number of words for silver color exist, but it had secondary importance next to gold, being sometimes called white gold.

Bronze

'Ayas' is the generic Vedic term for metal, as yava is for grain. Ayas meant iron in some Indo-European tongues. Hence scholars have identified the Vedic Aryans with the use of iron, which appears in the ancient world around 1500 BC. Yet ayas did not always mean iron. In old Latin it meant copper or bronze.[a] As the *Rig Veda* mentions only one metal it is unlikely that the first one developed was iron. While barley is an early grain, iron is not an early metal. Hence it is unlikely in the older texts that ayas meant iron; it was most likely bronze or copper. In the *Atharva Veda*, ayas is mentioned as either dark (shyama) or iron, or as red (lohita) or copper (AV IX. 5.4). As copper is a very common metal in India it is likely that both it and bronze preceded the use of iron, which is what the *Vedas* indicate.

> Twin kings of modest spirit, you uphold together a domain of a thousand pillars. Gold is its covering, the pillars are of bronze (ayas), it shines in Heaven like a whip for horses. Mitra and Varuna, you mount your golden form, a bronze pillar as a throne, at dawn in the rising of the Sun. From it you see the infinite and the finite (V.62.7-8).[19]

The comparison of ayas with the gold of the rising Sun also suggests that it originally meant bronze, not iron. Bronze has a golden lustre whereas iron becomes black. The ancient Nighantu or list of Vedic synonyms similarly makes ayas a synonym for gold.

This Vedic hymn also gives the metaphor of a great temple made with a thousand bronze pillars. Bronze implements like cauldrons are mentioned, as well.

> The metal cauldron that is heated at the ritual, we seers have gained (V.30.15).

Pillars

Pillars of stone (stambha, skambha, sthuna, or dharuna) are common objects of imagery and worship, much like the Shiva lingas of later times. They are particularly important in the Soma rites.

> The support pillar of Heaven, far extended, the Soma stalk encompasses the worlds from all sides (IX.74.2)[20]
>
> The prop pillar of Heaven and the support pillar of Earth, all people are in Soma's hand (IX.89.6).[21]

This worship of pillars reminds us of the obelisks of Egypt or the megaliths of Europe.

Swords made of stone are mentioned. Mortars and pestles are spoken of (ulukhala and musala; I.28) and Soma stones have entire hymns to them (grava; X.76, 95).

Gems

Apart from the numerous references to gold, there is reference to pearl or shell (krishana: I.35.4, I.126.4, VII.18.23; AV IV.10) showing some gathering of gems and shells from the sea. They were used as adornments for horses. While specific gems are not mentioned, the generic term for gems, 'ratna', is common. The first verse of the *Rig Veda* begins:

> I worship Agni, the priest, the God of the sacrifice, who works by the seasons, the invoker, the best holder of gems (I.1.1).[22]

This suggests knowledge of how gems are created or purified by fire. Soma and Rudra, the Vedic Gods of healing, are related to gems, showing the use of gems for healing.

> Soma and Rudra, you sustain a celestial power, holding seven gems in every house. Be auspicious to animals and men (VI.74.1).[23]

In a very cryptic reference the Dasyus are said to use the magic of gems to oppress the Earth, which the Vedic God Indra overcomes.

> Shining with a golden gem, extending a force-field over the Earth, though they moved quickly the Dasyus could not overcome Indra (I.33.8).[24]

Implements

Many other substances were used for making implements or clothes. Wood was fashioned into various spoons, bowls and implements. A vessel for the Soma, for example, is said to be fashioned out of wood (X.68.8). Leather was used widely for straps of various kinds. Soma holds together our joints like leather the chariot (VIII.48.5). Pottery appears mentioned as bowls (kumbha).

> Indra broke open the mountain like breaking a new pot (X.89.7).[25]

> Ashwins, you poured a hundred pots of wine from the hoof of the strong horse (I.116.7).

Wells (karta, avata) occur in a number of places, usually lined with stone. Irrigation methods or artificial embankments to direct the flow of streams and as walls or moats around towns also appear.

VEHICLES

The chariot, 'ratha', is commonly mentioned, apparently a two-wheeled vehicle, fast and good for battle, though several types are mentioned. A wagon, presumably a largely four-wheeled vehicle for carrying greater loads, occurs a number of times. Ships are common as we have already mentioned in regard to the ocean and river (nau, peru, dhi, and druma) with up to a hundred oars. Sometimes ratha means ship or any kind of vehicle.

WEAPONS AND ARMIES

Weapons included the bow and arrow, with points of stone, animal bone or metal, and also swords, knives, spears and axes made of stone or metal. Helmets and armor of metal and leather are mentioned. Drums were used in battle, as well as flags.

> Where men come together who hold flags, in which battle there is nothing good, where all the worlds that see the light are afraid, there Indra and Varuna bless us (VII.83.2).

Both war chariots and wagons were used, often apparently in great numbers. Several battles are mentioned in the *Rig Veda,* with many famous Vedic kings and heroes aided by the Gods. Large armies occur with from 10,000 to 100,000 troops defeated in battle. Up to a hundred cities of the Dasyus, the opponents of the Aryans, are said to have been conquered. Wars involved various small kingdoms and sometimes larger confederacies (like the Battle of the Ten Kings).

> Indra scattered fifty thousand of the dark people (IV.16.13).[26]
>
> Of the Dasa Varcin, Indra slew a hundred thousand times five like the turning of a wheel. Indra broke open a hundred stone cities for Divodasa. For Dabhiti, Indra put to sleep thirty thousand with his weapons (IV.30.15, 20, 21).[27]

> Indra, you scattered many thousands over the Earth and with strength saved Turvayana (VI.18.13).[28]
>
> Indra, that is to be lauded which by strength you did, when you destroyed the hundred thousand. You struck Shambara down from the mountain and aided Divodasa with manifold aids. Offering Raji to the Pithinas with strength you slew sixty thousand (VI.26.5-6).[29]

These wars exhibit numbers much higher than other battles in the ancient world down to the time of the Persians. They are battles between organized armies, not nomadic raids. In the battle of Sudas it is said:

> The ends of the world appeared with dust, the noise mounted to Heaven (VIII.83.3).

Prayer, ritual, and mantra were an important part of fighting and usually the side with the best seer, not the most men, won.

> Who, related to us or foreign, or who among us would attack us, may the Gods prevent him. Prayer is my inner armor (VI.75.19).[30]

Hence, occult or shamanistic powers were used in battle. It was often the ritual of the presiding Brahmin that made for the victory, not the size of the army. According to the modern Sanskrit sage Ganapati Muni, the *Rig Veda* contains special "astra mantras" or chants used as weapons. These could take an ordinary arrow and endow it with a fiery or lightning force, or they could just cast an energy of light or sound directly. We read of such power in the *Ramayana* also, where the warriors energize their arrows with mantric force.

These wars were for land, cattle, and, above all, for spiritual power.

> Indra, son of strength, grant us the thousand bearing of the wide lands with the destruction of the dragon (VI.20.1).[31]
>
> Heaven and Earth, your gifts are manifold, who gave us King Trasadasyu for the victory. You gave wide-yielding fields, and death to the Dasyus, an awesome victory (IV.38.1).[32]

VEDIC CITIES

Modern historians have described the Vedic Aryans as nomads. They point to the frequent reference to the Gods as "destoyers of cities" and the listing of the numbers of cities or fortresses they have conquered. What they fail to mention is that the *Rig Veda* also has many references to the Aryans living in cities or using them for protection. It should be noted further that other ancient kings styled themselves destroyers or conquerors of cities, including Narmer, regarded as the first pharaoh of Egypt, who was symbolized by the falcon, just like the Aryan kings of India. 'Conqueror of cities' is a common epithet for powerful ancient kings all over the world. There is no reason to make the Vedic people into barbarians and nomads because they also used it.

The most famous destroyer of cities is King Divodasa, who destroys the ninety-nine or one hundred cities of Shambara (II.19.6; IV.26.2). Sudas and others are said to destroy or conquer seven cities (VII.18.13). These cities of the enemy are said to be made out of stone (IV.30.20; II.14.6) or metal (ayas; II.20.8; IV.27.1), or plastered (dehya; as in VII.6.5). Perhaps the gates of the cities were reinforced with bronze.

The Aryans also have a comparable number of cities of their own. The Vedic seers pray for the Gods to protect them with cities.

> Oh Fire, protect us with a hundred metal cities (VII.3.7).[33]
>
> Agni, thus be like a wide unconquerable metal city multiplied a hundred times (VII.15.14).[34]
>
> Protect us with a hundred cities, oh Agni (VI.48.8).[35]
>
> With a hundred-fold cities protect us from evil and deceit, oh Maruts (I.166.8).[36]

The Vedic Gods and Goddesses are not only called destroyers of cities; they are also supplicated as cities.

> Agni, be like a wide, abundant and vast city (I.189.2).[37]
>
> Saraswati, a support like a metal city (VII.95.1).[38]

The Vedic Gods are not only conquerors of cities, they are styled rulers of cities, meaning that they not only took over those of the enemies they conquered (many of whom were Aryans in the first place) but also built their own.

> Oh powerful Agni, you have conquered all auspicious cities (III.15.4).[39]
>
> Indra rules all cities like a common single husband for many wives (VII.26.3).[40]

It was the practice of Vedic people to build cities or fortresses. After describing the practices of building boats (v.2), agriculture (v.3–4), digging of wells (v.5–6), and use of the chariot (v.7) another hymn states:

> Make an enclosure for cattle, for providing milk for people, sew a wide and thick armor, build unconquerable metal cities (X.101.8).[41]

The name of one of the cities is given, along with Agni lighting it up. The image may be that of the lights of a city, presumably largely from ghee lamps.

> Agni, who lit up the city Narmini, the seer, like a fast and conquering horse, is bright like the Sun with a hundredfold soul (I.149.3).[42]

Vedic battles are thus between kings and their organized armies and for the different cities or fortresses in which they dwell. There is no mention of random invasions or nomadic movements but an organized society centered around various urban centers. The metaphor of a hundred cities and a hundred thousand warriors suggests a thousand warriors per city. This would indicate cities of some size to have so many warriors. Probably there was a central fortress or city around which a larger rural population dwelled.

Dwellings are mentioned commonly in the *Rig Veda* (durona, dama) as well as doors and gates (dvara). The gates of Heaven are deified, Devi Dvara, in the common Apri hymns:

> Divine doors, invoked, open yourselves wide, be easy of access to prayer. Extensive, undecaying, spread yourselves wide, purifying the glorious heroic quality (II.3.5).[43]

In short, there is nothing in the *Rig Veda* showing a war between nomadic Aryan invaders and indigenous city dwellers. The wars were between kings with organized armies. In each kingdom there were cities or fortresses along with villages, and with farmers and herdsmen living outside the cities, just as we find up to the present time in India. We have, just as in later India, various kings and small kingdoms, with their respective cities, warring for larger areas. Sometimes a single king emerges as a kind of emperor, the renowned world-ruler. These appear to have been kings who ruled the known world or north India. Such kings, like Sudas, were conquerors of all cities in the Vedic style. They had large armies, groups of priests and other administrators to help them. Vedic literature shows a state of civilization and government at least on a par with anything in the rest of the ancient world down to the Greeks.

VEDIC SOCIETY

A division of society existed at least to the extent of three classes: the nobility, the priests and the common people.

> To him the people of their own accord pay homage, the king by whom the Brahmin is given precedence (IV.50.8).

There were also non-Aryans outside the structure of Aryan society but slavery does not appear to have existed, though certainly servants did.

Different trades are mentioned in the *Rig Veda*. King (raja), warrior (satva), priest (brahmin) and bard (kavi) are common. Doctors (bhishak) are also commonly mentioned, along with craftsmen, particularly chariot makers (taksha). Wool was commonly used for clothing and weavers and spinners are mentioned, along with looms (X.130). The favorite sport of the Aryans was chariot racing. Gambling is also mentioned a few times (X.34). Yet such references are quite rare relative to the importance of the ritual, mantra, and Yoga.

The Vedic social order appears to have been monogamous and patriarchal. Polygamy, however, was accepted at least among the kings and nobles. Indra is said to have many wives. On the other hand, the Maruts, Indra's companions, numbered between seven and one hundred and eighty, are said to have a single wife, Rodasi (I.167). The twin Ashwins and the Sun God Pushan also share a single wife, Surya Savitri. These metaphors of the Gods and Goddesses, however, may not reflect actual social relations but they do show an open society or such metaphors would have been offensive.

Women appear to have a better status in Vedic times than in later India.

> Many a woman is better and richer than a man who is ungodly and selfish (V.61.6).

The seers often compare themselves to women or wives of the Gods. The worship or high status of the mother is also found in Vedic hymns, even among the hymns to Indra, the most masculine of the Gods.

> Indra, you are greater than a father to me and greater than an uncaring brother. You appear as equal to my mother (VIII.1.6).[44]

Women could go to assemblies and choose their husbands. No mention of sati or widow burning is found in the *Rig Veda.* The only real explicit funeral hymn in the text directs the widow to return to the living.

> Arise, woman, to the realm of the living. His life is gone (X.18.8).

ART AND MAGIC

Poetry was common, as the *Veda* itself is poetry, though some love poetry can be seen in the hymns (X.93; the myth of Urvashi). A number of musical instruments were employed; drums, stringed instruments and flute-like instruments and sometimes large choirs.

> Let the gargara sound forth and let the godha resound,
> let the pinga vibrate the exalted prayer to Indra (VIII.69.9).

However, we are not certain exactly what these musical instruments are. Some type of wind instrument or bag pipe is mentioned,

> They blow the bakuram skin (IV.1.8).

Dance is often mentioned. Indra, like Shiva, is portrayed as a great dancer. The process of creation itself is likened to a great dance (X.72). Great artisans like the Ribhus are mythologized. They not only fashion the chariots of the Gods but have power over nature. Vedic poets and artists thus have magical powers.

The Gods have their special vehicles, as we have made reference to already. These magic vehicles travel in the atmosphere and have the power to go anywhere or encompass the worlds.

> No team of deer draws your chariot, oh Maruts, no horses and it goes without a driver. It does not stop and

has no reins, it moves through the atmosphere, it goes easily by its path through Heaven and Earth (VI.66.7).[45]

The ships of the Ashwins travel through the atmosphere, as do the golden ships of Pushan (VI.58). While this may be a metaphor for sailing vessels, some may be inclined to see in it some ancient technology or special occult vehicles, perhaps possessed by the priests and kept hidden from ordinary people. Yet in the *Vedas* such magical phenomena arise through the power of mantra and the meditative powers of the mind, not some outer technology. In later Puranic and epic texts, as in the *Vedas*, there is specific mention of a 'vimana', an aerial ship. It occurs in the *Rig Veda* related to the powers of the Sun and the Moon (Pushan and Soma):

> Soma and Pushan, the aerial ship in the atmosphere, which has a sevenfold wheel, the vehicle which is not disturbed by anything, which revolves easily employed by the mind, oh Bulls, energize it which has five rays (II.40.3).[46]

The Ribhus, as magic craftsmen, make magical things, like the cosmic chariot which encompasses all the worlds.

> Not born from a horse, without reins, worthy of praise, the three-wheeled chariot encompasses the region. Great is your Divine speech when, Ribhus, you nourish Heaven and Earth, who wise by the mind, according to the thought made the chariot that turns easily and does not waver (IV.36.1-2).

They also have the power to renew the Earth and further the forces of nature.

> For twelve days they slept in delight in the house of him who cannot be hidden (the Sun). They renewed the fields and led the rivers down. Plants spread over the deserts and the waters filled the depths (IV.33.7).

For these great accomplishments, including making the Soma chalice, delivering the cosmic cow and making the horses of Indra, the originally mortal become immortal.

> Here is your friendship by the mind, oh men. The priests came to these sessions with knowledge. By magic powers, equal to each form, the sons of Sudhanvan became holy. By magic powers they fashioned the chalice, by thought they drew the cow out of its skin, by the mind they fashioned the two horses of Indra. According to these actions the Ribhus became Divine (III.60.1-2).

The Ribhus thus symbolize the magic power of the priests. A similar case can be seen with the Vedic miracle workers, the Ashwins. They raise the dead, make the blind see, make the old young, and so on, as we note below in our section on Ayurveda.

AYURVEDA, VEDIC MEDICINE

Ayurveda is the traditional medicine of India and still practiced today. It presents itself as an aspect of Vedic science and looks to the *Vedas* for its origins and many of the terms that it uses. Most books on Ayurveda trace it to the *Atharva Veda,* the last of the four *Vedas,* as it more specifically mentions disease and its treatment through plants, mantras, and amulets. However, the real origins of Ayurveda are in the *Rig Veda,* the first of the *Vedas.* It is permeated with a symbolism that reflects the whole science of Ayurveda, particularly its more subtle or spiritual side. Doctors are commonly mentioned. Vedic Gods like Rudra, the Ashwins, Soma, Agni and Indra are lauded as doctors.

The central theory of Ayurveda is that of the three Doshas or biological humors: Vata, Pitta and Kapha, which correspond basically to the active elements of air, fire, and water. In the *Rig Veda,* we also have three great Gods or cosmic powers: Indra, Agni, and Soma. Indra is equated with Vata and Vayu in the *Rig Veda* itself as the God of the atmosphere. There are many verses and hymns to Indra-Vayu or Indra-Vata (i.e. IV.46, 47). Indra is called Prana in the *Upanishads* as the central life-force. Agni is equated with Pitta in Ayurvedic source books and is fire, combustion and transformation on all levels. Soma, as the fundamental liquid of life, is Kapha, the biological water humor. In Greek, another Indo-European language, Soma is another name for the substance of the body, which Ayurvedically speaking is Kapha.

While equatable with the three humors in this general sense, the Vedic Gods correspond more to their essential or inner forms. As we evolve spiritually these higher forms of the biological humors become developed and through them the old conditioned human brain is changed into the unconditioned mind, a vessel of cosmic intelligence. This is the Yoga of Ayurveda. It is the highest form of rejuvenation or rasayana treatment called "Brahma rasayana," the rejuvenation of cosmic awareness, which is essentially the rejuvenation of the mind.

As Vata is purified it gives rise to Prana, the higher state of life-force which brings with it the energy of the cosmic life. As Pitta is purified it gives rise to Tejas, which is the flame of truth perception, the power of the cosmic mind. As Kapha is purified it gives rise to Ojas, which is the most subtle and powerful vital fluid, our connection to the energy of cosmic delight. These three principles exist in the ordinary human state but in gross or unbalanced forms in which their true power is not revealed. The deeper side of Ayurveda is concerned with balancing the three humors in their subtle essences as Prana, Tejas, and Ojas. When Prana, the life-force, Tejas, the fire of the mind and Ojas, the essential fluid of the body are harmonized, then the mind is transformed. There is an actual mutation in the brain cells.

The three main Vedic Gods — Indra, Agni, and Soma — are nothing but these three pure forms of Prana, Tejas, and Ojas. The Vedic work or Yoga relates to the manifesting and balancing of Prana, Tejas and Ojas through the use of various substances and methods including herbs, rituals, mantra, and meditation. The term Ojas occurs a number of times in the *Rig Veda.*

> Then his Ojas shone, when he brought together as if in a skin both Heaven and Earth (VIII.6.5).

Indra as the power of the enlightened mind is able to bring Heaven and Earth together in the human body by the power of purified Ojas.

Vedic rituals are used for healing, as in the typical fire sacrifice (homa or Agnihotra), the ashes of which (bhasma) are still used in India today for healing purposes. Mantras, prayers, ghee or Soma were offered into the fire for healing purposes. On a yogic level, the main method of healing is the use of the mantra along with meditation. Included in the hymns to Indra are the mantras for purifying or transforming Prana or Vata. In the hymns to Agni are the mantras for purifying and transforming Pitta. In the hymns to Soma are the mantras for purifying and transforming Kapha.

While Vedic symbolism is complicated and multileveled, a few simple examples of its Ayurvedic meaning can be given. It is the great action of Indra to slay the dragon and release the seven rivers to flow into the sea. Indra is the pure life force that destroys the negative energy of ignorance and disease. He releases the seven streams of the seven Ayurvedic 'dhatus' or tissue-elements of the body (plasma, blood, muscle, fat, bone, marrow, semen) to flow into the ocean of bliss or God-consciousness.

The great Vedic Yoga involves first of all generating and sustaining Agni. He is the cosmic power of digestion, discrimination, and transformation. This fire is fed by Soma, which is the essence of all that we consume. According to the *Upanishads* all creation is nothing but Soma and Agni, which are the food and the eater of food, matter and spirit. The fire fed by Soma gives birth to Indra, who is the transformed life-force that comes forth from what we have assimilated.

The digestive fire or jatharagni of Ayurveda also has its origin in the concepts of the *Rig Veda:*

> This is that Agni in whose belly Indra holds the purified Soma as he grows (III.22.1).[47]

The jatharagni or the digestive fire is also the fire in the navel center or manipura chakra. Soma is the nectar that falls on it from the Moon or the third eye, the ajña chakra. When the fire fed by the Soma flares up it opens the crown chakra at the top of the head, the fontenelle which the *Upanishads* call the birthplace of Indra (AU III.12). Indra represents the awareness of the true Self. He is the perceiver (AU III.13-4), through whom the light comes forth out of darkness and the Sun of truth arises in the mind of man. He is the higher life-force that is really our sense of the Divine, our connection to the cosmic energy.

Various medicinal preparations occur in the *Rig Veda.* These are commonly made with milk (go, payas), yogurt (dadhi), ghee (ghrita; the most commonly used) or honey (madhu), along with the extracted essences of various plants. Agni is said to grow in the ocean of ghee (IV.58.1). Soma is the essential juice of various plants and is the main healing substance used. Various processes of fermentation and distillation are mentioned from which Soma was produced, the details of which have long been lost.

THE SOMA PLANT

There is much debate as to the identity of the original Soma plant in the *Vedas.* Actually it appears more as a preparation than a single plant. There is the heavenly as well as the earthly Soma. The true or heavenly Soma is not a plant, as is stated.

> They think they've drunk the Soma when they've crushed the plant, but the Soma which the men of wisdom know no mortal has ever drunk (X.85.40).

The heavenly Soma is a nectar secreted by the nervous system from Ojas (our primary vitality), which brings about the rejuvenation of the brain cells. The earthly Somas are different mountain plants generally of an aquatic nature. My feeling is that the earthly Soma plant was not a single plant but a mixture of various herbs purified or prepared with substances like milk, ghee, and honey, fermented and strained in various ways, apparently through wool (the golden fleece of Greek mythology). It was prepared along with Vedic mantras which were important in giving it power. I think that gold and possibly gems were used in its preparation. In this regard the original Soma may resemble some of the alchemical (rasa) preparations of later Ayurveda. I think there were a number of medicinal Soma preparations, most aimed at promoting longevity, rejuvenation, and purification of the body and mind for spiritual realization.

The magic of the Soma, extracting the essence of all herbs, permeates the *Rig Veda* and is its climax. Drinking of the Soma gives longevity, even immortality.

> We have drunk the Soma. We have become immortal. We have reached the light and found the Gods. We have gone to where our life is extended (VIII.48.3, 11).

The *Atharva Veda* relates Soma to the plant Kushta (Saussurea lappa), which is said to dwell together with the Soma as the universal medicine (AV XIX.39.5). It gives it a Himalayan home (AV XIX.39.1) and associates it with gold (AV XIX.39.7). This further relates the Soma to the Himalayas and possibly its usage along with gold. It reflects the Himalayan origin of the sacred herbs of the Vedic Aryans.

VEDIC HEALING METHODS

In the *Rig Veda,* we read of the use of herbs and gems (ratna), the laying on of hands, and the use of water (hydrotherapy).

> Your hand for me is health giving, for me it gives the best health, for me it is the universal medicine (X.60.12).
>
> In the Waters is immortality, in the Waters is the medicine, in the Waters the Soma tells me is all medicines, and the fire that gives peace to all, the Waters are the universal medicine (I.23.19–20).

The healing properties of the Himalayan rivers, like the Ganges, were well known in later times and appear to be mentioned here. No doubt certain herbs were used along with the sacred water.

The fashioning of artificial limbs, the restoring of sight to the blind, vigor to the impotent and even life to the dead are done by the wonder-working Vedic physicians, the Ashwins. The main references to their exploits are in the hymns of Kakshivan (I.116-119):

> The Ashwins made instantly a bronze leg for Vishpala (I.116.15).[48]
>
> Ashwins, you gave eyes to Rijrasva and made the light for the blind to see (I.117.17).
>
> Who was bound in the sea for ten nights and nine days by his evil father, Rebha who was cut and dismembered, you raised him up with a spoon of Soma (I.116.24).
>
> Ashwins, you made old Chyavana young again by your powers (I.117.13).
>
> Ashwins, you made whole the cripple woman (I.117.19).

Vedic Rudra, the Vedic prototype for the God Shiva of later times, the great father of the Gods, is also a great physician, of whom it is said:

> I know you as the best doctor of all the doctors (II.33.4).[49]

It is he who gives the cure to fever, the first and foremost of all diseases. His medicine is said to be his hand which is "jalasha" (II.33.7). I think that jalasha means leech, what dwells in water (jala). The later name for leech is jalauka. The leech is very important for curing infections and fevers that go with them (the diseases of Rudra).

THE VEDIC GOD OF MEDICINE

Traditionally Ayurveda is traced to Dhanvantari, the Hindu God of medicine. In the *Puranas* he is said to be the son of the great Vedic seer Dirghatamas (VP IV.8.2). The son of Dirghatamas in the *Rig Veda* is Kakshivan. In Kakshivan's hymns to the Ashwins (as above), we have the main references to medicine and miracles in the *Vedas,* including such great Ayurvedic figures as Chyavana. Hence Dhanvantari, the Hindu God of medicine, may be the same as the great Vedic seer Kakshivan. Kakshivan is the seer's seer. His hymns to the Ashwins (I.116-120) relate the exploits of all the major seers of the *Rig Veda.* He is mentioned in a number of the other books of the *Rig Veda.* Vamadeva, seer of the fourth book, says "I am the seer Kakshivan, the sage" (IV.26.1).

The connection of Ayurveda with the *Vedas*, particularly the *Rig Veda*, is not superficial or incidental. It reflects the essence of Ayurveda and its connection with the practice of Yoga. Once the mantric key to the *Rig Veda* is again known it can once more be used as a manual for inner transformation from the physical to the spiritual levels.

3
THE YUGA THEORY OF SRI YUKTESWAR

Sri Yukteswar, a great modern yogi and guru of Paramahansa Yogananda (author of *Autobiography of a Yogi*), has left us a very interesting theory of the time cycles of humanity. While we cannot prove all of it with the Vedic references we have found, we can find much that points us in the same direction. Yukteswar relates the yugic cycle, the four ages of ancient thought, with a precessional cycle of 24,000 years. He rejects the medieval Hindu idea that we are in a dark Iron Age or Kali Yuga of 432,000 years. The historical dates that correspond to the four Vedic World Ages are as follows. The 'Sandhis' or Transitional Eras fall between each of the the 'Yugas' or World Ages.[a]

SATYA YUGA/ Golden Age (descending)	11,501 BC	—	6701 BC
SANDHIS/ Transitional Eras	7101 BC	—	6401 BC
TRETA YUGA/ Silver Age (descending)	6701 BC	—	3101 BC
SANDHIS/ Transitional Eras	3401 BC	—	2901 BC
DWAPARA YUGA/ Bronze Age (descending)	3101 BC	—	701 BC
SANDHIS/ Transitional Eras	901 BC	—	601 BC
KALI YUGA/ Iron Age (descending)	701 BC	—	499 AD
SANDHIS/ Transitional Eras	399 AD	—	599 AD
KALI YUGA/ Iron Age (ascending)	499 AD	—	1699 AD
SANDHIS/ Transitional Eras	1599 AD	—	1899 AD
DWAPARA YUGA/ Bronze Age (ascending)	1699 AD	—	4099 AD

Yukteswar figures the precession to be 24,000 years rather than the modern figure of 25,900, equated with the Platonic 'Great Year'. This comes from taking literally the account of Manu in the *Manu Samhita* (I.69-72) which states that the four Yugas are composed of 4000, 3000, 2000 and 1000 years respectively, with a dawn and twilight of one tenth the length of the age. Yukteswar makes two such cycles of Yugas correspond to the precessional cycle. Yet instead of having a Golden Age follow the dark or Iron Age as in the medieval Hindu view, he has the cycle continue with a second or ascending Iron Age. He places the midpoint of the two dark or Iron Ages at 500 AD when the vernal equinox was at 0° Aries. He places the beginning of the ancient Golden Age at the opposite point when the vernal equinox was at 0° Libra.

In support of his view of this shorter Yuga period, we should note that the *Atharva Veda* states,

> A hundred to you, ten thousand years, two Yugas, three Yugas, four we make (AV VIII.2.21).

A Vedic Yuga is thus equated with ten thousand years instead of hundreds of thousands of years. It agrees with the base figure of Manu's Yuga cycle obtained by adding the ages of the four Yugas together. If on top of this we add the Sandhis or intermediate periods and double the cycle we get 24,000 years, just as Manu calculates.

By Yukteswar's account, the dates we have given for various astronomical positions would have to be reduced by a few centuries. By his system the later *Vedas* would be the teachings of the Bronze Age of 3100–700 BC, including the *Brahmanas* and *Upanishads*. The *Rig Veda* would be the teaching of the Silver Age of 6700–3100 BC. Yet Rig Vedic teachings in their creative or formative phase and the earliest mythical ancestors would come from the Golden Age. Yukteswar himself states that Manu is a figure of the Golden Age or Satya Yuga,[b] thus dating him and the Saraswati culture he established before 6700 BC.

The *Vedas* divide the year into two parts: one belonging to Agni, marked by the vernal equinox, and the other to Yama, marked by the autumn equinox. Perhaps the ancient seers marked the precessional cycle the same way, into a light and dark half, a Path of the Gods and Path of the Fathers. According to this theory of Sri Yukteswar, the point of the precessional cycle equivalent to the autumn equinox would have been about 5500 BC. This would be the time in which the vernal equinox was in the lunar constellation Punarvasu, which appears to be indicated in the Yama hymns of the tenth book of the *Rig Veda*. Here Yama would mark the middle of the Path of the Fathers for the great precessional or polar year. It is about this time we would expect Yama to become prominent. Perhaps most of the ancient religions had their seeds at this time, since it is at this time that the first need for codification of them would arise.

There are other references to the Yugas in Vedic literature. The *Upanishads* state that 'the karmas', the Brahmanical rites were envisioned by the sages in the Treta Yuga.

> That is the truth, the rites hidden in the mantras, which the seers saw in the Treta as a manifold system (MU II.1).[1]

This may refer to the Chitra full Moon period or the Libra solstice. It suggests that the Vedic mantras were already in existence in the Treta Yuga, at least in some basic form, when rituals were devised from them.

The *Puranas* state that a great Deva-Asura war occurred in the Treta Yuga in which the Gods were first defeated (VP IV.2.6). This may symbolize the defeat of the powers of light that occurs in the decline from the Golden Age, also suggesting some victory or temporary ascendancy of Asuric (Assyrian?) peoples. Perhaps after the Devas were defeated the *Vedas* had to be compiled and their ritual extended to save them from destruction.

There are also earlier astronomical positions in the *Rig Veda* going back perhaps to the Libra vernal equinox that Yukteswar uses to mark the midpoint between the two Golden Ages at 11,500 BC. The prominence of Abhijit in the *Vedas*, the lunar constellation which relates to the star Vega, is a case in point. Vega would have been the north pole star during much of the Golden Age. These references, however, are vague and as yet difficult to establish, so I have not included them in this book. Even to get the *Vedas* back to 6000 BC would be an extraordinary change for our historical view. I hope to deal with these earlier positions in other writings.

The difficulty with Yukteswar's view is that he figures the precessional cycle at 24,000 years, when by modern calculations it is more on the order of 25,800. He follows the precessional rate given in ancient Hindu astronomical texts like the *Surya Siddhanta,*[c] at 54″. This goes back to an ancient tradition that the Sun was at the first point of Aries at dawn of Feb. 18, 3102 BC, which would have only been possible at this precessional rate. The currently observed rate is about 50.3″ but it is based only on a few centuries of observation. Hence while Yukteswar's overall theory appears correct, the details of it may be harder to substantiate. On the other hand, the precessional rate may be variable through time, thus possibly eventually agreeing with Yukteswar's calculations.

APPENDIX B

ADDENDUM

1

THE LUNAR CONSTELLATIONS

NAKSHATRAS

NAME	EXTENT	RULER	DEITY
1. Ashwini	**00° 00′–13° 20′ Aries** Marked the beginning of the Path of the Gods or winter solstice in early Vedic times, c. 6500 BC	Ketu	The Ashwins
2. Bharani	**13° 20′–26° 40′ Aries** Marked the vernal equinox in *Vedanga Jyotish*, c. 1280 BC	Venus	Yama
3. Krittika	**26° 40′ Aries–10° 00′ Taurus** Marked the vernal equinox in parts of the *Brahmanas, Upanishads, Yajur* and *Atharva Veda*, c. 2000 BC	Sun	Agni
4. Rohini	**10° 00′–23° 20′ Taurus** Lauded in the male form as Rohita in the *Atharva Veda*. Related to myths in the later Vedic age relative to the vernal equinox, c. 3000 BC	Moon	Prajapati
5. Mrigashira	**23° 20′ Taurus–06° 40′ Gemini** Also called Agrahayana, and point of the vernal equinox in parts of the *Brahmanas* and later *Vedas*, c. 4000 BC	Mars	Soma
6. Ardra	**06° 40′–20° 00′ Gemini**	Rahu	Rudra
7. Punarvasu	**20° 00′ Gemini–03° 20′ Cancer** Equated with the nivartana or vernal equinox in the *Rig Veda* X.19, c. 6000 BC	Jupiter	Aditi
8. Pushya	**03° 20′–16° 40′ Cancer** Also called Tishya, prominent in the *Rig Veda*, perhaps related to the point of the vernal equinox, c. 6500 BC	Saturn	Brihaspati
9. Ashlesha	**16° 40′–30° 00′ Cancer** Marked the summer solstice in *Vedanga Jyotish*, c. 1280 BC	Mercury	Sarpa

10. Magha	**00° 00′–13° 20′ Leo** Marked the summer solstice in much of the *Yajur* and *Atharva Vedas*, c. 2000 BC	**Ketu**	**The Fathers**
11. Purva Phalguni	**13° 20′–26° 40′ Leo**	**Venus**	**Bhaga**
12. Uttara Phalguni	**26° 40′ Leo–10° 00′ Virgo** The summer solstice is placed between the two Phalgunis in the *Brahmanas* and parts of the *Rig* and *Atharva Vedas*,c. 4000 BC	**Sun**	**Aryaman**
13. Hasta	**10° 00′–23° 20′ Virgo**	**Moon**	**Savitar**
14. Chitra	**23° 20′ Virgo–06° 40′ Libra** May have marked the summer solstice in the *Rig Veda*, c. 6000 BC	**Mars**	**Twashtar**
15. Swati	**06° 40′–20° 00′ Libra**	**Rahu**	**Vayu**
16. Vishakha	**20° 00′ Libra–03° 20′ Scorpio** Marked the autumn equinox in *Vedanga Jyotish*, c. 1280 BC	**Jupiter**	**Indragni**
17. Anuradha	**03° 20′–16° 40′ Scorpio**	**Saturn**	**Mitra**
18. Jyeshta	**16° 40′–30° 00′ Scorpio**	**Mercury**	**Indra**
19. Mula	**00° 00′–13° 20′ Sagittarius**	**Ketu**	**Nirriti**
20. Purvashadha	**13° 20′–26° 40′ Sagittarius**	**Venus**	**Apas**
21. Uttarashadha	**26° 40′ Sag.–10° 00′ Capricorn**	**Sun**	**Vishwedevas**
22. Shravana	**10° 00′–23° 20′ Capricorn**	**Moon**	**Vishnu**
23. Dhanishta	**23° 20′ Cap.–06° 40′ Aquarius** Also called Shravishta, marked the winter solstice in later Vedic times, first within it and later at its initial point, c. 2000–1280 BC	**Mars**	**Vasus**
24. Shatabhishak	**06° 40′–20° 00′ Aquarius** May have marked the winter solstice in later Vedic times, c. 3000 BC	**Rahu**	**Varuna**
25. Purvabhadra	**20° 00′ Aquarius–03° 20′ Pisces**	**Jupiter**	**Aja Ekapat**
26. Uttarabhadra	**03° 20′–16° 40′ Pisces**	**Saturn**	**Ahir Budhnya**

27. Revati	**16° 40′–30° 00′ Pisces** May have marked the winter solstice in much of early Vedic literature, c. 5500 BC	**Mercury**	**Pushan**

Each constellation marks an area of the zodiac of thirteen degrees and twenty minutes. A twenty-eighth lunar constellation ruled by Brahma called "Abhijit" is sometimes placed between Shravana and Dhanishta, asterisms 22 and 23.

2
GLOSSARY OF TERMS

Aditi	Mother of the Vedic Gods, particularly the Adityas, the Earth
Adityas	Vedic Sun Gods, said to be seven, eight or twelve in number
Agastya	famous Vedic seer, associated with Vasishta, said to have brought the Vedic teaching to south India
Agni	Vedic fire God, outwardly the sacrificial or ritual fire, inwardly the flame of mindfulness and awareness
Ahi	the serpent destroyed by Indra, symbolizes egoism destroyed by the higher consciousness
Ahura Mazda	ancient Persian name of the Divine, cognate with Vedic Asura Mehda, "Wise Asura"
Angirasas	oldest group of Vedic seers from whom the others diversified; born from Agni
Anu	one of the five Vedic peoples, said to have been given the north of India
Apas	Vedic name for the Waters, particularly those of the cosmic ocean
Aranyaka	Vedic texts, intermediate between philosophical *Upanishads* and ritualistic *Brahmanas*
Arbuda	a demon destroyed by Indra; a mountain in Rajasthan
Arjika	famous Vedic Soma land in the region of the western Himalayas
Aryan	name of Vedic and many ancient Indo-European peoples, meaning noble, cultured or spiritual — not to be confused with modern European usage of the term
Ashwini	lunar constellation marking the beginning of Aries.
Ashwins	the twin horsemen, Vedic Gods, particularly of healing
Asura	Vedic name for God as the almighty; later name for demon

Atharva one of the early Vedic seers

Atharva Veda last of the four Vedas

Atman the Divine or inner Self

Atri one of the Seven Seers and father of the Atri family

Ayana Vedic and Sanskrit name for the solstice

Ayas Vedic for metal in general

Ayasya famous Vedic seer, related to Brihaspati and an Angirasa

Ayurveda Vedic system of medicine, "the science of life."

Ayus "the living one," sprung from Agni; early king of the Vedic lunar dynasty

Bactria Balkh region in Afghanistan

Balkh region in Afghanistan along the Oxus or Amu Darya, a western region of the Vedic people

Bharadwaja one of the Seven Vedic Seers and seer-families; son of Brihaspati, family priest of Divodasa

Bharata land of India, from the name of a Vedic king

Bhujyu ancient ancestor of the Vedic peoples, saved by the Ashwins from the middle of the ocean, also called Tugrya

Brahman the Divine Word, the Divine Reality, the Absolute

Brahmanas ritual texts of the late Vedic era

Brahmi the ancient Hindu script or alphabet

Brahmins the Vedic priestly class

Bhrigus one of the two oldest Vedic seer-families, founded by Bhrigu, son of Varuna

Brihaspati oldest of the Vedic seers, associated with the planet Jupiter and founder of the Vedic ritual

Chakras mystic centers in the subtle body, symbolized by various wheels in the *Vedas*

Dadhyak famous Vedic seer, son of Atharvan, identified with the sacrificial horse or the Sun at the winter solstice

Dasas cognate with Dasyus as unspiritual enemies of the Vedic people

Dasyu literally "destroyer," the unspiritual enemies of the Vedic Aryans

Deva name of God or the Divine, the shining one

Devayana Path of the Gods, the northern course of the Sun from the winter to the summer solstice

Dharma law, principle, or code of honor

Dirghatamas	famous Vedic seer, in whose hymns are hidden many of the spiritual and astronomical secrets of the Vedic people
Divodasa	famous king of the *Rig Veda* who destroys the hundred cities of the Dasyus
Dravidians	people of south India, ancient Aryans
Drishadvati	the second river after the Saraswati marking the central Vedic homeland
Druhyu	one of the five Vedic people, said to be given the west of India, Gandhara or Afghanistan
Dwapara Yuga	second or Bronze Age
Elam	ancient Susa region of Mesopotamia, now in western Iran, said to be Dravidian in language, land of Ila
Gandhara	Vedic land of the northwestern drainage of the Indus river
Gandharvas	celestial minstrels, perhaps cognate with the Greek centaurs
Ganga	Vedic and Sanskrit name for the Ganges river.
Ghee	clarified butter, Sanskrit Ghrita
Gujarat	southwest India by the Arabian Sea
Harappa	another name for Indus Valley culture
Hittites	ancient Aryans of Anatolia
Ikshwaku	legendary first king of the Vedic solar dynasty sprung from Manu
Il	Semitic name for God, as in Hebrew Elohim, Arabic Allah, and Phoenician Il; cognate with Vedic Ila
Ila	Vedic Goddess of speech and worship, the earth, a cow; eldest son or daughter of Manu and originator of the lunar dynasty of kings; region along the Saraswati river in India
Indra	foremost of the Vedic Gods, deity of self-knowledge and Yoga
Indo-Aryans	peoples of the same linguistic group as the Vedic.
Indus Valley culture	extensive ancient Indian civilization of the third millenium BC, possibly Vedic in origin
Itihasas	Hindu epic texts
Jyotish	Vedic astronomy and astrology, one of the six Vedangas or auxiliary branches of the *Vedas*

Kailas	the world-mountain; a mountain in Tibet across the Himalayas, near the source of most of the rivers of India
Kakshivan	famous Vedic seer, may be the same as Dhanvantari, father of Ayurvedic medicine
Kali Yuga	dark or Iron Age
Kanwa	one of the seven Vedic seers and seer families
Kapha	biological water-humor in Ayurvedic medicine
Karma	action, sacred work, Vedic rites
Kashyapa	a Vedic seer identified with the Sun
Kassites	Indo-Aryan rulers of Babylonia in the second millennium BC
Kelts	or Celts, ancient Indo-European people including the Irish, Welsh, and Scots.
Krishna	avatar, hero of the *Mahabharata.*
Krittika	lunar constellation marking early Taurus, indicated by the stars of the Pleiades
Kshatriya	the Vedic noble, kingly or warrior class
Kurukshetra	famous Vedic site west of Delhi in the Saraswati region, site of the Mahabharata War
Kurus	dynasty which ruled India at the close of the Vedic age
Lunar dynasty	one of the two main Vedic dynasties of kings, founded by Pururavas
Magha	lunar constellation marking early Leo
Mahabharata	the great Hindu epic of Lord Krishna and his era
Mahabharata War	the great war of the Mahabharata that marked the end of the Vedic age
Manasarovar	lake in Tibet below Kailas, near origin of the Sutlej river
Mantra	Vedic or Sanskrit chants or words of power
Manu	Vedic original man, cognate with English "man"
Maruts	Vedic Gods and seer family, friends of Indra, wandering sages
Meru	another name for Mount Kailas, the world-mountain or the north pole
Mithra	ancient Persian Sun God, cognate with Vedic Mitra
Mitra	Vedic God of friendship and compassion, form of the Sun God
Mohenjodaro	another name for Indus Valley culture, after one of its main cities

Mittani	ancient Indo-Aryans of Syria
Mrigashira	lunar constellation in Orion
Mujavat	famous Vedic Soma land
Nahusha	ancient Vedic king of the lunar dynasty; generic name for human beings, both Aryan and unaryan
Nakshatras	lunar constellations
Nau	Vedic for ship, also meaning the Divine Word
Netar	guiding God; Vedic name for God cognate with Egyptian Netar
Nimi	famous Vedic king of the solar dynasty, said to have been mummified
Ojas	spiritual vitality
Pani	literally "trader," unspiritual, commercial people who opposed the Vedic Aryans
Parashurama	a Bhrigu, seventh avatar of Vishnu, who defeated the Kshatriyas or warrior peoples
Parikshit	famous Vedic kings, particularly in the Kuru dynasty, which is sometimes called the Parikshit dynasty
Parushni	Vedic river, the modern Ravi, marking the western boundary of the Saraswati river system
Path of the Fathers	see 'Pitriyana'
Path of the Gods	see 'Devayana'
Phalgunis	lunar constellations marking the end of Leo and the beginning of Virgo
Pitriyana	Path of the Fathers, the southern course of the Sun from the summer to the winter solstice
Pitta	biological fire-humor in Ayurvedic medicine
Prana	the breath or life-force, identified with Indra
Pranayama	yogic control of the breath or life-force
Precession	backwards movement of the Earth on its axis through the zodiac, marking a period of about 25,800 years
Punjab	the five-river region of northwest India
Puranas	mythological texts of later Hinduism
Purisha	Vedic name of the heavenly ocean or source of the rains, literally a swamp, identifiable with the Bay of Bengal
Puru	youngest of the five Vedic people, related to the central region of India, the Saraswati or Ganges region

Purukutsa	famous Vedic king, father of Trasadasyu
Pururavas	ancient Vedic king of the lunar dynasty, father of Nahusha; associated with the Gandharvas or celestial minstrels
Pushan	"the nourisher," Vedic form of the Sun God as lord of the path
Pushya	lunar constellation marking early Cancer, where Brihaspati or Jupiter was born
Rahu	the north lunar node, a demon that causes eclipses, also called Swarbhanu
Rajas	the prime quality of energy or turbulence
Rama	Hindu avatar and form of the Sun God, king of the solar dynasty in the third age or Treta Yuga
Ramayana	the epic story of Rama
Rasa	famous large Vedic river, marking the division between the lands of the Gods and the demons; identifiable with the Narmada
Ratna	gems
Revati	lunar constellation marking the end of Pisces; name of the star marking the beginning of the zodiac at 0° Aries
Ribhus	Vedic seer family, magic craftsmen
Rig Veda	oldest of the four *Vedas* or scriptures of the Vedic Aryans, consisting of the mantras of the most ancient seers
Rishi	seer or sage
Rudra	early Vedic form of the God Shiva; father of all the Vedic Gods
Rudras	Vedic Gods, generally the Maruts
Sama Veda	second of the four *Vedas*, places mantras of the *Rig Veda* into a musical form
Salila	Vedic name for the ocean, particularly the boundless seas
Samadhi	blissful state of spiritual realization
Samudra	main Vedic and Sanskrit term for the ocean, particularly as the goal of all rivers
Sankhya	one of the systems of Vedic philosophy
Saraswati (Goddess)	Goddess of the Divine Word, mother of the *Vedas,* wisdom personified

Saraswati (river) main river along which the Vedic culture developed; west of the Yamuna, flowing from the Ambala hills to the Rann of Kutch; dried up around 1500 BC after several changes of course

Sarayu famous Vedic river, identified with the modern Ghaghara east of the Ganges; home of the solar dynasty

Sattva prime quality of light and clarity

Satya Yuga Golden Age or age of truth

Savitar Vedic form of the Sun-God governing creation and transformation, like the Greek Apollo

Scythians ancient Indo-Iranian people, Sanskrit Shaka

Shambara demon king of a hundred cities, destroyed by Divodasa with the help of Indra and a great Flood

Sharyanavat a famous Soma site; perhaps Lake Manasarovar at the foot of Mount Kailas in Tibet

Shiva the destroyer in the Hindu trinity; Vedic Rudra, often equivalent to Vedic Indra

Shukra Vedic seer in the Bhrigu line; name for the planet Venus

Shudras Vedic servant or labor class

Shutudri Vedic name of the Sutlej river; largest branch of the Saraswati river system

Sidereal zodiac zodiac of the observable stars, opposed to the Tropical zodiac or zodiac of the equinoxes

Sindhu Vedic name of the Indus river, generic name for river

Solar dynasty one of the two main Vedic dynasties of kings, said to be founded by Ikshwaku

Soma the mystic plant nectar of the *Vedas;* inwardly the nectar that flows from the head chakra

Sudas famous Vedic king who divided up the five Vedic peoples and brought the main era of the *Rig Veda* to a close

Surya the Vedic Sun God, Latin Sol, Greek Helios

Surya Savitri the Vedic Sun Goddess, married at the point of the winter solstice

Sushoma good Soma, the Vedic name of the Indus river in its upper regions of the mountains famous for Soma.

Tamas prime quality of darkness or inertia

Tilak, B.G.	Indian Vedic scholar of the turn of the century. Set forth the astronomical interpretation of Vedic hymns and proposed the theory of the arctic origin of the Vedic people
Tishya	lunar constellation, same as Pushya
Trasadasyu	famous Vedic king of the solar dynasty, a demi-god like Indra
Treta Yuga	third age or Silver Age
Turvasha	earliest of the five Vedic peoples, said to be given the east of India
Twashtar	Vedic Father God, a form of the Sun or Moon God
Upanishads	last portion of the *Vedas*, revealing the hidden spiritual meaning of the mantras
Ushas	Vedic Dawn Goddess
Vaishyas	Vedic merchant class
Vak	Vedic Word Goddess, Saraswati
Vamadeva	famous Vedic seer of the Gotama family, seer of the fourth book of the *Rig Veda*
Varna	Vedic class system, based upon spiritual values.
Varuna	ancient Vedic God, cognate with Greek Uranus, ruler of the ocean
Vasishta	one of the seven Vedic seers, priest of the solar dynasty, seer of the seventh book of the *Rig Veda*
Vasus	Vedic Gods of light
Vata	biological air-humor or Vayu in Ayurvedic medicine
Vayu	Vedic God of the wind, breath or life-spirit
Veda	spiritual knowledge
Vedanta	spiritual system behind the *Vedas*
Vedas	ancient spiritual texts of India
Vishnu	the preserver in the later Hindu trinity; in the *Vedas* a form of the Sun God
Vishuvat	Vedic and Sanskrit name for the solstice.
Vishwamitra	one of the seven Vedic seers, a famous Kshatriya or seer-king, seer of the third book of the *Rig Veda*
Vishwedevas	the Universal Gods
Vivaswan	name of the Sun God, particularly as father of humanity; father of Manu or the original man
Vritra	the dragon destroyed by Indra, symbolizes the ignorance destroyed by spiritual knowledge; holds captive the Waters

Yadu	one of the two earliest of the five Vedic people, said to be given the south of India (particularly modern-day Gujarat)
Yajña	Vedic sacrifice, inwardly the practice of Yoga
Yajur Veda	the Veda of sacrifice, adds ritualistic mantras to those of the *Rig Veda*
Yama	Vedic God of the dead and form of the original man, like Egyptian Osiris
Yamuna	river west of the Ganges, flowed into the Saraswati in early Vedic times
Yayati	early king of the lunar dynasty, father of the five Vedic peoples
Yima	Persian original man, cognate with Vedic Yama
Yoga	spiritual practices to bring about liberation or enlightenment
Yuga	World Age or cycle of World Ages, identifiable with the precessional cycle
Zoroaster	also Zarathustra, founder of the ancient Persian religion that goes by his name
Zoroastrian	ancient religion of Persia

3
NOTES

ANCIENT HISTORY FROM THE VISION OF THE SEERS

a. The Hindu calendar in ancient times started from a date of 3102 BC. It follows sixty-year cycles, which are used today. The ancient astronomer Aryabhatta in his *Aryabhattiya* states that when he was twenty-three years old the cycle of sixty years completed its sixtieth revolution. This would place him 3,600 years after the beginning of the older calendar or about 500 AD, to which time his text appears to date. It also shows there was a history of counting these cycles and that these ancient dates were not simply mythical.

b. Please see the books of Tilak in the Bibliography.

THE SARASWATI RIVER

a. *Nighantu-nirukta;* nadi, I.13.

b. AB III.II.19; KB XII.3.

c. G. Buhler, *The Laws of Manu* (Delhi, India: Motilal Banarsidass, 1988), pp.32–33.

d. *Saraswati River — Myth or Reality?*

The question has been debated for centuries: Is the river Saraswati a myth or has she been a reality at some distant point of the past? The debate may be coming to a close in the sand dunes of the Thar desert.

The researchers claim to have rediscovered at least part of the mighty river, which is described in the *Rig Veda* as "The mother of rivers."

A 3500 km. survey from the Adi Badri to Somnath in Gujarat which began in 1985 was conducted by a team under the leadership of noted archaeologist late Dr. V. S. Wakankar.

According to a team member, they sieved through the whole area, notably 150 prominent sites along the route. At the end of it all they had solid evidence to prove the existence of a highly developed culture on the banks of a river, which they say was Saraswati.

Apart from this circumstantial evidence, the existence of a mighty river, matching the Vedic description of Saraswati, has been scientifically proved. The multi-spectoral scanner (MSS), a widely used and relied upon instrument in archaeology, indicates various channels of the river in the region.

According to MSS observations of various channels, the Sutlej was the main tributary of the Ghaggar (the present name for Saraswati, now in Pakistan). But tectonic movements forced the Sutlej to flow in a different direction (at a right angle to its original channel), thus leaving the Ghaggar dry.

A study of the Landsat imagery of the Ghaggar reveals that the river had a constant width of six to eight kilometers (four to six miles) from Shatrana in Punjab to Marot in Pakistan. — *MLBD Newsletter* (Delhi, India: Motilal Banarsidass), Nov. 1989.

e. The river Saraswati takes its rise in the Ambala hills of the Punjab and flows past Kurukshetra, Thanesar and other ancient townships. After joining the Ghaggar near Shatrana it flows in a southwesterly direction and finally enters Bikaner. Beyond Shatrana it is presently known as Ghaggar, but in the Vedic and epic periods it was known as the Saraswati. The ancient bed of another river flowing in a westerly direction has been traced in the Bikaner division, where it is met by a nullah now known as Naiwali. The latter has been identified as an old bed of the Sutlej, which originally joined the Saraswati, not the Beas.

The flow-channel of a river flanked by sand-ridges and presently known as the Nali is traceable to the southeast of Hanumangarh up to Suratgarh, where it is joined by the Drishadvati, now a dried-up stream. The Nali flows past Anupgarh and enters the Bahawalpur state territory in West Pakistan. A long stretch of alluvium between the sand-ridges marks the ancient bed of the Saraswati and wherever irrigation facilities exist, it yields a rich harvest. The Drishadvati river which takes its rise south of the Saraswati in the Himalayan foothill region is presently known as the Chautang in the Punjab. Its ancient course traceable near Bhadra in Bikaner division of Rajasthan passes through Nohar and flows past the village of Rawatsar. Further west its bed is a wasteland, but five kilometers north of Suratgarh the Drishadvati joins the Saraswati. — S.R. Rao, *Lothal and the Indus Civilization* (Bombay, India: Asia Publishing House, 1973), pp. 32-33.

These dried river banks are marked in the modern Bartholomew map of India as several miles across. Yet they do not mark the original course of the Saraswati but a later deviation as it flowed to the west.

f. *Dried Saraswati Bed From Satellite Imagery:*

The American satellite Landsat has sent certain photographs of India. The analysis of these by the scientists of the Ahmadabad Space Research Centre revealed the dried bed of a big river from the Shivalik mountains near Simla up to the Rann of Kutch. *Earlier the rivers*

Yamuna and Sutlej were flowing into that river. The scientists found the width of that river at some places to be six kilometers.

Prior to these findings, many other scholars had also come to the same conclusion. Sri N. N. Godbole, an officer of the Rajasthan Government, had chemically analyzed the waters of the wells in this tract and found them to be the same; while the waters of the wells just a few furlongs away from the tract gave a different chemical composition. Research scholars have also found a thick bed of alluvial soil under the sand bed of Rajasthan proving that a big river was flowing there for a number of years and the alluvial soil accumulated because of it. — Sriram Sathe, *Bharatiya Historiography* (Hyderabad, India: Bharatiya Itihasa), pp.11-12.

g. Studies from the Post-Graduate Research Institute of Deccan College, Pune, and the Central Arid Zone Research Institute (CAZRI), Jodhpur, have discovered much important information about the Saraswati:

During Vedic times, Saraswati was a great river, perhaps rivalling even the Ganges and the Indus. The *Rig Veda* mentions a large river with a rapid flow from the mountains to the sea. The *Mahabharata* describes the same river vanishing in the sands. The reference obviously was to the Saraswati.

The original course of the Saraswati, which originated in the Himalayas, was southwesterly. It passed through present Nohar, Surjansar, Mathura, Tena and Pachpadra. When the climate became arid and massive sand dunes manifested themselves in western Rajasthan, the river changed course. It started flowing in between Sirsa and Nohar and through Lunkaransar, Bikaner, Mathura and Pachpadra. This course it maintained throughout the pre-Holocene period.

Further climatic changes in the region shifted the course of the river westward. It continued to flow in between Sirsa and Nohar, but turned west towards Rangamahal, Suratgarh, Anupgarh and Sakhi, all in the core desert region of Rajasthan. In the process it severed its connection with the Luni, though it still reached the Rann. The Hakra or Nara, now in Pakistan, is believed to be the remnant of part of this course.

Yet another shift took the river via Jakhal, Sirsa, Hanumangarh, Pilbangan, Suratgarh, Anupgarh and Sakhi. The second and third course changes apparently took place during the period of the Indus civilization.

The fourth and final major shift took the river further westward from Anupgargh to Fort Abhas, now in Pakistan, finally to merge with the Indus drainage system.

Though the courses of the Saraswati are now buried under desert sand, they still regulate the movement and supply of groundwater, soil scientists claim. The wells dug in such courses give perennial yield despite the meager rainfall in the region. — *Jaipur Correspondent*

h. *Why Same Date For 260 Harappan Sites? Indus-Saraswati Culture:*

Nearly 260 sites are now considered as belonging to the Indus or Harappan civilization. All these have the same date of destruction. Scholars were at a loss to explain why all these sites spread over a vast area were destroyed at the same time. Excavations have revealed that these sites were destroyed by natural calamities. What those calamities were nobody knows. The Indus river, after which these sites were named still flows perhaps pointing out that it has nothing to do with the destruction of these sites. Of the 260 sites, only about 20 are to the west of the Indus and the rest are on the eastern side. Any culture named after a river should thrive on both banks of the river. In the beginning, when only Mohenjodaro and Harappa were known, the scholars named the civilization after the river Indus because of its proximity to these sites. But now scholars are doubting the nomenclature. When we look at the dried bed of the river Saraswati as pictured by the Landsat imagery, the sites which were supposed to be part of the Indus civilization, appear to be on either of the banks of the Saraswati. *Hence the Indus civilization has to be renamed Saraswati civilization.*

This change in name will also solve another riddle. Because of the drying up of the river Saraswati, the sites might have been vacated and so all of them were destroyed at the same time. The thick bed of alluvial soil under the sands of Rajasthan can also be explained if we accept the drying up of the river Saraswati. The Saraswati civilization had flourished for thousands of years over a vast area and abundant waters of the rivers were helping the civilization in every way. But the drying up of the river, which was a natural calamity, forced the sites to be vacated. — Sriram Sathe, *Bharatiya Historiography,* op. cit., pp. 12–13.

i. Panini, the great grammarian of late ancient times (c. 500 BC), like other authors, divides the Aryans into eastern and western peoples. This appears to have been the standard practice of ancient Indian geographers. He mentions the Kshatriya or peoples of the East; the commentator Kashika notes (*Ashtadhyayi* IV.1.178), "Thus Pañcali, Vaidehi, Angi, Vangi and Magadhi, these being all eastern people." Their countries are the upper Ganges, mid-Ganges, Bengal and Bihar. Panini lists the eastern Aryan people as extending to the Bay of Bengal and the western Aryans to the Arabian sea. The Saraswati would thus appear to mark the central region of the Aryans by his account also.

This is the Vedic custom which lists the Saraswati as the central region, as we find also in *Manu Samhita* (II.17-22).

j. *Sacrificial Altars (Yajñashalas) In Harappan Sites*

Sacrificial altars have been discovered in Harappan sites from Baluchistan in the west up to Uttar Pradesh in the east and Gujarat in the south. This has helped Dr. Ahmed Hasan Dani, a Pakistani archaeologist, to prove that the whole of this area must have been under one culture in which the sacrificial altars had a place. Sacrificial altars are a special characteristic feature of Vedic culture. So the *Vedas* and Vedic culture must have been there in that vast part of India in Pre-Harappan times. Therefore, the theory that Aryan and Indus or Harappan cultures are separate fails to prove itself. — Sriram Sathe, *Bharatiya Historiography,* op. cit., p. 11.

k. Summing up the evidence from Lothal and Kalibangan it can be said that three types of fire-altars were built by the Harappans. They were rectangular, circular, or ovoid in plan and enclosed by a thin mud or brick wall. At Kalibangan seven rectangular fire-altars aligned in a row were found beside a well. Some were encountered individually in the houses of the Lower City also. The lumps of charcoal found in the lower part of the pits are said to suggest that fire was made and put out in situ. In most cases cylindrical or rectangular pre-fire block was found fixed in the center. Other contents of the pits, some of which are oval-shaped, are terracotta triangular cakes and ash. There is no doubt that these private fire-pits had a ritualistic use, but Lothal had the distinction of erecting large fire-altars in public places as well as private dwellings. — S. R. Rao, *Lothal and the Indus Civilization,* op.cit., p. 140; note also pp. 37 and 141.

Lothal is the great port city of the Indus Valley culture located in Gujarat at the mouth of the Gulf of Cambay.

l. *Affinities of Harappa and Vedic Civilizations*

The historical theories established hitherto consider Harappa (the Indus Valley) and Vedic civilizations to be opposed to each other. According to the popular contention the Aryans destroyed the Harappan civilization. At a conference recently held at Himachal Bhawan Delhi, Dr. Bhawan Singh, author of *Harappa Sabhyata Aur Vedic Sahitya,* opposed these theories. He said there are striking similarities between the two and gave arguments in favor of his opinion. Several scholars of history and Indology put their thought provoking views at the conference.

The Chairman of the Indian Archaeological Organization raised several questions on the archeological ground on so-called affinities between Harappa and Vedic civilizations. He asked whether there is any similarity between the evolutionary status and religions of the two civilizations. Expressing his doubts he said that the life of the river Saraswati ended with the Harappa civilization while there is mention of the river in the *Rig Veda,* proving its existence in the Vedic period as well.

Dr. S. K. Gupta, Dy. Direction National Museum, cited the similarity between the two on the basis of fire worship. In several excavations fire altars have been discovered at Harappan sites which indicates its closeness to Vedic Civilization. — *MLBD Newsletter,* op. cit., August 1987.

m. Bhimal Ghose, Anil Kar and Zahrid Jussain, "Comparative Role of the Aravali and Himalayan River-systems in the Fluviel Sedimentation of the Rajasthan Desert." Central Arid Zone Research Institute, Jodhpur.

n. *Dates of the Vedas Prior to Date of Harappa:*

The drying up of the Saraswati river must have taken place some centuries earlier to the scientifically decided date of the destruction of Harappan culture. This can be termed as the terminal point of the Saraswati culture. The Vedas contain several hymns and many verses about the river Saraswati. Thus the date of the Vedas, ie. the date of so-called Aryan culture goes earlier than the date of the Harappan culture and not after it. — Sriram Sathe, *Bharatiya Historiography,* op. cit., p. 13.

o. If we examine the ancient river flows we see that the Sutlej was the main stream in the Saraswati system, while the Yamuna, when it flowed west, would have been the main stream in the Drishadvati system. This suggests that the original Saraswati-Drishadvati region was the Sutlej-Yamuna when their courses were different. The Vedic Saraswati is said to break the ridges of the mountains with her powerful waves (VI.61.2). This could not be the Saraswati-Ghaggar as it starts in the foothills and has no mountain flow. It must be the Saraswati-Sutlej. This suggests great antiquity to the *Vedas* when the Sutlej and Yamuna formed a common river system into the Rann of Kutch. Research shows the the Ganges also once flowed west into the Saraswati.

THE LAND OF THE SEVEN RIVERS

a. Kunjalal Bhishagratna, *The Sushruta Samhita* (Varanasi, India: Chowkhama Sanskrit Series, 1981), p. 530, SS.CS XXIX.5-9.

b. Ibid., p. 537, SS.CS XXIX.27-8.

c. Ibid., pp. 537-538, SS.CS. XXIX.28-31.

d. The region of Badakshan/Mujavat was the prime ancient source of lapis lazuli, which was mined as early as perhaps 6000 BC. Gems from this region were taken through the Kabul (Vedic Kubha) region and then both west to the Middle East and east down into the plains of India. They were processed along the Helmand (Sanskrit Setumat) in southern Afghanistan. The lapis of the ancient Middle East thus probably came from trade with Vedic India and can be used as an index of the relationship between the two regions.
e. *Nighantu* I.13
f. James Darmesteter, *The Zend Avesta, Part I. The Vendidad* (Delhi, India: Motilal Banarsidass, 1980), p. 9., Fargard I.19-20.
g. *Mahabharata,* Bhishma Parva II.342.
h. James Darmesteter, *The Zend Avesta, Part III.,* op. cit., p. 317, *Yasna* LXV.3.
i. See VP II.2 for an extensive description of Meru.
j. See G. Buhler, *The Laws of Manu,* op. cit., pp. 32, MS II.22.
k. Ibid., p. 33. MS II.21 (note generally II.17-23).

STORIES OF VEDIC KINGS FROM THE *RIG VEDA*

a. Kunjalal Bhishagratna, *The Sushruta Samhita,* op. cit., p. 537.
b. James Darmesteter, *The Zend Avesta,* Part II, op. cit., p. 115. Gos Yast V.21.

STORIES OF VEDIC KINGS FROM THE *BRAHMANAS* & *PURANAS*

a. Note A. B. Keith, *Rig Veda Brahmanas* (Delhi, India: Motilal Banarsidass, 1971), pp. 330-331.
b. Note Ibid., p. 332.
c. Note Ibid., pp. 336-338.
d. Note Ibid., p. 45.
e. Note Ibid., p. 318. Note also that the *Shatapatha Brahmana* (I.4.1. 10, 17) describes how Mathava, the Videgha, is guided by the seer Gotama, one of the seven Rishis, from the Saraswati river region across the Shadanira (Gandhak) to the land of Videha. This shows the Vedic people in Videha (eastern Nepal) at the time of the *Brahmanas* and suggests their movement there in the time of the *Rig Veda* itself.
f. Note Ibid., p. 337.
g. The Angirasa Rishis appear in a limited way in the *Puranas.* Such great Vedic seers as Kutsa, Kakshivan and Vamadeva are not mentioned by name. Others like Atri occur in a mythological role. The name of the seer Dirghatamas occurs in several Puranic lineages in a major way.

Of the several kings in the Puranic lists called Divodasa, the earliest Divodasa is that of Kashi or Benares (VP IV.8.5). This is different from the Vedic Divodasa who dwells in the Saraswati region. The first Puranic Sudas is in the solar dynasty (VP IV.4.19) some generations before Rama. Another Sudas appears as a king of the Pañcalas in a dynasty that contains the names of other important Rig Vedic kings like Vadhryashwa, Divodasa, Srinjaya, Sahadeva and Somaka (VP IV.19.18). It is unlikely that the great Vedic Sudas was the last Puranic king of this name (particularly when his story, as we have seen, is related to that of Purukutsa, one of the earlier kings of the solar dynasty according to the *Puranas*). We should note that Vasishta, the priest of Sudas, also speaks of the Saraswati as flowing to the sea. Hence it is likely that the Vedic Sudas ruled at a time when the great river still flowed south. This would give him an early date whichever Puranic figure he might relate to.

h. Most notably F. E. Pargiter, *Ancient Indian Historical Tradition* (Delhi, India: 1962).

i. H. H. Wilson, *Vishnu Purana* Vol. II. (Delhi, India: Nag Publishers, 1980), p. 619, n. 4.

j. Ibid., p. 621, n. 8.

k. Ibid., p. 665, n. 80, VP IV.24.32. This yields a date of around 1415 BC for the Mahabharata War. Considering that the *Vedas* were already so old by this time that people didn't know what they meant anymore, such a date pushes the beginning of Vedic culture to a period very ancient to this. The tradition that Krishna dates to 3102 BC would push the Vedic age back yet further. Either way the Vedic tradition has a long literary and historical record that can take us back to very ancient times in India.

HINDU ASTRONOMY

a. E. Burgess and W. D. Whitney, *Surya Siddhanta* (Minneapolis: Wizard's Bookshelf, 1978), p. 244.

b. *Pancha Siddhantika* and *Brihat Samhita* III.1-2.

c. *Mahabharata* Anu.167, 26-28. See B.G. Tilak, *The Orion or Researches into the Antiquity of the Vedas* (Puna, India: Tilak Bros., 1986), see pp. 27-30 for a discussion of these various texts and references.

d. Note A. B. Keith, *Rig Veda Brahmanas* op. cit., p. 452.

The *Kaushitaki Brahmana* also mentions the summer solstice, where after moving northwards for six month he stops and begins to move south. "They perform the Ekavinsha day, the Vishuvat, in the middle of the year; by the Ekavinsha the Gods raised up the Sun to the world of Heaven" (AB IV.18).

e. B. G. Tilak, *The Orion*, op. cit., quoted p. 9.
f. Ibid., p. 38.
g. Ibid., p. 40.
h. A. B. Keith, *Rig Veda Brahmanas*, op. cit., p. 49.
i. Ekendranath Ghosh, *Studies In Rig Vedic Deities* (New Delhi, India: Cosmo Publications, 1983), p. 22.

ASTRONOMICAL REFERENCES IN THE *RIG VEDA*

a. Note A. B. Keith, *Rig Veda Brahmanas* op.cit., p. 513.
b. Quoted by T. H. Griffith, *The Hymns of the Rig Veda* (Delhi, India: Motilal Banarsidass, 1973), p. 570, n.3.
c. H. Jacobi, *Indian Antiquary* Vol.XXIII, p. 154.
d. B. G. Tilak, *The Orion*, op. cit., p. 51.
e. A. B. Keith, *Rig Veda Brahmanas*, op. cit. pp. 185-186.
f. W. D. Whitney, *Essays on Hindu and Chinese Systems of Asterisms*, p. 53 (out of print).
g. A whole book of the *Atharva Veda* (XIII) is dedicated to the Sun as Rohita, whose wife is Rohini (XIII.1.22-23). Rohini marked the vernal equinox before the Krittikas. This book could reflect that period (c. 3000 BC).
h. B. G. Tilak, *The Orion*, op. cit.; note pp. 98-118.
i. We discussed Sharyanavat as the lake below Kailas in our chapter on the rivers. Here it is a place hidden in the mountains, where the horse's head is hidden that contains the secret of the honey, madhu, the secret of Soma. This suggests that Vedic culture was prominent at Sharyanavat, at Kailas in the Himalayas, when the solstice was at the horse's head constellation or about 6000 BC.
j. B. G. Tilak, *The Arctic Home In the Veda*, op. cit., p. 247.
k. Note X.14.3-6 and X.15 as a whole, which are eulogies to the seers.
l. B. G. Tilak, *The Orion*, op. cit., pp. 155-156.
m. As in the *Isha Upanishad*, V.16, where Pushan and Yama, the God of death, are mentioned together.

VEDIC RELIGION

a. *Yoga Sutras* I.24-7.
b. i.e., *Prasna Upanishad* IV.
c. *Bhagavad Gita* X.26.
d. i.e., *Prasna Upanishad* III.8-9.
e. Kunjalal Bhishagratna, *The Sushruta Samhita* Vol.II, op. cit., p. 536.
f. Matthew 26:27.

g. Georges Dumezil, *Mitra-varuna* (New York: Zone Books, 1988), p. 26. Note also pp. 24–25 for their similar rules of conduct.
h. Eric Partridge, *Origins, A Short Etymological Dictionary of Modern English* (New York: Macmillan, 1979), p. 168.
i. Ibid., p. 179.
j. Ibid., p. 375.
k. Usha Choudhuri, *Indra and Varuna in Indian Mythology* (Delhi, India: Nag Publishers, 1981), p. 10.
l. *Shiva Purana* II.2.29, 31.
m. *Shiva Purana* II.2.29, 10.
n. The ucchishta of the *Atharva Veda* XI.7.
o. *Rig Veda Parishishtani* 11.
p. i.e., *Chandogya Upanishad* I.5–6.

ANCIENT ARYAN CULTURE

a. Colin Renfrew, "The Origins of Indo-European Languages," *Scientific American*, October 1989.
b. There is not the space to go into Tilak's theory here. Much of it revolves around the Sun Gods being seven or twelve as representing the different durations of the year in arctic regions. However, there are obvious reasons for the Sun Gods as seven or twelve. They are based upon the seven planets or seven days of the week and the twelve months. It hardly requires such an exotic solution as a seven month polar calendar. The idea of an arctic home, however, does appear in several traditions and may have some basis even apart from Tilak's interpretation of the *Rig Veda*. Moreover, Tilak's astronomical work on the *Vedas* remains important though his arctic interpretation has much that is questionable in it.
c. *Harappan Deposits Found in Delhi*

Delhi's history may date back as far as the Harappan period. Excavators at Mandoli Mound situated at a distance of 16 km. from Delhi railway station recently discovered deposits of the late Harappan period nearly 3700 years ago.

The excavations have brought forth information pertaining to the period 1700 to 1200 BC. The evidence of the antiques recovered from the site shows a continuous occupation by the people from the late Harappan period to the Gupta period (c. 500 AD). — *MLBD Newsletter*, op. cit., July 1988.

d. *Indus Valley and Central Asia*

New researches by Soviet archaeologists in South Turkemania have brought to light the existence of connections between the towns of the Indus Valley and the settlements of South Turkemania in the period of mature Harappa. Some of the finds in S. Turkemania have counterparts in the Harappa culture like metal and ivory articles, segmented faience, beads, pottery. Apart from objects imported from India, (ivory articles, beads) there are unmistakable traces of Indian influence, above all, a seal with Harappan inscription. There are also S. Turkemanian terracottas which resemble those manufactured by the Indus Valley Culture. — *MLBD Newsletter,* op. cit., Motilal Banarsidass), September 1988.

e. S. R. Rao, *Lothal and the Indus Civilization,* op. cit., p. 158.

f. *Remains of Krishna's Dwaraka Found*

Divers exploring the seabed off the coast of Gujarat have helped find the remains of an ancient civilization that once thrived in towns that now lie under the Arabian Sea. About 3,500 years ago, the Arabian Sea levels near the Gulf of Kutch rose and submerged two towns, Dwaraka and Bet Dwaraka, which are associated with lord Krishna. Krishna founded Dwaraka and Bet Dwaraka was his summer resort. The leader of the National Institute of Oceanography (NIO) team involved in the undersea quest, Dr. S. R. Rao said Dwaraka was built on the ruins of another city called Kusasthali. He believes his team has found evidence of the existence of this city also. The divers found ancient seals, fish beads, post Harappan pottery, and a jar inscribed with one of India's earliest writings. *Four of the seven letters on the jar are comparable with the later Indian script of Brahmi.* Dwaraka, which was built like a fort, represented the second phase of the urbanization in India, Dr. Rao said. The first Indian habitations appear in the Indus Valley Civilization sites, several hundred years earlier. — *MLBD Newsletter,* op. cit., May 1987.

g. *3500 Year Old Wall Of Dwaraka Discovered*

Marine archaeologists from the National Institute of Oceanography (NIO) have discovered a 3500 year old port wall off the Bet Dwaraka island in the Gulf of Kutch on Dec. 11, 1987. The 250 meter long wall located in the tidal zone of the island is the largest ancient marine structure found so far. It belonged to the now submerged city of ancient Dwaraka which gives an idea of the enormous dimensions of the city's architecture. The find also helps strengthen the belief that a large part of ancient Dwaraka now lies under the waters of the Gulf of Kutch. The team has found numerous artifacts like seals and pottery, but until now only small patches of structural remains had been discovered. The wall gets submerged by about four meters of water during the periods of high tide and is exposed only when the tides go down. The wall, which runs along the coast for 250 meters and curves around for another 50 meters, could also have served as a pier. The largest ancient structural remains of the time found so far had been the 230 meter long dockyard at Lothal, a relic of the Indus Valley Civilization.

Pottery found on the island and near the wall have been confirmed by thermoluminescent dating to be about 3500 years old. The artifacts include seals with post-Harappan inscriptions, pottery, stone-anchors and massive stone walls. The Indian epic, *Mahabharata,* mentions the imminent submergence of Dwaraka. These finds prove that the information contained in the epic is not all a myth. The wall found now is located roughly midway between two sections. It is made of seven sources of specially designed prism shaped stones. It will be possible to preserve the wall since it is not submerged all the time. — *MLBD Newsletter,* op. cit., Jan. 1988.

Note also S. R.Rao, "Excavation Of Submerged Ports — Dwarka A Case Study," *Marine Archaeology of Indian Ocean Countries, Proceedins of the First Indian Conference,* Oct. 1987, pp. 47-53. National Institute of Oceanography, Goa, India, 1988.

h. *Vishnu Purana* IV.24.32. There is also a tradition that Krishna came as early as 3102 BC. Some Hindu scholars would place the Dwaraka archaeological site from a later date than Krishna in order to support this. Yet either way the *Vedas* are much older than modern interpretations allow. Whether Krishna came at 1400 BC or 3100 BC is an important issue but even if he came at 1400 BC the antiquity of the *Vedas* and the Aryan nature of the Indus Culture are affirmed.

i. Jim G. Shaffer "The Indo-Aryan Invasions: Cultural Myth and Archaeological Reality," in J.R. Lukak's *The People of South Asia* (New York: Plenum, 1984), pp. 84-85. "At present, the archaeological record indicates no cultural discontinuities separating Painted Grey War from the indigenous protohistoric culture."

j. Ibid., p. 88.

k. R. H. Dyson, Jr., "Paradigm Changes in the Study of the Indus Civilization," in G.L. Possehl, Editor, *Harappan Civilization, a Contemporary Perspective,* (Warminister U.K.: Aris & Phillips, 1982). See also Allchin, B. and Allchin, R., *The Rise of Civilization in India And Pakistan* (Cambridge: Cambridge University Press, 1982).

l. See G. R. Hunter, *The Script of Harappa and Mohenjodaro and its Connection with Other Scripts* (London: Kegan Paul, Trench, Trubner & Co. 1934). Also see J. E. Mitchiner, *Studies in the Indus Valley Inscriptions* (New Delhi, India: Oxford and IBH, 1978).

Note particularly the work of Subhash Kak as in "A Frequency Analysis of the Indus Script," *Cryptologia*, July 1988, Volume XII, Number 3 and "Indus Writing," *The Mankind Quarterly,* Volume 30,

Nos. 1 & 2, Fall/Winter 1989. His work may provide the key for deciphering the Indus Valley Script.

m. Subhash Kak. "On the Decipherment of the Indus Script - A Preliminary Study of its Connection with Brahmi," *Indian Journal of History of Science* 22(1):51-62 (1987).

n. This rich site (Mehrgarh) provides an archaeological record with a long sequence of occupations. The sequence reveals a process of continuing elaboration that affected cereal cultivation, animal husbandry, crafts, architecture and even ideology. Step by step one can see the stage being set for the development of the complex cultural patterns that became manifest in the great cities of the Indus civilization in the middle of the third millenium BC. J. F. Jarrige and R. H. Meadow, "The Antecedents of Civilization in the Indus Valley," *Scientific American,* Aug. 1980.

o. C. Renfrew, *Archaeology and Language* (New York: Cambridge University Press, 1987), p. 182.

p. Ibid., p. 188.

q. Ibid., p. 190.

r. Ibid., p. 196.

s. G. Buhler, *The Laws of Manu,* op. cit., pp. 412-413. Note that a similar list occurs in the *Puranas* relative to the victory of Sagara over such inimical peoples (VP IV.3.18).

t. A. B. Keith, *Rig Veda Brahmanas,* op. cit., p. 307.

u. There are to this day various tribes in the mountain regions of India, including the Deccan, who are of different customs, many who are aboriginal peoples (not to mention the people of non-Vedic beliefs like the Buddhists, Jains and Muslims). That earlier texts show such different peoples in existence does not necessarily indicate that the Vedic people were new invaders into these regions. The idea is that some peoples fell from the Vedic teaching and were ostracized from it in various ways. This was an ongoing process. Some of them returned to the fold of the Vedic teaching, while other Vedic people in time fell from it as well (hence the temporary criticism of the Dravidians as unaryan).

PEOPLES OF THE MIDDLE EAST

a. P. D. Mehta, *Zarathustra the Transcendental Vision* (Dorset, U.K.: Element Books, 1985), pp. 7, 9.

b. T. Burrow. "The Proto-IndoAryans," *Journal of the Royal Asiatic Society,* No. 2, 1973.

c. Ibid., pp. 134-135.

d. James Darmesteter, *The Zend Avesta Part I,* op. cit., pp. 10-21, *Vendidad,* Fargard II.
e. Ibid., Vol. II, p. 254, Ram Yast XI.54.
f. Subhash Kak, "The Chronology of Ancient India," *Indian Journal of History of Science,* 22(3), 1987, p. 229.
g. T. Burrow. "The Proto-IndoAryans," op. cit., p. 123.
h. Subhash Kak. "On the Decipherment of the Indus Script — A Preliminary Study of its Connection with Brahmi," op. cit., p. 53.
i. E. A. Wallis Budge, *The Book of the Dead* (New York: Dover Publications, 1967), p. lxxxiii.
j. Ibid., pp. cxxxxv. & 246, n.4.
k. H. H. Wilson, *Vishnu Purana* Vol. II, op. cit., p. 553, n.2.
l. Samuel Noah Kramer, *The Sumerians* (Chicago: University of Chicago Press, 1963), pp. 281-283; note also pp. 163-164 for Flood myth.
m. As noted in Colin Renfrew, "The Origins of Indo-European Languages," op. cit.
n. V. G. Rahurkar, *The Vedic Priests of the Fire Cult* (Aligarh, India: Viveka Publications, 1982), p. 16.
o. *Upanisat-Samgrahah* (Sanskrit), Edited by J. L. Shastri (Delhi, India: Motilal Banarsidass, 1970), Part 2, pp. 392-393.
p. The Parushni river, one of the boundaries of the Saraswati region, is also known as the Iravati, from which its modern name Ravi appears to have derived. Iravati as a river occurs several times in the *Rig Veda* also (i. e., V.69.2). Vedic "ira" is an alternative form of "ila." Ilavati means abounding with Ila.
q. Pierre Grimal, editor, *La Rousse World Mythology* (London: Paul Hamlyn, 1965), p. 94.
r. The *Bible,* Genesis XI.27-32 & XII.1-5.
s. Ibid., Genesis II.8-15.
t. Ibid., Genesis IX.18-28.
u. The *Bible* resembles the Hindu *Puranas* in that it is similarly concerned with the genealogies of sages and kings. It also dates from the same era as the *Puranas,* being compiled from earlier material in the centuries before Christ. Thus the *Vedas* may also represent the original revelation from which the *Bible,* like the *Puranas,* arose as a mythological-historical text.

THE GREATER WORLD CULTURE

a. Eric Partridge, *Origins,* op. cit., p. 375.
b. Ibid., p. 259.
c. George Dumezil, *Mitra-Varuna,* op. cit., p. 26.
d. Colin Renfrew, "The Origins of Indo-European Languages," op. cit.

e. Vivian E. Robson, *The Fixed Stars and Constellations in Astrology*, (York Beach, Maine: Samuel Weiser, 1979), p. 88.

6. Note such passages as Clae Waltham, *Chuang Tzu: Genius of the Absurd* (New York: Ace Books, 1971), X.4, pp. 125-127.

7. E. Burgess and W. D. Whitney, *Surya Siddhanta*, op. cit., pp. 145-156 of volume. I.2.

APPENDIX

VEDIC CIVILIZATION

a. Eric Partridge, *Origins*, op. cit., p. 457, Indo-European root "ais- (a lump of) bronze or copper, later used to designate iron."

THE YUGA THEORY OF SRI YUKTESWAR

a. Sri Yukteswar, *The Holy Science* (Los Angeles, Ca.: Self-Realization Fellowship, 1984), pp. 12-13.

b. Ibid., p. 11.

c. E. Burgess and W. D. Whitney, *Surya Siddhanta*, op. cit., p. 244.

4
SANSKRIT QUOTES

For those passages to be emphasized, or those where the Sanskrit meaning may be questionable, I have included the Sanskrit transliteration. All quotes are from the *Rig Veda* unless otherwise specified. The Valakhilya hymns of the eighth book of the *Rig Veda* are counted in these references.

THE IMAGE OF THE OCEAN

1. IV. 58.11. dhāman te viśvam bhuvanam adhi śritam antaḥ samudre hṛdyantar āyuṣi
2. V.47.2. anantāsa uravo viśvataḥ sīm pari dyāvāpṛthivī yanti panthāḥ
3. I.11.1. Expansive as the sea: samudravyacasam
4. I.30.3. An extent like the sea: samudro na vyaco
5. I.52.4. Extensive as the sea: samudram na subhvaḥ
6. I.56.2. Like the ocean in their convergence: samudram na samcaraṇe
7. VI.36.3. As rivers to the ocean: samudram na sindhava
8. III.46.4. Like rivers into the sea: samudram na sravata
9. VIII.6.29. He looks down upon the sea: samudram ava paśyati
10. IV.16.7. The ocean-going floods: prārṇāṃsi samudriyāṇi
11. I.32.2. Directly the waters entered the ocean: añjaḥ samudram ava jagmur āpaḥ
12. VI.30.4. You released the waters to the ocean: avāsṛjo apo acchā samudram
13. VIII.3.10. By which you released the great floods to the ocean: yenā samudram asṛjo mahīr apas
14. III.36.6-7. Entered into the sea: samudram jagmuḥ; As rivers uniting to the sea: samudreṇa na sindhavo yādamānā
15. VI.72.3. You sent forth the flood of the rivers: prārṇāṃsi airayatam nadīnām; And filled manifold seas: ā samudrāṇi paprathuḥ purūṇi
16. VIII.40.5. The sea with seven foundations: saptabudhnam arṇavam
17. VIII.100.9. Within the ocean: samudre antaḥ
18. II.16.3. Not by the seas or mountains: na samudraiḥ parvatair
19. VIII.97.5. In the domain of the sea: samudrasyādhi viṣṭapi
20. VIII.65.3. In the ocean of Soma: samudre andhasaḥ

21. IV.21.3. From the ocean or the heavenly sea: samudrāt uta vā purīṣāt
22. X.89.4. From the bottom of the sea: sagarasya budhnāt
23. I.71.7. As seven mighty streams the ocean: samudram na sravataḥ sapta yahvīḥ
24. VIII.44.25. As rivers to the sea: samdrayeva sindhavaḥ
25. VIII.102-4-6. Whose vesture is the ocean: agnim samudravāsasam
26. X.5.1. A single ocean, the upholder of treasures: ekaḥ samudro dharuṇo rayīṇām
27. III.22.2-3. A brilliant ocean of light: tveṣaḥ sa bhaṇur arnavo; the ocean of Heaven: divo arṇam
28. VII.6.7. From the inferior and superior oceans, from Heaven and Earth: ā samudrād avarād ā parasmād, diva ā pṛthivyāḥ
29. I.97.8. As a ship across the river (or sea): sindhum iva nāvaya
30. I.99.1. As a ship across the river (or sea): nāveva sindhum
31. V.5.9. As a ship across the river (or sea): sindhum na nāva
32. I.116.5. In the supportless, foundationless, ungraspable ocean: anārambhaṇe anāsthāne agrabhaṇe samudre; A ship with a hundred oars: śatāritrām nāvam
33. I.116.4. To the other shore of the wet ocean: samudrasya dhanvan ārdrasya pāre
34. I.116.3. With ships of the nature of the wind: naubhir ātmanvatībhir; That travel through the atmosphere: antarikṣaprudbhir
35. I.117.14. From the flooding ocean: arṇaso samudrāt
36. I.118.6. Delivered across the ocean: pārayathaḥ samudrāt
37. VI.62.6. From the watery ocean: adbhyaḥ samudrāt
38. VII.69.7. Cast in the ocean: avaviddham samudre
39. I.174.9. Across the sea: samudram ati
40. VIII.83.3. As ships the waters: naubhir apo
41. VIII.42.3. As a saving ship: sutarmāṇam nāvam
42. IX.70.10. As a ship across the river (or sea): nāvā na sindhum
43. IX.73.1, 3. The ships of truth: satyasya nāvaḥ; Varuna takes us across the great ocean: mahaḥ samudram varuṇas tiro dadhe
44. X.44.6 The sacrificial ship: yajñiyam nāvam
45. I.46.7-8. The ship of our thoughts: nāvā matīnām; Your oar that is as wide as heaven: aritram vām divaspṛthu
46. VI.58.3. Ships that are within the sea: nāvo antaḥ samudre
47. V.73.8. When you cross the ocean: yat samudrāti parṣathaḥ
48. VII.56.24. Through whom we may cross the waters to good habitations: apo yena sukśitaye tarema
49. IV.24.4. The battle for the floods: arṇa sātau
50. X.49.9. I cross the floods: arṇāṃsi vi tirāmi
51. X.63.10. The Divine ship: daivim nāvam

52. X.63.15. svasti naḥ pathyāsu dhanvasu svasti apsu vṛjane svarvati
53. I.140.12. rathāya nāvam uto no gṛhāya nityāritrām padvatīm, asmākam vīrām uto no maghono janāṃśca yā pārayāccharma yā ca
54. VIII.10.1. In a house built upon the sea: samudre adhyākṛte gṛhe
55. I.19.7, 8. Who make the mountains shake across the flooding ocean: ye īṅkhayanti parvatān tiraḥ samudram arṇavam
56. V.55.5. udīrayathā marutaḥ samudrato yūyam vṛṣṭim varṣayathā purīṣinaḥ
57. I.25.7. He knows the ocean-going ships: veda nāvaḥ samudriyaḥ
58. VIII.41.8. A secret ocean: samudro apīcyas
59. V.85.6. When the diverse flowing streams cannot fill the one ocean with their water: ekam yad udrā na pṛṇanti enīr āsiñcantīr avanayaḥ samudram
60. VII.87.1. Led forth the ocean going floods of the rivers: prārṇāṃsi samudriyā nadīnām
61. VII.88.3. To the middle of the sea: samudram madhyam
62. I.161.14. Through the Waters and the oceans, Varuna moves: adbhir yāti varuṇah samudrair
63. VI.50.13, 14. The Earth with the oceans: pṛthivī samudraiḥ; The Earth and the Ocean: pṛthivī samudraḥ
64. VII.35.13. Peaceful the ocean: śam samudraḥ
65. VII.49.1-2. Whose eldest is the ocean: samudrajyeṣṭhāḥ; From the middle of the sea: salilasya madhyāt; Whose goal is the sea: samudrārthā
66. VII.95.2. sarasvatī śucir yatī giribhya ā samudrāt
67. III.33.2. As chariots they travel to the sea: acchā samudram rathyeva yāthaḥ
68. VIII.20.25. yat sindhau yad asiknyām yat samudreṣu yat parvateṣu bheṣajam
69. VI.61.8. yasyā ananto ahrutas tveṣaścariṣṇu arṇavaḥ amaścarati roruvat
70. IX.15.5. Lord of the rivers: patiḥ sindhunām
71. IX.86.8. The king of the river plunges into the sea: rājā samudram nadhyo vigāhate
72. IX.88.6. Like rivers down to the sea: samudram sindhavo na nīcīḥ
73. IX.89.2. Ship of truth: ṛtasya nāvam
74. IX.97.40. akrān samudraḥ prathame vidharman janayan prajā bhuvanasya rājā
75. IX.84.4. induḥ samudram idayarti vāyubhir
76. IX.86.29. You are the all knowing ocean, oh seer: tvam samudro asi viśvavit kave

77. IX.61.15. Increase the ocean of the hymn: vardha samudram ukthyam
78. IX.64.8, 17, 27. As the ocean you overflow: samudraḥ pinvase; As to the sea: vṛthā samudram; Enter the ocean: samudram ā viśa
79. IX.66.12. To the ocean: samudram; To the source of truth: ṛtasya yonim
80. IX.78.3. The ocean going angels: samudriyā apsaraso
81. IX.107.15. tarat samudram pavamāna ūrmiṇā rājā deva ṛtam bṛhat
82. IX.107.23. tvam samudram prathamo vi dhārayo devebhyaḥ soma matsaraḥ
83. IX.109.2. pavasva soma mahān samudraḥ pitā devānām viśvābhi dhāma
84. IX.33.6. From four oceans: samudrāṃścaturo
85. IX.80.1. samudrāso na savanāni vivyacuḥ
86. X.47.2. A fourfold ocean, the support of treasures: catuḥsamudram dharuṇam rayīṇām

THE SARASWATI RIVER

1. II.41.16. ambitame nadītame devitame sarasvati
2. VII.95.1-2. Saraswati like a bronze city: āyasī pūḥ; śurpassing all other rivers and waters: viśvā apo mahinā sindhur anyāḥ; Pure in her course from the mountains to the sea: śucir yatī giribhya ā samudrāt
3. VI.61.11-12. āpapruṣī pārthivāni uru rajo antarikṣam triṣadhasthā sapta dhātuḥ pañca jātā vardhayantī
4. I.3.12. maho arṇaḥ sarasvatī pra cetayati ketunā dhiyo viśvā vi rājati
5. III.23.4. ni tvā dadhe vara ā pṛthivyā iḷāyāspade sudinatve ahnām: dṛṣadvatyām mānuṣe āpayāyām sarasvatyām revad agne didīhi
6. I.31.11. They made Ila the teacher of men: iḷām akṛṇvan manuṣasya śāsanīm
7. VIII.21.18. citra id rājā rājakā id anyake yake sarasvatīm anu; parjanya iva tatanaddhi vṛṣṭyā sahasram ayutā dadat

THE LAND OF THE SEVEN RIVERS

1. X.35.2. The mountains of Sharyanavat: parvatāñcharyaṇavataḥ
2. V.41.15. Rasa, the Mighty Mother: mātā mahī rasā
3. IX.41.6. Like the Rasa around the world: raseva viṣṭapam
4. X.121.4. The ocean with the Rasa: samudram rasayā
5. V.55.7. na parvatā na nadyo varanta vo, yatrācidhvam maruto gacchathedu tat, uta dyāvāpṛthivī yāthanā pari
6. V.55.5. udīrayathā marutaḥ samudrato yūyam vṛṣṭim varṣayathā purīṣiṇaḥ

7. IV.21.3. From the sea or the heavenly ocean: samudrāt uta vā purīṣāt
8. X.64.8-9. The three times seven rivers: triḥ sapta nadyo mahīr apo; The Saraswati, Sarayu and Sindhu with their waves: may the great rivers with their great favors come, the divine Mother waters: sarasvatī sarayuḥ sindhur ūrmibhir maho mahīr avasā yantu vaksaṇīḥ devīr āpo mātaraḥ
9. V.54.9. pravatvatīyam pṛthivī marudbhyaḥ pravatvatī dyaur bhavati prayadbhyaḥ, pravatvatīḥ pathyā antarikśyāḥ pravatantaḥ parvatā jīradānavaḥ
10. VI.45.31. Wide girth as of the Ganges: uruḥ kakṣo na gāṅgyaḥ
11. III.58.6. Your ancient home, your auspicious friendship, your wealth is on the Jahnavi: purāṇam okaḥ sakhyam śivam vām yuvor narā draviṇam jahnāvyām
12. I.116.18. Yoked by a bull and a dolphin: vṛṣabhaśca śiṃśumāraśca yuktā
13. IV.54.5. To the vast mountains: bṛhadbhyaḥ parvatebhyaḥ
14. X.136.5. Nourishes both oceans, that which is eastern and that which is western: ubha samudrāvā kṣeti yaśca pūrva utāparaḥ
15. I.163.1. Arising from the ocean or the heavenly waters: udyan samudrād uta vā purīṣāt
16. AV IV.16.3. Whose flanks are the two seas: samudrau varuṇasya kukṣī

STORIES OF VEDIC KINGS FROM THE *RIG VEDA*

1. VII.75.19. brahma varma mamāntaram
2. VII.18.6. puroḷā it turvaśo yakṣur āsīd rāye matsayāso niśitā apīva, śruṣṭhim cakrur bhṛgavo druhayvaśca sakhā sakhāyam atarad viṣūcoḥ
3. VII.18.13. pūrum mṛdhravācam
4. VII.83.6. yuvām havanta ubhayāsa ājiṣu indram ca varuṇam
5. VII.6.3. akratūn grathino mṛdhravācaḥ paṇīr aśraddhāṃ ayajñān
6. VII.83.6. rājabhir daśabhir nibadhitam
7. VII.83.8. dāśarājñe pariyattāya viśvataḥ
8. VII.33.6. arbhkāsaḥ
9. VII.33.6. paricchinnā
10. VII.18.17. siṃhyāṃ cit petvenā jaghāna
11. VII.33.3. sudāsam prāvad indro brahmaṇā vo vasiṣṭhāḥ
12. III.53.11. rājā vṛtram jaṅghanat prāg apāg udag
13. III.53.11. vara ā pṛthivyāḥ
14. VII.6.7. From the inferior and superior ocean, from Heaven and Earth: ā samudrād avārād ā parasmād diva ā pṛthivyāḥ
15. VII.6.2. śam rājyam rodasyoḥ

16. VII.18.13. sapta puraḥ
17. VII.18.16. ardham vīrasya śṛtapām anindram parā śardhantam nunude abhi kṣām
18. VII.18.17. ava sraktīr veśyāvṛścad indraḥ
19. VIII.93.2. nava yo navatim puro bibheda bāhvojasā ahim ca vṛtrahāvadhīt
20. II.14.6. śatam śambarasya puro bibhedāśmaneva pūrvīḥ, yo varcinaḥ śatam indraḥ sahasram apāvapad
21. II.19.6. divodāsāya navatim ca nava indraḥ puro vyairacchambarasya
22. VI.26.5. ava girer dāsam śambaram han prāvo divodāsam citrābhir ūtī
23. VIII.32.3. ni arbudasya viṣṭapam varṣmāṇam bṛhatas tira
24. IV.27.1. garbhe nu sannanveṣānam avedam aham devānām janimāni visvā; śatam mā pura āyasīr arakṣam adha śyeno javasā niradīyam
25. IX.61.1, 2. avāhan navatīr nava puraḥ sadya itthādhiye divodāsāya śambaram adha tyam turvaśam yadum

STORIES OF VEDIC KINGS FROM THE *BRAHMANAS* & *PURANAS*

1. III.53.11. vara ā pṛthivyāḥ
2. IV.26.2. aham bhūmim adadām āryāya
3. AV IV.16.3. uto samudrau varuṇasya kukṣi
4. IV.42.8. Indram na vṛtraturam ardhadevam

HINDU ASTRONOMY

1. *Brihat Samhita* III.1-2. āśleṣārdhād āsīd yadā nivṛttiḥ kiloṣṇakiraṇasya, yuktam ayanam tad āsīt sāmpratam ayanam punarvasutaḥ
2. *Vedanga Jyotish* 5. prapadyete śraviṣṭadau suryācandramāsavudak
3. AV XIX.49.2. At her most extreme point: varṣiṣṭham
4. AV III.10.2-3. The wife of the year: samvatsarasya patnī; The replica of the year: samvatsarasya pratimām
5. SB II.1, 2, 3. etā — kṛttikāḥ — ha vai prācyai diṣo na cyavante sarvāṇi ha vā anyāni nakṣatrāṇi prācyai diṣaś cyavante
6. AV XIX.9.10. śam no grahāś cāndamasāḥ śam ādityaśca rāhuṇā
7. AV XIX.9.7. The planets that move in Heaven: grahas divicarā

ASTRONOMICAL REFERENCES IN THE *RIG VEDA*

1. I.24.10. ṛkṣā ucchā
2. X.22.10. kavīnām viśām nakṣatraśavasām

3. TB III.1.1.5. bṛhaspatiḥ prathamam jāyamanaḥ tiṣyam nakṣatram pradūrbabhuva
4. V.54.13. na yo yucchati tiṣyo yathā divo
5. I.105.10. pañcokṣaṇo madhye tasthur maho divaḥ
6. I.166.11. divyā iva stṛbhiḥ
7. II.2.5. dyaur na stṛbhir
8. IV.7.1, 3. As heaven with the stars: dyām iva stṛbhiḥ
9. II.34.12. With the great light of the luminous sea of milk: maho jyotiṣā śucatā goarṇasā
10. X.62.2. At the end of the year: parivatsare
11. II.37.4. turīyam pātram amṛktam amartyam
12. II.38.4. Divides the seasons: vi ṛtūn adadhar
13. VII.9.3. According to the seasons: ṛtuthā
14. II.13.1. ṛtur janitrī
15. I.25.8. veda māso dvādaśa vedaya upajāyate
16. III.56.2. ṣad bhārām eko acaran bibharti
17. I.164.15. sākamjānām saptatham āhur ekajam sāḷid yamā ṛṣayo devajā
18. VII.66.11. vi ye dadhuḥ śaradam māsam ād ahar yajñam aktum cād ṛcam
19. VII.103.1 vratacāriṇaḥ ... samvatsaram śaśayānā
20. VII.103.9. devahitim jugupur dvādaśasya ṛtum naro na pra minantyete; samvatsare prāvṛṣyāgatāyām taptā gharmā aśnuvate visargam
21. VII.103.8. The year long rite: brahma parivatsarīṇam
22. IV.33.7. dvādaśa dyūn yad agohyasya atithye raṇannṛbhavaḥ sasantaḥ; sukṣetrākṛṇvannanyanta sindhūn dhanvātiṣṭhan oṣadhībhir nimnam āpaḥ
23. I.164.11-12. dvādaśāram nahi tajjarāya varvarti cakram pari dyām ṛtasya; ā putrā agne mithunāso atra sapta śatāni vimśatiśca tasthuḥ; pañcapādam pitaram dvādaśākṛtim diva āhuḥ pare ardhe purīṣiṇam; atheme anya upare vicakṣaṇam saptacakre ṣaḷare āhurarpitam
24. I.164.48. dvādaśa pradhayścakram ekam trīṇi nabhyāni ka u tacciketa; tasmin sākam triśatā na śaṅkavo arpitāḥ ṣaṣṭir na calācalāsaḥ
25. I.164.43. śakamayam dhūmam ārād apaśyam viṣūvatā para enāvareṇa
26. I.155.6. caturbhiḥ sākam navatim ca nāmabhiś cakram na vṛttam
27. X.2.3, 7. The path of the Gods: devanānām panthām; He will arrange the sacrifice and the seasons: so adhvarān sa ṛtūn kalpayāti; Who knows the path of the Fathers: pāntham anu pravidvān pitṛyāṇam
28. VI.9.1. ahaśca kṛṣṇam ahar arjunam ca vi vartete rajasī vedyābhiḥ

29. I.95.3. purvām anu pra diśam pārthivānām ṛtūn praśāsad vi dadhā-vanuṣṭhu
30. I.31.4. ā tva pūrvam anayan āparam punaḥ
31. X.17.6. prapathe pathām ajaniṣṭa pūṣā prapathe divaḥ prapathe pṛthivyāḥ; ubhe abhi priyatame sadhasthe ā ca parā ca carati prajā-nan
32. VII.76.2. The paths leading to the Gods have appeared to me: pra me panthā devayānā adṛṣran
33. X.85.2. atho nakṣatrānām upasthe soma āhitaḥ
34. X.85.13. aghāsu hanyante gāvo arjunyoḥ paryuhyate
35. X.85.16. dve te cakre sūrye brahmāṇa ṛtuthā vidhuḥ
36. SB VI.2.2.18. eṣā ha saṃvatsarasya prathamā rātrir yat phālgunī paurṇamāsī
37. I.49.3. vayaścit te patatriṇo dvipac catuṣpad arjuni, uṣaḥ prāran ṛtūr anu divo antebhyaspari
38. I.117.22. ātharvaṇāyāśvinā dadhīce aśvyam śiraḥ pratyairayatam; sa vām madhu pra vocad ṛtāyan tvāṣṭram yad dasrāvapikakṣyam vām
39. I.116.12. tad vām narā sanaye damsa ugram āviṣkṛṇomi tanyatur na vṛṣṭim; dadhyaṅ ha yan madvātharvaṇo vām aśvasya śīrṣṇā pra yadīm uvāca
40. I.84.13-15. indro dadhīco asthabhir vṛtraṇyapratiṣkutaḥ jaghāna navatīr nava: icchannaśvasya yacchiraḥ parvateśvapaśritam tad vidaccharyaṇāvati: atrāha goramanvata nāma tvaṣṭur apīcyam itthā candramaso gṛhe
41. I.84.10. svādor itthā viṣūvato madhvaḥ pibanti gauryaḥ
42. X.24.6. madhumanme parāyaṇam madhumat punarāyanam; tā no devā devatayā yuvam madhumataskṛtam
43. I.183.6. By the paths of the Gods: devayānair
44. III.58.5. By the paths of the Gods: pathibhir devayānair
45. VII.71.1, 4. This most inferior breaking of the dawn: avamasyām vyuṣṭau
46. VII.71.5. niraṃhas tamasaḥ spartam atrim
47. V.51.14-15. svasti mitrāvaruṇā svasti pathye revati svasti na indra-ścagniśca svasti no adite kṛdhi: svasti panthām anu carema suryā-candramasāviva
48. X.19.1. ni vartadhvam mānu gātā asmān siṣakta revatīḥ; agnīsomā punarvasū asme dhārayatam rayim
49. X.19.4-5. yan niyānam nyananam samjñānam yat parāyaṇam āvartanam nivartanam yo gopā api tam huve: ya udānaḍ parāyaṇam āvartanam nivartanam api gopā ni vartatām
50. RVP 29.28. āvartadhvam nivartadhvam ṛtavaḥ parivatsarāḥ
51. III.47.3. uta ṛtubhir ṛtupaḥ pāhi somam

52. VI.6.6. sa citra citram citayantam asme citrakṣatra citratamam vayodham; candram rayim puruvīram bṛhantam candra candrābhir gṛṇate yuvasva
53. I.150.3. sa candro vipra martyo maho vrādhantamo divi
54. II.2.4. candram iva surucam hvāra ā dadhuḥ
55. I.23.13-15. ā pūṣancitrabarhīṣam āghṛṇe dharuṇam divaḥ ājā naṣṭam yathā paśum: pūṣā rājānam āghṛṇir apagūham guhā hitam avindaccitrabarhiṣam: uto sa mahyam indubhiḥ ṣaḍ yuktām anuseṣidhat
56. IV.58.4. yam devāso adaduḥ suryāyai

VEDIC RELIGION

1. BU I.IV.10 aham brahmāsmi
2. V.81.1. yuñjante mana uta yuñjante dhiyo viprā viprasya bṛhato vipaścitaḥ
3. KU II.3.11. sthirām indriyadhāraṇām
4. X.67.1-2. imām dhiyam saptaśirṣṇīm pitā na ṛtaprajātām bṛhatīm avindat turīyam svij jantayad viśvajano ayāsya uktham indrāya śamsan: ṛtam śamsanta ṛju dīdhyānā divasputrāso asurasya vīrāḥ vipram padam aṅgiraso dadhanā yajñasya dhāma prathamam mananta
5. I.164.5. ko dadarśa prathamam jāyamānam asthanvanta yad anasthā bibharti bhūmyā asur asṛg ātmā kva svit ko vidvāṃsam upa gāt praṣṭum etat
6. VIII.40.5. saptabudhnam arṇavam jihmabaram
7. IX.70.1. tri asmai sapta dhenavo duduhre satyām āśiram pūrvye vyomani chatvāranyā bhuvanāni nirṇije cāruṇi cakre yad ṛtair avardhata
8. III.26.8. tribhiḥ pavitrair apupodvyarkam hṛdā matim jyotiranu prajānan, varṣiṣṭham ratnam akṛta svadhābhir ādid dyāvāpṛthivī paryapaśyat
9. IV.30.3. viśve canedanā tvā devāsa indra yuyudhuḥ yad ahā naktam ātiraḥ
10. II.13.12. nīcā santam udanayaḥ parāvṛjam prāndham śroṇam śravayan sāsyukthyaḥ
11. I.164.50. yajñena yajñam ayajanta devās tāni dharmāṇi prathamānyāsan
12. II.56.8. dhunir munir iva
13. V.58.8. satyśrutaḥ kavayo yuvāno
14. Called brahma, vāk, nau, vaṇi, akṣara, dhī, medhā, gīr
15. V.40.6. turīyeṇa brahmaṇā
16. X.67.3. uta prāstaud ucca vidvān agāyata

17. I.163.1, 9. śyenasya pakṣā, hariṇasya bāhū, hiraṇyaśṛngo, ayo asya pādā, manojavā
18. VII.88.5. bṛhantam mānam sahasradvāram gṛham

ANCIENT ARYAN CULTURE

1. X.65.11. brahma gām aśvam janayanta oṣadhīr vanaspatīn pṛthivīm parvatām apaḥ sūryam divi rohantaḥ sudānava āryā vratā visṛjanto adhi kṣami
2. AV XIX.72.1. yasmāt kośād udabharāma veda tasim antar ava dadhma enam

PEOPLES OF THE MIDDLE EAST

1. V.50.1. viśvo devasya netur marto vurīta sakhyam
2. MP. suṣa nāma purī ramyā varuṇasyāpi dhīmataḥ
3. VII.88.5. bṛhantam mānam sahasradvāram gṛham
4. I.31.11. iḷām akṛnvan manuṣasya śaṣanim
5. III.29.3. iḷāyāsputra
6. III.29.4. iḷāyās pade, nabha pṛthivyā

THE GREATER WORLD CULTURE

1. AV XIX.39.8. yatra nāvaprabhraṃśanam; yatra himavataḥ śiraḥ

APPENDIX
VEDIC COSMOLOGY

1. I.89.10. aditir dyaur aditir antarikṣam aditir mātā sa pitā sa putraḥ, viśve devā aditiḥ pañca janā aditir jātam aditir janitvam
2. I.36.8. ghnanto vṛtram ataran rodasī apa uru kṣayāya cakrire
3. VII.69.1-3. ā vām ratho rodasī badbadhāno; hiraṇyayo vṛṣabhir yātvaśvaiḥ; paprathāno abhi pañca bhumā; trivanduro manasā yātu yuktaḥ; viśo yena gacchatho devayantīḥ; antān divo bādhate vartanibhyām
4. VII.67.8. ekasmin yoge samāne: pari vām sapta sravato ratho gāt
5. V.47.2. anantāsa uravo viśvataḥ sīm pari dyāvāpṛthivī yanti panthāḥ
6. VIII.8.23. trīṇi padāni aśvinor āviḥ santi guhā paraḥ
7. III.56.2. One unmoving: eko acaran
8. VI.30.1. bhūya id vāvṛdhe vīryāya eko ajuryo dayate vasūni; pra ririce diva indraḥ pṛthivyā ardham id asya prati rodasī ubhe
9. IV.54.2. devebhyo hi prathamam yajñiyebhyo amṛtatvam suvasi bhāgam uttamam; ādid dāmānam savitar vyūrnuṣe anūcīna jīvitā mānuṣebhyaḥ
10. VII.52.1. ādityāso aditayaḥ syāma pūr devatrā vasavo martyatrā, sanema mitrāvaruṇā sananto bhavema dyāvāpṛthivī bhavantaḥ

11. I.35.8. aṣṭau kakubhaḥ pṛthivyās trī dhanva yojanā sapta sindhūn
12. V.34.3. In heat or rain: ghraṃse, ūdhani
13. III.32.5. saraṇyubhir apo arṇā sisarṣi
14. VIII.20.4-5. vi dvīpāni pāpatan tiṣṭhad ducchunobhe yujanta rodasī; pra dhanvānyairata śubhrakhādayo yad ejatha svabhānavaḥ: acyutā cid vo ajmannā nānadati parvatāso vanaspatiḥ; bhūmir yāmeṣu rejate

VEDIC CIVILIZATION

1. II.14.11. Like a grainery with grain: ūrdaram yavena
2. III.45.4. vṛkṣam pakvam phalam aṅkvīva
3. VIII.1.33. daśabhiḥ sahasraiḥ
4. VIII.2.41. catvāri ayutā aṣṭa paraḥ sahasrā
5. VIII.4.20. ṣaṣṭim sahasra gavām
6. VIII.5.37. sahasrā daśa gonām
7. VIII.6.47. sahasrā daśa gonām
8. VIII.21.18. sahasram ayutā
9. VIII.46.22 ṣaṣṭim sahasra aśvyasya; uṣtrānām ayutā viṃṣatim satā
10. V.27.1 daśabhiḥ sahasraiḥ
11. I.126.3. ṣaṣṭiḥ sahasram gavyam
12. IX.107.1. śomo ya uttamam haviḥ
13. VIII.46.21. I.139.3. hiraṇyaya ratha
14. VI.58.2. nāvo hiraṇyayīr
15. V.54.12. śiprāḥ hiraṇyayīḥ
16. VII.57.3. rukmair āyudhais
17. VIII.1.5. mahe cana tvām adrivaḥ parā śulkāya deyām; na sahasrāya nāyutāya na śatāya
18. VI.47.23. daśo hiraṇya piṇḍān
19. V.62.7. A thousand pillars: sahasra sthūṇam; Gold is its covering, the pillars are of bronze: hiraṇya nirṇik ayo asya sthūnā
20. IX.74.2. divo skambho dharuṇaḥ svātata
21. IX.89.6. viṣṭambho divo dharuṇaḥ pṛthivyā
22. I.1.1. ratnadhātamam
23. VI.74.1. dame dame sapta ratnā dadhānā
24. I.33.8. cakrāṇāsaḥ parīṇaham pṛthivyā hiraṇyena maṇinā śumbhamānāḥ
25. X.89.7. bibheda girim navam inna kumbham
26. IV.16.13. pañcaśat sahasrā
27. IV.30.15, 20, 21. sahasrāṇi śata adhi pañca; śatam aśmanmayīnām purām; sahasrā tṛṃṣatam
28. VI.18.13. purū sahasrā
29. VI.26.5-6. śatā sahasrā; ṣaṣṭim sahasrā

30. VI.75.19. brahma varma mamāntaram
31. VI.20.1. Bearing of the wide lands: sahasrabharam urvarāsām
32. IV.38.1. Wide-yielding fields: kṣetrāsām urvarāsām
33. VII.3.7. śatam pūrbhir āyasībhir
34. VII.15.14. mahī na āyasi anādhṛṣṭo pūr śatabhujiḥ
35. VI.48.8. śatam pūrbhir
36. I.166.8. śatabhujibhis pūrbhī
37. I.189.2. pūśca pṛthvī bahulā na urvī
38. VII.95.1. sarasvatī dharuṇam āyasī pūh
39. III.15.4. puro viśvāḥ saṃjigīvān
40. VII.26.3. janīr iva patir ekaḥ samāno, nimāmṛje pura indraḥ su sarvāḥ
41. X.101.8. puraḥ kṛnudhvam āyasīr adhṛṣṭā
42. I.149.3. puram nārmiṇīm adīded
43. II.3.5. vi śrayantām urviyā hūyamānā dvāro devīḥ suprāyaṇā namobhiḥ; vyacasvatīr vi prathantām ajuryā varṇam punānā yaśasam suvīram
44. VIII.1.6. mata ca me chadayathaḥ samā
45. VI.66.7. aneno vo maruto yāmo astu anaśvaścid yam ajati arathīḥ, anavaso anabhīśū rajastūr vi rodasī pathyā yāti sādhan
46. II.40.3. rajaso vimānam saptacakram ratham a viśvaminvam ... pañcaraśmim
47. III.22.1. ayam so agnir yasmin somam indraḥ sutam dadha jaṭhare vāvaśānaḥ
48. I.116.15. sadyo jaṅghām āyasīm viśpalāyai
49. II.33.4. bhiṣaktamam tvā bhiṣajām śṛnomi

THE YUGA THEORY OF SRI YUKTESWAR

1. MU II.1. tadetad satyam mantreṣu karmāṇi kavayo yānyapaśyanstāni tretāyām bahudhā saṃtatāni

5
BIBILIOGRAPHY

LIST OF ABBREVIATIONS FOR TEXTS

Unless otherwise specified all references are to the *Rig Veda.*

AB *Aitareya Brahmana*
AV *Atharva Veda*
BG *Bhagavad Gita*
BU *Brihadaranyaka Upanishad*
CU *Chandogya Upanishad*
DM *Devi Mahatmya*
KB *Kaushitaki Brahmana*
MP *Matsya Purana*
MaiU *Maitriyani Upanishad*
MnU *Mahanarayana Upanishad*
MuU *Mundaka Upanishad*
PU *Prashna Upanishad*
RV *Rig Veda*
RVP *Rig Veda Parishishtani*
SP *Shiva Purana*
SS.CS *Sushrut Samhita, Chikitsasthana*
SYV *Vajasaneya Samhita, Shukla Yajur Veda*
TA *Taittiriya Aranyaka*
TB *Taittiriya Brahmana*
TS *Taittiriya Samhita, Krishna Yajur Veda*
VP *Vishnu Purana*
YS *Yoga Sutras*

MODERN BOOKS ON THE VEDAS

Aurobindo, Sri. *The Secret of the Veda.* Pondicherry, India: Sri Aurobindo Ashram, 1971.

Choudhuri, Usha. *Indra and Varuna in Indian Mythology.* Delhi, India: Nag Publishers, 1981.

Frawley, David. *The Creative Vision of the Early Upanishads.* Madras, India, 1982.

Frawley, David. *From the River of Heaven: Hindu and Vedic Knowledge for the Modern Age.* Salt Lake City, Utah: Passage Press, 1990.

Frawley, David. *Hymns From the Golden Age*. Delhi, India: Motilal Banarsidass, 1986.

Ghosh, Ekendranath. *Studies on Rigvedic Deities*. New Delhi, India: Cosmo Publications, 1983.

Gilbert, Kenneth. *The Wisdom of the Veda*. Pondicherry, India: Sri Aurobindo Ashram, 1973.

McClain, E.G. *The Myth of Invariance*. Boulder, CO.: Shamballa, 1978.

Mookerji, Dr. R. K.. *Hindu Civilization*. Bombay, India: Bharatiya Vidya Bhavan, 1977.

Pandit, M. P.. *Aditi and Other Deities in the Veda*. Madras, India: Sri Aurobindo Study Circle, 1958.

Rahurkar, V. G.. *The Vedic Priests of the Fire Cult*. Aligarh, India: Viveka Publications, 1982.

Rao, S. R.. *Lothal and the Indus Civilization*. Bombay, India: Asia Publishing House, 1973.

Sastry, T. V. Kapali. *Lights on the Veda*. Pondicherry, India: Sri Aurobindo Ashram, 1968.

Sriram Sathe. *Bharatiya Historiography*. Hyderabad, India: Bharatiya Itihasa Sankalana Samiti, 1987.

Tilak, B. G. *The Arctic Home in the Veda*. Poona, India: Tilak Bros., 1983.

Tilak, B. G.. *The Orion or Researches into the Antiquities of the Vedas*. Poona, India: Tilak Bros., 1986.

Waradpande, N. R.. *Aryan Invasion — A Myth*. Nagpur, India: Baba Saheb Apte Smarak Samiti Publication, 1989.

Yukteswar, Sri. *The Holy Science*. Los Angeles, Ca.: Self-Realization Fellowship, 1984.

ARTICLES OF INTEREST

Burrow, T. "The Proto-Indoaryans." *Journal of the Royal Asiatic Society*, No. 2, 1973.

Frawley, David. "Self-Realization and the Supermind in the *Rig Veda.*" Serialized monthly in *World Union*, May 1980-June 1982 and quarterly in the *Advent*, Aug. 1982-Nov. 1983.

Frawley, David. "The Heart of the Mystic Sacrifice (an interpretation of the *Yajur Veda*)." Serialized monthly in *Sri Aurobindo's Action*, Dec. 1982-Aug. 1983.

Frawley, David. "The First Chapter of the *White Yajur Veda*." Serialized monthly in *Sri Aurobindo's Action*, Jan.-April 1984.

Jarrige, Jean-Francois and Richard H. Meadow. "The Antecedents Of Civilization In The Indus Valley." *Scientific American*, Vol. 243, August 1980.

Kak, Subhash. "On Astronomy in Ancient India." *Indian Journal of History of Science,* 22(3): 205-221 (1987).

Kak, Subhash. "The Chronology of Ancient India." *Indian Journal of History of Science,* 22(3): 222-234 (1987).

Kak, Subhash. "On the Decipherment of the Indus Script — A Preliminary Study of its Connection with Brahmi." *Indian Journal of History of Science* 22(1):51-62 (1987),

Kak, Subhash. "A Frequency Analysis of the Indus Script." *Cryptologia,* July 1988, Vol. XII No. 3.

Kak, Subhash. "Indus Writing." *The Mankind Quarterly,* Vol. 30, Nos. 1 & 2, Fall/Winter 1989.

Kak, Subhash. "The Sign for Zero." *The Mankind Quarterly,* Vol. 30, No. 3, Spring 1990.

Rao, S. R. "Excavation of Submerged Ports — Dwarka a Case Study." *Marine Archaeology of Indian Ocean Countries, Proceedings of the First Indian Conference,* Oct. 1987, pp.47-53. National Institute of Oceanography, Goa, India, 1988.

TRANSLATIONS

Manu. *The Laws of Manu* (*Manu Samhita,* G. Buhler translation). Delhi, India: Motilal Banarsidass, 1988.

The Rig Veda (R. Griffith trans.). Delhi, India: Motilal Banarsidass, 1976.

Rig Veda Brahmanas: The Aitareya and Kaushitaki (A.B. Keith translation). Delhi, India: Motilal Banarsidass, 1970.

Surya Siddhanta (Burgess and Whitney trans.). San Diego, Ca.: Wizard's Bookshelf, 1978.

Sushrut. *Sushrut Samhita* (3 volumes, K. Bhishagratna trans.). Varanasi, India: Chowkhamba Sanskrit Series, 1981.

Vedanga Jyotish Of Lagadha (T.S. Kuppanna Sastry trans.). New Delhi, India: Indian National Science Academy, 1985.

The Vishnu Purana (2 volumes, H.H. Wilson translation). Delhi, India: Nag Publishers, 1980.

The Zend Avesta (3 volumes, J. Darmesteter translation). Delhi, India: Motilal Banarsidass, 1980.

SANSKRIT TEXTS

Atharva Veda
Badarayana. *Brahma Sutras*
Krishna. *Bhagavad Gita*
Mahabharata
Mihira, Varaha. *Brihat Samhita*
Patanjali, *Yoga Sutras*
Ramayana
Rig Veda
Sushrut. *Sushrut Samhita*
Taittiriya Aranyaka
Upanishads
Shukla Yajur Veda
Yaska. *Nighantu and Nirukta*

***

VEDIC ASTROLOGY CORRESPONDENCE COURSE

Vedic astrology, also called Hindu astrology or Jyotish, is the traditional astrology of India, often used along with Ayurveda and Yoga.

This course teaches the fundamentals of Vedic astrology through an explanation of the planets, signs, houses, aspects, harmonic charts, planetary periods and principles of chart interpretation. In addition, it sets forth the astrology of healing based upon the combined use of Ayurveda and Vedic astrology, explaining remedial measures of diet, herbs, gems, colors, mantras, yantras and deities. Spiritual and karmic aspects of astrology are stressed, astrology as a means of self-knowledge and attunement to the cosmic mind.

The course, perhaps the only one of its kind in this regard, presents the system in clear, practical and modern terms and is adapted toward western culture. Options for advanced study are also available.
For Courses send a S.A.S.E. to:

AMERICAN INSTITUTE OF VEDIC STUDIES
P.O. BOX 8357, SANTA FE, NM 87504-8357

* * *

BIODATA

Dr. David Frawley is a modern teacher of the comprehensive system of Vedic and Yogic Science, much like the Vedic seers of old. He is acknowledged as an Ayurvedic healer, Vedic astrologer, teacher of Yoga and meditation, and a Sanskrit scholar. Over the past twelve years he has written many books and articles on the different aspects of Vedic knowledge for publication both in the United States and in India.

His Indian books include *Hymns From the Golden Age* (1986), *Beyond the Mind* (1984) and *The Creative Vision of the Early Upanishads* (1982). His American titles include *Ayurvedic Healing, A Comprehensive Guide* (1989), *The Yoga of Herbs* (1986), *From the River of Heaven* (1990) and *The Astrology of the Seers* (1990). He also has a doctor's degree (O.M.D.) in Chinese medicine and is a published *I Ching* scholar both in the United States and China.

Dr. Frawley is the director of the American Institute of Vedic Studies, which aims to provide educational material for a modern restoration of Vedic knowledge, including Ayurveda, Vedic astrology, Vedic studies and Yoga. His forthcoming books through Passage Press are: *Wisdom of the Ancient Seers, Secrets of the Rig Veda; The Upanishadic Vision;* and *Beyond the Mind.*

The following are reviews of his various books on Vedic knowledge published in India:

> "Frawley is superb when he discusses in what sense the world is a creation of the word. His note on the Mantra is as chiselled as the Vedic Mantra itself." — M. P. Pandit, *The Mountain Path*

> "With such spiritual translation and interpretation of the Vedic mantras, he deserves a place amongst the great spiritual commentators of the Veda like Swami Atmananda, Swami Dayananda, Sri Aurobindo and V.S. Agrawal." — Prof. K. D. Shastri; *Haryana Sahitya Academy Journal of Indological Studies*

> "The work is an exceptionally admirable attempt to understand the Vedic vision. After Sri Aurobindo, it is perhaps the most original hermeneutical exercise in Vedic studies." — Dr. S. P. Duby; *Prabuddha Bharata*

> "The author discloses an acute sensitivity for the sound and spiritual meaning of the Vedic mantras." — P. Nagaraja Rao; *The Madras Hindu*

Index

O

P

R